Romans in Northern Campania

Romans in Northern Campania:
Settlement and Land-use around the Massico and the Garigliano Basin

Paul Arthur

"The first man who enclosed a field and thought of saying 'this is mine', and found people naive enough to believe him, was the real founder of society."

Rousseau, *Discours sur l'Inégalité*, 1755.

Archaeological Monographs of the British School at Rome No. 1

British School at Rome, London
1991

© *The British School at Rome, Regent's College, Regent's Park, London, NW1 4NS*

ISBN 0 904152 15 4

Cover illustration: the Roman road from Sinuessa to Suessa Aurunca (site S64)

Typeset and printed in England by Stephen Austin & Sons Ltd., Hertford.

Cover design: Three's Company, The Old School Hall, Perrin St., Headington, Oxford.

Contents

List of figures

Frontispiece: General map of Campania, showing the location of the North Campania Survey.

List of plates

General map of Campania, showing the location of the North Campania Survey

Introduction

To the historian Campania is often seen to be a paradigm for Roman land exploitation and, all things being equal, an area where opportunities provide near-ideal conditions in which to see the development of classical Roman settlement and agriculture at its best. The northern part of the region is one of the most fertile areas of the entire Mediterranean basin, composed of well-watered alluvial plains opening out directly to the sea and fertilized by the immission of rich minerals deriving from the volcanic complexes of Roccamonfina and Vesuvius. Its unique position led to a precocious phase of state formation at Capua which, at an early stage of development, entered the orbit of both Greek commerce and political interests from the south and Etruscan political domination from the north, thus assuming the position of a cultural interface area. Though a comprehensive archaeological study of Capua itself is still lacking, her political and economic position has been critically assessed at various times over the last century, and the Soprintendenza has carried out a great deal of field work. The same may not be said for certain adjoining areas, likewise of great agricultural potential, where both historical and archaeological data have rarely been compared. Indeed, with the proliferation of archaeological surveys in Italy over the last three decades, most notably in south and central Etruria, central Lazio, Molise, Puglia and around Luni in Liguria, northern Campania stands out as a critical unsampled area; a point made all too clear by its frequent omission in site and artifact distribution maps of peninsular Italy. It was with this imbalance in mind, and a realization of the fundamental importance of the territory to Rome's growth as an international power, that this research project was conceived.

My purpose in writing this volume is principally that of putting down on paper and making available to others basic data the collection of which cost me some three years fieldwork. It may have various defects, but I cannot rightly argue against the destruction of our common cultural heritage if I myself do nothing to save it. This book saves some bits, at least as far as crude information is concerned. I also attempt to do some cooking, though the outcome of this is mine and may not live up to everyone's tastes. I hope that I shall be able to return to some of the issues in the future, though for the time being the work exists for whosoever may be interested in it and want to expend some energy in directions of common interest. If the basic data are not felt to be good enough, I am happy to offer the contents of my unpublished work files to who should ask.

The text was completed in 1985 for presentation as a doctoral thesis, and examined on Christmas Eve of the same year. The year 1986 thus represented a clean break, and my copy and notes were subsequently stored so far out-of-sight as to permit me a clean conscience for over two years. Alarm bells rang from time to time when asked to prepare articles on the archaeology of the area for this conference or that volume and so, by early 1989, the text was back on my desk. With a mounting work load, I have decided to limit revision, and the bibliography has been integrated only with what I consider to be the most significant studies that have appeared over the last few years.

In the text I have chosen to use both Latin and modern Italian place names according to their context. In the case of *Suessa Aurunca*, modern Sessa Aurunca, where the town site has not shifted, this is of little importance. *Minturnae* and modern Minturno are, however, entirely different sites, whilst Sinuessa no longer exists and its equation with modern Mondragone, sustained by some scholars, is totally erroneous.

This study owes much to numerous individuals and it is most pleasant to remember the occasions in which I have derived benefit from the help and advice of people and institutions, all of whose interests I hope I have touched upon in this work.

The successive Superintendents of Archaeology of Naples and Caserta, Prof. Fausto Zevi and Dott.ssa Enrica Pozzi, and Dott.ssa Giuliana Tocco, once Inspector of Caserta and now Superintendent at Salerno, greatly encouraged my research and permitted access to state archives. Further encouragment was offered by the present Inspector of Caserta, Dott.ssa Luigia Melillo Faenza, especially as regards excavations carried out by Prof. Maurizio Gualtieri and myself at Sinuessa. The understanding of many of the landowners and coloni of Caserta permitted the formation of this study's archaeological base. My interest in Campanian archaeology, however, grew initially from discussions with the late Molly Cotton and with Martin Frederiksen, the two leading British scholars in the field and both well acquainted with the British School's survey project in southern Etruria. The occasion to participate in the Settefinestre and via Gabina villa projects, run by Prof. Andrea Carandini and by Profs. Philip Oliver-Smith and Walter Widrig respectively, stimulated my interest in the development of the Roman landscape in central Tyrrhenian Italy. Prof. David Oates, instead, steered me away from more dangerous ground. I am sorry that various limitations have meant that this study has fallen short of the marks that they have each set for their own projects.

A first season of survey was conducted together with Jean-Pierre Vallat in 1978. Hospitality, discussion and country treks in northern Campania were later provided by Gaetano Sperlongano and Luigi Crimaco (Mondragone), Franco Bevellino, Beniamino Petteruti, Mauro Volante, Albino Matano and Dante Di Cresce (Sessa Aurunca), and Adele Ceraldi and Father Zampi (Carinola). I was assisted on various occasions by Fiona Cameron, Chris Going, Geoff Marsh, Christopher Oliver, Pierfrancesco Talamo and David Williams. Claude Albore Livadie (prehistoric finds), Amanda Claridge (marbles), Jean-Paul Morel (Black Glaze ware) and Rosemary Powers (skeletal remains) kindly assisted in identifying material from field survey. In Britain and Italy I have benefited from exchanges of ideas with my friends and colleagues Brenda Bolton, Marisa De Spagnolis, Simon Keay, John Hayes, John Lloyd, Nicholas Purcell, Richard Reece, Alastair Small and the late Edith Mary Wightman. It is also with nostalgia that I remember my holding of the Rome Scholarship in Classical Archaeology at the British School (1981–1982) and the encouragement of the staff, in particular Amanda Claridge, Luciana Valentini and the Director at the time, David Whitehouse. Financially, the project was made possible by the British School itself, the Department of Education and Science and the Italian Ministry of Foreign Affairs. The Centro per l'Archeologia Medievale of the University of Salerno, through the offices of Prof. Paolo Peduto, kindly made available the use of their word processor (Olivetti ETS 1010) for the preparation of the doctorate. Having been converted to Olivetti, the present text has been prepared on my own M24, with a Microsoft package. Michele Varchetta has kindly inked-in some of my pencil drawings and, in particular, has prepared the map of sites.

Only five people have read through the final draft of the doctorate: my supervisor in London, Prof. John Wilkes, Prof. Graeme Barker whilst Director of the British School, my former history mentor, Dr. Brian Williams, and my examiners, Drs. Mark Hassall and Timothy Potter. I am particularly indebted to them all, although the person who has suffered most the trials of final preparation (apart, I think, from myself) is my wife Giuliana Miraglia, to whom this work is dedicated.

Paul Arthur
Naples, 1989

Chapter One

The Lie of the Land

The modern region of Campania, regarded as part of southern Italy, is composed of the provinces of Naples, Salerno, Avellino, Benevento and Caserta. The last, considered here, stretches from Naples and the Phlegrean Fields northwards to the river Garigliano.[1]

The *Casertano* is composed fundamentally of two major river basins opening out onto the Tyrrhenian sea, which have led to the formation of a sweeping stretch of sandy coastline from the slopes south of Formia to the volcanic hills around Naples and Pozzuoli. The larger Volturno basin lies to the south, with the smaller Garigliano basin to its north. These are separated by the spine of low-lying mountains known as the Massico, which reaches towards the sea running west of the volcano of Roccamonfina.

The Garigliano river basin, which lies in part within the province of Latina, is backed to the north by the Monti Aurunci, whilst the Volturno basin is backed to the east by Mt Maggiore and Montesarchio, preceding the even higher ridges of the Matese and the Campanian Appenines.

The Campania of this volume refers to the present region, and it is its north-western part which will form the subject of this study.

Available evidence suggests that there was little change in the major geomorphological features of the area, with the gradual establishment of a Mediterranean climate after the end of the last glaciation (Wurm) some 12.000 BP, though certain mutations in hydrology, flora and fauna were of no little importance to the way in which the land was eventually exploited.[2] Furthermore, an examination of the dynamics of change reveals how eventual mutations were frequently the result of human intervention and thus cast light on the opportunities which were grasped and successfully harnessed to man's ends or which were mis-managed, leading to eventual destabilization in the equilibrium between man and his environment.

The historian, said Braudel, 'tends to linger over the plain, which is the setting for the leading actors of the day, and does not seem eager to approach the high mountain nearby'.[3] Such reserve would be of no little consequence in northern Campania, where the potentials and constraints posed by the highlands have been decisive in the development of local affairs. They dominate and enclose the Campanian plain, emphasizing its nature and rendering maritime communication all the more significant. Of primary importance is the Massico, a Mesozoic calcareous formation of like nature to the Monti Aurunci to the north, rising at its highest point to some 813m asl and oriented in a NE-SW direction. Its northern and western faces are steep and difficult of access, compared to its southern side, possessed of far gentler gradients cut by numerous runoff and spring channels (known locally as rio in the singular). The whole forms a natural drainage system which contributes to the marked hydrological regime of the river basins. The western half of the Massico is dissected by a longitudinal valley containing the Canale Grande which, on debouching from the mountains to the north-east of Mt Cicoli, contributes largely to the Rio di S Limato. The ridge of the Massico now thrusts to within a kilometre of the sea, forming a narrow pass commanded at its northern extremity by the peak of Mt Cicoli (275m asl). A similarly narrow pass exists at the north-eastern end of the ridge, where the descending limestone has been overlapped by later Quaternary ash-flow tuff from the volcano of Roccamonfina to the north-east.

The Monti Aurunci to the north are bordered to their north and east by the Sacco-Liri-Garigliano river valleys, providing an internal communication route, whilst passes exist between the mountains and the sea and up the corridor of the river Ausente. The mountains rise to 1533m asl at the crest of Mt Petrella, and complete the cornice around the Garigliano basin.

At various points within the limestone area, where drainage is predominantly subsurface, caves have been shaped. One example, near Masseria Curti, Falciano, yielded Mousterian flints alongside the bones of a cave-bear.[4] Others were used as chapels in the middle ages.

The outstanding geological feature of the area, nevertheless, remains the slightly elliptical caldera of Roccamonfina, rising to a height of 1006m asl at Mt S Croce, majestically dominating the entire Garigliano floodplain. To the east it commands the gap which held the *Via Latina*, slipping down from Latium, and is divided from the limestone range of the Mt Maggiore to the south-east by the valley of the Savone. The body of the volcano, stretching to

---

[1] Alessio, 1977.
[2] For the C14 dates of the mesolithic in Campania and its related fauna see Tozzi, 1974.
[3] Braudel, 1975, I, 29.
[4] G Buchner, *Atti della Soprintendenza* C.2–37; Radmilli, 1961, 720.

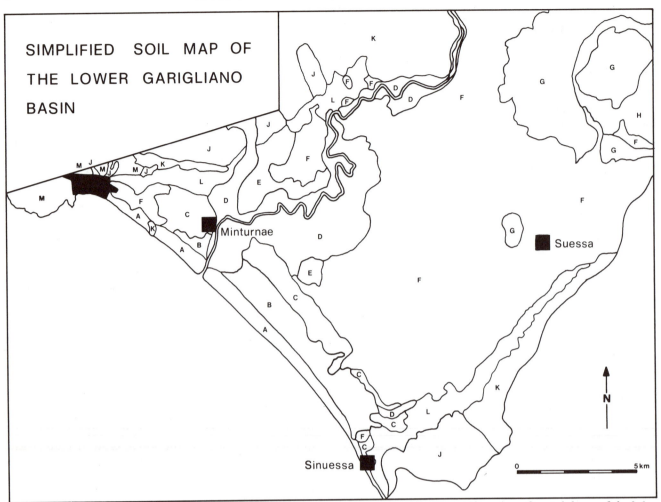

SIMPLIFIED SOIL MAP OF THE LOWER GARIGLIANO BASIN

Minturnae

Suessa

Sinuessa

N

0   5 km

Fig 1   Soil map of the Garigliano basin (after Remmelzwaal, 1978, with modifications). Key: A = Coastal dunes of the 0.1m Terracina level; B = Peaty lagoon deposits; C = Fossil beach ridges of the 16m Minturno level; D = River floodplain; E = Marine terraces/lagoon deposits of the 16m Minturno level; F = Tuff slopes; G = Lava outflows and domes; H = Roccamonfina crater bottom; J = Sandstones and shales; K = Limestones; L = Alluvial fans and colluvium (generally calcareous); M = Conglomerates

almost six kilometres in diameter, covers an area of some 200sq km, whilst the spread of pyroclastic debris is considerably greater, surpassing even that of the more notorious Mt Vesuvius, to the south. It came into existence during the pleicestocene at the junction of Appenine and counter-Appenine faults.[5] The distinct dissected landscape and tongue-like foothills to the north of the town of Sessa Aurunca are formed of the eroded ignimbrite or ash-flow tuffs deriving from overflows of the western caldera rim. Lavas are present predominantly in the crater and on the steep western slope down towards the Garigliano (Fig 1g).[6]

Roccamonfina is now dormant and there are no certain historical records of recent activity, though other localized volcanic events are recognized.

Orosius, in a description of portents which occurred in the years 269–268 BC, wrote that in the *ager Calenus* 'a flame suddenly burst forth from an opening in the ground and blazed frightfully for three days and three nights. Five *iugera* of land were burnt to ashes. The moisture which brought fertility was so completely exhausted that not only the plants of the fields but even the trees, so they say, were consumed to their very roots'. Science tells us that the event may now be identified as a freatic explosion leading to the formation of a *maar* or minor crater, perhaps to be identified as the Fossa dell'Annunziata near Falciano, just to the south of the Roman town of Forum Popilii, not, incidentally, in the *ager Calenus*.[7] Further *maaren* may be seen along the southern side of the Massico at Lago di

[5] Giannetti, 1979.
[6] The complex Roccamonfina depositions are now to be found treated by Remmelzwaal, 1978, 29ff.

[7] Scherillo *et al*, 1968.

Carinola, now a lake, Fossa Barbata, Fossa del Ballerino and perhaps also just north of Mondragone, in the depression known as Padule, now filled with some eight metres of clay, stratified above marine sands.[8]

Continuing post-volcanic activity in the area is attested by two particularly famous hot sulphur springs at Suio Terme (Aquae Vescinae), east of Suio, and Bagni Sulfurei (Thermae Sinuessanae), near Mondragone.

Seismic disturbance is also substantiated in the area.[9] The violent earthquake which wreaked major damage to a bath-building at *Allifae* and a *macellum* at *Aesernia*, both in Samnium, must have been felt further west.[10] One of the strongest recorded tremors, in 1688, reputedly led to the abandonment of what may already have been a decaying medieval village at S Maria la Piana, to the south of the Garigliano.[11] Furthermore, the toponym of the medieval village Trimenzulu, founded in 945, may witness a further, otherwise unrecorded, earthquake in the area. Even the recent earthquake of November 1980, the epicentre of which lay in Irpinia, left evidence of damage in northern Campania.[12]

Campania has suffered many of her problems and yet owes much of her fertility to an abundance of water. Though the sources have been harnessed at various times, they have always maintained a treacherous independence, thus earning veneration in the classical literature.

The region's major river, the Volturno, rises near Castel San Vincenzo in Molise at a height of some 548m asl and enters into the province of Caserta through a pass between the limestone mountains of the Matese and Le Mainarde. It is the greatest river of southern Italy, stretching for 175km, with a basin of some 5570km². A carrying capacity of some 100 cubic metres per second after its confluence with the Calore has made it vital to irrigation systems. February sees its carrying capacity doubled, whilst in August it is reduced to some 40 cubic metres per second.[13] Ovid noted the transportation of sand beneath its swirling waters. It was Lucan's swift and Virgil's shallow river.[14] In recent years numerous anthropogenic changes to its regime have taken place, including the establishment of hydroelectric installations, thus profoundly altering its natural hydrological characteristics.

A minor river, not without importance, is the Savone. Now heavily canalized, it rises on the eastern slopes of Roccamonfina and runs close to the southern base of the Massico, creating a basin of approximately 77km². Statius called it sluggish, and it was considered to be not much less turbid than the Volturno.[15]

The other major river of Caserta, whose lower reaches have since 1927 marked the divide between the regions of Lazio and Campania, is the Garigliano, to the north of the Massico range. It is Italy's sixth river in carrying capacity (122 cubic metres per second at Suio), followed by the larger Volturno. Flowing for 158km, with a basin of 4950km², it rises just above Sora as the river Liri.[16] Just to the south-east of Ceprano the Liri is met by the river Sacco and runs down the internal land corridor which joins Latium with Campania and once contained the Roman Via Latina.[17] After its confluence with the Gari, which collects water from La Mainarde, it assumes the name of Garigliano and changes direction to run between the Monti Aurunci and Monte Cassino, and then through the Roccamonfina/Monti Aurunci pass. Once through, it meanders for some 15 kilometres across a triangular basin before spilling-out into the sea. Various hydroelectrical plants have altered the river's regime, as well as Italy's first nuclear power station some 7km from its mouth. The Garigliano originally linked up with the Volturno by flowing in a south-easterly direction from the southern section of the Liri valley.[18] Its path was eventually blocked by an eruption of Roccamonfina, when it was made to forge its present course. Since classical times the river has altered its course to a slight extent, estimated at some 50m of lateral movement at Minturnae, close to its mouth.[19]

The early Quaternary coastline lay further inland. In the Garigliano basin it was at least up to two kilometres from the present shoreline in its central

---

[8] I should like to thank Jan Sevink for this information. The area seems to be totally devoid of antique remains, though the clay may have been extracted by Roman potters, and is now under plough.

[9] Cf Baratta, 1901; Kalby, 1982. See now the fundamental studies in Guidoboni, 1989.

[10] CIL IX 2338 = ILS 5588; CIL IX 2638. Cf. also CIL X 4858 for *Venafrum*.

[11] Borrelli, 1916, 22.

[12] Brancaccio, 1980.

[13] Ruocco, 1965, 135–136; *ibid*, 1970, 43.

[14] Ovid Met. XV, 714–715: *multamque trahens sub gurgite harenam Vulturnus*; Luc. II, 422–423; Vir. *Aen.* VII, 728–729; cf also Stat. *Silv.* IV, iii, 67–94, quoted in chap. 6 below.

[15] Stat. *Silv.* IV, iii, 66; cf Ippolito, 1930, 98.

[16] Almagià, 1966, 133–135.

[17] Quilici Gigli, 1970; Wightman, 1981, 275 and 281.

[18] Devoto, 1965.

[19] Ruegg, 1983; Brookes, 1974, 42.

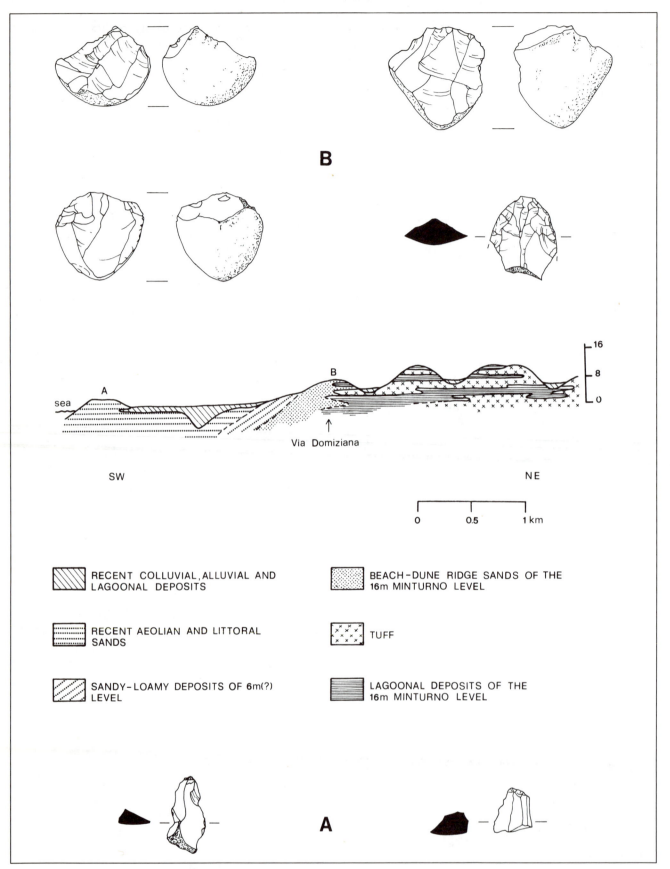

Fig 2   *Lithics from the recent littoral sands and from the 16m Minturno fossil beach ridge (after Remmelzwaal, 1978, with addition of the flints)*

section, and is marked by the littoral-aeolian deposits of the 16m Minturno level (Fig 1c). These, now fossil, beach-ridges were once backed by brackish marine lagoons (Fig 1e) and were frequented since, at least, the Upper Palaeolithic (Fig 2). The present coast (0–1m Terracina level. Fig 1, A) is also composed of beach-dune ridges, and emerged as a string of sandy barrier islands which, on merging, led to the creation of a lagoon (Fig 1, B). The actual formation of the beach ridges is complex and uncertain.[20] They had been formed and were actually frequented from, at least, the third millenium BC if not earlier, as is now archaeologically confirmed by finds of flints on the beach by the 'Swedish village' at Baia Domizia (Fig 2). Whatever processes were involved in their genesis, the most recent ones led to the formation of the lagoons and marshes which were to dictate the inland sweep of the Roman Via Appia.

In his 'Life of Marius', Plutarch refers to sailors who cast anchor at the mouth of the Garigliano, where the river expanded into a lake.[21] Further in the same passage, Marius proceeds through deep marshes and ditches full of mud and water. It is evident that already by classical times the lagoons were in existence. The area is now clearly visible as a non-calcareous peaty black soil between the Via Appia and Baia Domizia, and between the Garigliano to the north and Rio di S Limato to the south. It is, in fact, possible that the toponym S Limato derives from *limes* or *limites* referring to the edge of cultivable land in classical and later times. Much of the area which delimits the large lagoon now lies less than 5m asl. A smaller lagoon lay to the immediate south-west of the colony of Minturnae, between the Garigliano and the calcareous knoll of Mt D'Argento to the north. The two lagoons are clearly shown in the maps of A Bulifon (Naples, *c* 1692), de Rossi (Rome, 1714: pl I) and Covens and Mortier (Amsterdam, *c* 1720). The map drawn up by F Morghen around 1780, and all succeeding cartography, only shows the larger, southern, lagoon in the Piano di Sessa. The maps of Bulifon and Covens and Mortier both show two water courses feeding the southern lagoon at its northern and southern ends, whilst de Rossi's map indicates five water courses, the southernmost apparently deriving from Bagni Sulfurei. In this the map must

err, as the course is almost certainly the present Rio di S Limato, as opposed to an extinct course rising as far as Bagni Solfurei to the south. By the 1780s, according to Morghen's chart, the southernmost water course must have dried up, as only the northern one is illustrated. It may have been the Rio Travata, which, now partially canalized, flows into the Garigliano. It is marked on a road map of the mid eighteenth century as Rivo di Cascano.

When Scipione Breislak's map '*Topografia Fisica della Campania*', drawn up by Rizzi-Zannoni, appeared in 1797 the lagoon was no longer shown, although the whole coastal area is noticeably devoid of all human settlement and marsh conditions persisted in two major areas: the Pantano di Sessa (some 2000 hectares) running for *c* 9 km parallel to the coast, and the much smaller Pantano Corso (some 100 hectares) towards the interior.[22] King Ferdinand II of Naples attempted to drain the Garigliano basin between 1856 and 1859, without success.[23] The situation only began to improve at the turn of the century, but despite the formation of the Consorzio Aurunco di Bonifica in 1925, it was not until the programme of land reform set up in 1950 that the environment was rendered into its present state.[24] Apart from expropriation and re-distribution of properties, the programme saw to the draining, de-stoning and 'deep-ploughing' of much of the basin.[25] Altogether, some 127,000 hectares of land were effected in Campania, particularly in the floodplains of the Garigliano, Volturno and Sele rivers.

A further, small, lagoon once existed to the immediate north-west of Mondragone in a filled-in maar now known as Padule (*It* palude = marsh). The area is marked on the map drawn up by Baratta and published by the Marquis of Cusano in 1616 as a *stagno* or swamp. It also appears as such on a map by Bulifon labelled *Campania Felix* and prepared for the Duke of Maddaloni at the end of the seventeenth century.

Even though none of the maps illustrate lagoons between Mondragone and the Volturno to the south, until the 1950s the area had been one of the prime marshes of the country. Conditions were such that as early as 1471 the problem was raised in public parliament, though little of effect was achieved until the Bourbon programme of the Bonifica di Castel Volturno got under way in 1812.[26]

[20] Remmelzwaal, 1978, 47.
[21] Plutarch, *Mar.* xxxvii, 3.

[22] Giarizzo, 1965, 22.
[23] Pareto, 1865, 171 and 183.
[24] Legislation 841 of October 1st 1950: cf King, 1973, 49.
[25] It may be noted that some of the modern de-stoning machines are very effective in removing pottery sherds from a field. In fact, the agricultural reform programmes of this century marked a turning-point in the preservation of antiquities.
[26] Ippolito, 1930, 1; Afan de Rivera, 1847.

Cartography of the area demonstrates how the marsh in the right half of the floodplain was fed mainly by the 'sluggish' Savone and the meandering Rio delle Anze or Rio Lanzi. Conditions were further exacerbated by the Rio Fontanelle feeding the Lago di Carinola which, in turn, acted as a reservoir for the swamp which ran immediately to the south-east and parallel to a line drawn from Mondragone to Falciano. Baratta's map (Naples, 1616) shows some of the early, but relatively ineffectual, canals opened by Fontana for the Count of Lemos. The perennial flooding of the Volturno, noted already in classical times, was always a constant setback to drainage works, and despite some two thousand years of embanking operations it cannot yet be claimed that the problems of seasonal flooding are totally resolved.[27] The large scale works carried out in the first half of the nineteenth century were successful in transforming much of the higher floodplain into good agricultural land, whilst much fertile alluvial material was re-deposited, consequently raising the height of low-lying areas around the Savone. The effects are illustrated in a map of 1856, fruit of legislation for the systemization of marshlands ratified the previous year.[28] Part of the land came to form part of the *Real caccia del Savone*, or royal hunting grounds, whilst the area behind the coastal dunes between Mondragone and the Volturno remained stagnant.

The late 1920s and '30s witnessed a radical transformation of agricultural conditions in the Campanian plain with the final abolition of malaria and a spectacular increase in crop yield.[29] The affected areas were also totally drained and new agricultural and social services established. The programme of 1950 saw to the restoration of the ground lost during the war, and saw to the eventual completion of the final pages of what had been a long and unfortunate chapter in the history of the Italian landscape. The last canalizing works of note took place in recent times and have secured the drainage of land between Cellole and the sea which was often flooded in winter months. Such episodes are now rare (pl II), though vivid reminders are the farmsteads constructed above flood level on artificial hillocks.

The most significant geomorphological change in the area over the last two millennia, apart from the disappearance of the lagoons, would appear to be the loss of part of the classical coastline by a rise in sea level.[30] A recent examination, by Pirazzoli, of eighteen archaeological sites along the Provençal and Italian Tyrrhenian coast as far south as Formia suggests that the rise has not been more than a mean 0.5m, and that the 2–3m fluctuations suggested by some scholars should be 'ascribed to noneustatic causes: local tidal changes, storm surges, tectonics, climate changes, or misinterpretations'.[31] The effect may not have been greatly significant as far as Roman remains are concerned, though coastal towns could have suffered and it may have contributed to the degeneration of coastal marshes.

Nonetheless, it is a widely held belief that a good part of the maritime colony of Sinuessa now lies beneath the sea, on the basis of various structures visible at depths of, at least, eighteen metres.[32] The finds do not seem incompatible with harbour elements such as moles and possible warehouses, whilst other remains are reported offshore at the same latitude as the Thermae Sinuessanae. Bearing in mind the findings of Pirazzoli, the exaggerated depth of eighteen metres, even for harbour foundations, which were in any case below sea level, can only be explained by localized tectonic shifts. Perhaps seismic or volcanic activity, to which the area is not new, have resulted, as in the Phlegrean Fields, in the inundation of Sinuessa's port and related elements.[33]

'Yet before our iron cleaves an unknown plain, be it first our care to learn the winds and the wavering moods of the sky, the wonted tillage and nature of the ground, what each clime yields and what each disowns'.[34] An ignorance of the parameters of temperature, wind and rainfall can ultimately lead to gross misunderstandings, abuse and devastation. Most farmers have learnt this empirically and act accordingly.

Northern Campania has a Mediterranean climate. That is, it has the characteristics of the zone lying between the northern limit of the olive tree and the northern limit of the palm grove.[35] The area is moreover complemented its own particular set of micro-climatic characteristics formed by localized variations in geomorphology and situation. The flat lands of the Volturno basin and the coastal strip now lie above the 16° C isotherm, with a recorded maximum temperature for the years 1926 to 1955 of

[27] Stat. *Silv.* IV, iii, 79–80; Ippolito, 1930, 4–5.
[28] Savarese, 1856, pl. 2.
[29] The work carried out up to 1930 is usefully summarized by Ippolito (1930), though compare also Ciasca (1928).

[30] Schmiedt, 1972.
[31] Pirazzoli, 1976.
[32] Cf Cicala and Lao, 1958.
[33] For the Phlegrean Fields the bibliography is immense, stimulated further by the recent movements which have led to a partial abandonment of Pozzuoli and the creation of a new town at Monte Ruscello, though see, for example, Frederiksen, 1977.
[34] Virgil *Georg.* I, l-liii.
[35] Braudel, 1975, I, 234.

40° 1′ C at Caserta. The temperature cools progressively the higher one ventures, so that the heights of the Massico and Roccamonfina possess a 10° C isotherm. The coldest month is January with an average 8° 6′ C at Caserta, although the temperature can drop below 0°, even in February. These trends are partly caused by alternate winds from the Atlantic (libeccio and mistral) and from the northern continent (tramontana and grecale). Particularly in springtime, the warm and close African wind or scirocco affects the area, sometimes depositing a reddish desert dust. The maximum temperatures are to be found in July with the northward migration of tropical high pressures, whilst there is an almost negligible cooling-off in August.

Rain is particularly abundant in Campania, though irregularly distributed through the year. The summer months are usually very dry along the coast and in the Campanian plain, whilst the Sannio Appenines can receive between a sixth and an eighth of its annual precipitation of 800 to 1000mm. The Ferragosto rains (August 15th), however, are proverbial. The greater parts of the Garigliano and Volturno basins receive an annual aggregate of up to 1000mm, whilst Roccamonfina receives between 1400 and 1600mm of rain *per annum*. The majority of rain falls in autumn and winter, with a concentration during November, sometimes provoking severe floods.[36] Spring can be changeable. Though often producing light and beneficial showers, it does on occasion mark the beginning of a period of drought or yield enough cool rain to damage certain grains, vines and fruit trees.[37] It may be noted that the irregularity of Campanian precipitation has led to the formation of numerous seasonal runoff channels, particularly in the limestone hills.

The understanding of soils is equally important in assessing an area's potential and constraints in agricultural and industrial processes, as well as providing information on a landscape's genesis, development and man's effect on the environment. Their past form may now be masked by both natural and anthropic agents, and it is a truism to say that the ecological characteristics of the land have radically altered over the years.

Forest clearance, for example, has exposed soils and rocks to increased erosion and aided the deposition of sediments in valley bottoms, thus altering both natural and artificial drainage systems leading, in some cases, to the development of stagnant waters, marshes and malaria. Cultivation of particular crops

and hillside terracing, on the other hand, could have neutralizing effects, impeding the downward movement of erosion products. Efficient agrarian regimes can help to balance environmental deterioration, but the ancients were only generally aware of the natural processes, and most attempts at improving conditions stemmed from observation of direct cause and effect and were consequently often paliatives. In the long term, much of man's work was ultimately degenerative.

The fairly complex soil genesis in the area of the lower Garigliano basin has recently been the subject of an in-depth study by Remmelzwaal, from whose work figure 1 is drawn.[38] The predominant geological features have already been discussed, and local soil development is due predominantly to their presence.

The slopes of the Roccamonfina caldera (Fig 1, g and h) often present such steep gradients as to militate against efficient agricultural exploitation, and the soils consequently support a fairly dense forest cover. The same may be said for some of the steeper limestone slopes (Fig 1, k). However, most of the soils visible today may be considered light and easily workable by hand or animal traction. The most difficult areas, of alluvial fans and colluvium (Fig 1, l), which may have once necessitated plough-teams of two to four oxen, are generally restricted to the calcareous piedmont. Patches of the less easily worked clays on the south-eastern side of the Massico were nevertheless exploited in imperial times by a fairly flourishing pottery industry which has not totally disappeared today. Even the river floodplains, which may have created some difficulty on account of poor drainage, form only a small percentage of the available farming land.

The Garigliano itself does not seem to have shifted much across its floodplain since the formation of the 16m Minturno level. There are nonetheless traces of minor movements since Roman times which may have eroded part of its banks and, in one case, a developing meander has migrated some 50m or so northwards. The thick floodplain deposits consist of well-sorted silty to clayey sediments with fair drainage conditions. All in all, the lower-lying areas are to be considered excellent farming land, though it is to be noted that farmers today regard the area to the south of the Massico as preferable, with crops coming to maturity some twenty days earlier than those to the north, perhaps partly explaining the slightly differing densities of Roman sites in the two areas.

[36] See, for example, *Receuil des Gazettes*, Naples, 1650, 1557, cited by Braudel, 1975, I, 233, note 6, for torrential rains inundating Capua on November 2nd 1650.
[37] Ruocco, 1970, 31–42.

[38] Remmelzwaal 1978.

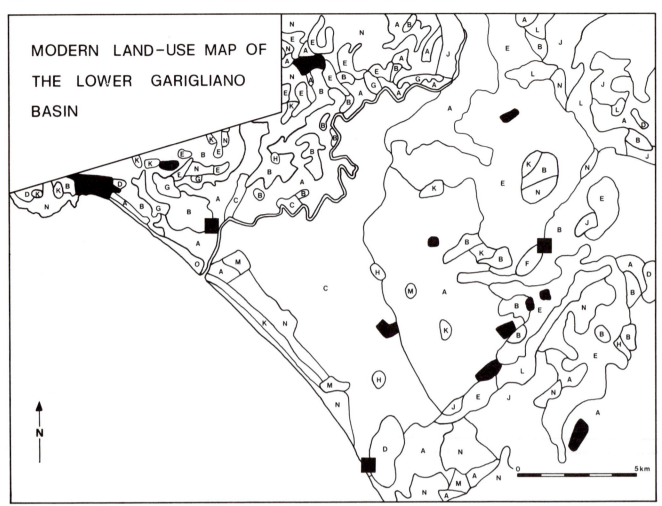

Fig 3   Land-use map of the Garigliano basin (after the Carta della Utilizzazione del suolo d'Italia, foglio 16, TCI, 1960).
Key: A = Seed crops (dry); B = Seed crops and trees (dry); C = Irrigated seed crops; D = Vineyard; E = Olive grove;
F = Orchard; G = Citrus fruit orchard; H = Fruit orchard; J = Coppice; K = Tall forest; L = Chestnut coppice;
M = Grassland; N = Pasture and land occasionaly used for seed crops; O = Virgin

Soil deposition since classical times may be partly gauged by depth of buried remains. Alluvial fanning and colluviation has accounted for a certain amount of burial of archaeological remains along the base of the Massico (in the area between Suessa and Sinuessa, marked 1, on fig 1). In a road section between Piedimonte and Carano, Roman tile was discovered beneath some two metres of clay, and probably derived from a site further up the slope to the south-west. In the Garigliano floodplain, however, erosion and alluviation do not appear to have destroyed or greatly buried much of the classical landscape. Roman sites are visible on the floodplain at Maiano, whilst a group of tile-tombs under only a few centimetres of soil was destroyed during construction of the nuclear power station in 1964.[39]

All told, the classical land-surface does not appear to have been much different from that of recent times.

Vegetation

Figure 3 illustrates the way in which the land around the lower Garigliano basin was divided according to crop types in 1960. It is immediately evident that the greatest surface area, and particularly the tuff slopes and alluvial floodplain, was covered with both dry and irrigated seed crops, amongst which the cereals predominated. The cultivation of cereals in Campania today is not greatly significant, taking up a value of no more than 10% of the aggregate yield, with wheat and maize predominating and divided up between dry and irrigated land.[40] The olive, instead, takes up a notable area, particularly on the higher tuff and limestone slopes, but also along the alluvial fans and colluvial deposits along the base of the Massico, though recently it has yielded ground to more cost-effective fruit-trees in the lower areas.[41] There are vineyards in the hills above

[39] In loc. Morelle: Soprintendenza archives S. 8–11.

[40] Ruocco, 1970, 100.
[41] Ruocco, 1970, 132.

Sinuessa and other patches around Scauri, Casanova di Carinola, Falciano and on the southern side of Roccamonfina. It would also seem as though every rural household has its own small crop for domestic use. Nonetheless it has a surprisingly limited distribution, almost certainly much less than in antiquity when land now abandoned or half-heartedly turned over to the olive was under cultivation. In fact, local wines have only a regional distribution and little reputation, in contrast to their antique status. The cultivation of citrus fruit is limited particularly to the north of the Garigliano. Other fruit orchards are found scattered mainly to the south of the river on volcanic tuffs, and to a large extent comprise peach trees.

Coppicing is found widespread on the lava outflows of Roccamonfina and on parts of the Massico, whilst a fair amount of chestnut survives. The coastal strip of infilled lagoons and modern dunes is given over to tall pines (pineta), backed by pasture and grassland, much of which has disappeared over the last twenty years because of the development of holiday resorts.

The present picture (pl III) is thus one of fairly intensive and rational agricultural exploitation of the lowland zones, which contrasts to the uplands turned over to coppice or small-scale olive cultivation, when macchia, on the limestones, is not the dominating feature.

Exaggerated growth-rings noted on beams recovered from the Garigliano seem to indicate the presence of oak woodland during the republic, whilst inscriptions from Minturnae make clear the survival of a significant amount of pine in the area at least until the first century BC.[42] It is difficult to gauge how much woodland was regenerated in later Roman and medieval times, though various toponyms reveal the more recent existence of woodland remnants composed particularly of oak (Cerquello, Cerqua, etc), elm (Ulmo) and other species. Much of their destruction is to be charged to the extension of surface area devoted to agriculture in post-medieval times and to the supply of timber and charcoal, particularly oak, to towns.[43]

The fauna

The exploitation of faunal resources is, with a notable exception, of little importance. In a recent work on transhumance in Italy it was stated that 'in Campania stock-raising must have been predominantly stable and subordinated to agriculture; the Campanian ager publicus was almost certainly wholly cultivated, it included mountainous areas and the marshy zones around Minturnae could have constituted good grazing lands'.[44] This may not be far from the truth as, given the general excellence of the land for agricultural purposes, sheep husbandry cannot have formed a significant part of the local economy save for in the lulls between periods of intensive cultivation, and as a medium for the successful practising of a fallow system alongside goats, cattle and geese. However, despite Juvenal's point that sheep-rearing was not becoming to the wealthy, even the medium and large agricultural estates may have maintained a number of sheep. Cato included 100 sheep in his list of farm equipment for an olive-plantation of 240 iugera. They must have formed an integral, if often minor, component of every fundus so as at least to provide for immediate needs, primarily in the way of wool, dairy produce and manure.[45] Given Juvenal's statement, it is further possible that certain agriculturalists owned sheep 'at a distance', and one may wonder whose money lay behind the immense flocks that are reported as grazing in the territory of Casinum, an area which 'may, despite Roman colonization, have remained in a state of relative underdevelopment throughout the republic'.[46] Livestock in general would be functional to an agricultural regime in furnishing fertilizers for the regeneration of heavily-worked soils such as Campania and, as far as sheep are concerned, it may be noted that a single beast can produce some 500kg of manure per annum, equal to about ten times its own weight. In such fashion, the controlled animal may have been viewed as a positive factor towards a healthy agrarian regime, as opposed to a farmer's pest leading to land degeneration through overgrazing.[47]

---

[42] For the oak: Brother D. Ruegg, pers. comm.; for the pine see Johnson, 1933, 126–128.
[43] Ruocco, 1970, 179; De Santis, 1945.

[44] Gabba and Pasquinucci, 1979, 75–182.
[45] Juv. Sat. I, 107–108; Cato de Agr. X, ii; Colum. RR VII, ii, 1.
[46] Wightman, 1981, 286; for the flocks around Casinum see Varro RR II, iii, 10. It may be noted that many late republican families attested in northern Campania, especially at Teanum Sidicinum, appear to come from the territories of Aesernia, Casinum, Venafrum, etc.
[47] Baticle, 1974; Lewthwaite, 1981, 61.

Though remembering M Antonius M.f. Claudia Terentus, *negotiator suariae et pecuariae* from Campania, in first century Rome, the sources for northern Campania are little more than silent.[48] It may be no accident that in a treatise on the agriculture of Sessa published at the turn of the eighteenth century the land's principal products are listed as oil, wine, cereals and legumes, whilst sheep, together with other animals, rate barely a mention.[49] Even today livestock are not common in the areas around the Massico, apart from the water buffalo which was a singular post-classical introduction intended to aid exploitation of the early medieval degenerated lands.[50] Few sheep are to be seen, although a number of people still remember a recent immigration of shepherds and their families from Longano (Campobasso) and Picinisco (Frosinone) to the *comune* of Sessa Aurunca. Before settling in the area they used to appear from the Mt Matese during the winter to peddle ricotta cheese and other ovine products. Their transhumant activities are recorded as recently as 1958, when they would arrive with their families and erect their camp of tents in the low-lying land around Minturno (see fig. 3 for pasture and grassland).[51] One particular family, living in the area of S Mauro, Mondragone, with a flock of some forty sheep, now obviates the transference of the animals over long distances by pasturing them up in the hills of the Massico during the summer months. Though perhaps not ideal, it indicates the capacity of the area for small-scale, perennial, sheep-rearing without recourse to transhumance.

On the archaeological side, the ubiquity of clay-loomweights suggests that household production of woollen objects was widespread throughout Campania, as in much of the rest of Italy. Extensive excavation at the small republican farm of Posto yielded six, although the author points out that they are not an indication that wool was produced directly on the property, whilst a Hellenistic farm at Botromagno, Puglia, in a more typical pastoral zone, yielded over a hundred and fifty.[52] In 1930, it was stated at Carmignano in Tuscany that 'today weaving is no longer diffuse; once weaving was

practised in every home'.[53] Morel seems to have reached a similar conclusion, claiming that in Roman times domestic production, to provide a percentage of a household's finished products, probably played a large role alongside that of the professional ateliers. This would seem contrary to Moeller's view of Pompeii, which may overestimate the quality of cloth requirements of a 'society as sophisticated as the Roman', although rural household production was presumably more frequent than urban household production.[54]

The production of a famous cheese (*caseus*) in the campus Caedicius is probably further indication of the presence of sheep in the area in Roman times, whilst the few shepherds present today produce small quantities of the strong and salty *pecorino* or *caso*.[55]

The importance of pig to the area's ancient economy is also difficult to assess, although it is the predominant species in most Italian faunal assemblages of Roman date, reaching 61% in a group of 567 identifiable bones recovered from late republican and early imperial contexts at Pompeii.[56] It is possible that there was a decline in proportions with the reduction of woodland through Roman times, particularly in favour of sheep, though again for much of Italy samples are few and results preliminary. The Theodosian Code registers the exportation of Campanian pork to Rome during the fourth century, although the quantity may well have been exceeded by that exported from Apulia and Lucania.[57] In more recent times the pig has been a feature of the Garigliano basin when, in the 1930s, it numbered second only to sheep. By 1960, however, its number had fallen dramatically below those of both cattle and horses, whilst its preferred oak woodland habitat had long since been destroyed.[58]

Both the lagoons and rivers of the area were also exploited for food. Lagoons and marshes offer fish and some wildfowl.[59] The potential importance of lagoonal fishing may be indicated by the angry protests at the proposal to drain the Lago Lesina in Puglia in 1923.[60] The river Garigliano is a significant source of eels, as it was in 1798, alongside bass and mullet, whilst trout could be had further

---

[48] CIL VI 33887 = ILS 7481; Plutarch *Crass.* IX, 3, refers to the many herdsmen and shepherds joining with Spartacus during the great slave revolt which had been initiated by gladiators at Capua. They too were presumably slaves and, though Plutarch's text does suggest that Spartacus received the reinforcements after he had departed the ager Campanus for the hills, may have belonged to Campanian estates.

[49] Gagliardo, 1814.

[50] Giarizzo, 1965, 71ff.

[51] Fedele, 1958, 132.

[52] Posto: Cotton, 1979, 76; Botromagno: Du Plat Taylor and Carter, 1969, 156.

[53] Scheuermeier, 1943, 285.

[54] Morel, 1976, 299; Moeller, 1976, 5.

[55] Pliny *NH* XI, xcvii, 241; Gagliardo, 1814, 24 (*cacio*).

[56] A King in Arthur and De Caro, report on excavations in and around the forum at Pompeii, forthcoming.

[57] *Cod. Theod.* 14, 4, 3, for AD 362/3; cf Chastagnol, 1953; Whitehouse, 1981; Barnish, 1987; and the interesting farming establishment at S Giovanni di Ruoti where pork appears to have been a major product: Small, 1981.

[58] Giarizzo, 1965, 74.

[59] Greco, 1927, II, 125.

[60] Colaccio, 1955, 55; cited by Delano-Smith, 1979, 388.

upstream.[61] Excavators of Minturnae were astounded by the amount of lead, hooks and weights connected with fishing to be found by the bridge over the Garigliano.[62]

Historical and archaeological evidence for the exploitation of seafood is meagre. To Pliny the Campanian shores were '*praeter...cetera in toto mari conchylio et pisce nobili adnotantur*'.[63] Athenaeus, in the late second and early third century AD, wrote of the gourmet Apicius who 'had lavished countless sums on his belly in Minturnae, a city of Campania, and lived there eating mostly high-priced prawns, which grow bigger there than the largest prawns of Smyrna or the lobsters of Alexandria'.[64] Pliny wrote that, under Claudius, wrasse were imported into the Tyrrhenian from the Carpathian sea and distributed between the Tiber mouth and the coast of Campania and, after a five year fishing restriction, they became native.[65]

Only two apparent fisheries are known, from the rockier northern section of the Garigliano basin, at Loc. Olmo and at Gianola, near Scauri.[66] The preparation of fish-sauces such as *garum* is not locally attested, whilst Spanish fish-sauce amphorae have been found on a number of survey sites and, indeed, seem to be more common than Baetican oil amphorae. In the absence of excavations, shellfish (*Donax (Serrula) trunculus*) are attested in abundance, associated with late republican pottery, on a surveyed site (M7) near Sinuessa.

In conclusion, it is difficult to deny the wealth of the land in and around the Garigliano basin as a natural resource area, and its suitability for successful employment in agriculture and certain basic manufacturing activities. Though the land was not fully harnessed before classical times, it may be suggested that the first sudden anthropogenic changes in the landscape occurred in the first half of the first millenium BC with the extension of Iron Age settlement into lower lying zones (see below). An acceleration in the process of change occurred as a direct result of Roman intervention from the end of the fourth century BC. Within the space of a few generations the land had been largely deforested, first so as to meet the demands of agriculture and building and subsequently to fuel a number of developing industries. With increasing demand the newly cleared slopes were turned over principally to the vine and olive. The low-lying areas were divided up into plots and used predominantly for the cultivation of cereals, though peaches and beans are also attested, indicating a rational involvement in polyculture to satisfy, at least, local demand. A certain amount of land drainage, though without doubt not on the recent scale, may have advanced cultivation into previously water-logged zones. The lagoons were generally avoided, though probably providing fish. Clayey soils, also farmed, were exploited by a flourishing pottery industry for the production of domestic wares, building materials and agricultural *instrumenta*, whilst the rocks of the area were quarried for pozzolana, marble, limestone, tuff and basalt or lava. It would thus appear that by the late republic, technology permitting, the opportunities offered by the land were exploited to the full, as seems further emphasized by a high population density. It will be the purpose of the following chapters to examine the archaeological and documentary evidence in detail in an attempt to extrapolate changing patterns of land exploitation through the course of time.

[61] *Corografia ....*, 1798, 110.
[62] Comfort, 1976, 583.
[63] Pliny *NH* III, v, 60.
[64] Athen. *Delp.* I, vii: Loeb text. To this day excellent lobsters, often from the island of Ponza, may be had in the markets of Formia and Minturno.
[65] Pliny *NH* IX, xxix.
[66] Aurigemma and De Santis, 1955, 59; Schmiedt, 1972, 142–145; cf also Schmiedt, 1981.

Chapter Two

The Archaeology

In 1938 the then Superintendent of Antiquities, Amedeo Maiuri, wrote that 'the Massico mountain chain, natural frontier between Latium novum and Campania, which in historical times was the natural bulwark between the Aurunci and the Campani, is still one of the least understood regions of Campania'. The situation had not substantially changed in 1976 when Werner Johannowsky published a seminal paper dealing above all with the classical settlement and communications on the southern side of the Massico ridge, save for the fact that bulldozing, levelling and deep-ploughing had, by then, become the order of the day.

It would be vain to attempt to date the beginning of an historical awareness of Campania, its importance being recognised as almost second only to Rome. However, in spite of the numerous surviving remains in northern Campania, archaeology stood for the most part neglected until the eighteenth century despite the fact that the 'grand tourists' regularly passed through the area on their way south.

On the 24th February 1787, Wolfgang Goethe crossed the Garigliano, heading for Naples: 'Nothing appears to us surprising'. A few kind words for the magnificent scenery of Sessa and a nice hotel at Sant'Agata on the Appia: 'Our room is cold. No window, only the blinds, which I hasten to close'.[1]

The first study of substance was, ironically, compiled by the noted falsario Francesco Maria Pratilli who, in 1745, published his *Della Via Appia riconosciuta e descritta da Roma a Brindisi*. Pratilli was a Capuan canon who set about the task of supplementing the existing evidence for the land through which the Appia passed with the aid of his fertile imagination. Even more damaging was his Lombard history, written as a revised edition of Pellegrino's *Historia Principum Langobardorum*.[2]

His work was followed not long after by a valuable study by De Masi, whose archaeological observations still appear to be a useful testimony of what had once been. His 'debt' to Pratilli may be gauged through his footnotes, and it is instructive to note how many inscriptions had been 'lost' between the publication of *Della Via Appia...* in 1745 and De Masi's *Memorie Istoriche degli Aurunci* in 1761, over a period of only sixteen years! Exemplary is a supposed funerary inscription of a *liberta* of C Nasennius, citizen of Suessa and, significantly, friend of Cicero.[3]

The finding of antiquities, with the sporadic re-use of architectural fragments in building projects, was a constant occurence, though the remains were rarely understood and received little attention in the literature. The initiation of excavations at Herculaneum in 1738, and those at Pompeii ten years later, lent impetus to the collection of classical pieces and persuaded Breislak in 1798, on the basis of Roman buildings revealed during construction works and well borings, that Suessa Aurunca likewise had been subjected to burial by volcanic eruption. Publication of discoveries was, more often than not, limited to the edition of inscriptions which were finally sifted by Theodor Mommsen for CIL X, which appeared in 1883.

Of note, however, is Ciuffi's *Memorie istoriche ed archeologiche di Traetto* (1854), for the area around Minturnae, and Menna's *Saggio istorico della città di Carinola* (1848), for the *ager Falernus*. Riccardelli, who also published a number of local inscriptions in 1873, was not lacking in fantasy by presenting a text supplying the date and number of slaves employed in the construction of the well-preserved aqueduct at Minturnae! It was about this time that the first rescue excavation took place in the lower Garigliano basin, and a large section of the Roman bathing complex at the Aquae Vescinae was unearthed in exemplary fashion by the engineer Fulvio between 1877 and 1892 prior to the construction of a hotel-spa complex.[4] Until then excavation had at most comprised the organised looting of *objets d'art* by figures as notable as the Austrian Marshal Nugent, whose discoveries at Minturnae between 1817 and 1819 now grace the collections of Zagreb Museum.[5] Early this century Minturnae became the protagonist of more methodological research, conducted by the University of Pennsylvania, which brought to light a substantial part of the town and a wealth of inscriptions.[6] The same years also saw important excavations by Mingazzini at the sanctuary of Marica, at the mouth of the Garigliano.[7]

[1]   Goethe, 1886.
[2]   Pellegrino, 1643; revised ed. by Pratilli, 1749–1754; cf Cilento, 1966, 24–29, and Mommsen, CIL X, p 373, for evaluations of Pratilli's work.

[3]   Pratilli, 1745, 221; De Masi, 1761, 174; Cic. *Ad Brut* I, 16.
[4]   NS 1887, 406–410; 1888, 460; 1892, 236–288.
[5]   Johnson, 1935, 13; Crema, 1933.
[6]   Johnson, 1933, 1935 and 1936; Kirsopp-Lake, 1935; Comfort, 1943.
[7]   Mingazzini, 1938. The data has been recently re-assessed in Talamo, 1985.

Sinuessa fared worse as the scene of wholesale destruction and depredation, particularly in more recent times, save for limited excavations by Werner Johannowsky, Luigi D'Amore and, ultimately, by Maurizio Gualtieri and the writer. Paradoxically Suessa Aurunca, as an example of urban continuity, is at least preserved beneath the modern town, save for its cemeteries which have witnessed a certain amount of destruction at the hands of tomb robbers and urban developers.

Unsystematic data collection has been practised this century by a host of amateur historians and archaeologists, of whom Pietro Fedele, pre-war parliamentary member, and Giuseppe Tommassino, once mayor of Sessa, are of especial note. The former formed a large collection of antiquities which was housed in a Lombard tower erected by Pandulf at the mouth of the Garigliano and blown up by German troops in 1943.[8] Others likewise amassed collections, the greater part of which have now been dispersed, though Tommassino diligently published the results of his studies in two volumes, *Aurunci Patres* (1942) and *Sulla Antica Dominazione degli Aurunci in Campania* (1925). A minor proportion of material, particularly epigraphic, has passed into the hands of the bishopric of Sessa and publication in the near future is promised by Giuseppe Guadagno.

To the south of the Massico two local historians have been particularly active, Biagio Greco (1927) and Antonio Sementini (nd), both publishing monographs on the history of the area around Mondragone, presenting valuable topographic information on sites no longer visible. As with most of the above-cited works, fact is to be divorced from the fiction of a too literal interpretation of the evidence.

Systematic archaeological and historical work, apart from some notable exceptions already cited, is principally confined to the last fifteen years or so. Preliminary fruits of Johannowsky's topographic studies appeared in 1975, one of his students published a thesis on pre-Roman fortified sites, whilst up-dated guides have appeared for Minturnae, Sinuessa and Suessa Aurunca.[9] The Ecole Francaise has been involved in research on antique land divisions, whilst even the efforts of local historians continue unabated, though most conspicuously for the territory of Sessa Aurunca.[10]

Despite this recent research fervour, controlled

excavation is virtually non-existent and confined principally to Roman sites. For what may eventually transpire to be typical of farming establishments in northern Campania we possess two excavated and published sites at Francolise.[11] A further villa, awaiting publication, has been excavated by Nunzio Allegro near Falciano. Pierfrancesco Talamo has trial-trenched an Iron Age settlement at Ponte Ronaco, near Sessa Aurunca, whilst the writer has excavated part of an amphora kiln dump, near Casanova di Carinola, and a section of Sinuessa together with Maurizio Gualtieri. Other excavations have been exiguous. To complete the panorama of previous work in the area it is necessary to mention the underwater projects carried out by the Istituto di Studi Liguri at Sinuessa, by the Centro Subacqueo Sinuessa on a Republican shipwreck and, most notably, by an American team working within the mouth of the Garigliano by the side of Minturnae.[12]

To provide an enlarged data base for the area, counterpoised with the historical scheme and pre-existing archaeological evidence, field survey was undertaken by the writer in an area of approximately 100 sq kilometres centered on the Massico, thus touching environments ranging from seabord to upland, and from calcareous to volcanic. This took place mainly between 1979 and 1981, through various months of the year, though in general the September/October ploughing seasons were found to be the best time for visibility on arable lands. The survey was to a large extent a single-handed effort, with periods of assistance from students of the University of Naples and British colleagues.

It was conducted on two levels:

A. Areas subjected to intensive survey, where total coverage was aimed at, using as far as possible walked transects of 5 metre spacing. This comprised virtually the entire map sheet of Mondragone (IGM F.171 II NE), a north-south strip of 2 kilometres width of the map sheet of Carinola (IGM F.172 IV SO) and the Massico piedmont area of the map sheet of Sessa Aurunca (IGM F.171 I SE).

B. Areas subjected to spot-survey aimed at supplementing information for the settlement and land-use pattern. This included much of the rest of the Garigliano basin, particularly to the south of the river, not subjected to intensive survey. This work proved to be especially useful in reconstructing

[8] D'Onofrio, 1980; Cecchelli, 1951.
[9] For the fortified sites see Conta Haller, 1978, and the alternative views of Guadagno, 1979; Minturnae: De Spagnolis, 1981; Sinuessa: Pagano and Ferone, 1976; Suessa Aurunca: Vallestrisco, 1977 and 1980.
[10] The work of the Ecole Francaise is presented in Chouquer *et al*, 1987, though see also Vallat, *passim*. For the local historians see Petterutti, 1983, and Villucci, *passim*.

[11] Cotton, 1979; Cotton and Metraux, 1985.
[12] Cicala and Lao, 1958; Randazzo, 1982; Ruegg, 1984, with bibliography.

communication networks and examining sites of key significance, such as Minturnae, which had a powerful bearing on the dynamics of the whole territory.

Constraints of time, money and manpower suggested this dual approach where, in certain areas, it would have been preferable to extend survey type A.

Three main difficulties were encountered:

I. Natural burial and erosion. The Massico is extremely steep and inaccessible in places, largely covered with *macchia mediterranea*, and occasionally thickly wooded. The extensive summer fires of 1981 improved visibility momentarily and permitted the examination of the surfaces on the southern slopes around the Conca di S Mauro, with limited finds.

The main factor in site alteration, however, is natural erosion, particularly on the steeper northern face of the Massico, causing:

1. obliteration of traces of human activity by the removal of archaeological material downhill;
2. redeposition of archaeological material and potential creation of new 'sites';
3. total or partial burial of archaeological material, especially in piedmont areas.

The scale of potential erosion is indicated by the discovery of modern rubbish beneath over 1m of soil, on the west side of Mt S Anna. A major phase of erosion seems to have taken place in late Iron Age and/or early Roman times, to judge by the position of archaeological finds in exposed sections around the base of the Massico. Otherwise, major erosion seems to be localised to areas of concentrated runoff.

II. Inaccessibility. A number of landowners and coloni in the area were hostile to archaeologists, up to the point of menacing with firearms. This condition seems to stem from high land prices and the awareness and hostility towards the government's prerogative to expropriate or temporarily sequester land bearing archaeological remains.[13] The local attitude towards archaeology appears far more negative than attitudes that I have encountered in other parts of Italy. Furthermore, there is an increasing tendency amongst absentee landowners (often from Naples), especially in the area to the north of the Massico, to fence off their properties as a precaution against theft of fruit.

It is further to be noted that, around the suggestively entitled locality of Monte Vallerovina, a NATO base restricts all forms of access. Modern nucleated settlement is also likely to obscure important data. Roman material has come to light in three areas of Mondragone, aside from the land to the sides of the Via Domiziana, whilst tile tombs have been found during road works at Falciano. What is urgently required for the small towns are material assemblages that will date their effective origin as

components of the nucleated settlement pattern that persists to this day.

III. Anthropic destruction. The 1960s saw the beginning of commercial interest in the coastal land for the development of tourist resorts. In the space of only a few years three new settlements have appeared: Baia Domizia, Baia Felice and Baia Azzura. Though the first was built, with all official sanctions, in an area largely composed of infilled lagoon and marshes, the last two have severly impinged on the suburban territory of Sinuessa. With the rise in land prices and the decrease in available space, clandestine construction has taken place within the Roman colony and around the western foothills of the Massico. As a corollary the 1970s witnessed an increment in the number of so-called *tombaroli*, who excavate illicitly to supply the antiquities market, to the point of becoming 'professional'. In one year they are alleged to have unearthed some 1000 Roman burials around Sinuessa in the space of just two months (pl IV).

To this destruction may be added the growth of a number of large agricultural estates in the hinterland, specialising in fruit crops and particularly peaches. To create the necessary flat open fields in hilly areas, large terraces are cut through the use of the bulldozer, successfully removing archaeological remains including Roman villas, foundations and all (pl V). Much of the Roman road between Sessa Aurunca and Cascano has been removed in this way, as has a portion of the town of Forum Claudii, though the area most seriously damaged appears to be that within the *comune* of Sessa Aurunca. The resources of the Soprintendenza Archeologica are obviously inadequate to cope with such wholesale devastation in just one small segment of the total area which falls under its jurisdiction. The field survey is thus particularly timely, though even so cannot keep abreast of the scale and rapidity of destruction.

Despite the drawbacks, over 300 archaeological sites have been examined of which at least 181 are datable to Roman times. To make any sense out of the rather disparate collection of material it was necessary to employ some sort of chronological framework which would allow quantification and comparison of relative figures of types of sites functioning at specific points over a period of time. At least in one way this would maximize the objectivity in identifying and evaluating trends in changing settlement patterns. It is inadvisable to place too much weight on relative figures as various factors might impede recognition of sites of varying type or period, in favour of others. For example, early medieval sites might be under-represented because

---

[13] Legislation no. 1089 of 6. 6. 1939, art. nos. 43 and 54–57.

of our limited knowledge of early medieval pottery types and distributions, palaeolithic sites may be under-represented because of substantial geological changes, including the deposition of eruptive material, whilst late Republican villas will be well represented because of the ease of recognition of surviving structures and contemporary material culture.[14]

In theory there is a certain safety in numbers; a breaking point above which the mistaken or failed attribution of a percentage of sites will not affect gross results obtained from statistical analyses of the whole. Unfortunately, this is not so simple in practice on account of the innumerable distorting factors. If it is true that surface remains on average represent only some 2% of buried assemblages, and this in itself is arguable, then of the 69 late African Red Slip sherds recovered from the near-total excavation of the villa at Posto, we should be fortunate in finding even one sherd through surface collection to represent a whole phase of late activity, and no one in their right mind would base a period of occupation on a single item.[15]

A further distorting factor is the degree of erosion to which surface material may be subjected. Thirty-nine sherds of black glazed wares, sigillata and other recognisable Roman fine wares, from a site which had been extensively ploughed, were measured across their maximum surviving length. The smallest sherds were 0.9cm, the largest 5.7cm, with a mean of 2.7cm. These fragments were identified through their characteristic surviving surfaces. Prehistoric and unglazed early medieval sherds, of similar size and often less resilient surfaces, will clearly pose great difficulties in identification. The most easily identifiable prehistoric and Iron Age sherds are those from colluvial deposits which have not been subjected to intensive agricultural activity.

A further drawback is that, to my mind, 100sq km is too small an area to be representative of the complex situation posed by northern Campania, though quite adequate in understanding the dynamics of the Massico and Garigliano basin. A larger area could not have been covered as the survey was executed mainly by the author, without the means to systematically monitor sites and the land over a sufficient arc of time. In this sense, the survey is far more similar to some of the earlier south Etruria surveys than those with greater resources conducted recently in Molise, the ager Cosanus and elsewhere.

It is important that such biases are borne in mind although they would probably not weigh too heavily on general trends deduced through gross changes in the number of sites obtained and subsequent figures calculated for each period (*infra*).

Settlement sites, excluding towns, have been divided into periods expressed in a chronological scheme based on that adopted for south Etruria, with adjustments for a northern Campanian context (table A).[16] The periods are not to be interpreted in any strict historical sense, but rather are to be considered instrumental in the handling of eminently datable artefacts or key chronological indicators, and thus of the sites themselves.

Period	Time span	Key indicator
I	Paleolithic–Neolithic	Lithic industries
II	Eneolithic–Bronze Age	Obsidian + ceramics
III	Final B.A.–primary Iron Age	Ceramics
IV	Protohistoric (C7th–C4th)	Ceramics
V	Roman colonisation–Second Punic War	Black glaze wares
VI	Late republic	Black glaze wares
VII	Early empire (C1st BC–C1st AD)	Italic sigillata
VIII	Mid empire (C2nd–C3rd)	African Red Slip
IX	Late empire (C4th–early C5th)	African Red Slip
X	Late antiquity (C5th–C6th)	African Red Slip
XI	Early medieval (C7th–C11th)	Painted wares
XII	Late medieval (C12th–C14th)	Glazed wares

Table A. Periods adopted for site handling.

The final interpretation of the archaeology of the area is intended to override this strict framework, devised essentially for ease of data processing. Each individual site may be present under one or more periods, according to the identified material remains, and it is site occurrence per period that is quantified. As each period differs in relative time span (IV, for example, covers some four centuries, whilst VII covers roughly a single century), each one has been calibrated by number of centuries represented and the quantification expressed as a relative percentage of the total site occurrence in the range of periods III to XI (Table B). Table B calculates non-urban settlement sites and thus excludes major settlements such as the fora or Cascano, as well as roads, burials and kiln sites. Periods I and II have been omitted from the final calculation on account of potentially heavily distorting factors, together with period XII which, in any case, is largely irrelevant to the main theme of this study.

[14] It may be noted that the site of a very important early medieval village, site M179, was discovered only after the field survey was completed (Arthur, Albarella and Wayman, 1989).

[15] The proportional representation of site assemblages as surface remains, estimated at an average 2%, comes from Barker and Symonds, 1984, 288.

[16] Potter, 1979, table I.

PERIOD	III	IV	V	VI	VII	VIII	IX	X	XI
No. of sites:	27	18	14	123	138	80	27	5	6
% of sites:	6	4	3	26	29	17	6	1	1
No. of sites per century:	7	5	7	82	138	40	18	3	1
% of sites per century:	2	2	2	27	46	13	6	1	0

Table B. Breakdown of non-urban settlement sites per period in the survey area.

The chronology of individual sites is based principally on data accumulated through artefact retrieval. Though I make no pretence at being able to date prehistoric material, basic subdivisions of such sites has been attempted in schematic fashion. In assemblages where pottery predominates over lithics, a general eneolithic/bronze age date has been assigned, whilst in exceptional cases it has been possible to define elements pertaining to specific facies, such as Apennine. In such cases, the refinement has been noted in the relevant site entry in the catalogue of sites. Scatters of very coarse hand-made pottery, with absence of flint or obsidian, are also classed as Bronze Age since clearer characterising elements seem to make their appearance in final Bronze Age and early Iron Age times. However, little burden is placed on these sites when they appear in discussion in later chapters.

Dating of later Iron Age sites, say from the eighth century BC, when subtle Greek influence tints the area, until the Roman conquest, seems less hazardous, also because of the appearance of ceramic forms which may be linked to established repertoires from other parts of western central Italy. The dating of periods of activity on classical sites is safer and has been based largely on pottery chronologies established for black glaze wares, Italic sigillata and African red slip ware.[17] Pottery post-dating the mass importation of African red slip ware up to the mid sixth century, and pre-dating the glazed wares of the twelfth and thirteenth centuries, is exiguous, though can in part be correlated with comparative material from excavations conducted by the writer in Naples, though again much work needs to be done before surface finds can be employed to date occupation with any degree of certainty.

Aceramic sites are problematic. Features such as terrace walls or rock-cut cuniculi are often not datable without excavation, and it is important to note that certain simple construction techniques may not have changed substantially over time, particularly in rural areas. Medieval masonry techniques have not yet received the attention they deserve, whilst even the chronologies of standard Roman masonry types, often based on buildings in the Rome area, must be used with caution.[18]

The most intractable problem was that of formulating a classification and hierarchy of settlement sites, a posteriori, in the hope that the evidence would break down into a recognisable grouped pattern. Some researches have resorted predominantly to size of surface scatters as the determining factor in site ranking. For example, a villa is distinguished from a farm by a surface scatter covering more than n m². Others have attempted to create a hierarchy through presence or absence of particular building features.[19] It is clear that the position of sites within such categories is to a certain extent arbitrary depending upon the state of preservation of a site, its location, cultural, environmental or technological constraints, and so forth, whilst the only 'real' answer to the interrogative of a site's nature is to be had through excavation. It should also be clear that a settlement's social position and function invariably altered with time, often quite dramatically. The structure of an abandoned wealthy villa could become the focus of squatter occupation, whilst a simple farm could develop into a major estate centre. Furthermore, various ranking criteria, expressed through material evidence, can be used, singly or combined: size, population capacity, productive capacity, social level, etc. Thus, no simple criteria can be used in meaningful site ranking or classification, and a bundle of criteria is preferred here, expressed as archaeological facts with their accompanying interpretations.

Definitions

Villa is a much-abused term, so much so that I am almost loath to use it. Many of the rural sites that I have discovered are, however, called villas by the Soprintendenza, local amateurs and other sorts of archaeologists, and it would probably cause more trouble than it is worth trying to coin a new term. To try and come to grips with the problem, I will define what *I* mean by a villa in the context of this study and, whilst I am about it, will define my other settlement-type terms.

Town (*Colonia, municipium*)
   Archaeological fact – concentration of archaeological material, sufficiently assorted as to indicate varied and distinct areas of activity (beyond those of a purely agrarian nature), such as exchange, manufacture and ritual, and

---

[17] Cf Morel, 1981; Goudineau, 1968; Hayes, 1972 and 1980.

[18] See now Adam, 1984.
[19] Cf Dyson, 1978, 257.

sufficiently large as to indicate the habitation of various family nuclei. Elevation above the rank of village is given by the presence of distinct public buildings, excluding those of a purely religious nature, thus indicating a centralised administration.

Interpretation – the basic Roman political and administrative unit; a diversified economic base with productive (not solely agricultural), marketing and mercantile facilities; presence of a sedentary population composed of various family nuclei; developed street system.

Forum

Archaeological fact – concentration of archaeological material, sufficiently assorted as to indicate varied and distinct areas of activity, such as exchange and ritual, and sufficiently large as to indicate the existence of various family nuclei. Evidence for manufacturing activities may be absent though, if present, are unlikely to outweigh evidence for agrarian activities, which should be preponderant.

Interpretation – public administrative centre; small nucleated settlement with productive and market facilities.

Vicus

Archaeological fact – undistinguishable, at present, from the evidence for fora save, perhaps, from the fact that their setting may seem to indicate spontaneous rather than planned development.

Interpretation – the smallest legally recognised unit of nucleated settlement, administered by *magistri vici* or *aediles*, with basic market facilities.[20] It is possibly similar to a hamlet, containing peasants or *coloni* dependant on agricultural estates (e.g. vicus Caedicius), or involved in rural activities such as mining.[21]

Pagus

Archaeological fact – not readily recognisable, and in this study identified through inscriptions or textual sources, though its central-place may have the same characteristics as a vicus.

Interpretation – 1) Territorial subdivision which could contain one or more *vici*, or small nucleated or scattered settlements. 2) As in the case of the *colonia*, its central place could be homonymous, which would help to explain the confusion arising from attempts to deduce a single definition from the sources (e.g. pagus Vescinus).

Thus, according to Festus, the *pagus* was constituted by a population sharing the same water source ('*eadem aqua utuntur*').[22]

Sanctuary

Archaeological fact – concentration of votive material.

Interpretation – site of religious congregation, usually assimilating political functions in pre-Roman times, and often used for the exchange of information and goods with controlled market facilities.

Villa

Archaeological fact – stone and/or tile built rural structure with clear and differentiated functional areas, including both those devoted to agricultural activities and those devoted to resident labour. The residential areas are themselves differentiated, by size and quality, indicating an internal social hierarchy between proprietor/manager and labourers. Thus, one should expect evidence for a certain degree of comfort, in the form of bath structures and interior decoration (mosaics, painted wall plaster, etc).

Interpretation – agricultural estate centre with a resident slave *familia* to provide the backbone of the rural workforce.[23]

Maritime villa

Archaeological fact – stone and/or tile built rural or suburban structure with clear and differentiated functional areas, including those devoted to resident labour and bath structures. The residential areas are themselves differentiated, by size and quality, indicating an internal social hierarchy between proprietor and labourers. There should be evidence of luxury, in the form of interior decoration (mosaics, painted wall plaster, marble revetment, etc.), and a proximity to the sea, for the site to be qualified.

Interpretation – vacational residence, sited to take advantage of the view of the sea, where eventual productive functions are, in any case, secondary.

Farm

Archaeological fact – stone and/or tile built rural structure with evidence of domestic occupation debris and areas of agricultural activity (scatters of dolia fragments, press blocks, etc). There may be evidence for a certain degree of comfort, in the form of bath structures and basic

20 Gros and Torelli, 1988, 54–55.
21 Festus, 402 L: '*vici ... cipiunt ex agris, qui ibi villas non habent, ut Marsi et Paeligni*'; Patterson, 1985, 67.
22 Festus, 247 L; Gros and Torelli, 1988, 54–55.
23 See, now, Carandini, 1989 (esp. p 108), for an analysis of the villa.

interior decoration (simple mosaics, painted wall plaster, etc), though there should not be evidence for the presence of an internal social hierarchy.

Interpretation – agricultural establishment for the residence and labour of a family, hired labour or tenants. Agricultural production should not be dependent on slave-labour.

Cemetery

Archaeological fact – distinct clusters of specific artefact types (tiles, pottery, etc), to be associated with tomb construction or grave-goods, within a well-definable area, where often two or more fragments of various individual objects are clearly recognisable. The clusters are often associated with human bone, though are not associated with heterogeneous fragmentary artefacts, indicative of rubbish accumulation.

Interpretation – group of burials (> 1).

Pottery scatter

Archaeological fact – not visibly any of the above. The term is used for artefact scatters where margins may be defined, thus indicating some form of intensive activity-area, in opposition to an area of extensive activity, predominantly field cultivation. Particular configurations of the scatter or characteristics of the material may lead to specific interpretations and denominations (*infra*).

Interpretation – potentially any of the above though, realistically, a small single family settlement site, outbuildings, temporary activity areas or cemetery. A punctual interpretation may be given by the nature of the material. For example, a kiln site may be suggested by the presence of pottery wasters.

Sites judged to be of particular significance are referred to in the text by the site code with which they were baptised during field survey. This is necessary so as provide unique identifiers and aid reference in future citations. Each numbered site bears the prefix C, M or S, referring respectively to the IGM map sheets Carinola, Mondragone and Sessa Aurunca, which bear no direct relation to the council boundaries of the same name.

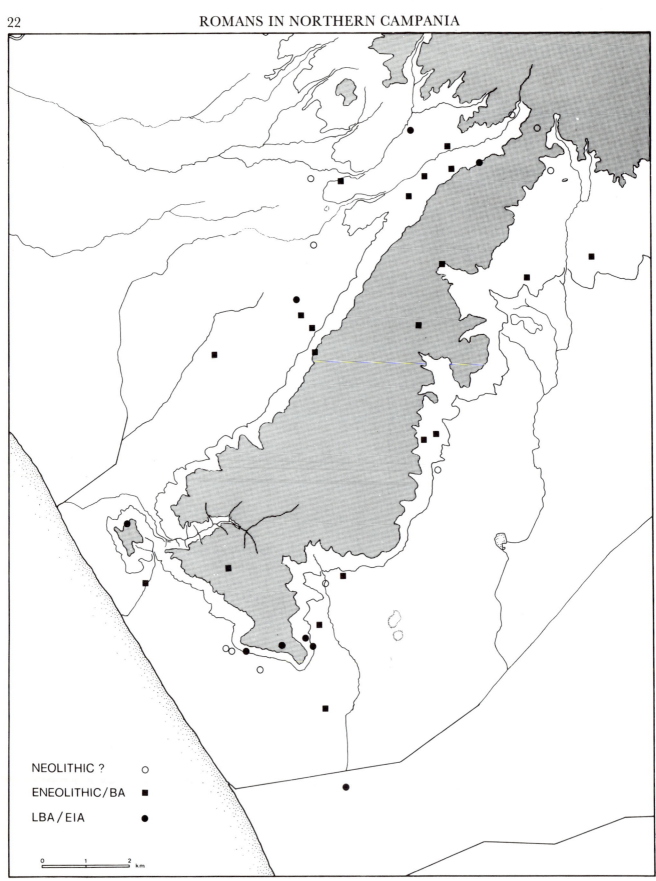

NEOLITHIC ?   ○

ENEOLITHIC/BA   ■

LBA/EIA   ●

0   1   2
km

Fig 4   The distribution of prehistoric sites around the Massico

Chapter Three

Prehistory and Pre-Roman Settlement

The preceding chapter traced the development of archaeological work in the area, from which it becomes clear that research was concentrated on the more evident and accessible classical remains to the virtual exclusion of prehistoric and Iron Age evidence. This state of affairs has now been partly rectified, as a corollary of the field survey, with recent assessment and publication of principal surface finds.[1] This present chapter thus serves only to outline the evidence for the evolution of the area in pre-classical times, thus setting the stage for the Roman conquest.

The known lithic assemblages of palaeolithic, mesolithic and neolithic times are either too few or too poor as to permit the elaboration of cultural models (Fig 4). Nonethless, the increasing frequency with which flint scatters and sporadic objects are being found does, at least, point towards a fair amount of exploitation of the land's resources from the neolithic, if not earlier, and augurs well for future appraisals. Even though the finds are concentrated in piedmont zones, the discovery of lithic material through well-boring in alluvial gravels in Loc. Quintola suggests that evidence of exploitation of lower-lying areas may now be largely blanketed by later alluvial and colluvial deposition.[2]

In eneolithic times, the area appears to have hosted a northern extension of the Gaudo group, first recognised around Paestum, which is represented by two burials in the Garigliano basin, neither recovered intact. From Masseria Sacconara comes a handled flask with cordoned neck and two pressure-flaked flint daggers, whilst more recently a flask, decorated with impressed dots, has been recovered near S Castrese.[3] Another very fine pressure-flaked flint dagger, from Ponte dell'Impiso, near Mondragone, could indicate the existence of a further Gaudo burial. Given the rather undiagnostic character of the ?neolithic site debris found during survey, and the distinct possibility that finer artifacts found their way into tomb groups, it seems at present impossible to correlate the material from the different contexts in order to be able to define the cultural entities of the area at that time.

The same could be said for much of the Bronze Age. Very eroded hand-made sherds are frequently

to be found amongst the macchia, though few characteristic fragments have been located, leaving the majority of sites with no fixed dating. Those few that may be more strictly defined appear to belong to the Apennine Bronze Age or to the final Bronze/early Iron Age. The most complete early assemblage comes from a bulldozed settlement sited on a fairly gentle north-facing slope of the Massico, near Piedimonte (site S51). Apart from the masses of pottery, of which a few fragments are decorated with 'pin-pricks' or incised lines, a loom-weight and fine blades of ?Lipari obsidian are of note. Whilst a minimal amount of pottery from the site appears assignable to an Apennine facies, the rest is dated through association, and clearly further work should be done. Much of the non-specific material, as at other sites in the area, can equally be paralleled amongst later sub-Apenninic assemblages, such as that which has come to light on the island of Vivara, off the coast of Naples.[4]

The evidence for the use of bronze, which only seems to have become common in Italy towards the later second millenium BC, is not surprisingly rare and numbers only two discoveries. A settlement to the south of Cascano has yielded the broken tip of a spearhead, whilst shortly before WW II a hoard of axeheads was unearthed near Ventaroli and rapidly dispersed amongst private hands. The only surviving piece which I have been able to locate appears to be of 'Savignano' type and similar to examples from Lazio dated to the early Bronze Age.[5]

The lack of diagnostic features amongst the mass of finds recovered from the area and suspected of dating to the Bronze Age does not permit us to relate the sites to cultural facies identified in other areas. Eventual evaluation of the dynamics of the area must await the collection of more eloquent evidence, including the analysis of faunal and palaeobotanical remains.

The pottery from Late Bronze or Early Iron Age surface scatters, likewise, does not appear to be particularly diagnostic, though it is generally well executed, with burnished surfaces and little in the way of decoration. The applied and finger-impressed cordons find parallels in both earlier and later ceramic complexes, though what does seem to recur

[1] Talamo, 1987.
[2] Tommasino, 1942, 37–38, pl 4.
[3] Barker, 1981, *passim*. The Gaudo remains from the Garigliano basin are described by Tommasino, 1942, 42–43, and Villucci, 1981c. See now also Marzocchella, 1980, for the discoveries around Naples.

[4] For Vivara see, for example, Cazzella *et al*, 1981, esp 147–149, figs 36–41. The finds from Piedimonte have been notified in Arthur, 1982c.
[5] Cf Peroni, 1971, fig 49.4; Carancini, 1979, fig 1, no 11.

on sites in the area are lug-handles with a simple, finger-impressed, central notch. Wares bearing a thick red slip are to be found from, at least, the eighth century BC. These are sometimes classed as *bucchero rosso*, and have been used to postulate early contacts with Etruria, though appear to have been locally produced.[6]

Northern Campania, as a pendant to *Megale Hellas*, strictly enters history with the beginning of Greek colonisation in southern Italy, first at the island of Pithecusae (Ischia) around 775 BC, and shortly afterwards at Cumae, when many of the prehistoric societies of the peninsula entered a period of more rapid social and economic development. This is particularly evident in Etruria on account of contacts stimulated through interest in the metal ores from Elba and elsewhere, as well as amongst communities in close proximity to the Greek colonies. Other areas, of limited natural resources, were only marginally affected by the new regime, being unable to enter into stable and fruitful exchange relationships with the colonies, though changes in the material culture of the societies inhabiting these backwaters underlines to some extent changes in social organisation brought about by cultural intercourse.[7]

According to Dionysius of Halicarnassus, the earliest attested colonisation around the Garigliano basin was by the Pelasgi who arrived from Thessaly to settle alongside the Aborigenes, themselves of Greek origin.[8] Now although Dionysius proposed to demonstrate the Greek origin of the Italic peoples, a thesis no longer tenable, archaeological discoveries have put Mycenean contacts with the Italian peninsula on a firm footing, suggesting that there is more substance to his legends than might at first sight have appeared.[9] Pottery assignable to Mycenean IIIA, dating to about the fourteenth century b.c., has been found on the islands of Ischia and Vivara in Campania. Thus, though we might now not discredit Dionysius outright, his reference to the abandoned Pelasgic city (*polis*) of Larisa, near Roman Forum Popilii, is hardly tenable.

Other Greek cities are supposed to have been sited along the coast north of Cumae. Livy gives an origin for the Roman colony of Sinuessa in the Greek town of Sinope. The former, according to Ribezzo, would have derived from the latter name through transcription of the Greek with subsequent addition of the Mediterranean suffix *-ssos* or *-ssa*: – Sinove – Sinovessa – Sinuessa.[10] To the north, along the coast, Pirae was said to have existed near Minturnae by Pliny.[11] Supporting evidence for such a site, by no means necessarily pre-Roman, may be given by the attestation of the local *gens Pirania*. It has often been identified with a series of Roman remains at Scauri with no sufficient reason.

The gulf upon which Scauri sits stretches southwards from Gaeta, and was known to Strabo as the *Caietanus sinus*.[12] It has also been known as the *Formianus sinus*, taking its name from Formiae which, following a false antique etymology, was held to have derived from the Greek *hormos* or harbour.[13] A further alternative name, *Sinus Amyclanus*, supposedly derived from the name of a Spartan colony Amyclae, founded near Terracina and abandoned subsequent to a mysterious invasion of serpents.[14] The existence of Sinope, Pirae, Amyclae and Formiae as pre-Roman Greek entities must be discounted, forming, according to Berard, part of a diffuse tradition of the Laconian origin of various Italic peoples. Though no Greek material is known from the sites, when they have been identified, the tradition must at least indicate the familiarity with which Greek maritime traders greeted the stretch of coast running northwards towards the entrepots of Latium and Etruria.

The earliest historically attested indigenous cultural group in the area was known as the Aurunci. As an historical reality they first appear in the pages of Livy as a people who had taken the Latin colonies of Cora and Pometia, in central Latium, only to lose them to Roman forces not long after.[15] These events occurred in the years 504–502 BC. If we accept the arguements advanced by Lepore, we may trace these people back, at least ethnically, to the late Bronze Age.[16] He would follow the identification of the Aurunci with the oft-cited Ausoni, through changes which the latter ethnic underwent in the Volscian dialect.[17] The Volsci were an osco-umbrian group using *-ci* as their most typical suffix. With the combination of this suffix with the rhotacism of a

[6]   Cf Johannowsky, 1983, 34–35 and 291.
[7]   Cf Renfrew, 1975.
[8]   Berard, 1963, 457.
[9]   Dion I; Berard, 1963, chap XII, esp pp 481–487.

[10] Livy X, xxi, 7. Verrengia, 1920, 2, note 4.
[11] Pliny *NH* III, 5.
[12] Strabo V, iii, 6.
[13] Coarelli, 1982, 359.
[14] Solin, II, 32. Cf Serv. *ad Aen.* X, 564. See Strabo V, 233, for the foundation of a Laconian colony at neighbouring Formiae.
[15] Livy II, 16–17.
[16] Lepore, 1977.
[17] That they were one and the same people was originally suggested by Cluverius in 1624, II, 1048ff.

mute to a sonorous *s* and finally to an *r*, the ethnic Auronici is created. Such an intermediate stage is to be found in Dionysius of Halicarnassus, when speaking of a people who had been expelled from part of the Campanian plains. Changes in the accentuation, the syncopation leading to the omission of the first *i* in Auronici and the vowel permutation by which the long *o* became *u* before the more guttural nasal *n* would have led to the final, historic, ethnic Aurunci. So spelt, it appears in the Latin texts and philologically its derivation would appear acceptable.

It has been suggested that the Ausoni once occupied a large area of central and southern Italy, which has been known as Ausonia.[18] Their identification with the Opici or Osci is also frequently argued.[19] How large an area was originally occupied by the Ausoni is hard to say. Pais collected and reviewed the textual sources, from which it is evident that the territory variously attributed to them stretched from Lazio, near the Pomptine plain, through Campania and Basilicata, down to the Chalcidian colony of Rhegium and Locri Epizephyri in southern Calabria.[20] Furthermore, Aristotle says that the people who had settled towards Tyrrhenia were Opici who bear the name of Ausoni.[21] From Aristotle's statement and the concentration of provenances for the Ausoni on the western side of Italy, we might imagine that the Apennines signalled the easternmost extension of their territory. However, one must be wary of postulating Ausonian presence purely on the basis of classical references to an area having formed part of Ausonia, a term often synonymous with Italy.[22] Lepore explained the classical references to Ausoni in Calabria and other parts of southern Italy as the name transference by Greeks who, having settled at Ischia and Cuma in the eighth century, came into contact with the indigenous population and lent their names to the land and inhabitants encountered in areas of later colonisation. Whatever the case, it is clear that the territory inhabited by the Ausoni, once spreading into southern Latium and into land later occupied by the Campani and Caudini, was gradu-

ally reduced until it became little more than an enclave centered on the lower Garigliano river and around Cales.

The first large-scale territorial restrictions may have occured with the expansion of the Etruscans into Campania after the mid seventh century BC. A princely tomb discovered at Cales, with Etruscan material dating to around 640–620 BC, may attest the presence of one of the first Etruscan notables in Campania.[23] At approximately the same date there was an increase in Etruscan material at Capua, which indicates far more than commercial contact, although it was not until the sixth century that the Etruscanisation of Campania was widespread though, according to Frederiksen, not 'excessively deep'.[24] The Etruscan occupation of Capua as an historical reality would seem to be preserved in the tradition of its foundation accepted by the elder Cato, although Velleius Paterculus' opinion about the actual foundation date seems closer to the truth.[25] Material found at Capua, especially in recent unpublished excavations, would seem to indicate stable settlement from the later ninth century and clearly earlier than distinct Etruscan intervention.[26] It may be that this pre-Etruscan stratum at Capua represents the presence of the so-called Ausoni, though affinities with the north Etrurian Villanovan facies, as early as the ninth century, cannot be denied.[27]

With the end of Etruscan hegemony in Campania, between about 474 and 424 BC, we find the area of Capua inhabited by a more clearly defined Oscan-speaking group known as Campani, who are distinguished from the Aurunci by the classical texts. The Campani, according to Diodorus, were formed as a nation in 438 BC and seem to have migrated into the promising Campanian plain after the rite of the *ver sacrum*.[28]

Thus, it would appear that by, at least, the seventh century much of Campania had been wrestled from the Ausoni by the Etruscans. When the Etruscans finally retreated, at least the land south of the river Volturno was principally in the hands of

[18] Eg Stat. *Silv.*, IV, v, 37. See also Strabo V, iii, 6, and Pliny *NH*, x, 95, for the application of the toponym to the Ionian Sea.
[19] Salmon, 1967, 28–29.
[20] Pais, 1908, 1–12; Strabo, *loc. cit.*; Val. Prob. *Verg. Buc. et Georg.*, ed. Keil, 1848; Oxyrh. Pap. III, 1903, no 408.
[21] Arist. VII, ix, 3.
[22] See, for example, Virgil *Aen.* VII, 795; McCail, 1978, 42–56, for a reference dating to as late as the fifth-sixth centuries AD to Ausoni as men from Italy.
[23] Valletrisco, 1972; Frederiksen, 1979, 298.
[24] Frederiksen, 1979, 299.
[25] Vell. Pat. I, vii, 2–4; cf also Polyb. II, xvii, 1.
[26] See Johannowsky, 1963, and 1965, 685–698. Heurgon, 1970, 485–495, on the basis of the source material felt that Capua was founded by the Etruscans during the eighth century.
[27] One of the commonest vessels found in Capuan tombs, for example, is a one-handled cup with an almost flat base and vertical or concave sides. It appears absent in other parts of Campania whilst being closely paralleled in northern Etruria. For the problem see Bailo Modesti et al., 1976, 24; D'Agostino, 1974, 11–26.
[28] Livy IV, xxxvii; X, xxxviii, 6; Diod. XII, xxi, 2. Frederiksen, *op. cit.*, 305–308.

groups of Samnite descent.[29] Pliny's list of the inhabitants of Campania, '*tenuere Osci, Graeci, Umbri, Tusci, Campani*', may thus be read as Ausoni, the coastal Greeks, the Umbri (?Sidicini), the Etruscans and the Samnite groups who descended into Campania in the fifth century.[30]

To the north, Ausonian territorial losses may have occured in southern Latium. It has been suggested above that land between the Volsci and the Hernici may once have been Ausonian. It is possible that the Ausoni had shared a border with the Latini prior to the move of the Volsci into the Pomptine plain. Lepore and Pallottino, following Devoto, would appear to date the Volscian move from the area around Rieti at the end of the sixth century BC, following the steady decline of Etruscan power in central Italy, with the ousting of the last Tarquin from Rome.[31]

The Romans' first recorded contact with the Aurunci seems to have been occasioned by the latter's occupation of Cora and Suessa Pometia (mod. Pomezia). The consuls Opiter Verginius and Spurrius Cassius besieged Suessa Pometia to little avail and returned to Rome, after having suffered heavy losses. Allowing enough time for their recovery, the Romans returned with greater determination, forcing the fall of the centre. Almost all of the Auruncan *principes* were decapitated, the inhabitants were sold into slavery, the town was destroyed and the land sold. A triumph was held in that year, 504/503 BC.[32]

Cora and Suessa Pometia, along with Signia, held the line north of the Volscian mountains/Monti Lepini and the agro Pontino.[33] It is possible that the Aurunci at that stage held part of the Monti Lepini and the valley of the Sacco, thus inhabiting land between the recently acquired territory of the Volsci, towards the agro Pontino and the sea, and the land of the Hernici in their eponymous mountains.[34] Conversely, the campaigns involving Cora and Suessa Pometia may have represented tentative Auruncan expansion northwards from homelands in the Monti Ausoni, Monti Aurunci and Campania.

In 495/494 BC, according to Livy, the Aurunci threatened war with Rome unless she withdrew from the recently occupied territory of the Volsci.[35] Yet again the land disputes were over the territory of Suessa Pometia and seem to indicate interest on the part of the Aurunci in an area which may have bordered their own possessions. Their forces marched into the area of Aricia, in the Alban hills, causing great consternation in Rome, but were promptly defeated not far from the town. The same events are recounted by Dionysius of Halicarnassus, where he adds that the Aurunci inhabited the most beautiful plain of Campania. Ogilvie, amongst others, is not prepared to accept these texts, claiming, in reference to Livy I, xli, 7, that 'the whole story arises from a mistaken attempt to connect the name Suessa with the false name for Pometia, Suessa Pometia'.[36]

By the mid fourth century the territory of the Aurunci was considerably smaller than the sources would seem to suggest for preceding periods, and seems to have been confined to the small Campano-Latian border zone within Latium Adiectum. In 346 BC they are mentioned at the conclusion of the war between the Volsci and Rome, and the taking of Antium and Satricum by the latter. It is possible that the Aurunci already felt threatened by Roman ambitions towards Campania, for in the following year they effected a raid which elicited Roman reprisals. The raid was seen as indicative of a general state of unrest amongst the peoples of Latium, which must have been largely stimulated by both Roman and Samnite ambitions for control of the middle Liri valley, an area of good agricultural land and significant mineral wealth, including iron.[37] Any tension in such close proximity to Auruncan possessions would have been seen as a threat to general security, despite the illusive Romano-Samnite treaty of 354 BC. As a consequence of the political tensions in Latium, Rome appointed a dictator in the person of Lucius Furius. With the appointment of Gn. Manlius Capitolinus as *magister equitum*, the courts suspended and troops levied, Furius marched against the

[29] Even Greek Cumae, by 419 BC, had been occupied – Livy IV, xliv, 12.
[30] Pliny *NH* III, v, 60.
[31] Lepore, 1977, 96; Pallottino, 1976, 39; Devoto, 1969, 114; cf Toynbee, 1965, 117–118.
[32] Livy II, 16–17. An apparent confusion in the sources indicates that Rome had already taken and slaughtered captives, including three hundred hostages, as well as holding a triumph, before the intervention of Opiter and Spurrius.
[33] Salmon, 1969, 172, note 53.
[34] It may be worth noting here the existence of evidence for kindred cultural traits between the northern Campanian area of the Aurunci and the so-called '*civiltà della valle del Liri*': Talamo, 1987, esp pp 162–167.

[35] Livy II, xxvi, 4 – xxvii, 1.
[36] Dion. VI, xxxii, 1–2; cf also VI, xxxvii. Ogilvie, 1965, 276.
[37] *Concilium omnis nominis Latini esset*: Livy VII, xxviii. Cf Salmon, 1967, 189–190.

Aurunci. The Romans brought the matter to a close in a single encounter and a temple to Iuno Moneta was dedicated on the Capitoline the following year.

In 343, the Samnites attacked the Sidicini who occupied the land on the eastern side of Roccamonfina. They evoked the assistance of the Campani, who must likewise have felt threatened by Samnite expansion. Their involvement only escalated the situation and, on the Campani's second defeat at the hands of the Samnites, they addressed an appeal to the Roman senate. This was at first ignored but, following the 'voluntary' subjugation of the Campani to Rome, the latter assumed the right to forbid Samnite expansion into Campania.[38] The ease with which Capua accepted Rome's yoke has been explained in terms of the political manoeuvres of the Campanian *equites* who feared the growing power of the plebeians.[39] The Romano-Samnite treaty, although respected over the middle Liri valley, had not forseen conflict over Campania. The rich grain lands which had attracted both Greeks and Etruscans could not escape the attentions of the land-hungry Samnites and Romans, and it was in neither's interests to let the territory fall into the hands of the adversary. Therefore, on the Samnites' rejection of the Roman prohibition, war inevitably broke out and the consuls M Valerius Corvus and A Cornelius Cossus took to the field.[40]

In the confused Livian account of events it is not clear as to whether or not the Aurunci took part. However, on conclusion of the First Samnite War the two major protagonists set about consolidating 'their' respective territories, through which they succeeded in destabilising smaller tribal groups who rightly saw themselves being subjected to the two super-powers. Thus broke out the so-called Latin War in which the Volsci, Sidicini and Aurunci, together with Latini and Campani, rose against both Rome and Samnium (c. 340–338 BC).[41] The episode concluded with two major battles, one near a place called Veseris, and the other at Trifanum, both almost certainly located in Auruncan territory around the Garigl`ano basin. The Aurunci surrendered to Rome to enjoy 'protection'.[42] The *Fasti Triumphales* record the ensuing triumph held by the

consuls C Titus Manlius Torquatus and Publius Decius Mus.

Rome's victory was of paramount importance as she was thus able to establish her power-base from which the eventual subjugation of the rest of southern Italy became almost a matter of course.[43] One of the consequences of post-war settlement was the incorporation of Capua as *municipium sine suffragio* and the expropriation of its prime land north of the Volturno to become the ager Falernus in 340 BC. As part of the new Roman policy, Latin colonies were set up in key spots outside of Latium Vetus. The first of these was Cales in 334 BC, established on old Auruncan land on the site of a pre-existing settlement.[44] It was, if anything, a primary bastion against the Samnites, controlling the southern end of the Sacco-Liri corridor from Latium and acting as a safeguard on the situation of Rome's new Campanian *socii*. The colony was also able to keep watch over the territory around Teanum Sidicinum, controlled by the Samnites, as well as the Garigliano basin which seems not to have been annexed at this stage.

In fact, according to Livy, the Sidicini raided the Auruncan enclave in 337, and before the consuls C Sulpicius and P Aelius could arrive with their troops, the Aurunci had abandoned their 'oppidum', which was razed by the enemy, and took refuge at another site which they also fortified and which, Livy tells us, was later called Suessa Aurunca.[45] These events are almost certainly a Livian creation or anachronism, partly used to explain the colonisation of Cales as a check on the Sidicini.[46] The consuls are surely those of 314 BC, C Sulpicius and Poetelius, who finally reduced the Aurunci and presumably razed their fortified sites (*infra*). The survivors may, in part, have moved back to their dispersed lowland farmsteads and villages, save for the areas in which land had been confiscated for the Latin colonists who were to arrive in 313 BC, though there is some evidence for synoecism.

Archaeology seems to confirm northern coastal Campania as an Iron Age fringe area, with communities focussing indirectly on inland central places such as Cales and, through Cales, Capua. The

[38] Livy VII, xxix–xxx, and VIII, xvii, 3.
[39] Bernardi, 1943; Toynbee, 1965, I, 334–335.
[40] Salmon, 1967, 195ff.
[41] But see Sordi, 1965, 13ff.
[42] Livy VIII, xv, 2. On Veseris see Salmon, 1967, 208, and now Frederiksen, 1984, 184–6, whose account of the Latin War and relative source material seems entirely credible. On Trifanum, never mentioned in later sources, see Livy VIII, xi. The area is perhaps to be found around Tre Ponti, if we are to imagine a settlement/sanctuary developing on the site of three small streams letting into the sea, just to the north of the modern junction of the Via Domiziana with a road leading to Sessa Aurunca.

[43] Salmon, 1982, 40–56.
[44] Johannowsky, 1961, note 12.
[45] Livy VIII, xv, 4.
[46] Salmon, 1967, 209, note 7.

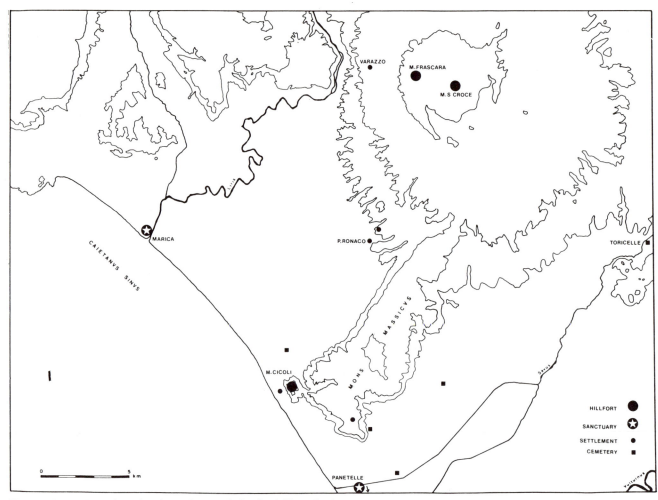

Fig 5   Later Iron Age sites in and around the Gargliano basin

almost embarassing dearth of Iron Age sites around the Massico would seem to militate against rapid internal development and demographic expansion in favour of a far more gradual development throughout the period down to the Roman conquest. However, most of the evidence for early Iron Age settlement derives paradoxically from the discovery of a small number of eighth and seventh century inhumation cemeteries, suggesting perhaps that the settlement sites themselves were located in areas now blanketed by alluvial or colluvial deposits, or in high positions subsequently eroded away or invaded by dense vegetation. Judging by the geomorphological evidence, it may also be suggested that the coastal areas and alluvial plains were usually avoided until land drainage took place under the Roman administration.

The cemeteries on the southern side of the Massico were, nonetheless, positioned in low-lying land,

indicating perhaps an extension of activity into more optimal farming zones where cereal cultivation and polyculture would have been facilitated by a broader and more varied catchment area or, alternatively, their positioning in marginal land, closer to the marshes.

They have yielded material more akin to Latian (Liri valley) cultural assemblages than Campanian ones from areas to the south of the Volturno, though aside from Capua which appears to possess more direct Villanovan antecedents, they may be grouped generically into what has been termed the *Fossakultur* of Cumaean type. A tomb excavated at Suessa, for example, dates to the late eighth century BC and contains a rather singular painted urn, as well as a tazza and cups akin to vessels from the Alban hills, central Lazio and Cassino.[47] All this would seem to add weight to the source evidence which suggests an Ausonian cultural substratum in parts of Lazio

[47] Mustilli, 1962, 185 and pl IV; Johannowsky, 1965, 686; Merolla, 1983, 209; Talamo, 1987, 51–60. For the *Fossakultur* see Johannowsky, 1983, and D'Agostino, 1974, 11ff.

and Campania which contributed towards the emergence of the later Auruncan cultural entity in northern Campania (Fig 5).[48]

On the south-eastern slopes of Monte Petrino, at the western extremity of the Massico, a further burial seems to have been covered by a tumulus constructed of limestone boulders, which yielded a black burnished olla bearing affinities with forms of local bucchero rosso, perhaps of later seventh century date[49] (site M120bis). Another probable tumulus has come to light in the section of a building site to the north of Casanova di Carinola (site C25). Though enigmatic in so far as both grave goods and skeletal remains appeared to be absent in the central inhumation trench, the discovery lies close to the site of a major Iron age cemetery which has yielded both bronze bracelets and ceramics datable to the eighth and seventh centuries BC.[50] Two further cemeteries of similar date, yielding bucchero rosso, were found on the southern side of Casanova di Carinola and between Falciano and Mondragone. Alongside imported Greek vessels, the latter yielded two iron swords, a fragmented spearhead and a bronze bracelet.

Though known imports are rare, an attempted opening towards a system of regional market exchange with neighbouring Greek and Etruscan territories seems to be indicated by the appearance of coastal sanctuaries at the mouths of the Garigliano and Savone around the seventh century (infra), though the narrow range and limited quantity of imported goods evidenced throughout the entire Iron Age suggests limited exchange opportunities. The iron artefacts reported from time to time are obviously imports, whether as finished objects or ores, as are the Greek pottery vessels. Etruscan wine amphorae, dating around the sixth century, have been found at Monte Ciçoli and at the sanctuary of Panetelle, indicating perhaps a minimal importation of prestige items.[51] Whether or not local viticulture was practised at this date is, for the time being, difficult to demonstrate, though the absence of any recognisably specific indigenous pottery vessels connected with the consumption of wine may be an arguement ex silentio against local production.

The almost total absence of black Campanian bucchero, particularly common in other areas of Campania during the sixth century, is striking. The only examples known from the area include a single sherd from an Augustan context at the Roman villa of Corigliano, from the site of another Roman villa near Mondragone, minimal quantities from the Iron Age settlement at Ponte Ronaco and scraps from the sanctuaries of Marica and Panetelle. This appears to echo the absence of Etruscan bucchero along the lower Liri valley, an area also claimed to have been controlled by the Aurunci, and might add weight to the suggestion that the Sacco-Liri corridor did not effectively act as a land route between Etruria and Campania until the construction of the Via Latina.[52] If so, the destruction of the Etruscan fleet in 474 BC by Hieron of Syracuse and the Cumaeans would assume even greater significance in the decline of Etruscan hegemony in internal Campania, with the truncation of their maritime route.

Extra-regional contacts during the final Iron Age are again indicated by small quantities of pottery, including Attic Black Glaze and Italic painted wares at few sites such as Ponte Ronaco and the cemetery of Mass. Tre Ponti. Native pottery is particularly plain and best illustrated at Ponte Ronaco where a number of jars present ovoid bodies, slightly everted rims and opposing lug-handles, of a type found in other parts of the region.[53] A number of vessels, particularly bowls, continue to bear a thick red slip, likening them to the later Pompeian Red Ware. Few of the ceramics appear decorated save for a series of large storage jars, well-represented at Ponte Ronaco, which bear incised wavy lines on their bodies. Almond-rim jars are indicative of contacts with Latian/Etrurian areas, where they appear already by the fifth century BC, though they may be post-conquest in northern Campania, whilst coarse pottery types from a Greek or Hellenistic milieu are totally absent in contrast to their presence on indigenous sites further south in Magna Graecia.[54]

Livy, in describing the final capitulation of the Aurunci in 314 BC, tells us that 'Ausona et Minturnae et Vescia urbes erant ex quibus principes iuventutis duodecim numero in proditionem urbium suarum coniurati ad consules veniunt'.[55] None of these Auruncan urbes have yet been securely located on the ground in spite of the efforts of numerous scholars. A basic fact, which is not to be overlooked, is that when Livy spoke of urbes he was chronicling events three hundred years

[48] Chap. 1 supra.
[49] Cf. Merolla, 1983, 234, no 2, from Cales.
[50] Finds early this century are recorded in Maiuri, 1925 and 1926. Further finds have been made recently by the local Archeoclub (ex inf. Carmine Di Lorenzo).
[51] Cf Ampolo, 1980, 32, on the value of wine in Etruria at the end of the seventh century B.C., and on early viticulture in general. For importation of Etrurian wine into Campania see now Albore Livadie, 1985.

[52] Wightman, 1981, 280–281, contra Quilici Gigli, 1970. On Campanian bucchero see Albore Livadie, 1979.
[53] Eg Bonghi Iovino and Donceel, 1969, 91–92.
[54] Early almond-rim jars from Veii, in south Etruria, are published by Threipland, 1963. A good selection of Greek and Hellenistic coarse ware types from an indigenous settlement in the south will appear in the report of excavations at Roccagloriosa (SA) by Maurizio Gualtieri and Helena Fracchia.
[55] Livy IX, xxv, 4–5.

old, of a non-Roman people and from the viewpoint of a citizen in Augustan Rome; and whatever he was, he was not a perceptic critic of his sources.

'In the Appenine areas inhabited by the Samnites urban conditions were affirmed in very recent times, and the phase of transition took place together with the gradual progress of Romanisation, between the end of the fourth and the first century BC'.[56] Despite the affirmation in the sources of Auruncan towns, as well as references to the presumably fictitious Greek foundations of Pirae, Sinope and Larisa, no material indication of large-scale nucleated settlement seems present in the Garigliano basin and contiguous areas prior to their colonisation by Rome. The immediate pre-Roman settlement would appear to fall into two principal categories: that of the small site, whether it be farmstead or hamlet, and that of the fortified enclosure positioned on a strategic prominence. In effect this was a pattern which repeated itself amongst various Italic peoples prior to their development under the influence of the more sophisticated urbanised societies of Italy.[57]

The immediate pre-conquest sites which have been discovered are few in number, and only a handful may be identified as villages or farms with any reasonable degree of likelihood. The site (S12) near the Roman bridge known as Ponte degli Aurunci (Ponte Ronaco) lies within an area of 1000m² and some 60 m asl, on a slight knoll which is truncated to the north and west by the steeply cut Vallone Grande. The associated pottery scatter would seem to indicate activity on site from the seventh century BC to about the mid third century, or some two or three generations after the foundation of the Latin colony at Suessa in 313 BC.[58] A trial excavation revealed part of the foundations of a structure in loosely-packed limestone blocks, which presumably functioned as footings for a wooden superstructure. Sherds of numerous storage jars testify the conservation of agricultural produce. Some 500m to the east of the site, and on the northern side of the Vallone Grande, a smaller pottery scatter refers to a contemporary cemetery. A number of tombs of the *tomba a fossa* type have been revealed.[59] A further settlement (site S14) lay less than a kilometre to the north of the cemetery, at some 101m asl, though has now been destroyed by a pozzolana quarry.

Two further settlement sites have been located near M Cicoli at the western end of the Massico. One, to the north of M Cicoli, lies on flat terrain where a sandy beach ridge is intercalated with colluvium, and is evidenced by a thin pottery scatter hardly larger than 200m². Its exiguous nature may indicate that it was little more than a farmstead.

The other site, which lies between M Cicoli and the sea, immediately to the south-east of the site of the later colony of Sinuessa, was revealed as a large scatter of material on a building site, covering an area of, at least, 100 x 50m. The positioning of the settlement is significant, as it lay on the coast, making use of the calcareous ridge of the Massico which only at this point drops to the sea, keeping the coastal marshes at bay. The pottery, buried within colluvial deposits of up to two metres, suggests a chronological span from about the sixth to the third centuries BC and, like the sites near Suessa Aurunca, it appears to have been abandoned a generation or so after the Roman conquest.

Three further sites, whose function is not clear, consist of very small scatters of material. One lies on the northern slope of M Petrino, and is revealed in a track through the macchia and grass immediately to the north-east of Colle Pezza di Caso (276m asl). The local coarse pottery and Italian Black Glaze ware from the site were associated with a fragment of a fifth century Attic ?column-krater and the handle of an Etruscan amphora. These last two items lend an unusual tone to the site, more easily paralleled amongst prestige grave groups than amongst settlement debris. A second site lies immediately to the east of M Petrino within some 20m², and has revealed pottery ranging probably from the fifth or fourth to early third century BC. Two groups of squared grey tuff blocks appear to signal the presence of, at least, two tombs, though the evidence is confused by the background noise furnished by a pottery scatter from an early medieval village. The material from the last site at Loc. Torone, to the south-east of M Petrino, is equally confused. The site lies within the area of a Roman villa and is also mixed with flints and obsidian of even earlier date.

[56] Writer's translation of La Regina, 1970, 191.
[57] Salmon, 1967, 50–52. For the urbanisation of Lazio see now Guaitoli, 1984, with references.
[58] The most closely dated find from the site is a bronze coin with obverse helmeted head of Minerva l. and reverse legend SVESANO and a cock standing r., of mid third century BC date. Small-scale excavations were carried out at the site in July 1980 by Pierfrancesco Talamo for the Soprintendenza: Talamo, 1987, 10ff.
[59] Villucci, 1980a, 49–55; Talamo, 1987. See sites S16, S17, S18 and S21.

The pottery, which includes Campanian bucchero and may run from the seventh/sixth century BC down to the Roman conquest, suggests the presence of a small domestic site.

Further farmsteads may be represented by terrace walls of drystone polygonal block masonry noted since the last century as present in various upland areas around the river basin. Almost all such sites which can be dated by surface pottery scatters are assignable to the late republic, whilst remaining examples generally yield little or no material, thus leaving open the question of their dating. The general impression gained is that polygonal and squared drystone masonry is on the whole a republican feature in the area, poorly represented in precolonial times and then mainly as a defensive expedient. One site, outside the bounds of the intensive survey, is of interest in this context as the mass of surface pottery similar to that found at Ponte Ronaco suggests stable settlement prior to the conquest. The site, close to the actual hamlet of Le Conche, just to the north of Fosso del Guarazzo, was noted as pre-Roman by Tommassino on the basis of the various tracts of roughly hewn drystone masonry.[60] The presence of extensive terracing, which date needs to be confirmed through excavation, and intermittent pottery scatters suggests a further approach towards settlement enucleation, though perhaps still a long way from the oppida known from more northerly lands or proto-urban sites such as Roccagloriosa in Lucania.

All in all, the summary evidence would tend to indicate that the Aurunci possessed a system of dispersed settlement composed of farmsteads and hamlets of a strongly agrarian character, cultivating mixed seed crops on the well-drained ignimbrite slopes. Even the burials, articulated in small, scattered and poor cemeteries, would appear to refer to individual family groups and differ substantially from the large nucleated cemeteries, with hierarchically distinct grave-groups, such as that found at Torricelle, near Teanum Sidicinum.[61]

Livy's accounts of the Aurunci may likely stem from the impression that the fortified enclosures made on the Roman conquerors. These fortified enclosures are characterised by circuit walls recalling those of some of the early *coloniae* and, in times of attrition, were presumably densely inhabited.

However, they may well have otherwise played only a marginal role in Auruncan daily affairs.

The most recent systematic study of hillforts in the Campano-Samnite areas charts three such sites above the Garigliano basin.[62] Two lie on the western lip of the Roccamonfina crater and the third is perched on the most westerly extension of the Massico range, M. Cicoli, overlooking two contemporary sites discussed above.

The most frequently cited enclosure is that known as Orto della Regina on Monte Frascara (M Cortinella), which has been the subject of erudite speculation since 1640 when it was 'identified' as the site of Aurunca.[63] It rests on the summit of part of the crater rim at the height of 933m asl, with access from the south, and commanding a view of the entire floodplain. It is elliptical in plan and delineated by a massive drystone wall of large polygonal lava blocks, some of which are up to two and a half metres in height, enclosing an area of 2.100m². The circuit is once broken by an entrance passage fitted to render vulnerable the right-hand side of would-be aggressors. Repeated walks over the site have proved fruitless in the recovery of dating evidence because of dense vegetational cover and a buildup of humus. Limited excavation was conducted by Conta Haller who reported a layer of carbonised material with coarse pottery and tile, above another layer of sterile yellowish soil.[64]

The second enclosure, on Monte S Croce (Monte Fino), lies just over a kilometre to the east of the first, at 1006m asl, and on the terminal cone of the volcano. The site suffered bulldozing in the early 1950s when several human skeletons were brought to light.[65] A surviving tract of enclosure wall on the northern side shows that this site also possessed a drystone wall built of massive lava blocks and based on a foundation with an offset. Perrotta referred to the existence of a paved road, three cisterns and the remains of a staircase known as the 'Scala Santa' (perhaps all of medieval date), which may be that indicated in a photograph taken by Thomas Ashby.[66] The site is even better placed than Orto della Regina for the view that it commands not only of the floodplain but, on a clear day, of the land to the north east and south as far as Vesuvius. The ideal defensive position was taken up again in the middle ages with the construction of a castle.

[60] Tommasino, 1942, 213ff, pl XIX: loc. Varazzo.
[61] For Torricelle see Tocco Sciarelli, 1981. The cemetery appears to stretch from the late fifth century BC, through the fourth century, and has yielded over 200 tile and tuff built tombs.

[62] Conta Haller, 1978, 45–58, and bibliography.
[63] Sacco, 1640, 124.
[64] Conta Haller, 1978, 50.
[65] I owe this information to Dott B Petteruti.
[66] Perrotta, 1737, 86. The photograph is in the archives of the British School at Rome.

Monte Cicoli, commanding the narrow pass along the coast where Sinuessa was sited, is crowned by a small fortified enclosure of rough limestone block walling which, according to Conta Haller, was quarried from nearby Monte Pizzuto.[67] The site was re-used for the placement of a medieval turret, to which a track paved with squared limestone flagstones on the northern side of the hill may have led, and later for a WW II observation post. Little of the ancient site is visible, although the surface is littered with pottery, mostly of republican date. There is also a small quantity of pottery which could date to the fourth century BC or earlier.

The hilltop enclosures seem not to have been centres of municipal life. They were badly positioned for exploitation of all but the meanest land, and their habitable surface area was restricted in size, comparing unfavourably to enclosures in Samnite and Lucanian areas. The sites may instead be seen as a reaction to conditions created by Roman expansion and the Samnite wars, and seem to have functioned mainly as centres of refuge for congregations of what was essentially a dispersed agricultural population. Despite massive defensive circuits, the labour for the construction of which is at least indicative of tribal unity and a centralised directive, the quantities of domestic rubbish to be found on the sites are limited. An excavation intended to provide dating evidence for a similar enclosure at Poggio Cesi in the territory of the Aequi proved downright embarassing with its absolute lack of finds.[68] The evidence available implies limited temporal occupation of the sites, constructed presumably through the joint efforts of the farmers who occupied the piedmont farmsteads and villages around Roccamonfina, the Massico and the Monti Aurunci.

A last point worthy of note is the apparent interrelationship of the hillforts in the area between the Garigliano and the Volturno. The position of nineteen such sites permitted reciprocal visual communication, thus ensuring a network similar to that found linking the enclosures of the Matese.[69] Because of their geographical location it is impossible that all the hillforts belonged to a single cultural entity. Nevertheless, it is not unreasonable to suppose a certain amount of joint tactical planning amongst the various hillfort-building peoples, in defense against a common enemy.

The situation in the territory of the Aurunci would thus appear strikingly similar to that observed in certain Samnite areas of the Apennines and Adriatic coast, where true urban conditions appeared hand in hand with the processes of Romanisation. A significant difference would seem to have been the Roman process of municipalisation of certain pre-existing centres in Samnium, which did not occur in the Auruncan territory. Rather, the pre-Roman settlements were abandoned at the time of the conquest or gradually absorbed through a process of synoecism some two or three generations after the foundation of the Latin and Roman coloniae. The archaeological evidence suggests a demographic shift to the new Roman centres, which bore no apparent relationship to the preceding distribution of society.

The limited territory held by the Aurunci in the immediate pre-conquest period has so far yielded evidence for only one sanctuary in the Garigliano basin, dedicated to the deity Marica, who is also attested at Pesaro and Laurentum.[70] It was sited on the right bank of the river and lies now some 400m from the sea in an area which at the time of its foundation may well have been malarial. The site appears to have first been frequented around the eighth century BC although, according to the excavator, it was not until the end of the sixth century that the first temple was erected with grey tuff masonry, deriving probably from deposits to the immediate south of the Massico.[71] A number of plain and painted architectural terracottas, similar to examples from the sanctuary of the matres at Capua, were found associated. In contrast to what little else is known of Auruncan craftmanship, their working is extremely fine suggesting either direct importation of the pieces or their commissioning to alien hands. They contrast notably with the votive clay figurines, which were crudely fashioned, primitive and presumably native, though an Ionic statuette of a seated woman, dated to the sixth century BC, probably indicates sporadic importation even of minor objects.[72] This is perhaps what is to be expected of such a site placed at the mouth of a river which not only penetrated the Auruncan heartland, but offered a safe anchorage, confirmed by the later siting of the Roman colony of Minturnae at the same site, thus opening the territory to maritime contacts with other cultural groups up and down the coast. In the absence of recognisable major settlements in the basin during the late Iron Age, the site may well have acted as a focal point for the

---

[67] Conta Haller, 1978, 59.
[68] Tata, 1981, 224–225.
[69] La Regina, 1970, 196; Conta Haller, 1978, fig 1.

[70] Pesaro: CIL I, 175. Laurentum: Serv. ad loc. For the sanctuary at the mouth of the Garigliano see Giglioli, 1911; Mingazzini, 1939; Talamo, 1987; and for the terracottas, Forti, 1950. On a legend of the statue of the deity being the stolen Artemis of Cumae see Augustine Civ. Dei II, 23.
[71] For the tuff deposits see Stanzione, 1966.
[72] Johannowsky, 1978, 139.

scattered population, serving the processes of exchange of goods and information at inter and extra-regional levels, as well as that of a rallying point for the formulation of political stances and, of course, the celebration of religious rites.[73] Thus the sanctuary, at one and the same time, expressed and reinforced local cultural identity. Given however the overall scarcity of imported pottery, despite the presence of what has otherwise the characteristics of a port of trade, one may suggest that attempts towards external intercourse were largely unsuccessful. At Pompeii, for example, evidence has recently been set forth for brisk exchange during the sixth century BC at a cultural interface area where Greeks, Etruscans and native communities had much to gain through reciprocal exchange.[74] If the picture presented here, of a relatively backward state of affairs in and around the Garigliano basin, bears any semblance to reality then the site at the mouth of the Garigliano may have served conceptually as a port of trade, though to relatively little practical advantage since the area was at that time relatively poor in marketable resources and surplus.

The imported pottery, the one inscription known from the territory (*infra*) and the external political contacts attested at the eve of Rome's conquest all seem to indicate the first steps towards what might otherwise have been a veritable boom in cultural development, once full agricultural potential had been realised. However, it needs to be stressed again that the number of Iron age sites known are few and that sample excavation is urgently required. We are as yet unable to make proper distinctions in northern Campania between Iron Age ceramic assemblages from domestic, ritual and funerary contexts. It is consequently possible that imported pottery, whether as table ware or commodity containers, was considered prestige material and will be found only in particular social contexts and not generally amongst the material debris deriving from ploughed-out or eroded settlement sites or run-of-the-mill cemeteries.

Very little is actually known concerning both the social and political structures of the Aurunci, and whether or not they differed appreciably from those of superficially similar groups such as the Samnites. Livy's account of the twelve Auruncan *principes* seeking to voice their people's grievances at Rome does, at least, hint at the existence of a social and political hierarchy which might subsequently be reinforced through analyses of cemeteries and internal hierarchies of grave-goods and burial patterns.

In fact, on cimiterial evidence from Suessa Aurunca, Piedimonte d'Alife and Ruviano, the group of the Ausoni has been considered as a decidedly conservative and relatively poor peasant culture of the '*tombe a fossa*' type.[75] If to this one is to add the information concerning the apparent difficulty that Rome experienced in subduing the Aurunci, it may be suspected that the populace was both characteristically strong and hardy, more akin to the peasant-soldier Samnites of the Abruzzi than to Polybius' Campani.[76]

As noted above, the construction of the hill-forts, and implicitly also that of the sanctuary of Marica, further indicates the possibility of amassing a labour-force under a centralised directive. The existing pre-Roman toponyms of Vescia, Minturnae and Ausonia indicate territorial subdivisions, perhaps into *pagi*, and it may be suggested that Livy's *principes* in some way functioned towards the administration of these sectors of Auruncan territory. In whatever way the land was organised, it does seem clear from the available evidence that the overriding settlement pattern is that of dispersed hamlets and farmsteads based on a subsistence agriculture.

Evidence is almost equally scarce for an assessment of the archaic material culture of the area, making it difficult to establish cultural contrasts with better known neighbouring territories, where regional ceramic assemblages have been produced, at least, in part.[77] Material is available from a fairly substantial seventh century cemetery near Mondragone, though whether or not it is equally representative of the land to the north of the Massico is difficult to say. What is certain is that the material collected during field survey is relatively poor, dominated by a narrow range of coarse wares, and displaying a singular lack of imported or local fine wares. The votive statuettes from the sanctuary of Marica vary between primitive hand-modelled examples and more elaborate moulded figures of clear hellenistic derivation, presumably almost all of local manufacture, though the mass-production encountered at the sanctuary of Panetelle, is not to be found here. Only a single example of relief carving is known, represented by a stone head of rude workmanship.[78]

Epigraphic material consists of a sole inscription on three blocks of tuff discovered re-used in the covering of an aqueduct by the village of Roccamonfina.[79] It is uncertain whether it should be considered Auruncan or Sidicine because of its discovery close to the town of Teanum Sidicinum, and its value as evidence of Auruncan literacy is thus

---

[73] Cf Livy I, xxx, 5, for the celebration of both sacred and secular at the pre-Roman shrine of Feronia, to the north of Rome.
[74] Arthur, 1986.

[75] Johannowsky, 1983.
[76] Polyb. VII, i, 1; cf Sen. *Ep. Mor.* LI, v.
[77] Cf. now Johannowsky, 1983.
[78] D'Onofrio, 1980, pl IV.
[79] Antonini, 1977, 343–344; Poccetti, 1984.

commensurately reduced. The text, running to eight lines, is both dextral and sinistral in a script formed from both Latin and Oscan elements. Stops are used between words though, sadly, their meaning is not clear. One word apparently reads *mefineis* which, it has been suggested, may be the genitive form of an antroponym connected with the celebrated Sabellian deity Mefitis, and forming the base of the toponym Roccamonfina.

In sum, the information available for the immediate pre-conquest systemisation of the land around the Massico is scarce, though perhaps indicative of a relatively poor and primitive social group. Research in this sector is thus of great importance towards clarifying the character of a fringe-area of the Campanian heartlands and in explaining the factors that seem to have led to a more precocious level of state-formation in adjoining areas of ?Auruncan Cales and Capua. To this end, large-scale excavation of at least one village is needed to verify the model suggested here or to see alternatively whether Livy's Auruncan *urbes*, in the sense of a substantial organised nucleated settlement pattern with a diversified economic base, did indeed start to make their appearance prior to Roman intervention.

Chapter Four

The Process of Romanisation

After the defeat of the Samnites, in 313/312 BC, the Romans were able to turn their interests once more to the fertile lands of Campania. In the same year the Aurunci were defeated and Caius Maenius re-subjugated the town of Capua. At that stage it became vital that Rome, once and for all, consolidated her hold over the access to the Campanian plain, which was partly achieved by the establishment of the Latin colony at Suessa Aurunca and by the laying out of the via Appia.

Apart from the positioning of the colonies and the courses of the roads, there is not much evidence for the early colonial systemisation of the area. In the years immediately following the deduction of Suessa Aurunca, the political situation was precarious and Samnite raids are recorded for 305 and 296 BC.[1] The indigenous population may have remained hostile for many years, and acts of unrecorded, localized, violence and sedition may well have been frequent.

Two colonies were founded in the lower Garigliano basin, Suessa Aurunca (313 BC) and Minturnae (295 BC), whilst Sinuessa (295 BC) and the ager Falernus (340 BC) occupied the territory to the immediate south.

Nominally the earliest, the ager Falernus was created from land, north of the Volturno, to the immediate south of the Massico ridge and west of the campus Stellatis and the ager Calenus, confiscated from the Campani after their defeat in the Latin war.[2] This was Rome's first major step in the fight for control of the Campanian plain. The organization of the territory appears to have been a protracted affair, possibly because of its size, environmental conditions and unrest amongst the native population. It was not until 318 BC that the tribe *Falerna* was created specifically for the colony, and it is perhaps not until that date that actual allotments were assigned.[3] Viritane distributions were made to Roman plebs in lots of three and a quarter *iugera*, slightly larger than the usual recorded allotments owing to their distance from Rome, whilst further distributions were probably made to the Campanian *equites* who had received the citizenship for collaboration.[4]

Traces of centuriation relating to the ager Falernus have been identified extending largely to the east of Rio Fontanelle as eight *decumani* running in a north-south direction. A recent paper by Jan Sevink apparently shows that the area in question was originally marshy and that ancient drainage took place through canals used in the redeposition of soil (colmatage) derived from higher areas to the north-east.[5] An overlay of Sevink's map with that of the centuriation system elaborated by Vallat indicates that a fair proportion of the centuriation of the ager Falernus extended over the area of former canals, such as Rio Forma/Rio Roda Vecchio, Rio di Volante Vecchio, the upper part of the Savone and the Savone Vecchio, as well as over the resulting colmatage deposits (Fig 6).[6] It follows that, if the colmatage deposits of the ager Falernus are indeed of classical date, as are the similar examples in the ager Pomptinus, then land drainage took place prior to actual colonial settlement in the area.

Various interesting observations follow. First, this very area, which we now know as prime agricultural land linking the fields around Capua and the Volturno with the foothills of the Massico, was not only relatively uncultivable in pre-Roman times, but would also have acted as an effective geomorphological barrier between the Aurunci and the Campani, perhaps explaining the visible cultural diversities between the two groups. This could go further towards explaining the rather slow and insular cultural development of the former, illustrated in the preceding chapter. Furthermore, either we imagine the drainage project as pre-Roman, effected by the Campani, or we should probably view it as part of Rome's overall scheme of colonising the northern Campanian plain. If the latter is the case, then the time necessary in which to carry out the project could explain the discrepancy between the confiscation of the ager Falernus from Capua in 340 BC and the creation of the *tribus Falerna* in 318 BC, surely a premise for material settlement, and the hypothesized appearance of nucleated settlement at Forum Claudii around 312 BC with the laying out of the via Appia (*infra*).

The ager Falernus appears to have had no clear administrative nucleus. Even if it may have been partly served by neighbouring Cales, which had been created as a Latin colony in 334 BC, the latter would not have expleted administrative functions.[7]

---

[1] Livy VIII, 44; Diod. XX, xc, 3.
[2] Livy VIII, xi.
[3] Vallat, 1980a.
[4] Livy VIII, xii, 12; IX, xx, 6. On the Campanian *equites* see Livy VIII, xi, 16: *Equitibus Campanis civitas Romana data.* Cf Ross Taylor, 1960, 67.

[5] Sevink, 1985.
[6] Vallat, 1980.
[7] On the significance of Cales, with its 2.500 settlers, see Mommsen, CIL X, p 460; Ross Taylor, 1960, 56; Johannowsky, 1976, 3. Cales was augmented with further settlers in 184 BC – Livy XIII, iii, 70.

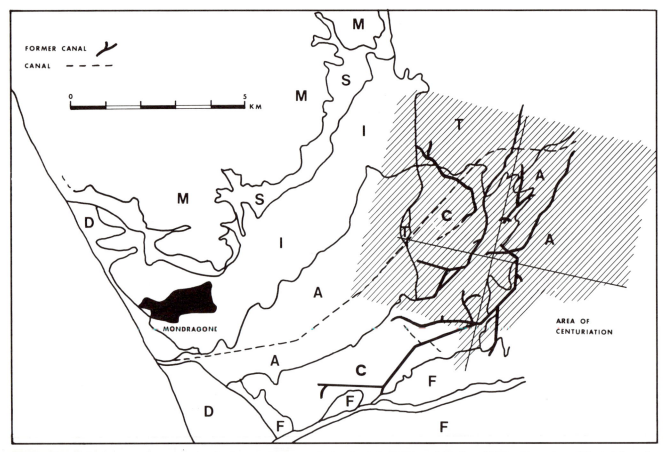

Fig 6   Land drainage and centuriation in the ager Falernus (after Sevink, 1985, and Vallat, 1980). Key: A = Fluvial deposits of local rivers; C = Colmatage deposits; D = Dunes; F = Fluvial deposits of the river Volturno; I = Ignimbrite; M = Massico mountain range; S = Slope deposits; T = Volcanic tuffs

In view of the unsettled conditions of the time and Rome's patent concern over the land's security, it is possible that the *coloni* were settled *en bloc* in the two *fora* attested in the area. Unfortunately, the foundation date of neither site is known. Johannowsky was prepared to see them as Gracchan, which is probably too late, whilst Forum Claudii (site C21) is in fact only perhaps attested for the first time in AD 499.[8] The *forum* may, in effect, have been named by Appius Claudius Caecus in 312 BC during the laying out of the via Appia. The fact that the textual and epigraphic sources make no mention of it may be pertinent. If it was founded in 312 BC, close to an original route for the via Appia through the Sessa/ Cascano pass, and Forum Popilii was established as an alternative centre with the re-direction of the road through the pass at Sinuessa from 295 BC, then the former may soon have become redundant as the local administrative and market centre. The rarity of republican material on the site, and the lack of sources would then be explained by the fact that it was effectively deserted only seventeen years after its foundation. Radke would instead have a preliminary stretch of the Appia built in 316 BC by M Popillius Laenas, with homonymous Forum Popilii as the primary foundation. This diverges unnecessarily from the original source for its construction.[9] Johannowsky's thesis has Forum Claudii founded by Appius Claudius Pulcher, consul in 143 BC and *triumvir agris dividendis colonisque deducendis* with Tiberius Gracchus in 133, and Forum Popilii by P Popillius Laenas, consul in the following year. Needless to say, this thesis is also attractive, though archaeological evidence may be called into play, at least, to demonstrate earlier occupation at the sites.

In many instances the naming of a *forum* seems to have been a Roman process of inserting a pre-existing indigenous settlement into an official

[8]   In AD 499 Forum Claudii was represented by its bishop at a synod in Rome (Cass. *Acta Syn.*). However, the reference may be to the homonymous site near Bracciano. For the *forum* see Johannowsky, 1974, 274; 1976, 30–31.

[9]   Fron. *Aq.* I, iv; Cf Wiseman, 1970, 130 and bibliography for Radke and the arguments against his thesis.

administrative hierarchy. The possible pre-existence of two nucleated settlements in the area, possibly even linked with the pro-Roman *equites* of Livy, may have made it undesirable to create a further colonial centre.[10]

Both sites have revealed a small amount of republican material, though neither have been excavated and, as suggested above, Forum Claudii may have been effectively abandoned shortly after its creation to re-emerge only in late antique times. Early settlement at Forum Popilii (site C43) is perhaps attested by the clandestine discovery of a number of late fourth or early third century tomb groups which, unfortunately, have now been dispersed.

The courses of two phases of the via Appia are also presumably of early date, though the surviving remains seem to date for the most part to late republican and early imperial times. The early surfaces are unlikely to have been systematically paved, though clearance and engineering works must nonetheless have been conducted by Appius Claudius during this early phase of Roman establishment in the south, as communication was of paramount importance in the military security of the area. The sole tract which may still preserve traces of the original early third century layout lies to the east of Mondragone, where the road takes on the form of a deep scar through the landscape, embanked with large squared drystone tuff blocks on both sides, later restored in part with *opus incertum* (pls VI and VII). Though less impressive than examples existing to the north of Rome, the engineering involved possessed valid precedents in Etruscan road-cuttings.[11]

On account of the lack of controlled archaeological excavation in much of northern Campania, even the three colonies have yielded few datable elements for early phases of Roman intervention.

Suessa Aurunca

Suessa Aurunca was founded as a Latin colony in 313 BC to control the heartland of the Aurunci.[12] It is situated on the crest of a ridge formed from the spoil of Roccamonfina, sloping upwards from *c* 143 to 205m asl, and providing a vantage point over much of the Garigliano basin (Fig 7). The defensive position also controlled the Cascano pass which leads southwards into the ager Falernus and the Campanian plain. The colony was bounded on the

north-western side by the depression of the Rio Fossitiello, and on the eastern side by the Vallone Grande.

Livy claims that it had been an Auruncan settlement.[13] There are few enough archaeological elements even for the Roman town, but up to now nothing has come to light to suggest that there was a significant pre-Roman occupation of the ridge.[14]

Little is known of Suessa Aurunca's early colonial history prior to the Second Punic War. In 211 BC, Hannibal's troops ravaged the territory along with the lands of Casinum and Allifae and in 209, like Sinuessa and Minturnae two years later, it refused to supply Rome with money and manpower towards the war effort. It continued to avoid the demand until 204 BC when, on repeated refusal, it was forced alongside other recalcitrant colonies to supply twice the maximum number of infantrymen that had ever been requested, along with 120 horsemen.[15]

Minturnae

Shortly after the foundation of Suessa Aurunca, Roman control of the area was strengthened with the foundation of the Roman maritime colonies of Minturnae and Sinuessa in 295 BC. Both were enrolled in the *tribu Teretina*. Minturnae was established on the right bank of the river *Liris* (Garigliano), with the same scope as later Liternum on the *Clanis* and Volturnum on the *Vulturnus*, as a maritime colony with the additional function of controlling river traffic. The Liris was certainly navigable in Roman times, as indeed it still was in the

---

[10] On the *fora* see Ruoff-Vaananen, 1978, 16–23. Livy VIII, xi, 16.

[11] Potter, 1979, 79–83. Johannowsky, 1976, 15, notes a stretch of road between Minturnae and Suessa Aurunca with *opus quadratum* terracing, which he dates no later than 313 BC.

[12] Livy IX, xxviii.

[13] Livy IX, xxviii, 7.

[14] The vague reference in the Soprintendenza archives (S. 9–19) to hand-made vases discovered in 1931 during lowering of the road level of Via Porta Carrese is by no means proof.

It is unlikely that any of the coins attributed to Suessa Aurunca were struck before 313 BC, whilst a large number, both in silver and bronze, are datable to the third century. Their distribution outside of the Garigliano basin includes sanctuaries and votive deposits at Panatelle, near the mouth of the Savone, Teano, Pompeii, Campochiaro, and hoards from Pietrabbondante, Cava dei Tirreni, Morino, Canosa and Carsoli. For the coins, which are in need of reassessment, see Sambon, 1903, 345–349, who dated them *c* 280–268 BC; Borelli, 1921, and 1935. The finds are published accordingly: Pietrabbondante, Cava dei Tirreni, Morino and Canosa in Crawford, 1969, hoards 24, 52, 54 and 86 respectively; Caroli in Cederna, 1951, 181; Campochiaro in Cantilena, 1981, 80; Pompeii in Maiuri, 1973, 118; Panetelle and Teano, unpublished excavations by G Tocco and J-P Morel respectively, whilst other examples have come to light at an extra-urban sanctuary at Sinuessa – *ex inf* M Pagano. Their contexts seem to suggest that they formed little part of a true monetary economy at this date, although their distribution may be partly conditioned by their survival, dependant in many cases on the function that they may have assumed as part of the sacred possessions of sanctuaries, and publication.

[15] Livy XXVI, ix, 1; XXVII, ix; XXIX, xv.

SUESSA

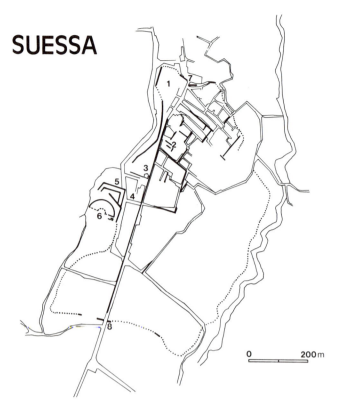

0   200m

Fig 7   Plan of the Latin colony of Suessa Aurunca (after Johannowsky, 1973, and Valletrisco, 1980). Key: 1 = Arx; 2 = Public baths?; 3 = Nymphaeum; 4 = Area of forum?; 5 = Cryptoporticus; 6 = Theatre; 7 = North gate (Porta Ercole); 8 = South gate

age of the Arab geographer Idrisi of the mid twelfth century, whilst today it is recommended to vessels not exceeding 0.9m in draught.[16] The colony also commanded the north-western territory confiscated from the Aurunci.

It was originally rectangular in shape, defended by a large wall of roughly squared blocks with four square angle towers (Fig 8). The via Appia formed the *decumanus maximus* before leaving the southernmost gate to cross the river. There is no evidence to suggest that the colony was founded on the site of a former Auruncan settlement despite earlier interpretations that the rectangular *castrum* wall was pre-Roman. The primary plan does, in fact, bear close comparison to to the plan of the early republican *castrum* at Ostia.[17]

Sinuessa

Twelve kilometres to the south of Minturnae, Sinuessa was founded as a Roman maritime colony on the south-western extremity of the Garigliano basin to command the coastal pass into Campania proper, and closing the triangle with Minturnae and Suessa for control of the entire basin. It was enrolled in the voting tribe *Teretina*.[18] The date of foundation, 296 or 295 BC, is given by Livy and Velleius, the former also noting that it had previously been known as the Greek town of Sinope. There is no evidence for the period and its existence should probably be discounted. There seems equally little truth in a presumed Auruncan town called Vescia, a hypothesis based on Livy and a suggested etymological derivation of Sinuessa from *Sinus Vesciae*.[19]

The two colonies were founded some seventeen years after the final subjugation of the Aurunci and the planting of Suessa Aurunca as a buttress to the consolidation of Rome's hold over Campania. Furthermore, Sinuessa and Minturnae were established during the Third Samnite war, shortly after the Samnites had raided Latium Adiectum by stealing up the coastal strip. They had already raided and been defeated in the ager Falernus in 305, and their incursion the year following the foundation of Sinuessa was likewise foiled. For these reasons it would appear that Rome had difficulty in enrolling the colonists who regarded the sites as a *stationem se prope perpetuam infestae regionis*.[20] Such could also suggest that the lowlands, prior to careful drainage and working, were largely insalubrious and that relations with the natives would have been rendered even more uneasy on expropriation of the more fertile and workable tracts. Sinuessa's positioning, strategic motives aside, was fundamental in initiating exploitation of the rich hinterland.[21]

Perhaps, as at Terracina, some 300 male citizens were originally planted at both Sinuessa and Minturnae.[22] In fact the *castrum* wall at Minturnae encompassed about the same area as that of mid fourth century Ostia, which covered just over 2 hectares and provided for some 300 families. A similar figure of 300 *coloni*, or roughly 1.100 people has been advanced for the Latin colony of Cosa founded in 273 BC.[23] Each *colonus* of Sinuessa would

[16] The work of Idrisi is published by Amari and Schiaparelli, 1883, 94. For the current navigability of the Garigliano see Aldridge, 1978, 203.

[17] Johnson, 1935, 1–2; Aurigemma and De Santis, 1955, 41–42. For the early plan of Ostia see, for example, Castagnoli, 1956, 86–87.

[18] Palmieri, 1977.

[19] Livy IX, xxv, 4; X, xxi, 7–8; Vell. I, xix, 6; Philipp, *RE* XV, 2, 1935; Cicala and Lao, 1958.

[20] Livy VIII, xliv; X, xx and xxi, 10; Diod. XX, xc, 3–4; Toynbee, 1965, 184–186; Salmon, 1967, 79–81, and 1969, 77.

[21] Pliny *NH* III, v, 4: *terrarum....tamquam iuvandos ad mortales ipsa avide in maria procurrens*.

[22] Livy VIII, xxi.

[23] Brown, 1980, 18.

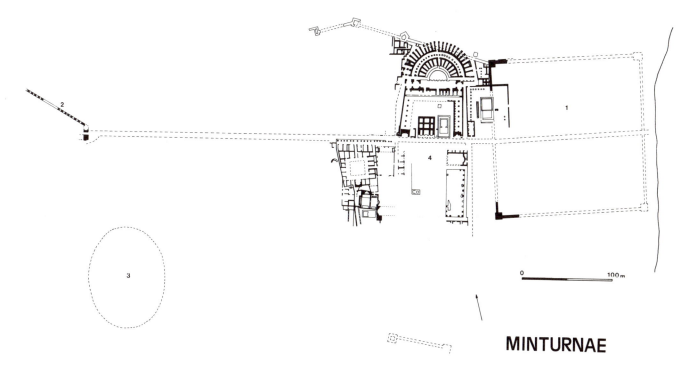

Fig 8   Plan of the Roman colony of Minturnae (after De Spagnolis, 1981). Key: 1 = Site of original colony; 2 = Aqueduct; 3 = Amphitheatre; 4 = Forum

probably have been allocated about 2 *iugera* of centuriated land situated mainly in the triangular plain stretching southwards through the areas of Incaldana and Mondragone, down to the Savone.

Sinuessa is next brought to our attention during the Hannibalic Wars when, in 217 BC, Carthaginian troops devastated much of the country south of the Massico and struck both Sinuessa and a settlement at the Thermae Sinuessanae. Two years later it appeared as a base for mobilization of part of the Roman forces under Sempronius, when a scorched-earth policy was being effected before the arrival of the enemy.[24] Later, on the arrival of Hasdrubal in Italy, Rome felt it necessary to enlist extra manpower from the coastguard colonies, who were usually exempted from supplying soldiers. On refusal, the consuls called the recalcitrant colonies to the Senate to voice their dissension. Of the colonies which had declined contributions, only Ostia and Antium were permitted to retain their traditional exemptions. A similar reluctance, by both Minturnae and Sinuessa, to supply manpower for maritime service is noted for 191 BC, during the war against Antiochus I.[25]

Surprisingly little archaeological work has been carried out at the site, despite the fact that it is largely under plough, and consequently knowledge

about the form that the settlement possessed is meagre (Fig 9). It is perhaps likely that, as at Minturnae, it was originally rectangular with the Appia traversing the site in a north-south direction as the *decumanus maximus*. A 54m long tract of wall, belonging to the colony's original southern defenses and constructed of roughly squared tuff blocks, was discovered running in a straight line towards the sea and at right-angles to the *decumanus*. The excavations, conducted by Werner Johannowsky, also revealed a square tower and a pomerial road. Both a portico and a kiln complex were built to the south of the wall in late republican times, whilst numerous burials indicate the presence of one of Sinuessa's cemeteries. Sadly, a published description of the excavations is lacking. A further section of wall near Mass. Morrone, referred to by Sementini as a *muro ciclopico*, probably indicates the eastern extension of the circuit.[26]

Peripheral fortified sites

The creation of the three colonies in the Garigliano basin seems to have been part of a carefully planned defensive scheme. It may be suggested that the two coastal colonies were created as prime bulwarks at the vulnerable sea/land interface and, therefore,

[24] Livy XXII, xiii, 10; xiv, 5; XXIII, xxxii, 14–15; xxv, 5; Polyb. III, 90. Cf Brunt, 1971, 270.
[25] Livy XXVII, xxxviii, 3–5; XXXVI, iii, 4–7.

[26] Sementini, n.d., 48. The term '*ciclopico*' was often used by local antiquaries and farmers to denote drystone masonry composed of large ashlar or polygonal blocks. Cf also Pagano, 1981b, 109–110.

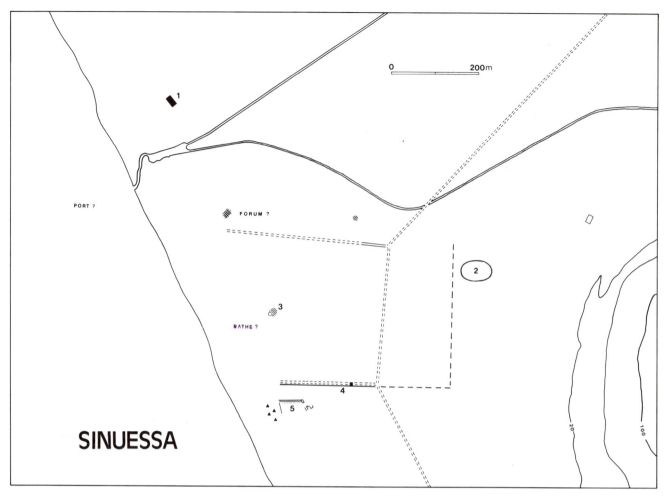

Fig 9   Plan of the Roman colony of Sinuessa. Key: 1 = Villa of S Limato (site M1); 2 = Amphitheatre (site M23);
3 = Kiln waster dump and well; 4 = Town walls; 5 = Sanctuary (site M20)

carefully manned with loyal Roman *coloni*. They not only controlled north-south maritime traffic, but also any movement of goods out of the hinterland. Suessa Aurunca, instead, was a colony which may have had the role of 'hen-coop' for the re-settlement of the local Auruncan peoples, diluted with a population of Latin colonists. Access from the Campanian plain, to the south, was instead monitored by the creation of two small nucleated sites, perhaps acting as part of an early-warning system, at the two passes at either end of the Massico chain: Cascano (213m asl) and Monte Cicoli (275m asl).

In 1978 building works in the centre of the modern hamlet of Cascano brought to light substantial Roman remains, a large part of which are of imperial date (site C5). However, a short but striking tract of probable early ashlar wall was also revealed. It consisted of a drystone construction of closely-fitting squared grey tuff blocks, bearing comparison to the early walls of neighbouring Suessa Aurunca, as well as fourth or early third century

walls at such sites as Cales, Minturnae and Pompeii. Unfortunately, the few scraps of Black Glaze ware found on site were not closely datable, and only excavation can prove the point. Cascano did however develop into a small settlement controlling the strategic passage from the ager Falernus through the gap between the Massico and Roccamonfina and into the Garigliano basin by Suessa, which lay only three kilometres distant.

The site on Monte Cicoli was based on the pre-existing Iron Age refuge overlooking the position of the colony of Sinuessa, and commanding a view up and down the coast (site M27). Roman use of the site is indicated by a dense spread of pottery, some of which appears to be of late fourth or early third century date. The site remained in use down to, at least, the mid second century BC, presumably as a lookout, given its inadequate location for most other forms of exploitation, and may in its later stages have assisted in warning Sinuessa against the pirates who were only finally cleared from the seas after Pompey had been given a special command against them in 67 BC.[27]

[27] Plut. *Pomp.* XXV; Vell. II, xxxi; App. Mith. xciv.

The land schemes

The environment which the Romans encountered at the moment of conquest, in the later fourth century BC, must already have suffered numerous anthropogenic changes since prehistory but, given the somewhat backward state of affairs amongst the Aurunci when compared with other coastal cultures of Etruria, Latium and Campania, may still have appeared particularly inhospitable.[28] Both thick woods and pestilential marshes find echo in later accounts of the area. Roman and pre-Roman colluvial deposition indicates a certain amount of deforestation of mountainous areas with concomitant erosion and denudation during the last few centuries BC. Examples of datable colluvial deposits are available in thc area, though one particularly distinct case will suffice to illustrate the nature of the evidence.

At the north-eastern end of the Massico chain runoff between two limestone crests, Mt Crocefisso (468m asl) and Mt Vallerovina (436m asl), led to the downcutting of a wide seasonal rio through the soft mantle of ignimbrite (site C46: Fig 10). The rio was eventually totally backfilled and obscured until revealed by recent bulldozed terracing of the slopes. Examination of the section showed its fill to be composed of a fairly homogeneous red-orange colluvium with some intercalated lenses of yellow soil and gravel brought down from the eroded limestone slopes. The central fill contained several weathered sherds of late Bronze or early Iron Age pottery, whilst occasional Roman sherds were present exclusively in the uppermost centimetres of humic topsoil. In view of the evidence it may be suggested that the greater part of the stream cutting was filled by the time that the Romans started to cultivate the upper slopes. The increased erosion testified by the colluvial deposits both here and elsewhere indicate an altered environmental situation which may be attributed to later Iron Age or early Roman deforestation in the absence of evidence for other causative agents such as climatic deterioration. A soil column extracted for pollen analysis unfortunately yielded no appreciable results.[29]

The actual extent of deforestation around the basin is impossible to gauge, although it is quite probable that much of the area around the Garigliano and the Massico was still heavily wooded by the middle of the first millenium BC, whilst the slopes of Roccamonfina probably remained a constant source of timber right through to the present day. With the Roman colonization the lowlands, below 100m, were centuriated. Frontinus explains that there was no forest adjacent to the plots, so that stretches of woodland on Mons Maricus (*sic*) were divided up and defined by boundary markers. The presence of holdings in the mountains will already have signalled further deforestation, which must have accelerated with the growth of larger rural properties through the second and first centuries BC. Not only are traces of villas and farms with great stone retaining walls found in hill and mountain areas now covered with macchia, but abandoned agricultural terraces with drystone revetment walls and thin Roman pottery scatters are still to be seen over the 300m mark, where woodland was made to give way to the olive and the vine, and the latter later to the macchia.

Evidence survives for the centuriation of the three colonies and, although originally considered by Castagnoli, new material makes a brief reconsideration necessary.[30] Both Minturnae and Suessa are illustrated by miniatures which were drawn up to accompany the codices of the gromatici. The diagram of Suessa shows the walled *colonia* lying within a grid of square *centuriae* which run up to the foot of the *Mons Aricius*, probably to be identified with the Massico chain and not Roccamonfina. The accompanying text follows the diagram obviously by mistake.[31] It is best referred to by a closely preceding passage: *Et sunt plerumque agri, ut in Campania in Suessano, culti, qui habent in monte Marico plagas silvarum determinates; quarum silvarum proprietas ad quos pertineat debeat vindicatur. nam et formae antiquae declarant ita esse adsignatum, quoniam solo culto nihil fuit silvestre iunctum quod adsignaretur*, based probably on Frontinus and agreeing with a passage of the *De Controversis* indicating that forested lots on the hills were assigned to complement the lots of low-lying cultivable land.[32] Frontinus further indicates that the territory was divided by *centuriae* in the plain and *ad strigas* in the highlands.[33] Such details are not shown on the schematic diagram of Suessa Aurunca, though the uneven lie of the land would certainly argue against a single grid system surrounding the town on all sides.

The diagram of Minturnae is richer in information, showing the walled colony backed by the Mons Vescini and divided by the *flumen Liris* which runs into an elliptical expanse of water representing the sea. The centuriation is shown as a rectangular grid labelled *adsignatio nova*. A passage of Hyginus

[28] Talamo, 1987.
[29] I should like to thank Helen Porter for having processed the sample.

[30] Castagnoli, 1944, 102–105.
[31] I.e. the illustration accompanying the text of Agennius Urbicus: Lachmann, 80, 3; Thulin, 39, 8.
[32] For the two passages see Lachmann, 79, 13; Thulin, 39, 8, and Lachmann, 15, 1; Thulin, 6, 3.
[33] Lachmann, 3, 2; Thulin, 1, 4. Cf also *Lib. Col.* 237, 11.

SESSA AURUNCA

KEY: POTSHERDS ▲

SOIL COLUMN ·······

STONES ·°₀°°

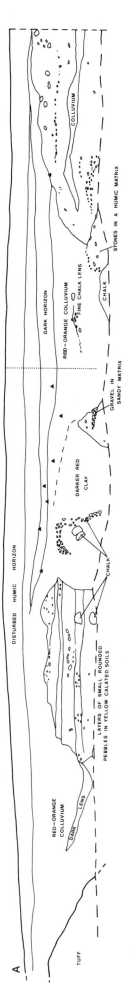
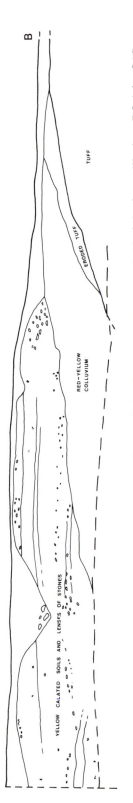

Fig 10   Section through a seasonal stream-bed choked with colluvium, probably during the second half of the first millenium BC (site C46)

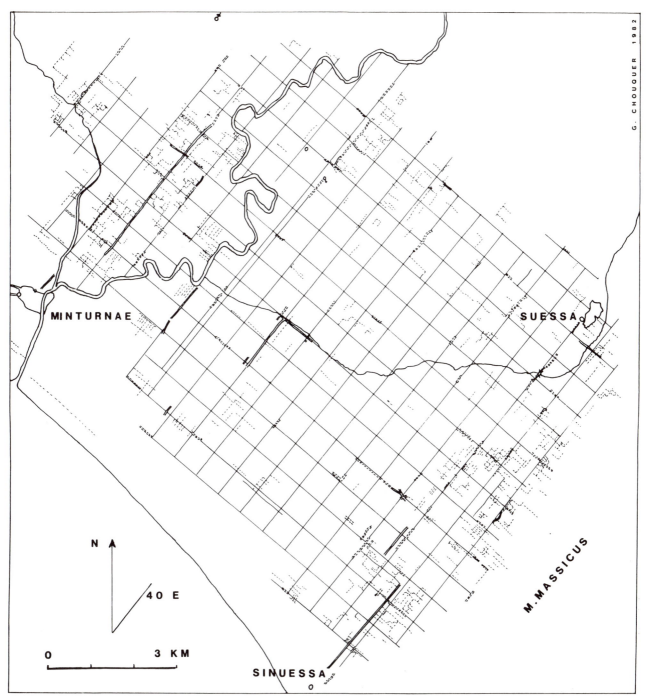

Fig 11   Hypothetical reconstruction of the centuriation system in the Garigliano basin (after Chouquer and Favory, 1982)

accompanies the illustration.[34] It is obvious that the town of Minturnae was never actually divided by the Liris, as a passage of Pliny might also at first sight suggest: *colonia Minturnae Liri amne divisa*.[35] This does not, of course, preclude the development of suburbs on the south bank. The *colonia* of Pliny's text is intended as the whole territory assigned to the *coloni*, and it is clear that this had to extend to the left bank of the river on account of the restricted land available on the right bank.[36] Whether or not such was the case with the original *centuratio* is not known, although the *adsignatio nova* of the miniature on the

---

[34] Hyginus: *...in Campania finibus Minturnensium: quorum nova adsignatio trans fluvium Lirem limitibus continentur: citra Lirem postea adsignatum per professiones veterum possessorum, ubi iam opportunarum finium commutatione relictis primae adsignationis terminis more arcifinio possidetur.*

[35] Pliny *NH* III, v, 39.

[36] Coarelli, 1982, 369–370, interprets Livy as referring to the actual town being divided in two by the river. I have seen very little archaeological material on the left bank to support such a hypothesis, though some constructions there undoubtedly were.

left bank of the Liris, and Pliny, may well refer to later Caesarian or Augustan assignations.

A good part of the texts of the *gromatici* and the miniatures can be verified on the ground. Indeed, six different systems have been proposed.[37] The initial colonial *centuriatio* of Minturnae has apparently been detected along the Via Appia to the west of the colony (Minturnae I). Between Suessa Aurunca and Sinuessa, Chouquer and Favory propose the existence of pre-Roman land divisions based on a grid of 8 by 8 *versus* (Suessa I – Sinuessa I), which chronology I find inherently unlikely, whilst other divisions, *per strigas*, extend to the north of the Minturnae-Suessa road (Suessa II). These last could be contemporary with regular systems to the immediate north of Sinuessa (Sinuessa II) and to the west of Suessa Aurunca up to the town of Cellole (Suessa III).[38] If, as has been suggested, the town of Cellole marks the boundary between the territories of Suessa Aurunca and Minturnae, on account of the discovery there of inscriptions referring to both the *tribus Teretina* of Minturnae and the *tribus Aemilia* of Suessa Aurunca, then it would also mark the northernmost possible point of extension of the land plots assigned to coloni dependant upon the latter.[39]

The most clearly surviving *centuriatio* invests almost the entire river basin (Minturnae II – Suessa IV – Sinuessa III; Fig 11).[40] It is formed of a grid lying parallel to the NE-SW axis of the Massico and for the most part below the 50m. contour, and extending to the north, over the Garigliano. It is likely that this was the latest major system imposed on the area, perhaps in Augustan times, as it seems to have conditioned the development of the medieval villages of S Maria la Piana, Quintola (site S41), Carano (a praedial toponym!), Piedimonte Massicano and Piedimonte Rivoli. The reconstructed grid furthermore coincides with various scatters of Roman road blocks which, because of their apparent random distribution, have in the past

posed many problems in the interpretation of the course of the road linking Suessa Aurunca and Sinuessa.[41]

No certain traces of land divisions have been identified between the presumed site of the pagus Sarclanus (*infra*), to the immediate east of Mondragone, and Sinuessa, although tracks stretching at right-angles to the north-east of the via Appia, in the area of Incaldana, may indicate division *per strigas* because of limited arable land. It has been suggested that the area presents evidence of at least three *cardines* spaced at intervals of 20 *actus*. Further rectilinear road systems to the south of Mondragone, delimited by the river Savone and recent marshes, betray divisions of about 568 metres or 16 *actus*.[42]

The traces of various centuriation systems to the south and east of the Massico and in the ager Falernus are the subject of various further in-depth studies carried out by Chouquer, Favory and Vallat (*passim*).

Markets, vici *and* pagi

The development of the Campanian road system will have greatly advanced the possibilities of communication and exchange.[43] The gateway ports of Sinuessa and Minturnae were linked not only to their own territories, but also to those of the more inland towns, making possible a somewhat cheaper and efficient two-way supply network than that which had existed before. The improved network must have been a positive factor in the development of small-scale trade and exchange which, in Campania as in much of the empire, depended greatly on small markets and fairs. All the towns possessed their own shops, often supplying manufactured goods such as those listed by Cato, or items deriving from long-distance trade.[44] A large proportion of materials produced in neighbouring rural areas however, must have circulated through a system of temporary

---

[37] Chouquer *et alii*, 1987, 169–180, presenting a full discussion.

[38] Land divisions to the immediate north of Sinuessa are hypothesized by Pagano, 1981b, 116–117, on the basis of the discovery of a paved Roman road running NW-SE to the west of the via Appia and parallel to a number of modern country tracks, permitting a reconstruction of land strips of *c* 14 *actus* width. On the basis of the estimated area subjected to *centuriatio*, approximately 2.100.000m², and the absence of *cardines*, which appears to be a feature of early colonies such as Alba Fucens, Cosa and Luceria, Pagano proposes that the system may date to the foundation of the colony in 296/295 BC, satisfying some 300 *coloni* at 2 *iugera pro capite*. If so, it may be further suggested that the decision to farm the land initially to the north of the town was dictated by reasons of security, particularly as that to the south was better drained and thus more favorable to agricultural exploitation.

[39] Castagnoli, *op. cit.*, 105. For the inscriptions see CIL X 4776 and 4777.

[40] See also Arthur, 1982a.

[41] It is of interest to note the presence of the toponym Pertecara, probably derived from *pertica*, in the area between the site of Sinuessa and Piedimonte. The same toponym also appears to the north of Casanova di Carinola at a point at which gentle slopes meet the salient Massico. Cf Prop. IV, I, 130; Grom. III.

[42] Chouquer *et alii*, 1987, 180–181. Cf Dilke, 1971, 95.

[43] See pp. 47–54 below.

[44] Cato Agr. CXXV, 1–3.

markets held at regular intervals, the *nundinae*, well-attested in Campania.[45] These clearly developed from pre-Roman rural markets and fairs, often focused on occasions and sites of religious observance. Macmullen's thesis that 'urban fairs are less often heard of because they were less necessary than rural ones' is disputable in the context of areas like Campania during the late republic and early empire.[46] The close-knit pattern of distribution of the Campanian agro-towns would probably have rendered rural markets inconceivable, as the regional market-day calendars may indicate. Rather, farmers, bailiffs and itinerant merchants would have slotted themselves into the market-day schedules which saw to avoiding clashes of dates by allocating successive days to each town in the area. Such is the system still practised in parts of rural Italy today. The modern artisan potters at the village of Cascano, for instance, sell many of their wares through attendance at the markets of towns such as Teano, Sessa, Caserta, Capua and S Maria Capua Vetere, held on different days. The distance that itinerant salesmen decide to travel to each market depends on various factors of supply and demand. Cascano has no regular market, availing itself of that held every Thursday morning at Sessa, four kilometres along the road and well within walking distance, for supply of goods not otherwise locally available. Thronging with people, the centre of town becomes temporarily closed to traffic, and the day is turned into a social event with the opportunity for inhabitants spread over a certain area to get together and exchange goods and gossip.

It is probably unlikely that *vici* played a great role as markets, except perhaps in the early days when the Roman urban/administrative system was new to many parts of Italy, and in areas where towns were thinly sown, as in much of North Africa.[47] Above all, the *vici* served rural population groups, acting as a central dwelling-place for the farmers and peasant labourers whose properties or land were relatively distant from any town. In some cases, as in that of the vicus Caedicius, internal organization may have been provided by a local notable or landlord. Alternatively, a *vicus* may have formed part of a *pagus*, or subdivision of a larger administrative unit such as a town.

The problem of the origin and definition of the *pagus* is vexing, particularly as they are rarely mentioned in the sources. Indeed, the two known in the area under examination, the pagus Vescinus and the pagus Sarclanus, are each attested by a single inscription. Both may pre-date the Roman conquest and be indicative of the form of territorial organization of the Aurunci. Recently, Frederiksen suggested that the Campanian *pagi* were Roman creations because of their names, their developed financial procedures and dating based on the Roman calendar, and cited as an example the pagus Herculaneus of Capua. He thus dismissed his earlier belief in the resurgence of ancient tribal *pagi* after the Second Punic War, though the same may not hold true for the area of the Aurunci where even the toponyms appear to betray pre-Roman origins.[48]

If the original *pagi* were destroyed or subsided as territorial subdivisions with the new administrative regime brought with Romanisation, we do not know precisely when they began to acquire renewed significance. The inscription of the pagus Vescinus can be no earlier than the end of the republic, whilst that of the pagus Sarclanus dates to as late as AD 43, though both attest financial transactions and would accord with the suggestion that the *pagus* as a financial unit was a growth of the late republic and more specifically Augustan in Rome, when they were used for the taking of the census.[49] If used as a centre for tax-collection, as in Diocletianic Egypt, they would have acquired greater significance with Augustus' virtual elimination of the *publicani*. The inscription of the pagus Sarclanus records a donation of HS 2000 to the decurions of the *pagus* by a certain P Crusius Germanus.[50] That of the pagus Vescinus refers to an expenditure of HS 12000 by members of the *pagus* towards the construction of an amphitheatre, perhaps at Minturnae.[51] All this helps to underline their financial stability, independent from that of the local *municipium*, during the late republic and early empire. Furthermore, the singular nature of the pagus Sarclanus is underlined by the fact that it possessed *decuriones*.[52]

[45] Macmullen, 1970.
[46] Macmullen, *loc. cit.*, 337.
[47] Cf Shaw, 1981.

[48] Frederiksen, 1976, 351, which retracts Frederiksen, 1959, 90. See also Mommsen CIL X, p. 367; Kornemann, 1905, 72ff.; Heurgon, 1942, 115ff. Sarclanus is unlikely to derive from the Latin *sarculum* or hoe: Andrei, 1981, 50.
[49] Frederiksen, 1976, 346–347.
[50] Pellegrino, 1978.
[51] Pontecorvo, 1979. Cf the financial contribution by the pagus Felix Suburbanus towards the Sullan amphitheatre at Pompeii for the provision of steps: CIL X 853.
[52] This is noted by Patterson, 1985, 68, who, however, wants to assimilate *pagi* and *vici*.

The sanctuaries

If the pre-Roman settlement pattern was dismembered by Roman synoecism, at least the continuity in use of traditional cult-centres was tolerated. Two religious sanctuaries have been excavated in northern coastal Campania: that of the deity Marica (*supra*), and an unattributed one near the mouth of the Savus, in loc. Panetelle, on the coastal road later to become the via Domitiana.[53] Their comparable settings at the mouths of major rivers are repeated frequently in Magna Graecia, as at the Heraion at the mouth of the Sele near Paestum, and though in part intended as placatory to local water sources upon whose regime the burden of a successful agriculture was largely placed, highlight the rivers' importance as communication routes. Both of the northern Campanian sites were bordered by marshes, and it is probable that at such focal geomorphological interfaces, accessible to both maritime and riverine traffic, they may have continued to function as market centres or 'half-way' meeting points between communities into the early days of Roman colonisation. Though market functions were eventually forgotten, ritual continued into the early empire as must their role as focal points for the exchange of ideas and news.[54]

Both sites were established well prior to Roman colonisation, though only the former has been tolerably well published, with the presentation of archaic material.[55] The architecture revealed at both sites appears to be little, if any, earlier than the Roman conquest. At Panetelle the excavated temple was of Italic type with a *podium* measuring 18 x 15m and a *pronaos* and *cella* between closed *antae* and divided in two by transverse walls. The visible remains seem to be datable to around the later second century BC.[56] The earliest recognized phase of the Italic temple of Marica was built of roughly cemented grey tuff blocks which cannot be as early as the late sixth century date proposed by Mingazzini.[57] Both sites seem to have flourished during the second century BC, though the deposition of the abundant ex-voto appears to have terminated by the period of the

Social War. The sanctuaries remained in use at least into the late first century AD, with the coin sequences running up to Tiberius and Claudius and a reconstruction of the *cella* of the temple of Marica effected in brick-faced concrete. The latter site may also have been rededicated through assimilation with Isis and Serapis, underlining Minturnae's later status as 'international' entrepot.[58] Nonetheless, the disappearance of votive offerings around the beginning of the first century BC, a phenomenon repeated in various parts of the peninsula, indicates a fairly radical change in the dynamics of sanctuary use.[59]

The factors of change are difficult to discern, but may be linked to Italy's altered social and political structure after the Social War. With definitive *official* Romanisation of the country came the added importance of the state cults, located primarily in and around the *fora* of the various municipalities. More to the point, the sanctuaries were above all a phenomenon strongly linked to indigenous rural populations, which had themselves been undergoing radical transformations and assimilation ever more swiftly from the time of the Second Punic War. It may not have been so much the disappearance of the small and medium property owners, as Pensabene seems to indicate, but rather changes in their composition, status and outlook that altered their rapport with the traditional deities.[60] These people were no longer Aurunci or Sidicini or Campani, but members of an ever-more Roman world, and citizens to boot from 90 BC. That is not to say that pilgrimages to sanctuaries ceased in the early first century BC, which archaeology seems to contradict, but that with the population's altered composition and status, and a steadily diminishing number of faithful, it became no longer viable to produce and market traditional ex-voto for a changed clientele. As one scholar has recently put it, in a slightly different context, 'the process of social evolution and the mere passage of time ensure that certain rites will get overlooked, neglected or forgotten'.[61] Religious observance was also becoming more introverted, perhaps as a result of increasing social complexity, with less emphasis on congregation and more on the

[53] The sanctuary at loc. Panetelle was excavated on two separate occasions by Werner Johannowsky and by Giuliana Tocco respectively. The site remains substantially unpublished and clandestine excavation now continues unabated.

[54] Cf Pugliese Caratelli, 1962, 243; Grenier, 1959, 950.

[55] *Supra*. Johannowsky, 1975, 31, note 107, claims that the site at Panatelle was 'un importante santuario risalente ad età arcaica' and, in another paper (1978, 138), signals the presence of at least one sixth century BC 'Rhodian group' B2 cup. See now Talamo, 1987.

[56] Johannowsky, 1971, 467, note 30; *ibid.*, 1974, 273.

[57] 1938, 695ff.

[58] Mingazzini, 1938, 930ff.

[59] Cf Rizzello, 1980, 202, for evidence of the process in the nearby middle Liri valley.

[60] Pensabene, 1979, 222.

[61] North, 1976, 12. Parallel changes were also occurring in towns. Excavations by the writer at Pompeii have revealed an enormous number of ex-voto made at and for the Temple of Apollo overlooking the forum (Arthur, 1986). These had been discarded in cisterns and *favissae*, and sealed by the time the area of the forum was reorganized under the burden of the increasing wealth entering local hands in the second half of the second century BC. There is no indication of continuity in the practice of making and selling similar objects after that date, even though the temple functioned until its destruction by the eruption of Mt Vesuvius in AD 79.

role of the *pater familias* and the importance of the domestic *lares*. As with present survivals of pagan superstitions, that the appeasement of local river deities, for example, was not forgotten throughout imperial times may be indicated by the continued deposition of coins in the *Liris*.[62] Thus we might suggest that despite the enforced synoecism in the early years of the Roman conquest, true social integration had not been achieved locally until, at least, the Social War or when the autochtonous religious rites had become an echo of the past with the abandonment or marginalisation of the sanctuaries.

Other sanctuaries and shrines are known from the area and help to emphasize the nature of rural and urban religious observance in early Roman times. A prolific votive deposit was located under the coastal dunes, in loc. Le Vagnole, just to the south of Sinuessa: coins, terracotta heads, statuettes, animals and anatomical members were brought to light by bulldozing operations for the construction of the tourist village of Baia Azzura.[63] A further group of votive offerings, comprising terracotta feet and young male heads, which have been dated to the third and second centuries BC, was found just to the south-east of Sessa Aurunca.[64] A rural shrine may be indicated by a find of two terracotta feet, a face and part of the back of the neck of an all-round head, just to the south-east of Falciano. This may well date to around the second century BC and could be the same site that Johannowsky refers to as Starzatella, where ex-voto of fourth century BC date were discovered.[65]

What is immediately striking from the combined evidence is the relative 'poverty' of these sanctuaries when compared to the two major sanctuaries discovered in the neighbourhood of Teanum Sidicinum, one of Campania's richest towns, lying to the east of the Garigliano basin. The two Sidicine sanctuaries both present material datable to the Roman occupation of the region.[66] The Santuario Loreto was constructed on four terraces overlooking the Savus river. It underwent four major building phases from the third century (drystone tuff block masonry) to Sullan times (opus incertum tending to quasi-reticulatum), eventually covering an area of over two hectares, and including a group of four small temples. After the early first century BC, evidence for continued activity at the site diminishes drastically, with a little further building at the end of the republic or Augustan times and under the Julio-Claudians.[67] The other site, at Fondo Ruozzo, was similarly terraced above the Savus. It seems to have undergone two major construction phases, one of late fourth or early third century BC date (drystone tuff block masonry) and the other dating to the first half of the second century BC (opus incertum). Despite the discovery of a little later material, the Black Glaze A pottery suggests a date of around 150 BC for the end of ritual deposition.[68] Both sites have yielded a vast amount of terracotta statues and statuettes, pottery, and numerous silver and bronze coins, of a range far wider than those from either of the two excavated coastal sanctuaries described above.

The road network

The constraints that will dictate the route of any road or track between two given points are usually twofold: geomorphological and political. Taking heed of these constraints, the road will generally follow the most direct route between points A and B. In attempting to reconstruct prehistoric communication systems, the geomorphological factors may be tolerably well understood and taken into account, whilst the political may often remain unknown. Factors such as religious observance of consecrated territory may be considered political and will usually contribute to the unknown. Once a route is

[62] Frier and Parker, 1970; Metcalf, 1974. Later, unpublished, finds are in possession of the Soprintendenza.

[63] Pagano and Ferone, 1976, 30–31 and pl V, for a photograph of one of the male heads. Another is illustrated in Cuomo *et alii*, nd, 24, where the site is identified as 'Tempio di Mercurio'. Much material was seen and photographed by Dott. Andrea Nerone, of Mondragone, to whom I am indebted for information, including the fact that one of the terracottas bore a dedication to Mercury. Other terracotta fragments have been found underwater (Michele, 1971).

[64] Villucci, 1981b, 160 and 162. Unfortunately none of the finds are illustrated and the exact find-spot seems not to have been recorded!

[65] Johannowsky, 1975, 28. Other Hellenistic ex-votos were unearthed near Croce di Casale.

[66] A third sanctuary, at Mass. Iastavello, in the territory of Teanum Sidicinum, dates to the early Iron Age and has yielded numerous miniature pottery vessels, bronze rings and articles of glass paste. It is located by a spring and could testify to the veneration of a minor water deity. See Albore Livadie, 1981.

[67] Johannowsky, 1963.

[68] J-P. Morel, Conference on Magna Graecia, Taranto, 1980.

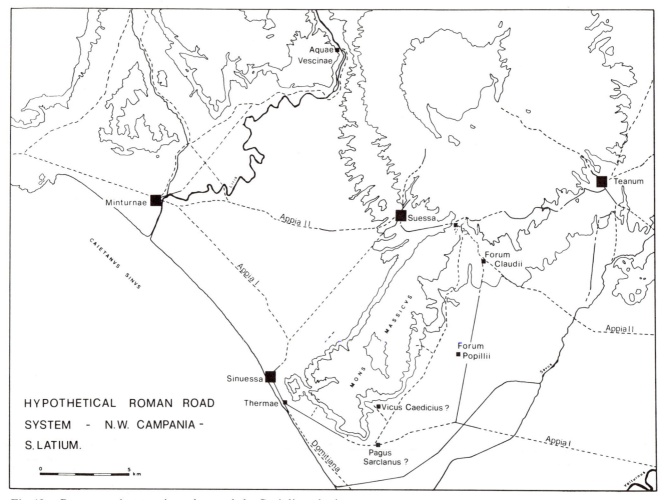

Fig 12   Roman road system in and around the Garigliano basin

established sites may, in the first place, tend to concentrate along it, thus producing archaeological elements which may be interpreted in relation to its reconstruction. Such evidence is, at best, circumstantial. Periods of unrest, for instance, may encourage avoidance of established thoroughfares.

Communication will generally relate to settlement and food supply, though military movement and administration can be significant factors in determining the existence of communication networks. In the past, provision of food will have involved seasonal migration of peoples according to movements of game as well as the establishment of tracks providing access to water sources and other resources. With the domestication of animals and the establishment of agricultural regimes seasonal migration will have come under control. In the event, *tratturi* will have been established between uplands and lowlands, and between exhausted and fresh vegetational systems. In a large part of Italy these will have formed the basis for future communication systems.

Though the only principal surviving *tratturo* in the area under study is probably the road leading from Casino/Interamna to Minturno, major movement in the territory is noticeably either north-south, along or parallel to the coast, or east-west, up and down the valleys. The Roman road system is the first to have left identifiable marks on the landscape and is, of course, recorded to a fair extent through the sources. Though it may in part be based on earlier systems, these are no longer readily distinguishable. The only Iron Age thoroughfare which is recognizable with any degree of certainty seems to be the hollowed-way at Ponte Ronaco, where a concentration of pre-Roman burials was probably linked north-eastwards to Suessa Aurunca and south-eastwards to the Iron Age village of Ponte Ronaco (see The Suessa Aurunca-Sinuessa road *infra*). It is therefore the Roman system that will be considered here, under its separate components (see Fig. 12).

The Via Appia – I

This was begun by Appius Claudius Caecus, though apparently he did no more than trace its course from Rome to Capua in 312 BC.[69] The surface was

[69] Livy IX, 29; Front. *Aq.* I, 4.

probably not paved until 191 BC. The actual course of the Appia between Minturnae and Capua is still in doubt for the period between its layout and the foundation of the colony of Sinuessa in 296 BC. Even though it later ran to Sinuessa and crossed the ager Falernus to the south of the Massico, it has been suggested and disputed that its original course, once over the river Garigliano at Minturnae, veered inland direct to Suessa Aurunca.[70] This would have avoided the lagoon or *pantano* along the coast and more significantly would have made much more tactical sense in the siting of Suessa Aurunca at the mouth of the pass at Cascano.

Other major Roman roads are known to have changed course for strategic reasons, such as the nearby Via Latina. The original and later roads were subsequently referred to as the *Via Latina vetus* and the *Via Latina nova*, the former deviating from the direct Aquinum-Casinum route so as to take in Interamna Lirenas, founded in 312 BC, ensuring its communication with Campania during the bitter struggle with the Samnites.[71]

As the Appia dropped down from the hills it would have passed to the area of Forum Claudii, which name could thus derive from the *gentilicium* of Appius Claudius Caecus.[72] There is perhaps little hope of confirmation for such an hypothesis, although the pass at Cascano was certainly in use long before the Romans presided over the area and became the major route in late antique times, remaining such down to the present day. The coastal route would have become necessary with the foundation of the colony and gateway port of Sinuessa, to protect the pass and act as an opening for the surplus produce of the hinterland.

At this point we may consider the remains, even though considerably less is visible now in respect to what was visible only a hundred years ago. The Via Appia, from the evidence of a milestone, appears to have formed the *decumanus maximus* of Minturnae. After leaving the colony's east gate it broached the river Garigliano with a bridge known to Cicero as the *pons Tirenus*.[73] The original bridge, which prior to the foundation of the colony at Minturnae may have crossed slightly further downstream, was built wholly in wood on account of the unstable underlying alluvial gravels.[74] At a later stage, probably during the second century BC, it was reinforced by the construction of at least one pier in faced *opus caementicium*. Having crossed the river, the road skirted the eastern side of the lagoon at Pantano di Sessa where occasional polygonal road blocks can still be seen to the south-east of Masseria S Giuseppe, on the eastern side of the via Domiziana. They appear on a raised embankment about half a metre above the surface of the field indicating, probably, that the road was designed to avoid the marshes and floods. A large part of the road was destroyed during works on the modern Domiziana, especially between kms 5 and 6.[75] It continued over the flat land alongside the modern route up to Mass. Ulivella, where blocks can still be seen across the fields. It is at this point that Cresce located a junction with a branch road to Suessa Aurunca, which would seem to be preserved in a modern track labelled Le Colonne (*nota bene*) on the IGM map.[76] At the same juncture it would seem that the Appia turned virtually due south towards Sinuessa, having effectively by-passed the lagoon, and again its trajectory is marked out by the modern road. Near Mass. Tre Ponti (?Trifanum) the road was set on a substructure composed of three arches, presumably to cross over the torrents feeding the lagoon. Nothing remains visible *in situ*, although road blocks are to be observed dumped in various places. The Appia departed from the line of the modern road just south of where the latter crosses the Canale D'Auria, swinging south-westwards to pass immediately to the east of Mass. della Signora. Once over the Rio di S. Limato, the Appia turns directly south through a cemetery area (site M21) and enters Sinuessa to form its *decumanus maximus*.[77] Upon leaving the town it deviates to the south-east, where its line may be picked up in a modern track.

During construction of the tourist resort of Baia Felice, along the track immediately to the west of Mass. Santoracco, a stretch of the road was unearthed in the area of a cemetery containing at least two cylindrical mausolea (site M22).[78] A further tract was brought to light at the height of the via Domiziana's 13.7km mark.[79] It was closer to the sea than the present road and once again found preserved beneath a modern lane. It measured some 20m in length, and was *c* 4m wide. At Bagni Solfurei,

[70] Johannowsky, 1976, 14–15; *contra* Radke, 1964, 216; Wiseman, 1970, 130.

[71] Ward Perkins, 1964, 20–22.

[72] There is no reason why Forum Claudii should have been called Forum Appii from the *gentilicium Appia*, as Johannowsky, 1976, 15, maintains, for the town to have been named after Appius Claudius, as *praenomina*, *gentilicia* and *cognomina* are all found used as forum names: Ruoff Vaananen, 1978, 32.

[73] Cic. *Ad Att.* XVI, xiii, 1; cf Frier, 1969, for an unconvincing interpretation of *pons Teretinus* as the name of the bridge.

[74] Brookes, 1974, 46.

[75] Sementini, nd, 14.

[76] Cresce, 1914, 44.

[77] Pagano and Ferone, 1976, 19–20.

[78] Pagano and Ferone, 1976, 20 and 24, where there appears to be some confusion between the remains of the Appia at Mass. Santoracco and a *cardo* of Sinuessa which was excavated between the intra-mural Appia and the sea. Their plate III, 1, in fact details the *cardo* discussed on pp. 26–28. On the cemetery and two associated bas-reliefs see Ruggiero, 1888, 405; Greco, 1927, I, 8; Pagano, 1981a, 876–881.

[79] Gallina, 1971.

the site of the Thermae Sinuessanae and antique junction with the via Domitiana, the Appia swings inland to cross the piedmont plain, running parallel to and for the most part immediately to the east of the present internal route to Mondragone.[80] At about 400m south-east of Mass. S Rocco, the modern road veers due south to enter Mondragone. Instead, at this point the Appia coasted M. Petrino, directly below the abandoned tuff quarries, to appear in front of the modern cemetery of Mondragone (site of the Pagus Sarclanus). Here, a number of disturbed polygonal road blocks show that the line of the Roman road is yet again preserved in the line of a country lane, heading towards the lake of Carinola. As Johannowsky points out, there would appear to have been a junction of two or three Roman roads by the modern cemetery.[81] The Appia would be the southernmost, heading due east across the flats and contained partly within a sunken road-cutting revetted with squared blocks of grey tuff and, later, with opus incertum (pl VI). At this point it appears to have been about 10m wide. It crosses beneath a modern road in the area of Mass. Pioppara and Mass. Pucci, where its surface and a number of tile tombs have come to light. Further to the east the Appia must have crossed the river Savone over the pons Campanus and near a staging-post (villula) where Horace once rested overnight in the company of Virgil and Maecenas.[82] Some three miles further on, the Appia reaches the area of the Sullan colony of Urbana, to proceed to Casilinum (mod. Capua) and over the Volturno to Capua (mod. S Maria Capua Vetere). This last tract is not particularly well-known. It has, so far, yielded one milestone, of Constantinian date, re-used during the reign of Valentinian I and Valens, and signalling the 126th mile from Rome.[83]

The Via Appia – II

The next section of road to be considered is that departing from Minturnae for Suessa Aurunca, tentatively identified as the original Via Appia (supra) superseded around 296 BC by the road built to link the new foundations of Minturnae and Sinuessa.

A mid-eighteenth century Rome-Naples road map marks existing Roman roads as secondary routes (pl VII). One of the latter, labelled 'Antica Via Appia per Sessa', suggests a course for the Appia between Minturnae and Suessa Aurunca.

Having crossed the river Garigliano from Minturnae, the Roman road would appear to continue in a south-easterly direction on the line of the modern via Appia, the *Strada Statale 7*. As it meets the confluence of the Rio Travata with the Garigliano it bends slightly further south so as to coast the Travata's left bank. It then crosses over just to the south of the confluence with the Rio dei Fasani from the east, although the antique map suggests that the road crossed the Travata prior to its confluence. We may of course be dealing with two different roads, although a cartographic error is perhaps more likely. After the Appia crosses the Travata it is marked by the recently enlarged Sessa-Fasani road, which appears as a track on the latest IGM map, revised in 1957. Scattered limestone blocks are visible along a line from Mass. Travata, past Mass. Volana, to about the height of Mass. Colonello. Halfway along this stretch a small cemetery, composed of tile tombs of imperial date, was found, whilst a section of road surface in situ and discovered during the construction of the Sessa-Fasani road has been preserved by the authorities.[84] Just after passing Mass. Colonnello the Appia may have crossed another small rio and continued in a straight line through the localities of Padre Eterno and Il Campo, where its line is traced by a track just to the south of Rio Fossitiello.[85] Immediately before reaching Sessa it veers due east, leading on to the main *decumanus* of the colony where a housing estate (*case popolari*) is situated, whilst a branch road apparently met the town just to the north of the theatre complex.[86] During the construction of the housing estate in the '60s various road blocks and an extensive cemetery came to light.

Just prior to reaching Sessa, the Appia bifurcated. One section of road entered the colony on its north-western side after having passed below the terraces of the theatre and cryptoporticus. The other, for a short length coincided with the *decumanus maximus* (present viale Trieste), and just before reaching the area of Porta Cappuccino, turned right to follow a steep gradient down to the seasonal river known as Vallone Grande. Here it departed from the site of the town's south-east gate to traverse the river bed, in which numerous Roman coins have been found in the past. Once over the Vallone a stretch of road, rising sharply up the left bank to meet the modern road departing eastwards from Sessa, may still be seen in situ for some 50m. Its polygonal lava blocks

[80] Sementini, nd, 25 and 27. Part of the paving may still be seen *in situ* in the escarpment immediately to the west of the modern asphalted road.

[81] Johannowsky, 1976, 18.

[82] Hor. *Sat.* I, v; Fraenkel, 1957, 15–18; cf Pagano, 1978.

[83] Johannowsky, 1986, 18–20.

[84] Valletrisco, 1977, 63. The tombs were seen by the writer in 1980 during bulldozing operations in the field immediately to the north of the road. Little datable pottery was noted, but included a fragment of the North African casserole form Hayes 197.

[85] Tommassino, 1925, 128.

[86] Valletrisco, 1977, 63 and fig 2.

bear parallel score marks intended to aid the grip of traffic on the gradient. The road, once flanked by mausolea, continues on the northern side of the present Appia through the area of S Agata. It then deviates slightly to the north coasting the northern bank of the Rio delle Cammarelle (literally 'little rooms'), so-named presumably because of the many small rectangular tombs of early imperial date which were brought to light in 1979, during levelling of the land for agricultural purposes.[87] The last few years have witnessed the destruction of much of the Roman road between S Agata and Cascano, although dispersed blocks are visible in the rio and in adjacent fields up to the chapel of S Antuono.[88] The Rio delle Cammarelle must have been crossed just before the road reached the *vicus* at Cascano. Having reached Cascano, it bifurcated, with a well-preserved *diverticulum* continuing eastwards through the areas known as Capitolo and I Tre Vescovi, to Teano. The Appia itself, however, would appear to swing south-eastwards, probably once again on the line of its medieval and modern successors. A stretch of paving is to be found immediately to the south-east of the Strada Statale 7 and the abandoned railway line at the 176km mark. After crossing the Rio Annone it disappears into an area which has recently undergone heavy agricultural earth-moving operations, to reappear, having crossed the Rio Persico, on the line of the modern highway. Johannowsky interprets this section as the northernmost *decumanus* of a centuriation system, and does not appear to accept it also as the Suessa Aurunca-Capua road.[89] Its exact course is then not known until it reaches Francolise, though instead of running beneath the modern SS 7 it may have turned south-eastwards to follow a direct line through Mass. Cento Finestre to meet the SS 7 again around Mass. del Fievo on the opposite side of the Savone. Immediately to the east of the masseria it may have been crossed by a road running south from Teanum Sidicinum towards the area of San Andrea, which appears largely preserved in modern roads and tracks.[90]

In the frontispiece map to the Posto excavation report, Ward Perkins has the road running in a direct line from Francolise to Sparanise and Cales,

where it joined up with the Via Latina.[91] The latter appears to have been constructed in 127 BC by L Cornelius Cinna, presumably following an earlier route which must have connected Cales and Capua even prior to the Roman conquest.[92] From Cales the road ran in an almost unbroken line down to Casilinum and then over the Volturnus to Capua.

The roads from Minturnae

The road departing from the north-east gate of the original *castrum* of Minturnae, its *cardo maximus*, seems to have provided the route along the river Ausente and through the hills to Interamna Lirenas, Casinum and Aquinum, linking up with the via Latina. Upon leaving the town it bifurcates, with a southerly section departing from the Aquae Vescinae (*infra*). The northern section heads in a north-easterly direction following the Ausente on its right bank, and at the height of Taverna Cinquanta it crosses the river and breaks into three roads.

One heads south-east, intersecting the road from Minturnae to the Aquae Vescinae, to proceed to the Garigliano, which it crossed at Ponte dell'Epitaffio, continuing until it met the original course of the Appia between Minturnae and Suessa Aurunca.[93] Figure 12 shows the road traversing the Garigliano and turning south to avoid the river's meander, although it is possible that it continued in a straight line and that the meander is a post-classical development. Another road seems to run parallel, at just under a kilometre and a half to the north-east, to cross the river in the centre of an upstream meander.[94] Although most of its surface has been destroyed by modern drainage works and the construction of the now disused Gaeta-Sparanise railway, some broken road blocks are visible near the site of a very rich villa (?of the Caii) situated on the left bank of the river.

The second road, leaving the junction at Taverna Cinquanta, heads in a south-easterly direction to meet up with the Minturnae-Aquae Vescinae road south of Castelforte.

The last road proceeds in a north-westerly direction towards modern Ausonia, following the river Ausente. According to De Rossi this road, like the

[87] Cf Cresce, 1914, 68–69; De Masi, 1761, 184–185. The rediscovery of the site by the writer was followed by salvage operations directed by Dott. Nunzio Allegro for the Soprintendenza. The remains have been preserved and include, in section, part of an unpaved *diverticulum* turning northwards towards the hamlet of Marzuli.
[88] Fiorito and Villucci, 1980, 34.
[89] Johannowsky, 1976, 35.
[90] For the road network south of Teanum Sidicinum see Cocozza, 1981, *passim*.

[91] Cotton, 1979, frontispiece. This section of road may have been that which became known as the via Falerna: CIL X 3910.
[92] Wiseman, 1970, 139.
[93] Cf Brookes, 1974, 41, note 5. The bridge, of which part of the limestone ashlar basement still survives, was also known as Ponte degli Schiavi, not to be confused with the bridge of the same name marked on the IGM map 171 I S.O. which crosses the Canale Trenta Palmi: De Spagnolis, 1981, 29 and figs 55–56.
[94] *Ex inf.* Dott. Del Vecchio.

Sinuessa-Puteoli coastal route, was known as the via Domitiana.[95]

Another Roman road departs from the Appia at S Croce, some seven kilometres to the north-west of Minturnae, to travel northwards up the valley between S. Maria Infante and Spigno Saturno and on to Ausonia and Interamna Lirenas. A sanctuary dedicated to Hercules was discovered along its course at Ausonia, which seems to have been situated in the territory of Interamna. This discovery, coupled with Cicero's mention of the via Herculanea, which he would take from Minturnae to Arpinum, suggests that it was one and the same road. He considered it a long and bad thoroughfare and would stop for the night at Aquinum.[96]

The road leaving the north-west gate of Minturnae for the Aquae Vescinae coasts the Garigliano, traversing a stretch of marsh over a causeway of which three arches in opus caementicium still survive. At about one and a half kilometres from the town the road disappears into the river, engulfed by a meander which has been developing since classical times.[97] At the same point various remains have been located, including a structure in brick-faced concrete and an amphora dump. The road then continues in a straight line to meet up with a branch from the supposed via Herculanea just south of Castelforte. It then runs beneath Suio and coasts M Castelluccio to meet the Garigliano opposite Casale Arco. At this point the road appears to have crossed onto the left bank of the river over a bridge whose foundations, according to locals, are visible in the river bed on the rare occasions of low water. The bridge may be that mentioned in the text of an inscription discovered at the nearby villa of the Maesiani Celsi at Corigliano, on a slope overlooking the left bank, perhaps indicating that the wealthy villa owner had decided to erect a bridge in privato so as to connect his estate with the market and port at Minturnae.[98] On crossing the bridge the road continues alongside the river, where it was lined by amphora kilns and other structures, to pass a modest late republican villa at Mass. Petrolio. Three kilometres further on it crossed back onto the right bank of the Garigliano by means of another bridge, of which three piles were still visible earlier this century, and eventually reached the Stabilimento Duratore where the Aquae Vescinae were located.[99]

The Suessa Aurunca-Sinuessa road

An inscription from Sessa records the building of a road to the town by Hadrian in AD 122.[100] As in the case of the via Domitiana, this almost certainly refers to the paving or improvement of a pre-existing route. Indeed, it may be identified with the decumanus maximus of the centuriation system of the colony and as such is unlikely to have been paved when it was first laid out. Tradition would have it that this road connected with Sinuessa, which would now seem confirmed by archaeological evidence.

It departs from Sessa on the line of the present Corso Lucilio and angles to the south-west shortly after its junction with the modern road crossing the Vallone Grande, linking up with the SS 7 to Capua. A stretch of paved surface is still to be seen between the junction and the Roman bridge of Ponte Ronaco. It is flanked to the north by a series of brick-faced mausolea, a tuff sarcophagus and tile tombs.[101] The road continues in a hollowed way cut during Roman or pre-Roman times, flanked to the south by Iron Age tombs, until it reaches the bridge of Ponte Ronaco which spans the Vallone Grande. The bridge is formed of twenty-one arches of reticulate and tile masonry which, on building technique, could date to the principate of Hadrian, supporting the attribution of the road as via Hadrianea. Once over the bridge the road disappears below ground to the east of Mass. Irace and a small ploughed-out mausoleum. The route is then conjectured as running in a straight line up to the deserted medieval village of Quintola. The one upstanding casale of the village, Mass. degli Aitani, is to be found re-utilizing a large number of basalt road blocks. Though the road no longer surfaces, its course appears marked by a singularly straight dirt-track to the south-west of Quintola, running for over two kilometres and passing through an area known as Le Colonne, possibly named after a nearby Roman villa where fragments of tile-built columns may still be seen. The road must finally have met the Appia by Mass. Ulivella, where a number of road blocks are still to

---

[95] De Rossi, 1980, 300.

[96] Cic. de lege Agr. II, 4; ad Att. XVI, 10 and 13; De Azevedo, 1947, 43–44. For the sanctuary of Hercules see CIL X 5396, and Beloch, 1926, 532.

[97] Brookes, 1974, fig 1.

[98] The villa has been the subject of two seasons of excavation by the writer, in 1979 and 1980, on behalf of the Soprintendenza and partly financed by The Society of Antiquaries of London, to which I am indebted. For the Maesiani Celsi see chap 5 infra. See Villucci, 1979, for a brief discussion of the villas in the area.

[99] Giglioli, 1911, 43.

[100] CIL X 4756.

[101] The Roman cemetery was partly brought to light in 1980 and further excavated in 1985 by Dott. Luigia Melillo. See Perrotta, 1980.

be found in the fields amongst a thin scatter of republican pottery.

The other roads from Suessa Aurunca

Further roads departing from Suessa Aurunca are treated by Valletrisco, though the evidence for their existence is generally insubstantial and will not be dealt with here.[102] Of particular note, however, is the westernmost of the two routes debouching from the northern gate of Suessa Aurunca, by the side of the 'arx'. It is well attested running almost due north, probably towards the volcano of Roccamonfina to coast its western flank and, perhaps, reaching Valogno with its possible Roman lava quarries, to continue on to the Aquae Vescinae. A particularly well-preserved stretch, of almost half a kilometre in length, is visible on the eastern side of the present road to Ponte, overlooking the Rio della Selva, and seems to have been flanked by at least one monumental mausoleum.[103]

The ager Falernus road

The other major artery of the area, which does not appear to be mentioned in textual or epigraphic sources, (though like the Appia and the Domitiana it is also marked by the course of a modern road) is the Roman road coasting the southern foothills of the Massico and linking both the first and second phases of the Appia at the cemeteries of Mondragone and Cascano respectively.

Its junction with the Appia in loc. S Pietro at Mondragone came to light during construction works at the cemetery in 1937. Subsequently its route is to be reconstructed on the basis of scattered paving blocks. These follow a line roughly between the areas of Saraceno and Pietragrossa (lit. 'large stone'), parallel, though slightly to the south, of the present Mondragone-Falciano road. In the area of S Rocco, just to the south of Falciano itself, a section of paved road of republican date flanked by tombs was revealed in 1981. This section appears to lie in a NE/SW direction, whilst a diverticulum was noted departing southwards. After Falciano the evidence is scanty, though further blocks have come to light at Mass. Dragone, to the north of Casanova, and close

to the present Casanova-Cascano road, thus closing its presumed course.

The diverticula

Aside from the main thoroughfares linking the major settlement and administrative foci, there must have been innumerable diverticula, many of which were private or municipal, permitting access to estates, quarries, fields and the like. As today, the majority will have been dirt-tracks, often lying in hollowed ways intended to assist controlled movement of livestock. In summer they would have formed localized dust-bowls, and during the autumn and spring rains virtual quagmires, though assisting in the drainage of surrounding fields. Most of these diverticula will remain elusive, but on occasion they were provided with a surface either of small stones, broken tile or even standard limestone or lava road blocks. A number of well paved examples have been found.

Traces of limestone paving have been noted amongst the macchia on both the northern and southern sides of M Cicoli, and may form part of a winding road of republican date constructed so as to provide access to the site on the hill's summit.[104] Another track struck off through the fields in a north-easterly direction and at right-angles to the section of the Appia between the Thermae Sinuessanae and the supposed site of the Pagus Sarclanus. On meeting the hills it began to wind its way up in the direction of · the abandoned Benedictine monastery of S Anna. A particularly well-preserved section, found at over 150m asl, was composed of close-fitting limestone blocks and possessed a carefully made kerb of rectangular stones set end to end. The road's make-up consisted of the local limestone and clay scree containing a large number of Tunisian amphora sherds of late republican date.[105] Slightly higher up the hill, to the south-east of the preserved road, is a large terraced villa heavily covered with macchia which may have been the road's destination.

A paved diverticulum, now evidenced by scattered road blocks, led to the hypothesized site of the vicus Caedicius (infra), and possibly proceeded in the direction of the marble quarry at S Mauro.[106] Yet a

---

[102] Valletrisco, 1977.
[103] Cf De Masi, 1761, 162.

[104] Cf Conta Haller, 1978, 55. I have only been able to trace the northerly section.
[105] Though no rims or handles were noted, the sherds would appear to pertain to amphorae of form Cintas 312–313, the commonest imported type to the area.
[106] For the quarry, possibly originally of Roman date, see Arthur, 1985b.

further paved road left modern Falciano Capo for the hills towards Canale S Maria, passing the area of the later early medieval Benedictine monastery of S Maria a Fauciano. A large section was destroyed in the late 1970s, but it is reputed locally to have led to the large Roman villa known as Castellone, lying at c 270m asl.[107]

A further paved road, which I have not been able to trace in its entirety, appears to have departed from the via Appia to service the intra-montane republican farms of Campopiano and S Croce. According to Maiuri, it followed the right bank of the Canale Grande, probably more or less on the course of the present track.[108] Part of the road may be seen on the shoulder of a republican terraced farm, shortly after which it bridged a stream letting onto the Canale Grande. Traces of the bridge are still visible. Once over the 400m contour, it probably linked up with a section of road traced in the area of Pietrascivola, which may have been maintained in early medieval times as an aid towards land exploitation by the Benedictine community that inhabited the wilderness of S Croce.

Finally, of particular interest are the road blocks found scattered close to the northern bank of the river Savone, which may already have been canalized in Roman times. These appear to signal the line of a road along the river's course which may have been intended as a tow-path to facilitate the movement of barges carrying agricultural produce down to the coast.

Aside from the via Appia, the via Domitiana and the road built by Hadrian, we possess little in the way of dating evidence for the construction or paving of the various tracts and, though in many cases they will have formalized pre-existing communication networks, the foundation date of a given road is often little more than conjecture.[109] The via Appia itself is fairly well documented and must have been paved by, at least, the mid second century BC. It was improved during the late republic, prior to Horace's trip to Brundisium, at least in the stretch through the Pomptine marshes.[110] During the reign of Augustus the maintenance of Italy's principal arteries became the direct responsibility of the emperor, and conditions, at least for a while, must have greatly improved. Milestones suggest that road works took place under Vespasian, Nerva, Trajan, Severus, Caracalla, the Tetrarchs, Valentinian I and Valens, and Valentinian II, Theodosius and Arcadius. Trajan, perhaps in particular, seems to have been concerned with embanking the via Appia along its marshy stretches.[111] By the age of Procopius, the via Appia between Rome and Capua seems still to have been in fair condition. The wonder it caused suggests that the construction of such a road surface was no longer thought to have been possible.[112]

---

[107] De Stasio, 1975, 55–56.
[108] Maiuri, 1934, 302–303.

[109] Unfortunately, little excavation has been conducted along the roads and, when they are brought to light, there is often no attempt made to explore beneath their surface. For a tentative reconstruction of pre-Roman routes in the Terra di Lavoro, see Guadagno, 1976.
[110] Heurgon, 1942, 18; perhaps the milestone CXII found near Mondragone and set up by one of the consuls by the name of Cn. Domitius refers to these works: CIL X 6872–3.
[111] CIL X 6869–6878; cf also Villucci, 1980b, 2–5, and Johannowsky, 1976, 14, note 5. On Trajan: Galen de methodo medendi IX, 8, in Kuhn, 1965.
[112] Proc. de Bello Goth. XIV, 6–11.

Chapter Five

'Pax Romana'

With the close of the Second Punic War Campania may justly be regarded as having entered a strict Roman political and administrative orbit, necessitated above all by state security. Capua's position was redimensioned following her allegiance to Hannibal, whilst firm control of the ager Campanus and the Phlegrean Fields was obtained with the establishment of new coastal colonies at Volturnum, the maritime outlet of Capua, Liternum and Puteoli, in 194 BC. It is from this time that both historical and archaeological sources appear to concur in demonstrating the entrance of Campania into an international Mediterranean market, and the fruits of her new position seem indicated by intensive building activity in both urban and rural contexts which probably gathered increasing speed throughout the course of the second century. Though never quite reaching the standards set by Capua and Puteoli, the remains from the more provincial northern Campanian towns likewise date principally to the late republic and early empire.

Nucleated Settlements

Suessa Aurunca

Sometime during the first century BC Suessa Aurunca was raised to the rank of *municipium*, an event which may be inferred from two texts of Cicero. This may have occured with the *lex Iulia* of 90 BC when both Teanum Sidicinum and Cales were awarded municipal status following the Social War. At the same time it appears to have been enrolled in the *tribus Aemilia*.[1]

Suessa Aurunca is also known to have possessed sympathies for Sulla during the Civil War in 83 BC. It was captured by Sertorius during an armistice, which event led ultimately to the defection of Scipio's troops and the consul's capture by Sulla. It is possible that the town's sympathies were generated by interests and landholdings that the dictator had in the area. A certain A Opinius C.f. Sulla, cited in a local inscription, bore his *cognomen*, whilst freedmen

of the dictator living at Minturnae were responsible for erecting a statue in his honour.[2]

Suessa Aurunca is later remembered during the wars following Caesar's assassination as the *lautissimum oppidum* which lost a number of its inhabitants in a massacre conducted by the troops of M Antonius.[3] Finally, an assignation of colonists took place, possibly under Augustus, when the town became known as *Colonia Iulia Felix Classica Suessa*, with its last epithet perhaps referring to the settlement of veterans of an uncertain *legio classica*.[4]

Little is known of the actual plan of Suessa Aurunca as it is now largely built over. The most recent reconstruction, although presenting some inaccuracies, shows the maximum extent of the walled area to have been larger than the area enclosed by the later medieval walls.[5] The early Latin colony seems to have been positioned on the higher, northern, part of the tufaceous ridge, with a possible *arx* in the area later occupied by the Lombard castle. In fact this whole area presents a street grid which preserves the original urban network *per strigas*. Later expansion led to a reorganization of the street grid of part of the lower town. Whilst the primary walls were constructed of squared tuff blocks, as at Minturnae, subsequent enlargements of the colony were enclosed by different types of walling, including at least one tract in opus reticulatum. At a point on the north-western side of the town, the walls may have been abutted by vaulted structures in reticulate masonry once visible beneath the church of St Benedict.[6]

Apart from the walls, the only major visible monument dating to republican times which survives is the ⊓-shaped cryptoporticus built of opus incertum, on the western side of the town. Johannowsky would not date it earlier than c 70 BC, although it would seem in any case earlier than the adjacent theatre built of careful opus reticulatum, possibly Augustan.[7] Many of the remaining traces of the Roman town consist of fragments of walling encased in later buildings. One well-preserved structure, which has been variously identified as part of a

[1] Cic. *Phil.* XII, ix, 1; XXVII, ix; XXIX, xv.

[2] App. *Bell. Civ.* I, x, 85. For A Opinius Sulla see Villucci, 1980c, 40. Cornelius Sulla's freedmen at Minturnae appear in CIL X 6007 = ILS 871. Dessau suggested that the piece could have been brought from Rome in the Middle Ages.

[3] Cic. *Phil.* XII, viii, 18; IV, 2.

[4] CIL X 4832; Keppie, 1984, 143.

[5] Valletrisco, 1977 and 1980; Sommella, 1988, 44–45.

[6] Smith, 1873, 1043.

[7] Maiuri, 1961; Johannowsky, 1973, 144ff; Della Corte, 1938, discusses the numerous graffiti present on the internal plastered walls of the cryptoporticus.

public bath-building or a monumental fountain-nymphaeum, lies parallel and to the north of a Roman road or *cardo* crossing at Piazza Tiberio. It consists of a trefoil vaulted structure, lined with opus signinum, which opens into a vaulted rectangular room. The remains, in both reticulate masonry and brick, are probably to be dated to the later first century AD. Another building, conserving parts of two vaults and constructed largely of quasi-reticulate masonry with later additions of brick and reticulatum, lies immediately to the north of Via Ferranzio.[8]

The town apparently possessed an amphitheatre, *extra moenia*, which is buried in the area of market gardens to the south.

At least one aqueduct was built around the first century AD to bring water from Roccamonfina to the town. Its construction might be seen as an indication of urban growth and demand. Hadrian may have been responsible for the construction of the bridge known as Ponte Ronaco, particularly if the road along which it lies is correctly identified as that commemorated by an inscription from the town, whilst the emperor's grand-niece Matidia, a very wealthy municipal benefactress, provided Suessa with a library in the later second century AD. Four statues dedicated in her honour are recorded from the town.[9]

There is little evidence for later Roman building works apart from tombs. A small palaeochristian catacomb, cut into the tuff to the immediate north-west of the town, is dedicated to saints Castus and Secundus.[10] The cemetery to the south-west of the town, on the road to Fasani, has yielded an early imperial brick-faced concrete mausoleum and various tile and amphora burials. In 1951 a small late Roman tomb was found at Località Semi-cerchio during the construction of council flats. It consisted of a semicircular structure with four steps leading down to a chamber with three *loculi*. One bore painted stucco decoration with the name GALATIA moulded upside-down, whilst three late Roman lamps and a coin of Diocletian were also found.[11] Other cemeteries were discovered recently

on the roads to Sinuessa and Teanum Sidicinum, but have not yielded material dating later than the early second century AD. The continuity of habitation at the town through the early medieval period is discussed in chapter VIII below.

Cascano and Quintola

The only apparent evidence for a *vicus* or *statio* in the territory of Suessa Aurunca is provided by abundant archaeological material from modern Cascano, even now within the council boundaries. Though the name of Cascano in classical times is uncertain, it is of interest to note that sometime before the last century the hamlet was also known as Gallicano or Galligano, like the homonymous site in the Alban hills near Praeneste. The toponym Cascano is, however, attested as early as 1280.[12]

The site may have commenced life as a lookout on the Appia at the time of the colony's foundation in 313 BC, at a point already frequented in Neolithic or early Bronze Age times.[13] Whereas the colony over-looked the Garigliano basin, Cascano overlooked a pass into the ager Falernus. As well as traces of a possible early defensive wall, discussed above, and a paved road, the immediate neighbourhood of the town appears to have yielded three inscriptions. Two are funerary, one referring to a C Valerius Rufus, whilst the third bears a list of freedmen of the *gentes Pontia* and *Popilia*.[14] Burials have been found to the north and west of Cascano since at least 1858. Various coins have also been recovered from the town, dating from the late republic to the later third century AD.[15] Recent demolition in the town centre has revealed a number of archaeological features including a vat lined with opus signinum and frag-ments of stone and brick-faced concrete walls. Part of the site was covered with a dump of wasters from a nearby kiln site, indicating pottery production from the first or early second centuries AD until about the fifth century, exploiting the rich local clay beds which still support a small community of potters.

---

8   For the fountain/nymphaeum see Carafa and Colletta, 1978, and Valletrisco, 1977, 66–67. The building north of Via Ferranzio is discussed by Valletrisco, *op. cit.*, 70, where she wrongly identifies the construction technique as opus incertum. Cf also Valletrisco, 1980, where an attempt is made to locate suburban baths to the north of the town on somewhat dubious evidence.

9   The remains of an aqueduct in opus reticulatum are visible half way up the north-western scarp of Costa Malegrano, but cannot refer to the example noted in Valletrisco, 1977, 71–72, as she questions its Roman date. For the road built under Hadrian see CIL X 4756, whilst for Matidia see CIL X 4744–7 and Duncan-Jones, 1974, 31 and 228.

10 Valletrisco, 1977, 72; Diamare, 1906, 59–64; Marucchi, 1897, 140–141.

11 Soprintendenza archives S.8–13; *Il Mattino* 61. 2 March 1951.

12 Menna, 1848, I, 134 and 138; Leccisotti, 1972, 1509.

13 Numerous flints have been found in gardens within Cascano by Albino Matano and the writer.

14 CIL X 4764, 4775 and 4773 respectively.

15 For the burials see Ruggiero, 1881, 411. As for the coins, I have been able to examine a few small bronzes, a sestertius of Gordian III and a republican denarius of the moneyer C Iunius Brutus – cf Crawford, 1974, 433/2. All are in private possession.

It is also possible that the deserted medieval village sited almost halfway between Suessa Aurunca and Sinuessa on their link-road may have had its origin in a small Roman settlement. Its name, Quintola, is suggestive. A few Roman imperial pottery sherds have been found on the site, whilst more conclusive remains may be obscured by the medieval material and grass which effectively blankets most of the site.

Minturnae

Little is known of the later republican history of Minturnae. Appian, writing of the proscriptions of 43 BC, tells of the assassination of the ex-consul Varus at the town.[16] Colonial settlement took place under both Caesar and Augustus. An inscription from Cellole, recording a L Magius Sex.f. Urgulanianus, who held posts in the IX Hispana, V Macedonica and IIII Scythica during Augustus' Illyrian campaigns, may attest one of the veterans who received land plots.[17] It has its place secured in history, however, by the part it played in the episode of Marius' escape from Sulla (*infra*).

Conversely, the archaeological evidence for late republican and early imperial Minturnae is particularly rich, following the excavations conducted by Jotham Johnson from 1931 to 1933 and briefer campaigns by others in 1942 and 1955 to 1957.[18] Apart from the defences, remains of the initial colonial settlement have yet to be identified. Later in the republic, possibly prior to the Second Punic War, the defences were extended and provided with pentagonal towers so as to enclose a larger area to the north-west. The new forum was laid out parallel to the western defences of the early colony, with the Appia dividing the actual market-square from the portico enclosing the capitolium. The latter may have been the *aedes Iovis* which, according to Livy, had been struck by a bolt of lightning in 207 BC along with the *lucus Maricae*. Sixteen years later it was hit a second time along with a group of *tabernae*. Curiously, the portico, enclosing the temple area, appears to have replaced a series of *tabernae* no earlier than c 211–208 BC, according to the *terminus*

post quem supplied by a coin hoard found in a layer of burnt debris beneath it.[19] Under the empire part of the portico was converted into a series of rooms opening onto the back of the Augustan theatre. The *summa cavea* eradicated part of the late republican defences of the colony. Johnson's temple B, built to the east of the capitolium and tentatively identified as having been dedicated to Rome and Augustus, as well as two fountains inserted into the wings of the portico, may also be Augustan in date. Further imperial constructions include a large temple complex to the east of the forum, an amphitheatre and an impressive aqueduct rising in *località* Capo D'Acqua at the foot of Mt Spigno Saturnia and entering the colony through the *castellum aquae* sited over the west gate.[20] The remains of the Via Appia bridge over the river Liris were discovered in 1967, and indicate that no solid masonry bridge was ever constructed at this point of the river because of the instability of the alluvium. Cicero informs us that it was known as *pons Tirenus*.[21]

The port of Minturnae, though unexcavated, must have been quite substantial. Part of it was situated within the mouth of the river, immediately in front and to the south of the town. Early this century a row of some fifteen shipsheds constructed in opus reticulatum were apparently still visible, whilst amphora deposits have been found on the right bank of the river slightly upstream. The greater part of the harbour, however, may have lain within the small lagoon which once existed to the south-east of the town and which may have been in part artificially adjusted. Remains of Roman ships are claimed to have been found in the northern section of the lagoon beneath two metres of peat and clay.[22] The *socii picarii* attested in the magister lists from the town may indicate local ship-building during the late republic. The activity appears substantiated by an inscription found by the Garigliano near the town of SS Cosma e Damiano, recording a certain Q Caelius, *architectus navalis*. Another inscription, from Minturnae, honouring Q Planius, patron of the town and tribune of the *legio XX Valeria Victrix*, was set up by a *collegium fabrum tignuarium* or college of carpenters who are likely to have been involved with the

[16] *Bell. Civ.* IV, xxviii.
[17] Lachmann and Rudorff, 1948, 234; Hyginus 141.
[18] Chapter 3 *supra*. Cf particularly Johnson, 1935; Aurigemma and De Santis, 1955; Crema, 1933; Adriani, 1938. The most recent summary of the site is to be found in De Spagnolis, 1981.

[19] On the successive lightning bolts see Livy XXVII, 37, and XXXVI, 37. Newell, 1933; Richmond, 1937, 292; Crawford, 1969, 68.
[20] Butler, 1901, 187–192; Richmond, 1933, 154–156.
[21] Cic. *ad Att.* XVI, xiii, 1.; Frier, 1969; Brookes, 1974; Ruegg, 1983.
[22] Remmelzwaal, 1978, 76–77. On the shipsheds see Johnson, 1933, 128, and also Ruegg, *op. cit.*

shipyards.[23] The inscription must post-date AD 60 when the *legio XX Valeria Victrix* received the epithet for its part in suppressing the Boudiccan revolt in Britain. The Planii were a northern Campanian family attested once at Capua and twice at nearby Cales. The sources refer to an M Planius Heres, equestrian and friend of Cicero.[24] Further evidence of shipbuilding and overhauling may be represented by a particular series of bronze nails recovered from the bed of the Garigliano and paralleled in comparable contexts at Ostia, Nemi, Frejus and Richborough.[25] By the end of the first century AD the port of Minturnae seems to have been sufficiently thriving to enable it to receive a society of *negotiatores* from eastern cities, including Berytus, Heliopolis, Ephesus and Tyre, which set up a dedication to the deified Nerva.[26]

The exploitation of local salt-pans along the coast is recorded by the late republican lists from the town giving four slaves as *socii salinatores*.[27]

Minturnae was also the centre of an iron-working industry by the mid second century BC. Cato recommended the town, along with Cales, as a source for iron tools and particularly agricultural *instrumenta* such as scythes, mattocks, axes and small chains.[28] There are no known ore deposits in the lower Garigliano basin, and the metal was probably imported from the Meta region around Atina, where iron foundries may still be found today. Of undoubted significance is the discovery of abundant iron slag at the colony of Fregellae, along the Liri valley route. That the river Garigliano was itself used in the transport of raw materials may be indicated by Dominic Ruegg's discovery of good quality haematite on the river bed.

The Aquae Vescinae, the Pagus Vescinus and Pirae

The ancient sources are of little aid in understanding the organization of the territory of the colony and what, if any, *vici* it possessed. One settlement lay at the Aquae Vescinae, a site of mineral water springs on the right bank of the Garigliano, sandwiched between the river and the escarpments of the Monti Aurunci (Fig 13). The hillside was partly contained by a revetment wall of opus incertum, over 70m in length. Part of the site has been excavated and consists of a large, highly ornamented bath building fronting onto a paved road and facing a colonnaded portico, behind which were further buildings possibly catering for visitors to the waters. The site appears to have accommodated cults to Hygeia and to a genius of the Vescinian waters. A dedication to Geta and Caracalla by two imperial slaves and *dispensatores* indicates that the springs had become part of the imperial *patrimonium* by, at latest, the early third century AD.[29] The springs appear not to have been as renowned as the Thermae Sinuessanae, although they may have been known to both Lucan and Pliny.[30] The latest dated find from the excavations was a gold coin of Justinian. Nothing is known of later activity until mention is made of the waters in medieval documents, possibly from the tenth century. Traces of an aqueduct are visible in the hills about a kilometre to the north of the site in *località* Vaglie, on the left bank of the Garigliano, though it is not known whether or not it served the waters.

A further settlement in the territory of Minturnae is indicated by a recently discovered inscription referring to a pagus Vescinus, clearly deriving from the toponym Vescia, having contributed HS 12.000 from the coffers of the cult of Mars towards the construction of a theatre. The text, carved on a block of limestone, was discovered in *località* Cisterna, near the towns of SS Cosma and Damiano and Castelforte, and would seem to date no later than Augustan times.[31]

Pliny mentions another centre called Pirae, which apparently lay between Formiae and Minturnae and which, by his time, had been deserted. There is no archaeological indication of the site's existence, though one assumes it is linked to the noted local

---

[23] On the inscription of Caelius see CIL X 5371. The inscription to Planius reads:

> Q.PLANIO
> FELICI
> PATRON[o] COL[oniae]
> TRIB[uno] LEG[ionis] XX VAL[eriae]
> VICTRICIS
> COLLEG[ium] FABR[um] TIGN[uarium]
> QVIB[us] EX S[enatus] C[onsulto] C[...] L[...]
> L[oco] D[ato] D[ecreto] D[ecurionum]

and is inscribed on a statue base discovered by Johnson in 1931. Cf De Spagnolis, 1981, 48–49 and fig 29.

[24] *EE* VIII, 551; Cic. *Fam.* IX, 13; CIL X 4289. Cf Frederiksen, 1959, 119.

[25] Arthur, 1976; Feugère, 1981.

[26] Riccardelli, 1873, 22, if he is to be believed.

[27] Johnson, 1933, 126.

[28] Cic. *de Agr.* CXXXV, 1.

[29] Giglioli, 1911, 49–50. See also the appendix for an inscription from Minturnae attesting paving of the road to the Aquae Vescinae under Severus and his sons.

[30] Lucan *Phars.* II, 424–425; Pliny *NH* II, 227. It has been suggested that the Aquae Vescinae may have been the locality of Plotinus' projected Platonopolis, though the thesis has been convincingly rejected in favor of Cumae: Giglioli, 1911, 53; Pugliese Caratelli, 1980.

[31] Pontecorvo, 1979, 6; Ionta, 1985, n.19. Of the three dignitaries recorded by the inscription, Valerius M.f. Paetus, Sex. Flavius Sex.f. and [...]vius L.f., the first named may also appear in the dedications to Mars, CIL X 5998–5999, from Minturnae.

It would be very interesting to know if any connection existed between him and the L Valerius Paetus attested on a lead-pipe found at the port on the river Tiber, and with the prefect of the fleet at Misenum in AD 145 (Rodriguez Almeida, 1984, 89).

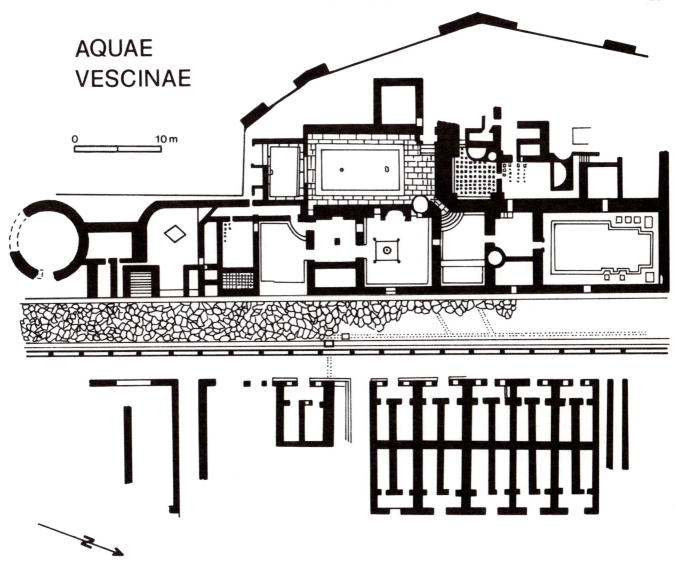

AQUAE
VESCINAE

0   10 m

Fig 13   Site plan of the complex at the Aquae Vescinae (after Giglioli, 1911)

gens Pirania. Various scholars have attempted to identify it with the impressive remains of polygonal walling visible by the coast at Scauri (pl VIII). Coarelli accepts the masonry as pre-Roman and states that the remains were later enveloped by a large villa probably to be identified as a property of Marcus Aemilius Scaurus, consul in 115 BC, hence the toponym Scauri. There is little to buttress these conjectures, though two principal periods of construction may, nonetheless, be recognized in the drystone terrace wall and in the well-preserved remains of a cryptoporticus in opus incertum (pl IX).[32] This must be one of the largest villas in the whole of the Garigliano basin.

Sinuessa

Following the Second Punic War, there is evidence for urban expansion at Sinuessa. A censor for 174 BC, Fulvius Flaccus, is recorded as having contracted for the building of *magalia* out of public funds at the town, as well as sewers, an enclosure wall, a market place surrounded by porticoes and shops, and three statues of Janus. If *magalia* are taken to mean suburbs, it is possible that this refers to expansion of the town outside the original colonial *pomerium*, as at Minturnae, resulting from further colonisation or a general increase in population.[33]

It was sometime later, in 133 BC, that the town

---

[32] Aurigemma and De Santis, 1955, 58 and pl XXXVI; Riccardelli, 1873, 61–68; Coarelli, 1982, 368. The site has now been re-examined by Rosi, 1989, 99–110.

[33] Livy XLI, xxvii, 12: *Sinuessae maca[lia addenda] aviariae in his et clo[acas et mur]um circumducendum [....] et forum porticibus tabernisque claudendum et Ianos tris faciendos.* Note the corrupt text and emendations by Roth in brackets.

was the focus of a slave uprising. One may also incidentally note the death of the poet Sex. Turpilius at the town in 103 BC.[34]

The colony appears to have been strengthened with an assignation of veterans, possibly under Vespasian, when it received the title *Flavia* attested in an inscription dating to the time of Septimius Severus.[35] Slightly earlier, Vitellius, with his posting to Germania Inferior in AD 60, robbed the town, along with Formia, of its *publica vectigalia* so as to strengthen his power-base.[36] One may also note a series of rich benefactions during the later republic and early empire. A well-known inscription attests the provision of gladiatorial games and a feast by L Papius Pollio on the occasion of his father's death (*infra*). These presumably took place in the local amphitheatre, whose *podium* was built by Sex. Caecilius Birronianus. A further feast was offered by a local *duumvir*, M Cacius Cerna, whilst during the late republic C Clodius Adiutor paid towards work on the forum and possibly the capitolium. The same man is also attested in inscriptions from the amphitheatre at Capua, where he appears to have been involved in the upkeep of regional roads.[37]

All in all, the evidence suggests increasing prosperity from, at least, the early second century BC.

The urban layout of Sinuessa has been partly reconstructed on the basis of scattered elements for the period of the late republic and early empire. Pagano sites the forum to the west of the *decumanus maximus*, where two dedicatory inscriptions to the Clodii were unearthed.[38] To the west of their find-spot is a dense scatter of marble and alabaster veneer which could signal the presence of an important public building. Clandestine excavation in the area of the colony has revealed much over the last few years. In an area to the south of the forum part of a building in brick-faced concrete came to light. The walls were pierced vertically with box-flue tiles and bore marble veneer, suggesting its identification as a bath-building. Slightly to the north-east of this building another illicit construction site yielded a well in opus incertum by the side of a dump of smashed local amphorae, forms Dressel 1B and 2–4.

As it is perhaps doubtful that the vessels signal the presence of a kiln within the walls, the dump may have been associated with ancient building work, as Sinuessa has its own characteristic construction technique of walls built out of discarded amphora sherds.

The town's amphitheatre, located by means of an air photograph, is represented on the ground by part of a subterranean vaulted structure (?*cuneus*), in reticulate masonry with tile courses, near masseria Morrone. It appears to have lain outside the original colonial *pomerium* and is the only structure to have been recognized to the east of the Appia apart from a stretch of the defensive circuit. It may be dated around Augustan times when Sex. Caecilius Birronianus, who seems also to have possessed property in Rome, paid for the construction of its *podium*.[39]

Unlike Minturnae, Sinuessa does not appear to have possessed a civic aqueduct. However, control of the water of the Canale Grande, a seasonal river rising in the Massico range and opening into the sea as the Rio di S Limato immediately to the north of the colony, is suggested by the discovery of what appears to be a dam (site M180) between Mt Cicoli and *località* Campopiano. It remains as a broken wall, 1.55m wide, faced with bands of yellow and grey tuff reticulate masonry, standing to the east of and perpendicular to the river (pl X).[40]

The written sources for Sinuessa terminate in the fourth century and the latest pottery discovered dates no later than the early fifth century AD. It appears to be concentrated along the *decumanus maximus*/Via Appia, perhaps indicating contraction and concentration of the settlement along the principal thoroughfare. The site was presumably abandoned soon after (chapter eight below).

The Vicus Caedicius, the Vicus Petrinus, the Thermae Sinuessanae, the Pagus Sarclanus and Trifanum

The territory of the colony seems to have accommodated at least three *vici*, the vicus Caedicius, the

---

[34] Bigott in *RE* VII, A2, 1428–1430.

[35] Lachmann and Rudorff, 1948, 237; Sirago, 1958, 14. Vallat, 1980a, 398, sees an assignation of triumviral or Augustan origin.

[36] Suet. *Vit*. VII, ii.

[37] For L Papius Pollio: CIL X 4727; M Cacius Cerna: CIL X 4736; C Clodius Adiutor: *AE* 1926, 143; cf also *AE* 1926, 142; *PIR* 906; CIL X 3851 and 3852; Sex. Caecilius Birronianus: CIL X 4737. The Caecili, including L Caecilius Secundus, an *augustalis*, are attested in a monumental funerary inscription from Minturnae: Giglioli, 1908, 397. Various slaves and *liberti* of the *familia* are recorded through the Minturnae magistrates lists. A L Caecilius produced lamps at Cales: Morel, 1989, 558.

[38] Pagano and Ferone, 1976, 32.

[39] CIL X 4737; see CIL VI 1808 for his activity in Rome.

[40] The remains are not published. They are known locally as Ponte Vecchio and lie between two concrete dams erected since the war and still functioning.

vicus Petrinus and the Thermae Sinuessanae, as well as the pagus Sarclanus and a locality known as Trifanum. The problem of the location of these sites, aside from the Thermae, is still debated.

In 1937 an inscription was discovered at the modern cemetery of Mondragone (site M124). It records a P Crusius Germanus who donated HS 2000 to the decurions of the pagus Sarclanus in AD 43, so that they could celebrate his birthday with the interest from the sum which was to be invested.[41] The find-spot fronts a small country road which preserves the line of the Via Appia. Various fragments of walling and a grain mill were also discovered and are supplemented by further finds which came to light during extension works in 1979 and 1980.[42] Together with the numerous other finds from the area, the inscription suggests that the *pagus* possessed an administrative centre in the region of the modern cemetery. Johannowsky, who appears certain of the attribution, suggests that the *pagus* was originally sited on the coast near the Savone, at the site of the sanctuary in *località* Panetelle. He dates a shift of the *pagus* from Panetelle to the cemetery of Mondragone from the end of the second century BC. All that remains visible today is a large two-tiered terraced villa, which Johannowsky takes as the forum of the settlement, and various scattered elements including a monumental marble architrave and a terracotta bath bearing the stamp LVE or LVF, which had been found used as a sarcophagus in the Roman cemetery.[43] A funerary inscription from the site records C Plotius Salvus, whilst ceramic evidence suggests activity from, at least, the second century BC until the fifth century AD.[44] A small aqueduct brought water down from the spring rising at Colle Pezza di Caso, north of Mt Petrino. The centre of the *pagus* lay at *c* 4.5 Roman miles from Sinuessa.

The vicus Caedicius is attested by Pliny, '*Faustianus circiter IIII milia passum a vico Caedicio qui vicus a Sinuessa VI M passum abest*', and by Festus, '*Caediciae tabernae in via Appia a domini nomine sunt vocatae*'.[45] An inscription inserted in the bell-tower of Carinola cathedral refers to *colonis Senuisanis et Caedicianeis* (pl XI), whilst a *campus Caedicius* is cited by

Pliny.[46] On the basis of this evidence Johannowsky has suggested that the *campus* comprised the *Caediciae tabernae* at some six miles from Sinuessa along the Appia, and that the *vicus* itself lay further into the hills. The identification of the *vicus* would thus have to be made with a site some 1.5 miles further on from the pagus Sarclanus and presumably along the road leading in the direction of the estate named after Faustus Sulla, rather than along the Via Appia. The next major concentration of material of Roman date after that at the cemetery of Mondragone lies in an area known as Ponte dell'Impiso, which is itself a Roman bridge (sites M59–60). The site was accessible along a *diverticulum* which struck a course northeastwards from the Roman road which coasted the southern foothills of the Massico, passing through Falciano to meet up eventually with the Suessa-Teanum route. It lies about 6 Roman miles from Sinuessa and some 4 Roman miles from Falciano whose toponym, it has been suggested, derives from *Faustianum*. Its identification with the vicus Caedicius of the sources is at least plausible.

Today all that may be seen at the site is an impressive double-terraced villa built in opus incertum, another late republican structure to its east encased in a modern farmhouse, and a tile-built wall to the side of the Ponte dell'Impiso. The *ponte* is a single vaulted gallery which forms a bridge and contains the Canale del Fico, which rises at a spring-line some 400m up in the hills. In the past, at least one mosaic floor was discovered, as well as a structure with cipollino marble columns, one of which is still visible on site. A singular discovery was a large pit brimming with human bones, obviously representing a mass-burial and closely resembling a plague-pit. Unfortunately, without controlled excavation, its exact nature and date must remain uncertain. The ceramic evidence from the site as a whole takes occupation into the sixth century AD.[47]

The vicus Petrinus has not yet been identified. The locality is mentioned by both Cicero and Horace, the latter suggesting that it was situated in the territory of Sinuessa.[48] The toponym survives today in Mt Petrino, the mountain rising above Mondragone, which points at least to the approximate area in which the *vicus* may have lain.

[41] Pellegrino, 1978.

[42] Sementini, nd, 32–33. I personally witnessed the destruction of remains in 1979.

[43] Cf Johannowsky, 1976, 31, note 107, and 1973, 150–151. The terracotta bath, noted by Sementini, nd, 33–34, was photographed by the writer in 1980, but had disappeared when the site was revisited in the company of Enrica Pozzi and Antonio Rigillo. I am grateful to Dott. Adele Ciaraldi for the transcription of the eroded stamp.

[44] For the inscription see *EE* VIII 567.

[45] Pliny *NH* XIV, viii, 62; Kubitschek, 1889, 30; Festus–Lindsay p 39.

[46] CIL X 4727. Palmieri, 1977, 306–309. The *campus Caedicius* is in Pliny NH XCVII, 241.

[47] A stamped tile reading MICO[... comes from the site. For the *gens Caedicia* and its economic activities see below.

[48] Cic. *ad Fam.* VI, xix, 1; Hor. *Ep.* I, v, 5. Cf Johannowsky, 1976, 25–26; Frederiksen, 1984, 50, note 51.

Probably the most developed, whilst certainly the most celebrated, *vicus* of Sinuessa was the so-called Thermae Sinuessanae (site M37), a *statio* at the 109th milestone from Rome.[49] The site may be located straddling the Appia in the pass just over a quarter of a kilometre wide between Mt Pizzuto and the sea. It attracted attention because of its mineral water springs, including sulphur springs which now surface at a temperature of 46°C. It is not known when the site was first frequented for its waters, but Pliny and Strabo both mention them as having the quality to cure sterility in women and insanity in men. A Livian passage recording the devastation by Hannibal's troops of land around the ager Falernus and up to the *aquas Sinuessanas* is not conclusive for the presence of a settlement there by the end of the third century BC.[50]

Indeed, the abundant archaeological remains at the site suggest that large-scale settlement and exploitation did not get under way until the last century of the republic, whilst its heyday was attained perhaps under the early empire (*infra*). Standing structures, apart from a monumental mausoleum, are of tile or reticulate masonry, whilst the pottery examined runs from the first century BC until about the sixth century AD. It is probable that the site possessed its own small anchorage and, in fact, archaeological remains do run down to the shoreline to extend, apparently, beneath the sea.

The Thermae Sinuessanae are remembered by a dedication to Aphrodite in Greek. Narcissus, an ailing *libertus* of Claudius, is recorded as having visited the site to seek cure. Ofonius Tigellinus, Nero's infamous praetorian prefect, committed suicide on his estate at the Thermae Sinuessanae, which may subsequently have passed into imperial hands. Martial also records the accidental death there of a drunken Philostratus. Finally, an inscription from the Temple of Aesculapius at Lambaesis carries a dedication by T Caunius Priscus, dating to about AD 186, possibly to the healing cult of the

Thermae Sinuessanae.[51] The bulk of the evidence, as can be seen, points to a floruit of the site under the early empire. It may well have been the subject of imperial patronage, if indeed it did not become part of the *patrimonium*, like the somewhat similar site of the Aquae Vescinae (*supra*).

The Fora and Urbana

For a supposed early republican foundation of the *fora* see chapter five above.

Forum Popilii appears in the *Liber Coloniarum*, for the first time, as a town from whose territory Augustus distributed land plots. It is also present in Pliny's list of *oppida*, where it would appear to bear the status of *municipium*. Its suggested elevation to *colonia*, based on an inscription found re-used near the site and mentioning *duoviri*, is more doubtful.[52]

The site eventually appears to have extended over an area of some five hectares, with a roughly trapezoidal plan.[53] Only late republican and early imperial remains are visible. They consist of a stretch of wall in limestone opus incertum some one and a half metres thick, possibly representing part of a late republican defensive circuit, and the smashed remains of an arcade in opus incertum, tuff reticulate and brick, perhaps representing a public building dating to the late republic or early first century AD.

Little is known of Forum Claudii, and archaeological work is urgently required as the site is undergoing destruction. Visible remains, principally in brick-faced concrete, include part of a bath-building on a hill and remains incorporated in the church of S Episcopio below, beside a cistern in opus vittatum. Excavations were undertaken by Margherita Asso in front of the church, in 1969, though they remain unpublished.[54]

Another colony, Urbana, was founded in the ager Falernus by Sulla as a consequence of the Civil War. In the first century AD it passed to Capua, possibly on the occasion of the settlement of veterans in the

---

[49] Lugli, 1944, 286; CIL X 6870.

[50] Pliny *NH* XXI, iv; Strabo V, iii, 7; Livy XXII, xiii, 10; Cf Greco, 1927, II, 108ff. for the modern waters.

[51] For the Greek inscription: CIG 3, 5956. Narcissus: Tac. *Ann.* XII, lxvi. Tigellinus: Plut. *Otho* II, 3; Tac. *Hist.* I, lxxii. Philostratus: Mart. *Ep.* XI, lxxxii. Cf also *Ep.* VI, xlii and XI, vii. The inscription from Lambaesis is CIL VIII 2583.

[52] *Forum Populi, oppidum muro ductum. iter populo debetur ped. XV limitibus Augusteis ager eius in iugeribus est adsignatus. nam imperator Vespasianus postea lege sua agrum censiri iussit.* Lachmann and Rudorff, 1948, 233; Cf Nissen, 1902, II, 691; Thomsen, 1947. Astrom, 1969, suggests that the numeral following the phrase *iter populo debetur* may refer to the total width of centurial *cardines* in feet, or rather to that proportion of the delimited *centuria* that was to remain a public passageway. For the *municipium*: Pliny NH III, v, 64; Ruoff-Vaanen, 1978, 49–50. For the *colonia*: Johannowsky, 1976, 4; Vallat, 1980b, argues for the attribution of the inscription to Sinuessa.

[53] Johannowsky, 1976, 7.

[54] I have searched in various archives, in vain, for the documentation of the excavation. See the plan in Guadagno, 1987, tav. III.

ager Campanus in AD 53.[55] Otherwise the site remains obscure. Even its location is not certain, though it is listed in both the Peutinger Table and the Ravenna Cosmography.[56]

Further colonisation or viritane distribution in the ager Falernus under Claudius might be attested by an inscription honouring the veteran and local decurion Ti. Iulius Ti.f. Fal. Italicus, centurion in the legions *VII Macedonica*, *XV Primigenia* and *XIII Gemina Pia Fidelis*. The second legion had been raised under Caligula or Claudius, whilst the last had received its epithet in 42 for its part against the revolt of Scribonianus, thus probably dating the text to the reign of Claudius.[57]

As has been argued above, these small nucleated settlements undoubtedly served as local market centres from their inception. However, unlike the two *fora*, which must have been official foundations pertaining to the Romanisation of the area, the other lesser centres may have appeared spontaneously at key road junctions. Cascano appears at the junction of the Suessa-Teanum road with the link road descending to the Appia and to the *diverticulum* which coasted the southern foothills of the Massico. Both the *Thermae Sinuessanae* and the *Pagus Sarclanus* were sited on the Appia at its junction with the Via Domitiana and the aforementioned Massico *diverticulum* respectively. Their expansion dates predominantly to the late republic, probably reflecting rising levels of agricultural production, and they are to be viewed as part of a complex economic system, in part also expressed by the more dispersed ribbon-development along the Viae Domitiana and Appia attested through dense scatters of both domestic rubbish and amphora kiln waste. The paradigm of the *tabernae Caediciae* is treated below.

Villas and farms
If the first tendency of the Roman population in the area was towards nucleated settlement, presumably above all induced by insecure conditions in the fresh

ager publicus, a system of dispersed settlement may already have begun to make itself felt prior to the Second Punic War. Unfortunately, current knowledge of the chronology of Black Glaze wares and perhaps their limited shape development over short periods of time, do not permit us to use surface finds alone in distinguishing between sites founded during the later third century or during the first half of the second century BC. All that can be affirmed at present is that substantial numbers of rural villa and farm sites were already in existence during the second century, and that a few of these sites yield occasional fragments of earlier pottery.[58]

Inevitably, without excavation it is not possible to estimate the social or economic standing of these early rural sites with any degree of certainty, or to examine whether small farmsteads were transformed into grandiose villas with the passage of time and influx of capital. However, already by the Second Punic War the general Fabius Maximus owned a fairly well-appointed estate in Campania. He sold it in 217 BC in order to pay the ransom of 247 Roman prisoners, which indicates that it was of some commercial value and that Fabius had further estates to which he could turn. Not long after the war, Scipio Africanus went into voluntary exile at Liternum where he possessed a villa which he may have acquired when the state sold land in Campania in 205 BC, the year of his consulship, to raise money for the war effort. A later proprietor of the villa, Seneca, has left us a description of the apparently rather sombre original structure.[59]

Few such early villa sites have been excavated in Italy and they must, on the whole, have been fairly modest affairs such as the first period at Via Gabina site 11, near Rome, and the villa at Tolve, Basilicata.[60] Some of these early sites may already have been involved in the direct cultivation of wine as a cash-crop with the use of small slave *familiae* and hired labour, though neither the villa at Tolve nor that at Via Gabina possessed the characteristic grape and olive pressing equipment which became so

---

[55] Pliny *NH* XIV, viii, 62; Tac. *Ann.* XIII, 31.
[56] Miller, 1916; Cuomo, 1974, 29–36.
[57] CIL X 4723.

[58] I should like to thank Prof. J-P Morel for having examined some of the Black Glaze pottery from the field survey and confirming my impression that a small quantity of material dates to the third century BC. Whether these pieces date the foundation of sites to the third century, or represent survival pieces in possession of the second century inhabitants is another matter to be resolved.
[59] On the villa of Fabius Maximus see Livy XXII, xxiii. For that of Scipio see Livy XXVIII, xlvi, 4–5, and Shatzman, 1975, 246–248. Seneca *Ep.* LXXXVI describes it:
'*vidi villam extructam lapide quadrato, murum circumdatum silvae, turres quoque in propugnaculum villae utrimque subrectas, cisternam aedificiis ac viridibus subditam, quae sufficere in usum vel exercitus posset, balneolum angustum, tenebricosum ex consuetudine antiqua; non videbatur maioribus nostris caldum nisi obscurum*'.
[60] For Gabina site 11 see Widrig, 1980, and for Tolve, Tocco *et al*, 1982.

typical of agricultural estates during the later republic. Moreover, in northern Campania the amphora evidence, as will be shown below, does not support a hypothesis of significant commercial production until, probably, the second quarter of the second century BC. Indeed, Frederiksen postulated a primary phase of slave-run establishments in Campania oriented towards cereal cultivation and pastoralism, preceding the appearance of the 'classic' villa with its intensive production.[61] In this light, it is worth noting that there had already been a revolt of slave *pastores* in Italy as early as 198 BC, and in 206 BC there had been difficulties in restoring farm lands owing to a scarcity of slaves (*inopia servitiorum*) and a loss of free farmers.[62] The consuls of the day coerced what 'free' farmers they could to return to their lands which, presumably, had until then been worked principally from the colonies.

The small number of possible third century sites found during field survey could certainly not have accommodated the *coloni* of Suessa Aurunca and Sinuessa, though some archaeologists might argue that the flimsy nature of early colonial rural dwellings has led largely to their subsequent obliteration. A similar absence of third century rural sites has, nonetheless, been encountered in the ager Cosanus.[63] Livy's reference to Hannibal's burning of villas in the ager Falernus is probably an anachronism, alluding to a scorched-earth policy, as must certainly be his reference to villas during the war against the Sabini in 470 BC.[64] Of certain third century date are the rural sanctuaries, founded in pre-Roman times, though these are hardly likely to have had a large resident population.

Even if leading Roman families had begun to acquire land outside Latium by the Second Punic War, it was the second century overseas conquests that fired the large-scale, profit-oriented, intensive agriculture with market expansion and the concentration of capital, land and slaves in the hands of individuals. Tenney Frank estimated a total of 161.600.000 *denarii* entering the public treasury as spoils down to 157 BC. Some 70.000.000 were said to come from the East alone. This figure does not include the incalculable amount which entered private hands, nor the amount of slaves who entered Italy. Some 250.000 may have arrived as prisoners in

the first half of the second century. To these should be added those acquired on the market, those from the peninsula itself and those who were the products of breeding.[65] In the context of the post-war scene, it is significant that it was at this very time that Cato compiled his agricultural notes which later materialized as *de agricultura*.

An impressive multiplication of the number of sites around the Massico, from 2% to 27% of the whole, during the course of the second century is evidenced by the archaeological remains. Many of the new sites would appear to have been villas terraced onto the hillsides with conspicuous dry-stone, polygonal-block retaining walls. Others, similarly terraced but with less impressive remains, sometimes consisting only of scattered dolium, amphora and tile fragments, may indicate dependent structures or small-holdings occupying marginal zones, now more often than not, heavily clothed with the macchia (Fig 14). These latter sites, which seem to have been abandoned during the late republic, may indicate pressure on land during the second or early first century BC, and the ensuing need to exploit less favorable resources in the struggle for olive and vine lands. Yet further villas were sited along the coast, though these appear to be predominantly of first century BC date, or later (*infra*). The shrine at Monte D'Argento, towards the northern limits of the territory of Minturnae, which yielded three dedicatory inscriptions to the rustic deity Silvanus by members of the *gens Caecina*, probably lay within the bounds of one of these coastal *fundi*.[66]

The picture of a multiplication of rural sites, and of more intensive land exploitation, from the second century is one that seems to repeat itself in various other parts of the peninsula. Potter speaks of an 'extremely impressive' figure for south Etruria 'with its implication of a dense concentration of small-holdings'. In the ager Cosanus, from the second half of the second century, 'circa 90% of the small settlements of the second century disappear' to be replaced by large villas. In Molise, republican sites appear in great quantity to start disappearing under the empire.[67] It is immediately apparent that the pattern is not straightforward and, despite a clear leap in the scale of production, numerous local

[61] Frederiksen, 1981, 285–286.

[62] Livy XXXIII, 26, and XXVIII, xi, 8–10, respectively.

[63] Celuzza and Regoli, 1982, 37.

[64] Livy XXII, 14; II, 62. For the somewhat different phenomenon of Greek colonial settlement compare the important work by Carter *et al*, 1985, in the *chora* of Metapontum.

[65] Frank, 1933, 138. Cf Brunt, 1971, 121ff and 702–703; Carandini, 1979, 187; and Toynbee, 1965, II, 171–173 for the recorded cases of mass-enslavement from 264 to 133 BC.

[66] Laurent-Vibert and Piganiol, 1907, 497–498. A similar case may perhaps be made for the dedication to Silvanus by C Valerius Martialis, found near the left bank of the Garigliano (CIL X 5999). Perhaps these are also to be taken as indicative of surviving stretches of woodland in the basin in late republican times?

[67] Potter, 1979, 125; Celuzza and Regoli, 1982, 41; Barker, Lloyd and Webley, 1978, 42.

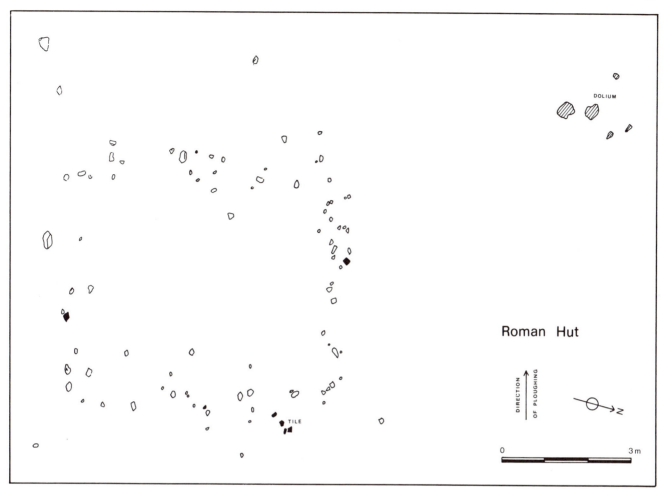

Fig 14   Traces of ploughed-out limestone footings and dolium emplacement of a second century BC Roman building (site M93)

variations to a general trend in the multiplication of rural sites or in the scale of productive units occurred under the late republic.

The concentration of small-holdings in south Etruria is not paralleled by the archaeological evidence available in northern Campania. This may largely be due to differing land values between the two areas, leading to larger properties in northern Campania, as well as more intensive urban settlement where small-holders and tenants were more likely to reside.[68] The properties of the wealthy late republican landowners indicated in the area were not necessarily *latifundia* or extensive tracts of land. The large landowner may equally well have possessed a series of smaller holdings in the same area or dispersed within and without the peninsula. Finley indeed believed that 'the dispersed holdings of a Pliny, a Herodes Atticus or a Symmachus represented the usual pattern'.[69] In a period of land hunger it is easier to accumulate dispersed holdings than contiguous ones, and avoids too many eggs in one basket. Numerous proprietors of dispersed holdings could be cited, particularly amongst landlords of the Ciceronian age, but also going back to Cato.[70] The archaeological evidence for wealthy landlords might thus be in part obscured by a proliferation of

[68] Furthermore, the pattern of dispersed holdings is often alien to the south, where agro-towns predominate, on account of a complex series of factors including unequal distribution of resources, particularly water, violence in the countryside and possibly what has been termed an urban culture pattern, in which distaste and disrespect for agrarian life forms a part. The scattered *masserie* that developed from the sixteenth century were the centres of large estates which may be likened more to the Roman villa than to the peasant farm, despite the differing labour conditions. Cf Blok, 1969, 127–128.

[69] Finley, 1980, 133–134; Cf, Kuziscin, 1957, 61–63. Shatzman, 1975, lists the various holdings of individual senators. Cf also White, 1967, for a discussion of the meaning of *latifundia*.

[70] Thielscher, 1963, 6–9.

medium-sized holdings, so that a modest villa/farm need not necessarily imply a proprietor of modest means. It must also be remembered that contiguous villas could theoretically belong to a single *dominus*. Only such articulated situations can explain the list of wealthy proprietors recorded around the Massico and the proliferation of medium to large villas, particularly on the southern slopes, sometimes less than 500m distant one from the other.[71]

In 133 BC a slave revolt in Sicily appears to have been the spark for a more extensive uprising which, to judge from the figures recorded, was far more severe in and around the lower Garigliano basin than in any other part of Italy. Some 500 slaves were crucified at Minturnae, and a reputed total of 4,000 were captured and presumably executed at Sinuessa by Q Metellus and C Servilius Capio.[72] It is not known where the insurgents were originally employed, although their eventual concentration at Minturnae and Sinuessa suggests that a fair number were local. It seems safe to assume that the majority were agricultural labourers coming from the large estates. Furthermore, a certain weight might be given to the figures if one considers that the late republican Minturnae *magister* lists total 312 individual slaves who must have been in the minority to those tied to the plantations.

Landlords and Labourers

In the early first century BC even the southern Latian and northern Campanian coasts were attracting wealthy residents seeking temporary political asylum from the political jostling of Rome. From the second half of the century a number of maritime villas appear. The hinterland establishments seem to have remained essentially productive, though not without embellishments that may indicate the transient visits of their owners, such as the famous Sinuessa Venus (pl XII), a lifesize Hellenistic statue bringing to mind the trade of L Cornelius Lentulus Crus, landlord at Minturnae.[73]

Both textual and epigraphic evidence increases dramatically, and supplements the archaeological evidence of the villas. Particularly noteworthy is the list of proprietors adduced from the 29 Minturnae lists, dedicated to various deities by *magistri* of local corporations, and analyzed by Munzer.[74] Though the town's territory cannot have been particularly extensive, the large number of powerful and widely-connected *gentes* represented must surely indicate its importance in the late republican economic network. Together with other textual and epigraphic references, it is possible to build up an impression of the composition of local proprietors and inhabitants and their social standing, particularly for the closing years of the republic.

The land of the ager Falernus and the neighbouring territory of Sinuessa seems to have been particularly attractive to 'capitalist' landowners, perhaps more so than the territories of Minturnae and Suessa Aurunca.[75] Amongst villa owners one may count both Cicero and some of his acquaintances. In a letter to Lepta in 45 BC Cicero refers to his friend's Petrine villa: '*nam et villa et amoenitas illa commemorationis est, nam deversori*'. Its appellation suggests a location in the area of Mt Petrino, within a couple of kilometres from the sea. Lepta was Cicero's *praefectus fabrorum* in Cilicia, and is cited as Q Lepta in a letter to Mescinius Rufus. He is almost certainly to be identified with the Q Paconius Q.f. Lepta who had been *quattorvir quinquennalis* at Cales, thus indicating that he had at least two properties in northern Campania. Furthermore, the burial of a certain Paconia Helpis at Sinuessa may refer to a *liberta* of his *familia*. The *gens Paconia* probably originated in Etruria, though is first attested at Cales in a stamp on the base of a third century BC Black Glaze bowl, reading C. PACO. C.F.Q.N. This is of great interest, and we may surmise that Cicero's friend was a descendant of one of the original Latin colonial families whose acquisition of wealth may have commenced through interest in pottery manufacture. The *gentilicium* also occurs at Misenum, whilst a republican wine amphora of form Lamboglia II,

[71] La Penna, 1971, 360. Cf Skydsgaard, 1969, for a general assessment of the evidence for the size of holdings.

[72] Oros. V, ix, 4.

[73] Munzer, 1935, 325; Gianfrotta, 1981, 75–77. For the Venus of Sinuessa, coming from a villa four kilometres to the southeast of Sinuessa, see Napoli, 1957, and Greco, 1927. A maritime villa, at S Albina, to the north of Minturnae, yielded a large headless statue of Minerva and the mutilated marble of a nymph with a shell, probably from a fountain (Aurigemma and De Santis, 1955, 59).

[74] Munzer, 1935. Cf also Staedler, 1942, for the view that the lists represented crossroad dedications. His interpretation has little or no following amongst modern scholars. The texts were originally published by Johnson, 1933. The slaves and *liberti* of the lists must have come from families whose means were a sufficient guarantee to the secure funding of the cults in question. In general terms, the number of members of an individual *familia* represented amongst the *magistri* may reflect the relative importance or wealth of that *familia* in the area. Cf Staerman and Trofimova, 1982, 215.

[75] Some of the evidence is presented by Shatzman, 1975, although I can find little to support his assertion that L Aemilius Paulus, consul in 50 BC, owned a house at Gaeta, and much less at Sinuessa.

stamped L. PACONI, was found in Spain and was probably produced around Brindisi. The abundance of Paconii in the East from the late second century BC, at Athens, Rhodes, Cos and Delos. suggests a very substantial interest of the family in commerce. In fact, Cicero was probably involved in trying to secure a contract for Lepta to supply wine for Caesar's *munerum regiorum*, thus indicating how Lepta himself was involved in the commercial production of wine, likely on his Campanian estates.[76]

Of the villa of another friend, Macula, Cicero wrote '*Eius Falernum mihi semper idoneum visum est deversorio, si modo tecti satis est ad comitatum nostrum recipiendum*'. He was probably P Pompeius Macula, one of the lovers of Sulla's daughter Fausta and ancestor of an aedile at Pompeii in AD 25/25, Q Pompeius Macula.[77]

The senator L Quinctius also owned property in the ager Falernus. The Quinctii may have come from Praeneste, and are well represented in the East, especially at Chalcis and Delos. Other members of the *gens* may have possessed land in the neighbouring Garigliano basin. It is worth noting that a slave, Eudamus Quinctius, appears on list 21 from Minturnae, whilst a tile stamp discovered beneath the villa of the Maesiani Celsi at Corigliano appears to read L. QVIN.[78]

Faustus Sulla, the son of the dictator, owned important land in the area. Pliny mentions a locality known as Faustianum some four Roman miles from the vicus Caedicius. At about the right distance lies modern Falciano, which is found labelled *Faustianum* on maps dating back as early as 1679, and the transmutation of one toponym to the other seems a distinct possibility. The local wine known as Faustinianum, from the southern slopes of the Massico, was recognized for its quality during the late republic, and adds further evidence for commercial interests in the vine by members of the late republican élite.[79]

Gnaeus Pompeius Magnus may have acquired his Falernian property through L Cornelius Sulla, but what is certain is that his estates were auctioned-off by Caesar after his murder in Egypt in 48 BC. His Falernian holding was bought up by the poet Anser and, not long after, fell into the hands of Pompey's son Sextus, who also had estates in Sicily and Macedonia.[80] The presence of such figures as P Pompeius Macula, Faustus Sulla and Gn. Pompeius Magnus in the ager Falernus permits the hypothesis that they acquired their property through the Sullan confiscations in the first half of the first century BC.

Epigraphic material adds further names to the list of proprietors, including the Papii and the Caedicii. The Papii appear to have been an important family from Lanuvium, a member of which became a moneyer in *c* 78 BC and one of the *novi homines* in the Senate. The *gentilicium* is attested over much of central Italy, whilst a branch settled around Narona in Dalmatia. Papii are represented around the Massico, where they must have had landed property, as well as at Capua. A well-known sepulchral inscription walled into the bell-tower of Carinola cathedral attests a Papius L.f. and his son L Papius L.f. Ter. Pollio *duovir*, presumably of Sinuessa, of late republican date. The inscription further refers to a donation of *mulsum et crustum* (sic) to the *colonis Senuisanis et Caedicianeis* and a *munus gladiatorium* to the *colonis Senuisanis et Papieis*. One of the family's freedmen is known through an inscription from the area of

[76] For Cicero's property: *ad Att.* XIV, viii, 1. For the question of Lepta see Cic. *ad Fam.* VI, xix, 1–2, and V, xx, 4; Horace *Ep.* V; Shulze, 1904, 359; CIL X 4654 = ILS 5779; Munzer, RE XII, 2071. Paconia Helpis is cited in an inscription from the northern cemetery of Sinuessa, now in private possession, carved on white marble, length 30cm, height 22.3cm, reading:

DM
PACONIA HELPIS
CBM
SEIO SEVERO

The Black Glaze pottery stamps from Cales are, in part, published by Pedroni, 1986, 381–382; Morel, 1983, 23, note 10, gives one from Teanum, whilst Morel, 1981, 85, attests a stamp reading M.PACO.C.f.Q.n. from Rome. How long after the third century BC the family continued its involvement in pottery manufacture is unknown. Given, however, the ever-increasing evidence for links between Campanian Black Glaze and sigillata production, it may be worthy of note that a L. Paconius appears amongst the few *gentilicia* attested in the production of sigillata at Montans, Gaul, in Augustan times, as does the *cognomen* Lepta: cf Martin, 1986, 7.

The *Gabinii*, possibly from Gabii, may represent another colonial family that produced pottery at Cales and later expanded in the area, eventually generating the senator A Gabinius, *cos.* AD 58, at Venafrum: Ross Taylor, 1960, 217. For a Paconius at Misenum: CIL X 3419; for the Brindisi amphora: A. Hesnard, conference at the Finnish Institute in Rome (2.5.1979). For the *gens* in the East see Hatzfeld, 1919, 399; *ibid*, 1912, 62–64. For Caesar's *munerum regiorum*: Cic. *ad Fam.* VI, xix, 2.
Did Mescinius Rufus or members of his family also have property in the area?: cf Johnson, 1933, no 16, and Tommassino, 1925, 349.
[77] Cic. *ad Fam.* VI, xix, 1; Macrob. *Sat.* II, ii, 9; Castren, 1975, 110 and 205.
[78] Cic. *Cluent.* 175; Livy XXX, 17. For the Quinctii in the East: Hatzfeld, 1919, 400–401. At Minturnae: Johnson, 1933. For the tile stamp: Villucci, 1979.
[79] Pliny *NH* XIV, viii, 62–63. Cf the anonymous map of the diocese of Teano dating to 1679: Rosi, 1979, plate following p 91. For the toponym see Gentile, 1955.
[80] Cic. *Phil.* II, xxvi, 64; IV, iv, 11; XIII, v, 11; *PIR* 1 P450.

Quintola in the territory of Suessa.

The wealth of the Campanian branch of the family is partly indicated by the HS 12,000 cited in the Carinola inscription for funerary costs. Furthermore, a certain Corellia Galla Papiana, who must almost certainly have been related to the northern Campanian/southern Latian branch of the family, was buried at San Cesareo near Rome, but not without bequeathing HS 100,000 to both Minturnae and Casinum. Such suggests local interests in the two towns, with a strategic residence near the capital, focal point for most major families with both political and commercial investments.

The family must have been involved in the commercial cultivation of the vine. A certain L Papius L.l. Phaselus is cited as *mercator vinarius* on an inscription found near Rome, whilst a wine amphora from the city bears the stamp L.PAPI.SABI..[81]

Epigraphic and textual evidence also informs us of the *gens Caedicia*. The *gens* was of Latian origin, attested already at the siege of Veii in 390 and producing consuls as early as 289 and 256 BC. By the first century BC the Caedicii were established at both Sinuessa and Minturnae. A late republican inscription from Sinuessa refers to a Caedicius as *duovir*, whilst a C Caedicius C.f. held a like post at Minturnae. Also from Minturnae are two slaves, Pamphilus Caed. C.s. and Barnaes Caed. C.s., recorded through the *magister* lists. C Caedicius Agrippa, *cur. rip. alv. Tib.*, reached the senate under Tiberius. Finally, a Caedicia M.f. Victrix, attested through amphora stamps and an inscription from Sorrento, might be identified as Caedicia, wife of Flavius Scaevinus, exiled from Italy by Nero in AD

65. If these first century members of the family were also landlords in northern Campania, the Caedicii would be the sole family attested as holding land in the area continuously from the late republic, through the troubled years of the civil wars, down to Julio-Claudian times, with no appreciable diminution of status.[82]

On the evidence it is likely that the family possessed at least two *fundi* in the area, one near Minturnae and one near Sinuessa. The latter is best attested as both the vicus Caedicius and *campus Caedicius* of Pliny and the *Caediciae tabernae* of Festus (*supra*). The *tabernae*, on the Via Appia to the south of Sinuessa, could have been an extension of the property towards the commercial outlet represented by the thoroughfare.[83] The texts inform us of the local production of a renowned cheese, the *caseus Caedicii*, presumably from the *campus*. The principal product must, however, have been the wine represented by the containers stamped CAEDICIAE M.F. VICTRIX, distributed at Rome, Fondi, Florence, Carthage and in Spain.[84] Though not particularly abundant, a few Caedicii of late republican date have been traced in the eastern Mediterranean. The funeral stele of a probable Caedicius Firmus comes from Cos, whilst an ephebe is known at Naxos.[85] Neither are necessarily linked with the Campanian estates.

The evidence for proprietors in the territory of Suessa Aurunca is far less satisfactory, but may to a certain extent reflect the lesser attraction of the area when compared to that south of the Massico with its gentler, more bountiful, south-facing slopes. The texts yield C Nasennius, a friend whom Cicero

---

[81] For the moneyer: Wiseman, 1971, 249. The Yugoslav branch is treated in Wilkes, 1969, 299–300, and CIL III 1869, 9258, 14625 and 14824. For the important Carinola inscription see CIL X 4727 = ILS 6297 = ILLRP 667; Palmieri, 1977, 306, note 3; Menna, 1848, 49–50, claims that it came from the area near the Garigliano towards Sinuessa. The *libertus* from the territory of Suessa is the subject of the inscription:

L.PAPIVS L.L.
TABVLARI
O.H.S.S.

published by Sementini, nd, 15.
For Corellia Galla Papiana see CIL XIV 2827 = ILS 6294; Duncan Jones, 1974, 231, no. 665. CIL X 5159 = ILS 3784 refers to a M Papius M.f. *duovir iure dicundo* from Casinum. For the *mercator vinarius* see CIL X 6493 = ILS 7483. The amphora stamp is CIL XV 3083 = Callender, 1965, no 909. It may further be noted that a form Dressel 1A wine amphora bearing the stamp PAP (retrograde) was found in Milan (Baldacci, 1969, 119 and fig 8), and a wreck bearing Dressel 1B's stamped PAP was discovered at La Roche Fouras, off the south coast of France (Joncheray and Rochier, 1976, 179–180). For the local amphora stamps and the Spargi wreck, probably from Sinuessa, see below.

[82] For the early republican Caedicii see Basanoff, 1950. For the Caedicii at Sinuessa: Johannowsky, 1976, 24, note 85; CIL X 6017; cf also CIL X 6025a; at Minturnae: Johnson, 1933, no. 24. For C Caedicius Agrippa: Wiseman, 1971, 218, no. 76. For Caedicia: Tac. *Ann.* XV, 71; ILS 8573; PIR 2, no. 116; *IG* XIV, 722.

[83] If the vicus Caedicius is to be placed around S. Mauro, and the *campus Caedicius* behind, in the hills of the Massico, I wonder if one should not search for the *tabernae* by the supposed pagus Sarclanus (*supra*) or road junction between the Appia and the artery which coasts the Massico to reach Cascano. The positioning would be excellent as outlet to the *fundus*. In the area, immediately to the south of the Appia, is a large concentration of kiln waste comprising, almost exclusively, unstamped amphorae of form Dressel 2–4. For a recent discussion of the problem see Manacorda, 1985b, 143–144, and Di Porto, 1984, 64, for *tabernae* within the context of an agricultural 'company'.

[84] On the stamps see Callender, 1965, no. 218; Panella, 1980, 255 and note 34; Manacorda, 1985b, 143. I would express a slight reserve on the attribution of the stamps to northern Campania. Other areas are possible, and it is worth remembering the *vinea Caediciana* attested at Strongoli, Calabria (CIL X 114), and the inscription to Caedicia found at Sorrento and possibly from Naples.

[85] CIL III 12261, and Hatzfeld, 1919, 86.

considered *fortem virum*, and C Lucilius, the poet, native to the town. The Papii may also have owned property in this area along with, or opposed to, estates on the southern side of the Massico.[86]

The Ofillii or Aufillii seem also to have had interests in the area, and possibly around the hill to the west of Suessa Aurunca, now known as Monte Ofelio! The inscription L.OFELLI/O.H.S.S. from a *columbarium* near the hill is probably to be regarded as genuine, despite the fact that it is recorded only by Pratilli. Credence may be added by the fact that the *gens* is attested in an unpublished magistrates list from neighbouring Teanum, whilst two of the family's *liberti* were buried around Castrociclo in southern Lazio during the late republic or early empire. The family appears frequently at both Capua and Delos, and was undoubtedly involved in commerce.[87]

Turning to Minturnae, we may note the *gens Cahia* or *Caia*, of Oscan derivation, involved in the wine trade. The *magister* lists yield the slave Philomusus Cahi L.s. and the *libertae* Cahia l. Astapium and Caia Eleute. Commercial activities are revealed by two *dolia* bearing the stamps *in planta pedis*, CASSIVS/ CAHI C[ai] S[ervus] FEC[it] and ABIN[n]AE[us]/ CAHI C[ai] S[ervus] F[ecit], recovered from the sea in the areas of Monte Argentario and Civitavecchia respectively. Stamps in *planta pedis* on *opus doliare* are rare and the discovery of a morphologically similar stamp on the rim of a terracotta *puteal*, reading C.CAIVS/CRATES FECI[t], and found on the site of a rich villa sited on the alluvium south of the Garigliano, near Maiano, would seem to confirm the provenance of the *dolia*.[88] Further families attested in the *magister* lists also produced stamped *dolia* including the Piranii, and probably the Helvii and the Calicii.

Marius himself may also have had local property, though little may be made of the slave Philemo Mari C.s. in the lists.[89] Whatever the case, the destination during his flight from Sulla in 88 BC was Minturnae,

where he was aided by an indebted Fannia, the wealthy wife of C Titinius whose slaves and freedmen are listed amongst the *magistri*. Following Marius' defeat Sulla may have confiscated the property of Fannia, and other Marians, as he appears to have done in the ager Falernus, thus explaining a heavy presence of his slaves and *liberti* in the area. We know, also, that in 83 BC nearby Suessa Aurunca displayed clear sympathies for the dictator.[90]

Amongst other notables at Minturnae, one may add a member of the *gens Gellia*, a senatorial family to which the historian Aulus Gellius belonged.[91] All in all, some 121 late republican *gentes* are recorded in the Minturnae lists. Imperial landlords will be treated in chapter seven below.

The Land

Given an unbalanced hydrological regime between low-lying and upland areas of northern Campania, one of Rome's priorities, particularly during the phase of expansion following the Second Punic War, must have been to render the land salubrious and extend its agricultural capacities.[92] Once the regime could be more ably controlled, low-lying areas would have become suitable for arable and grazing. Organized drainage and irrigation of parts of the Garigliano, Savone and Volturno floodplains during the late republic and early empire seems proven and, indeed, some of the banks and ditches amongst the palimpsest of eroded earthworks visible even on 1:25.000 maps appear to be of classical date.[93] Clearer evidence of drainage works is provided by the presence of colmatage deposits formed by the redeposition of sediments in marshy areas through their transportation by a series of canals which, unfortunately, has not yet been dated. Sevink infers a classical date for the network on the basis of the abundant evidence for Roman interest in the area and, indeed, part of it seems to pre-date the centuriation systems.[94]

---

[86] Cic. *ad Brut.* I, 16. Cf Frederiksen, 1959, 120; Juv. *Sat.* I, 20. For the Papii see above.

[87] Pratilli, 1745, 219; cf De Masi, 1761, 175. The Teanum inscription is to be published by the writer, but for a C Aufillius Suavis from the same town see CIL X 4792. The funerary *cippi* from Castrociclo are published by Diebner, 1983, nos. 24 and 46. Cf Frederiksen, 1959, 119, for Capua and Delos.

[88] It may be suggested that the villa, on toponomastic grounds, belonged to the *gens Maia*, attested at Minturnae. Various finds from the site include a richly decorated marble Corinthian helmet, a stag and hound group similar to those from the House of the Stags at Herculaneum (Maiuri, 1975, 118, pls. 59–60) and various marble mouldings. Amphorae stamped CAI have been found at both Rome and Naples: Callender, 1965, 88, no. 227a.

[89] Cf Badian, 1973, 123–124; Cic. *ad Att.* II, xiv, 2 and xv, 3; CIL X 5614.

[90] Plut. *Mar.* XXXVIII; Johnson, 1933, nos. 7, 12, 13, 18, 19, 21 and 22. Cf Carney, 1961, for a full account of Marius' episode at Minturnae, though some of his conclusions appear a trifle forced. For Sulla see the statue dedication CIL X 6007. His slaves and *liberti* are also recorded through Johnson, 1933, nos. 5 and 7; CIL X 6028; Fabré, 1981, 138, no. 35. Sulla's slaves may have included confiscated slaves of Marius, as suggested by Gabba, 1967, 275–276, as well as slaves of the Fanii and Titinii. The good number of Cornelii at Minturnae recall Sulla's power-base formed, in part, of 10,000 Cornelii or enfranchised slaves ready to defend the dictator in Rome: Appian I, civ, 489.

[91] CIL X 6017; Wiseman, 1983, 305.

[92] Livy X, xxi, 10.

[93] *Ex inf.* J Sevink

[94] Sevink, 1985.

A precedent for such drainage works in low-lying Campania may have been established by the Greek colonists of Cumae. Livy refers to a *fossa graeca*, which might be connected with the apparent ditch-cutting ordered by Aristodemus at the end of the sixth century BC in the Cumaean *chora*. It may be remembered that large scale drainage works seem also to have been practised at Metapontum after 466 BC, whilst recent studies by Ing E Cerlesi suggest that the Etruscans may have been involved in land drainage through a series of rock-cut *cuniculi* at Capua.[95]

The formation of a port out of the marshy lagoon of Minturnae must have involved a considerable amount of engineering. We know little concerning work on the larger marshy lagoon, or *pantano di Sessa*, to the south of the Garigliano, which was so rigorously skirted by the via Appia, though banked amphorae were apparently unearthed in its midst. Similar banks of intact late republican or early imperial amphorae were also brought to light by the present mouth of the Savone, which originally entered the sea further south.[96] The drainage channels from the *pantano di Sessa* to the sea, indicated in post-medieval maps, may well have possessed Roman antecedents. Furthermore, the tales of Plutarch's marsh-dwellers, together with the discovery of a coin hoard, dating to the third century BC, at *località* Costera, suggest that land improvement schemes along the coast went hand in hand with colonization.[97]

At a later date, the emperor Nero is recorded as having dug the *fossa Neronis*, a canal extending along the stretch of coast from south of Sinuessa to the Phlegrean Fields, ostensibly to aid communications. Though an unpaved route was already in existence connecting the maritime colonies, the canal will have facilitated transport by barge as well as improving land drainage.[98] This work was followed in AD 95 by the construction of the via Domitiana. As it departed from the via Appia, at Sinuessa, it was commemorated by an arch. It then proceeded to Volturnum, crossing the river over a brick-faced concrete bridge, still partly preserved, to reach Cumae and the Phlegrean Fields. Hand in hand with the road construction, Domitian's engineers erected

a series of protective dykes in the Volturnus flood-plain. The scale of works necessary to control the river can only have been tackled by centralized government, and the success obtained by the Roman state in these works seems evident by the distribution of Roman sites along the coast.[99]

Lesser operations of water-management may have been the responsibility of local landowners or cooperative projects under the aegis of the local community, *colonia*, *municipium* or *pagus*. These were innumerable and are to be detected archaeologically. Municipal aqueducts and the dam at Sinuessa are mentioned above. A minor aqueduct is also known, supplying the area of the supposed pagus Sarclanus, which may also have been an official construction. Its original form has, unfortunately, been altered by both later medieval and modern attempts at exploiting the water source which rises as a spring about 290m asl. in the slopes to the north of Mt Petrino. The water runs just below ground level in a *cuniculus* around the eastern side of the mountain, and may originally have debouched at the large Roman complex at Casella della Starza, being extended towards the centre of Mondragone at a later date. Part of the way along its course, at some 200m asl., are the remains of a small Roman building in opus incertum with a signinum floor. Just below the building lies a well-head opening into the vaulted *cuniculus* which, at that point is about 2m high. Part of the lower end of the *cuniculus*, if it is one and the same, is now preserved in a conical, late or post-medieval cistern or distribution tower at Casella della Starza. The base of the *cuniculus* is now obscured by silt, though it has a minimum height of 70cm and a maximum width of 42cm with a vaulted ceiling. This type of *cuniculus* is very common in the area, and is found cut through both limestone and volcanic tuff. It may be regarded as one of the simplest forms of underground water conduit.

Water control in the low-lying land around the large villa at Ponte dell'Impiso (?*vicus Caedicius*) seems to have been effected by a network of small *cuniculi* either running below ground as vaulted channels or above ground as open-air conduits. Their irregular plan suggests that they were originally natural stream-channels, often seasonal, adapted so

[95] Livy XXVIII, xlvi, 4, and Plut. *Mor.* 262 B. For Metapontum see Uggeri, 1969, whilst for Capua see Cerlesi, Cerlesi and Cerlesi, 1984.

[96] Cf for example, Hesnard, 1980, for a similar deposit at La Longarina, Ostia.

[97] For the coin hoard see Breglia, 1946.

[98] Stat. *Silv.* IV, iii; Tac. *Ann.* XV, xlii; Hor. Sat. I, v, 3–24. An inscription recording republican road maintenance by two *duoviri* of Volturnum is published in CIL X 3276 and Pellegrino, 1977, 44–45.

[99] For the road see Dio LXVII; Romanelli, 1819, 486; Beloch, 1926, 376. A commemorative inscription from Puteoli is published in AE 1973, 137. On the Volturnus and Roman drainage operations see Maiuri, 1928, 181; Dio *loc. cit.*; Mart. *Epig.* VIII, lxv; Stat. *Silv.* IV, iii, 67–94. On a flood necessitating reconstruction of the ?Appia in AD 212 see CIL X 6876.

The Roman technological capacity in drainage is indicated, amongst other things, by the ambitious project to drain the Fucine lake (Pliny *NH* XXXVI, xxiv, 124). On 'large productive and protective water works that are managed by the government' cf Wittfogel, 1956, 153.

as to avoid unnecessary erosion or flooding. Although precise dating is often in doubt, the vaulted sections look suspiciously Roman and at one point, close to the villa, where an open-air conduit disappears into an underground leat, the sides are revetted with *opus latericium* of first or early second century AD date.

Even smaller conduits in the form of clay or lead pipes have been revealed around the Massico.[100] At one point, above the abandoned monastery of S Sebastiano, near Mondragone, bulldozing operations have revealed a pipe-line probably intended to drain what is now an abandoned agricultural terrace wall, or to conduct water onto the terraces from a spring-line above, at some 150m asl. One small overground cistern at Mass. Falco in the flat area known as Incaldana, between the mountains and the sea, was fed by a terracotta pipeline descending from the hills in the area of the spring (sorgente di Lavino) at *c* 180m asl. The cistern's capacity could no longer be measured, although its surface area cannot have been much larger than 25m^2. As it was not directly attached to a habitation or villa, it may be suggested that it functioned as a water source for livestock and/ or for field irrigation. Another free-standing cistern is situated on the side of the Padule depression, perhaps thus profiting from a gain in height of some fifteen metres or so, to feed irrigation channels below. The cistern has two barrel-vaults and a capacity of some 300m^3. This may be compared to the period II farmyard cistern at Posto, which had a minimum capacity of some 346m^3.[101] Conversely, a villa much larger than Posto, at *località* Grella, between Cascano and Casanova, had a smaller set of cisterns with a capacity of *c* 170m^3 (Fig 15). The disparity may have something to do with relative heads of livestock or differing farming requirements between the two sites. It may be observed that Posto is in a low-lying area devoted now to seed crops and orchards, whilst the Grella villa lies in a hilly area suited more to the less-demanding olive and vine.

Most, if not all, of the villas in the area possessed cisterns but, unlike the two free-standing examples described above, they were often located below ground or beneath the main body of the villa, forming part of the *basis villae*. Although these cisterns were often supplied with rain water through a system of *compluvia*, *impluvia* and leats, they may

also have acted as recipients for run-off or spring water from the hills, as at the villas of Corigliano and Gusti. Much of the water on villa sites must have been destined for domestic use, and bath-suites will have required a fair amount. In one case the discovery of a new spring, which was used to supply a rich villa near Sinuessa, was celebrated by an inscription.[102] Little has, however, been written about water control on villas and farms and one must await more complete excavation and publication before a general picture will become available.

Further indications of Roman attempts to control the hydrological regime may be suggested by the parallel linear channels draining the hills above Incaldana. The channels, running straight towards the sea, have been re-cut at various times and dating is thus difficult. Given, however, that run-off channels would have to have been contained at the points where they intersected the Appia and Domitiana, and given that their organization would have assisted in giving regularity to the ploughed fields, a Roman origin is probable. Cato, in fact, notes that drainage-ditches on the hillsides should be kept clean and that land should be drained in winter.[103] I would add the proposition that not only were the channels cut to control run-off in classical times, but that they were also harnessed for irrigational purposes. Even though Delano-Smith rightly asserts that 'neither Roman nor Arab engineers were able to reach the acquifers or to build the dams of the size that today ensure Mediterranean Europe's water supply', the extent of Rome's exploitation of the natural hydrological regime must not be overestimated. Indeed, it now seems that increasing neglect and miscomprehension of water systems through the late empire was an important factor in incipient land degradation.[104]

The Produce

The success of republican manipulation of the natural regime may be partly gauged by the combined textual and archaeological evidence for an unprecedented scale of cultivation of grain, vines and olives. Of grain, however, little is attested in the immediate study area, underlining, perhaps, Varro's statement that '*ad victum optima fert ager Campanus frumentum, Falernus vinum, Casinas oleum...*'.[105] Only

[100] Vitale, 1939, 248.
[101] Cotton, 1979, 27.

[102] CIL X 4734. Cf Pagano and Ferone, 1976, 35.
[103] Cato *de Agr.* CLV, 1.
[104] The hypothetical abandonment of a network of classical drainage-ditches has been called into play as a factor of decline in a similar coastal situation in the *ager Lunensis* (Ward Perkins, 1978, 318–319).
[105] Varro in Macrob. *Sat.* III, xvi, 12.

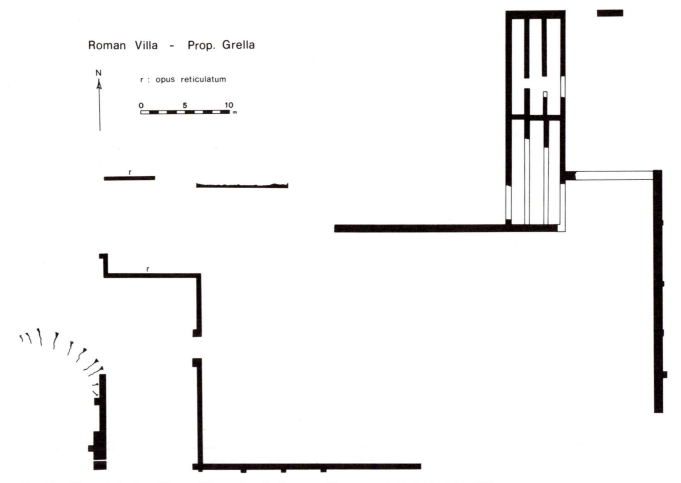

Fig 15   Plan of the Republican villa at Loc. Grella, near Casanova di Carinola (site C12)

one Pompeian-type donkey-mill has turned up in field survey, in contrast to various presses, on a rural site which lies some 2.5kms to the north-east of Sinuessa.[106] Another was found at the Roman villa of Corigliano, and a third example comes from the hypothesized centre of the pagus Sarclanus.[107] However, their apparent rarity on rural sites in the area does not counter the possibility of large-scale grain production.

If one considers the intra-mural area of Pompeii, where the archaeological evidence is somewhat clearer, there appear to be twenty-six *pistrina* or bakeries, each of which contain a number of donkey-mills. However, of the thirty-six *villae rusticae* examined by Carrington, only one contained a donkey-mill, which was set beside a hand-mill in a complex of two rooms devoted specifically to the preparation of flour and the baking of bread. Elements for subsistence baking were revealed in a couple of other villas.[108] The evidence is rather slight but it could suggest that some form of centralized milling of grain was in operation. A passage of Apuleius refers to an Attic country property which possessed a mill used also to grind neighbours' corn. The passage would presumably refer to a large mill capable of processing significant quantities of grain, and one might assume that the neighbours, unable to acquire their own mills, turned to that of the ?wealthier country property either to prepare a year's supply of flour for

[106] The mill is badly damaged and presents a minimum height of 0.44m. Originally it cannot have been much larger than 0.60m and thus almost the height of the normal Pompeian mill. Analysis by D.P.S. Peacock, whom I wish to thank, suggests that it is made of a grey lava or leucitophyre from the region of Orvieto. Cf Peacock, 1980, 44–46. Moritz, 1958, 75, notes sizes of Pompeian mills.

[107] Villucci, 1979, 50; Sementini, nd, 32.

[108] The mills in and around Pompeii are noted in Eschebach, 1970, 176; Carrington, 1931; Della Corte, 1923, 280.

domestic use or, more possibly, to prepare their saleable surplus. Small quantities of flour, when needed, could of course be prepared on a hand-mill. Conversely, a donkey-mill would presuppose a large resident population on an estate or commercial production of flour. Even the large slave-run villas of Settefinestre and Lucus Feronia have not yielded donkey-mills, even though the proprietors of the latter owned the *horrea Volusiana* in Rome. This would seem to suggest that the grain from the estate of the Volusii north of Rome may have been stored and processed in the city. The concentration of mills in Pompeii points to the reception of local grain, and not flour, by the town, whilst the evidence on the whole indicates that rural sites would usually send their threshed grain as soon as possible to the local urban centre for sale and final processing.

On any account, the ager Falernus and Garigliano basin seem to have been relatively unimportant as regards grain yield, and probably even more so by the second century BC, when evidence begins to surface for commercial wine production. By the beginning of the century, Campanian wine amphorae were already being exported to Carthage. Some, though not all, examples came from the Bay of Naples, where numerous 'Punic' type oil amphorae from Pompeii may indicate one of the exchange commodities.[109] The evidence of Graeco-Italic amphorae from kiln waster dumps at Mondragone suggests that northern Campania was involved in commercial production by the first half of the second century BC and, although the scale does not as yet seem to have been large, similar vessels already appear as far afield as Ampurias.[110]

It is not until the mid first century BC that a local wine, the Falernian, is noted in the sources, though its title *vetuli Falerni* indicates that it had already made its mark.[111] Indeed, it was the latter part of the second century BC that witnessed a boom in the production of local wine amphorae, of type Dressel 1A, at various sites along the coast (pl XIII). Sophisticated pressing equipment (*torcularia*), identified through the discovery of a number of characteristic limestone blocks bearing two rectangular socket holes, makes its appearance with the numerous villas of this date and indicate an increment, by at least one third, on the juice obtained by manual pressing. Though the date of individual *torcularia* can only be obtained through excavation, a number come from sites abandoned prior to the empire.

Petronius had his protagonist Trimalchio serve up Falernian of the consulship of L Opimius (121 BC), presumably vintage stock.[112] That the wine was both well-known and desirable is indicated by many classical references, often purposeful backdrops to scenes of taste and luxury. Given, however, the quantity produced during the first century BC, we may surmise that it became a "Chianti" of the late republic. It was divisible into at least three categories according to the location of the vineyards and quality of the fruit. *Caucinum* came from the hilltops, *Faustianum* or *Faustinianum* was a white wine from the middle slopes, whilst *Falernum* proper was a piedmont wine. The *Massicum* came from an adjoining area of the Massico and could be confused with *Falernum*. *Statanum* was also produced locally. Nothing is known about the wine produced in the Garigliano basin, though neighbouring Formiae yielded a pleasant, though not particularly noted, drink.

The earliest securely attested local amphorae, dating to the first half of the second century BC, are late Graeco-Italic vessels from a kiln dump revealed by the side of the via Domiziana, at Mondragone.[113] Earlier production may have taken place at Minturnae if the Graeco-Italic vessels stamped VALERIO, from a context no later than the mid third century, are local.[114]

In the early first century BC, the scale of amphora production reached vertiginous proportions, with serried ranks of kilns up and down the coast from Minturnae to Mondragone, servicing a hinterland that may have stretched inland as far as Cales. The scale of production is further indicated by such a quantity of waste that Sinuessa was able to perfect an endogenic building technique based on amphora sherds.

Towards the late first century BC various Roman notables, such as *Q Paconius Lepta*, *L Cornelius Lentulus Crus*, *Faustus Sulla*, the *Caedicii* and probably also the *Papii*, were involved in viticulture and the commerce in wine. Lentulus appears to be attested through the stamp L[*uci*]. LENTV[*li*]. P[*ubli*]. F[*ili*]. on Dressel 1B type amphorae, possibly indicating interests in the trade of wine from an estate at Minturnae.[115] The Caedicii are represented by the stamp mentioning *Caedicia Victrix M.f.*, whilst the Papii might hide behind the stamps ΓΑΓΑ and Γ, known from finds in the area of Sinuessa. However, only the stamps of Lentulus and Caedicia are explicit, and neither have

[109] *Ex inf* Dr. M. Fulford, and excavations by the writer at Pompeii.
[110] Hesnard *et al*, 1989.
[111] During the second century BC, Polybius referred to a particular wine from Capua which may have come from the Falernian district, given that at that stage it was considered Capuan territory (Polybius XXXIV, II, 1; Catull. XXVII, 1).
[112] Pet. *Sat*. XXXIV.
[113] Hesnard *et al*, 1989, 27, fig 11.
[114] Kirsopp-Lake, 1935; Hesnard *et al*, 1989, 31. The gens Valeria was important at Minturnae right down to the late republic.
[115] Paterson, 1982, 152; Gianfrotta, 1981, 75–76. On the commercial interests of Lentulus see Coarelli, 1983.

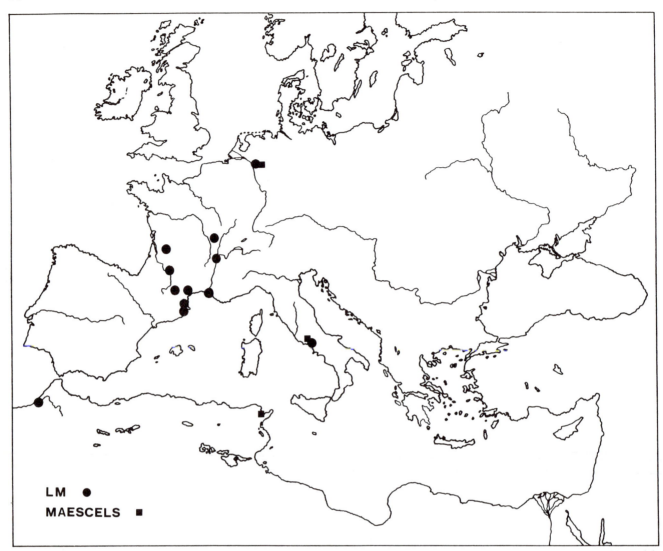

Fig 16   Known distribution of the late republican amphora stamps L.M. and MAESCELS (after Hesnard et al., 1989, with additions)

yet been found in the area.[116] The stamps so far found on the coastal kiln sites are indecipherable, without exception, and it is doubtful whether they were ever meant to be legible outside the immediate sphere of production.[117]

Of the few stamps for which a distribution is known, we may cite L.M., on Dressel 1B amphorae produced at Sinuessa, found at Oberaden, Mont Beuvray, Périgueux, Ruscino, Ensérune, Bordeneuve de Bory (Lot et Garonne), Essalois in the Loire, the Gulf of Fos, Ampurias, and Sala in Morocco (Fig 16).[118]

Further information is provided by the discovery of amphorae stamped MAESCELS, associated with the stamp (?)CALI, on the sites of a Roman villa

and a neighbouring kiln site, almost certainly within the same *fundus*, in *località* Masseria S Donato, near Corigliano, in the *ager* of Suessa Aurunca. The stamp MAESCELS may be attributed to the family of the *Maesiani Celsi*, which yielded a senator from the town.[119] The stamp is known from Oberaden and, in various examples, from Carthage, on amphora types Dressel 2–4 and Oberaden 74, and at the latter site is associated with the stamps (?)CALI and CER.[120]

The distribution of the kiln sites along the coast (Fig 17), exploiting the alluvial and colluvial clays, and giving immediate access to the ports of Minturnae, Sinuessa and Volturnum, through the Appia and the course of the later Domitiana, suggest that

---

[116] To the references to stamps of Lentulus listed by Gianfrotta, 1981, one may add Amar and Liou, 1984.

[117] Cfr. Panella, 1980. Amar and Liou, 1984, 160, list other stamps, on amphorae of type Dressel 2–4, for which a northern Campanian provenance is hypothesized.

[118] See Hesnard, *et al*, 1989, 33–35.

[119] Cebeillac Gervasoni, 1982.

[120] CIL VIII 22637.68 a–b; Loeschcke, 1942, Taf. 19,2; and F Rakob, unpublished excavations at Carthage.

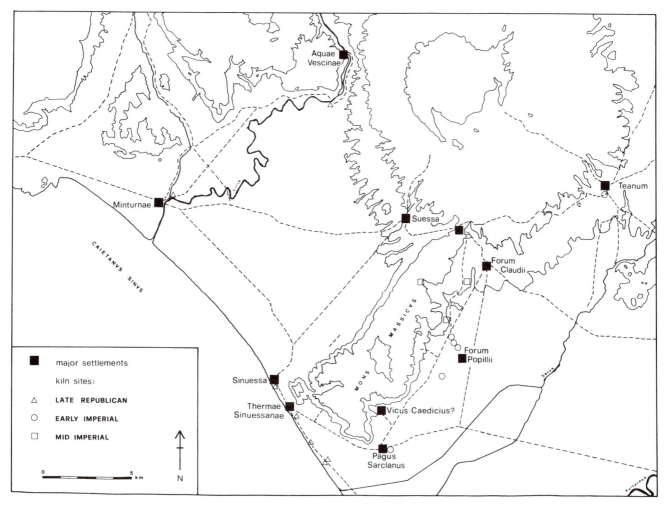

Fig 17   The distribution of amphora kiln sites

they were not located on the wine-producing *fundi*.[121] In fact, to judge by the distribution of villas and presses, the latter lay predominantly in the hinterland, on the slopes of the Massico, in the ager Falernus proper and in the Garigliano basin. The lower-lying coastal areas were more likely utilized for seed crops. During the course of the first century AD, no later than the Tiberian period, the distribution of kiln sites was radically altered with their migration into the heart of the wine producing districts to the south of the Massico.[122]

The coastal kilns were probably owned or managed by independent potters or *negotiatores* who produced containers for those whose wine they were eventually to carry. A single atelier could use numerous distinct stamps as in the case of the site found by David Peacock which has, so far, yielded seven.[123] The only kiln site that has yielded explicit

stamps is that of the Maesiani Celsi which, furthermore, seems to have been located directly on the family's *fundus*.[124]

Perhaps around the same time, or not long before the migration of kilns inland, the typical local late republican wine amphora, type Dressel 1B, was replaced by the lighter type Dressel 2–4, imitating Koan containers. With the change there appears to have been a significant diminution in the use of stamps, such that no inland kiln has yet yielded a stamped vessel, save for the peculiar case of the Maesiani Celsi, where both production and *negotiato* may have been in the same hands. If the migration of production sites from the coast inland signifies a relocation directly onto the individual *fundi*, passing from independent management by ceramicists or *negotiatores* to management by individual *domini*, then the disappearance of stamps on amphorae may

---

[121] It may be noted that the volcanic maar or Padule depression immediately to the north of Mondragone constitutes an enormous clay quarry, with an eight metre thick layer of clay. However, it remains to be shown that this was so exploited in Roman times.

[122] Arthur, 1982; Panella, 1989.

[123] Peacock, 1978; Panella, 1980.

[124] If such stamps were a guarantee of the quality of the product, amphora or wine, why were not all vessels stamped? See Manacorda, 1989.

perhaps be explained by their being no longer necessary for the identification of the produce of individual vendors.

The stamp *Π* from Mondragone, has been identified on the Spargi wreck, in Sardinia, where it was associated with containers bearing the stamps SAB and others in Greek and Oscan.[125] The hypothesis that the ship came from Sinuessa may be supported by its cargo of Black Glaze ware which is very similar to material from Cales which, furthermore, is common in excavations at the maritime colony. The date of the wreck is still debated. Pallares, in the last excavation report, suggests a date little after 126 BC, whilst Lyding Will prefers a date around 75 BC.[126] If Pallares' so-called 'presigillata' may be identified with eastern sigillata A, then the wreck is unlikely to date earlier than 90–80 BC when the class seems to make its appearance in Italy. The thin-walled wares seem also to be of first century BC date, in particular Pallares, 1986, fig 8d, which has so far not appeared in second century contexts at Pompeii.

Amongst the amphorae from the wreck is a type claimed to be similar to type Dressel 28, which is of Spanish origin.[127] A few years ago, André Tchernia showed me a photograph of an amphora from a kiln site at Mondragone, morphologically similar to amphorae from a kiln at Velaux, Bouches-du-Rhone, which in turn probably derive from the same prototypes as the Dressel 28.[128] Furthermore, stamps reading MAESCELS, from Carthage, were apparently present on amphorae recognized as type Dressel 28, whilst the stamp from Oberaden was on a vessel of type Oberaden 74.[129] We now know that these vessels were produced in the Garigliano basin. On the basis of this evidence we can say that vessels similar, though certainly not identical, to type Dressel 28/Oberaden 74 were produced in northern Campania, and thus the Spargi finds may indeed have had the same provenance as the more typical amphorae of type Dressel 1B, also present amongst the cargo.[130]

In conclusion, it may be suggested that the prototypes of both Spanish and Gaulish ring-foot amphorae with double-ledged rims were Italian and came from the same areas as the prototypes of the Spanish and Gaulish Dressel 1/Pascual 1 and Dressel 2–4 types, further reinforcing the concept of the exportation of a whole productive system (including the slave mode of production and techniques of viticulture) by Italian landlords who acquired properties in these provinces.

The kiln sites in the ager Falernus also produced flat-based and miniature Dressel 2–4s. The appearance of these ring-foot amphorae in Italy is probably to be explained by a diversification in the function of amphorae, rather than in their contents. Whilst the amphorae with pointed stubs were ideal for maritime transportation, the ring-foot types were more suited to transportation by river barge or cart. What seems to have been a moment of trial and experimentation in northern Campania was further developed in Gaul, with the production of numerous ring-foot vessels for transportation along the Rhone-Rhine axis, at first to satisfy the demands of the *castra* along the *limes* that had been used to the consumption of Italian wines. Towards the second century, ring-foot types developed in Italy, as is demonstrated by the productions of Forlimpopoli, Spello and Santarcangelo di Romagna.[131]

The scheme presented here seems to support certain speculations advanced by Laubenheimer.[132] May we speak of competition between Gallic and Italian (and Spanish) merchants? How likely is it that the same figures lay behind the initiatives in both Italy and the provinces? May we imagine that the production of ring-foot amphorae at Fréjus and Marseilles, at least at an early stage, was motivated by the need to transfer Italian wine from maritime transport containers (amphorae or *dolia*) to river and land transport containers?

The actual discovery of a vineyard (Fig 18), adding further testimony of Roman vine cropping, not only indicates the sort of land that was exploited, but also allows for comparison with the dictates of the ancient agronomists. It is situated over 100m asl., just beneath a Roman villa on a south-easterly slope, in an area which now consists of olives within scrub. The vineyard, exposed by construction of the *strada panoramica* above Falciano, consists of a series of fifteen parallel trenches (*sulci*) cut into the soft volcanic ignimbrite. Their spacing varies from 2.53 to 3.23 m, with a mean spacing of 2.76m. Columella recommended a spacing of between 4 (1.20m) and 10 *pedes* (3m) between rows of vines, depending on whether hoes or ploughs were to be used. A similar distance of 2.5m between rows of vines permitted inter-cultivation of vegetables in Piemonte early this century. Columella also gave

[125] Lamboglia, 1961, 158–9; Pallares, 1986.
[126] Pallares, 1986, 99; Lyding Will, 1984.
[127] Pallares, 1986, 94, fig 6d-e.
[128] Tchernia and Villa, 1977, fig 6.
[129] Zevi, 1966, 225–226. For Oberaden see Loeschcke, 1942.
[130] Amphorae belonging to the same strain seem now also to have been produced at the *portus Cosanus*: Lyding Will, 1987, 213–216, type 24.

[131] For the whole problem of ring-foot amphorae see now Panella, 1989. The Gaulish vessels are presented by Laubenheimer, 1985, *passim*.
[132] Laubenheimer, 1985, esp. 455.

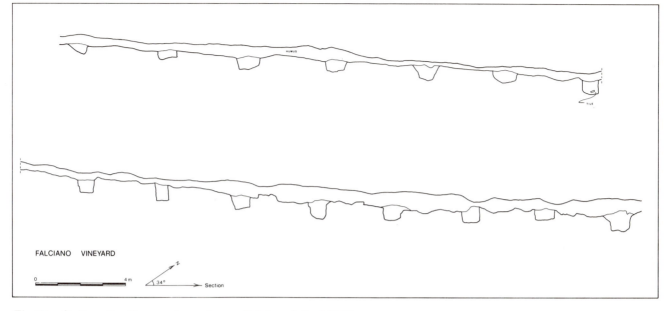

Fig 18   Section of a Roman vineyard near Falciano (site M166)

a width for the *sulci* of 2 *pedes*, which is the minimum width found for one of the best-preserved *sulci* at Falciano. Their mean width, bearing in mind that some examples are partly eroded, is 0.79m. Depths are given by Columella as 2 and 2.5 *pedes*, comparing favourably with the deepest preserved example of 0.64m. Such trenching, particularly on slopes, would help to ensure uniform drainage and aeration of the soil.[133]

The Falciano vineyard, sadly, is not well dated. At present, the land is abandoned. The topsoil contains abundant post-medieval brown glazed pottery which is totally absent from the *sulci*, whilst Roman finds comprise a tile fragment and a local imitation of North African Red Slip Ware of Hayes type 8 (Flavian to second century). An imperial date is thus indicated.

The other major crop of the area must have been the olive, ideally suited to the limestone uplands where soil cover is frequently quite shallow. Numerous abandoned orchards and terraces, often fairly inaccessible, probably testify to the large extension that the crop enjoyed in the past.[134]

Indeed, the farmsteads sited on the loftiest slopes and crests of hills, and especially those towards the coast, most of which were deserted in the late republic, were almost certainly devoted to olive cultivation. The prevailing winds, detrimental to the vine, would not only have left the groves unscathed, but could have assisted in the fall and collection of the fruit in maturity.

There is however little indication that olive oil was exported from Campania and, despite the reputation that Venafrum and Casinum enjoyed, no local oil amphorae have been identified from western central Italy. The olive yield of these inland towns could never have been large enough for overseas exportation, and presumably satisfied local demand and perhaps major consumer centres in the form of limited high quality produce.[135] Self-sufficiency may, on the other hand, be witnessed by the relative scarcity of Baetican oil amphorae at both Pompeii and Naples, where sufficient collections of contemporary amphorae exist, and through the field survey which has yielded only five fragments, three of which come from Sinuessa.[136]

[133] Colum. *RR* IV, 3; V, v, 3; XI, ii, 28; Scheuermeier, 1943, 146–152 and pl 264; White, 1970, 237; Carandini, 1980. For the specifications of the vine-trenches of an early republican vineyard at Tor Pagnotta, near Rome, see Valenzani and Volpe, 1980. Another possible vineyard, at Ponte di Nona, near Rome, presents spacing of 0.5m between *sulci* (*pers. comm.* T Potter).

[134] Despite state intervention, the last century has witnessed a significant decrease in the farming of this labour-intensive crop. In '30s Italy produced some two hundred million kilos of olive oil over a surface area of 2.300.000 hectares, underboth promiscuous and intensive cultivation, whilst Spain, with a lesser surface area devolved to the crop, yielded some three hundred and fifty million kilos of oil (Morani, 1933, 80). The country is obviously well-suited to the olive and, save for abnormal consumer centres such as Rome, must for most of its history have been self-sufficient.

[135] Sirago, 1958, 225. A distinction might be made, as in modern Italy, between the rather expensive *olio extra vergine*, and mass-produced cheaper oil. Some of the oil may have also gone into the production of secondary products such as unguents. On Mediterranean oil and Roman Italy see now Mattingly, 1988.

[136] For Pompeii see Manacorda, 1977, 131–132, *contra* Tchernia, 1964, 447–449, who argued that olive oil production around Pompeii may already have become insufficient to cope with local demand by the first century AD. The data from Naples is not yet published. It may be noted that no identifiable fragments of Baetican oil amphorae were found at the Francolise villas.

Panella has demonstrated that Tripolitanian (?)oil amphorae appear at Pompeii in larger proportion to Baetican ones, with a ratio of 41:6. The quantity of imported oil still seems low, though the necessity to import has been argued as the result of insufficient local production to cope with demographic expansion. Recent excavations at Pompeii have shown, however, that North African amphorae, particularly from Tunisia, already appeared in significant quantities from the early second century BC. These are the same vessels that appeared with great frequency during field survey in northern Campania, second only to local containers, suggesting importation of African ?oil into much of the region from the second century BC down, perhaps, to Augustan times. Thus, though the villas at Posto and San Rocco seem to have imported Tunisian oil during the republic, from the first century AD they improved their own oil producing capacities and imported oil containers no longer appeared on site.[137]

It may be suggested that even the olive gave way to the vine during the scramble for cash-cropping in the second century BC, and that it was only with the eventual decline in Italian wine production from the first century AD that the olive could make a partial comeback, capable of satisfying local demand. If the evidence cited above for the abandonment of olive cultivation in marginal upland areas during the later republic is faithful, the appearance of expanded oil production in the more optimal zones of the Francolise villas at a slightly later date may indicate a downhill movement of the plant into areas of redundant vineyards.

The three principal crops, the vine, the olive and the grain, must have competed for surface area in their respective marginal zones, though they could have coexisted in close proximity, utilizing high slopes, foothills and plains respectively. The pattern is often repeated today in other areas but, whilst both the olive and the vine can be cultivated on the plain, grain cannot be adequately cultivated on the slopes. These were obviously the predominant crops, often farmed for cash returns, though polyculture was undoubtedly practised, if only to satisfy local

demand for the fruits and vegetables needed to integrate diet, particularly in market-garden areas in and around towns. References are scarce, though it is known that pears were grown in the ager Falernus and used to prepare a beverage. Marcus Aurelius used to enjoy Campanian peaches, whilst Palladius noted a particular preparation of dried figs in the region. It is not known where they were farmed. Mention may finally be made of the cultivation of the broad bean (Lat. *faba*) around Minturnae, and of four *liberti* of the *gens Cominia* who were involved in its commerce.[138]

The *magister* inscriptions from Minturnae refer to the *socii picarii* who were responsible for the preparation of pitch, which seems to be a clear indication of the survival of a significant amount of pine in the area at least until the first century BC. Furthermore, exaggerated growth-rings noted on beams recovered from the Garigliano seem to indicate also the presence of oak woodland during republican times in the more low-lying, moist areas of the basin.[139] Coupled with the inscription referring to an *architectus navalis*, one may hypothesize ship-building activity at Minturnae relying on substantial quantities of locally available wood, and in particular fir and pine.[140] In the Phlegrean Fields, to the south, the *Silvae Ami et Gallinaria* survived down to the empire, and it seems only to have been Agrippa's need to construct a fleet of ships that led to the large-scale stripping of the wood around the Lake Avernus.[141] Significant quantities of wood were also required for iron-smelting and potting, whilst it may be remembered that Cato recommended Suessa for the purchase of wooden agricultural machinery, including carts (*plostra*) and sledges (*treblae*).[142]

Cato also lists Suessa Aurunca, together with Casilinum, on the Volturno, as a source for baskets (*fiscinas*), implying a readily available supply of reeds and canes, which may also have been used in thatching.[143] In the tenth century the craft appears to have been in the hands of Benedictine monks.[144] The artisanal industry is still alive today at SS. Cosma and Damiano, where use is made of *Ampelodesma stricta* from the limestone hills.

---

[137] Cotton, 1979; Cotton and Metraux, 1985.

[138] Pears: Pliny *NH* XV, 53. Peaches: *SHA Clod. Alb.* XII, 3. Beans: AE 1922, no. 123. It is worth noting that, though figs are not greatly abundant, peaches now constitute the principal crop of the lower Garigliano basin, with about 37,000 trees recorded under cultivation in 1965 (Giarizzo, 1965, 70).

[139] For the *socii picarii* see Johnson, 1933, 126–128; Giardina, 1981; for the oak from the Garigliano: Brother D Ruegg, *pers. comm.*

[140] Meiggs, 1980. The inscription of the *architectus navalis* was housed in the Lombard tower to the south of the Garigliano, destroyed during WW II. It has recently been recovered by the archaeological group of Minturno.

[141] Ruocco, 1965, 190.

[142] Cato, *de Agr.* CXXXV, 1 and XXII, 3.

[143] *de Agr.* CXXXV, 3.

[144] Giarizzo, 1965, 80 and note 97.

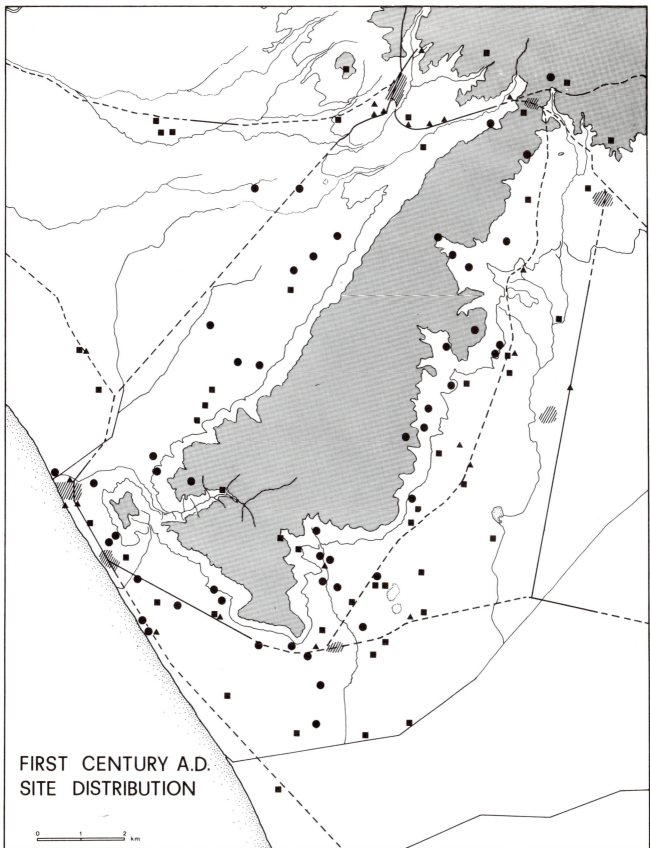

FIRST CENTURY A.D.
SITE DISTRIBUTION

0   1   2 km

Fig 19   First century AD site distribution around the Massico. Key: hatching = Nucleated settlements; dots = Villa sites; squares = Farms/pottery scatters; triangles = Cemeteries/burials

Chapter Six

Imperial Settlement: an 'Indian Summer'

With the advent of more stable political conditions under the early empire, many Campanian towns seem to have enjoyed a significant, though brief, period of intense building activity, road development and general prosperity. This seems not so clearly reflected in the archaeological evidence from the countryside, where gross capital expenditure may have occured somewhat earlier. It may perhaps be maintained that, in imperial times, the region remained 'healthy' for as long as it was able to rely on its heritage, bequeathed by the economic system set up under the late republic. The signs of sustained and partially renewed economic success were a consequence of the new directions permitted after the close of the Civil Wars and the fall of the republic, though they were not to last for long.[1]

The material evidence for the towns, presented in the previous chapter, consists largely of traces of buildings in reticulate and brick masonry which may be dated principally within the last decades of the first century BC and the beginning of the second century AD. Subsequently, urban building on any substantial scale seems to have ceased, partly because of the adequacy of early imperial construction in withstanding the ravages of time, though perhaps predominantly on account of financial recession and a consequent decline and redirection of civic and private spending and munificence.[2] Dedications rarefy, though it is worth remembering one by the *populus civitatis Foropopiliensium* dating to as late as AD 367.[3]

Monumental tombs lining the roads, such as the large cylindrical mausoleum along the via Domitiana, or the box-like examples radiating out from Suessa Aurunca, are of the early empire and indicate the continued flamboyant spending of various wealthy local families. Though road maintenance, at least along the Appia, was kept up into the fifth century as attested by the milestones, most of the paving seems to have been laid down during the late republic or early empire, to be marveled at by later generations.[4]

The major road building project was that of the coastal via Domitiana, linking Sinuessa with Puteoli and thus bypassing Capua and the tiresome internal route (*supra*). This official sanctioning by Domitian of what was a pre-existing thoroughfare suggests land improvement and concern over communications between the agricultural reservoir of northern Campania and the node of the Bay of Naples and Puteoli. Furthermore, it underwrote the unsuccessful project of the *Fossa Neronis*, intended to ease movement by barge, avoiding thus the currents of the open sea.

Two other substantial road building projects are indicated by bridge constructions. One of these, along the road from Minturnae to Suessa, still exists to this day as Ponte Ronaco. It is often attributed to Hadrian, which is possible on architectural technique. The other bridge crossed the Garigliano and is attested by a monumental inscription, perhaps originally set up on an arch, which indicates that it was erected privately, *ex senatus consulto*, during the reign of Vespasian.

A certain amount of maintenance of centurial road systems under the empire may be assumed given the partial preservation of centuriation networks down to the present day, both to the north and the south of the Massico. Their survival, however, was probably conditioned more by practical considerations of field access, than by any particular continuity in property configurations.

After the late republic the evidence for private estates is drastically reduced. What textual and epigraphic evidence that does survive may provide an even more distorted sample of ownership than that for the late republic. The drop in the number of proprietors may be more apparent than real, though various families dominant under the late republic disappeared, and others came to the fore. A similar decrease in the number of known landowners occurs in the Bay of Naples, and the pattern seems to be repeated in other parts of Italy.[5] Large estates appear in the hands of senatorial families or people within imperial court circles. In their case, as with recorded municipal notables, there appears to be little continuity of land ownership, underlining the profound social mutations which had taken place

---

[1] Cf Syme, 1939, 451–456.

[2] See, most recently, Ward Perkins, 1984, chap 1; similarly in south Etruria – Potter, 1979, 116.

[3] CIL X 4725.

[4] We are told, for example, of a Tiberian senator of local origin, M Vinicius, patron of Velleius, who paid for the upkeep of roads at Cales: Tac. *Ann.* VI, xv, 1; *AE* 1929, 166.

[5] Cf D'Arms, 1977.

within the decades that saw the Civil Wars and the stabilisation of the empire. These apparent qualitative and quantitative changes in properties and proprietors may also signal the agglomeration of holdings to culminate in the imperial *latifundia*.

Horace chose the ager Falernus when he wanted to refer to an estate of a thousand *iugera* which Octavian had assigned to one of his partisans.[6] The size and location of the estate was exemplificatory of the increasing wealth of some *liberti*. Another such man was Domitius Apollinaris, a friend of Martial, who could number a holding at Minturnae amongst his possessions. Other men, such as Ofonius Tigellinus, Nero's praetorian prefect who perished at Sinuessa, may also have acquired local land through imperial patronage.[7]

However, the largest number of properties attested under the early and mid empire was in senatorial hands. Whether the senator and mentor of Marcus Aurelius, Q Iunius Rusticus, was a landowner at Sinuessa is impossible to say, although he was certainly acquainted with the town.[8] Both the senators C Appius Eunomius Sapidius and C Clodius C.f. Quir. Adiutor, however, were local landowners and patrons of Sinuessa, Adiutor being probably of second century date. The *Balneum Clodianum* of Teanum, if truly financed by a branch of the family, not only underlines the wealth, but also the extension of the family's interests to the neighbouring town.[9] The M Maesius, attested as decurion at Suessa Aurunca in 193, seems to have been related to the Maesii who had reached the Senate.[10] The *gentes Sosia* or *Pompeia* may have possessed land around Minturnae in the mid second century AD. A dedicatory inscription from the town to Pompeia Q.f. Sosia Falconilla records her family ties with four consuls, including Frontinus, over a period of one hundred years.[11]

It seems probable that consuls of AD 64 and 70, C Laecanius Bassus and his adoptive son C Caecina Paetus, also both had properties in the territory of Minturnae, around Monte D'Argento, where mem-

bers and freedmen of their families made dedications at a shrine of Silvanus, and at Ausonia on the road to Interamna Lirenas. Apart from a residence at Rome, which C Laecanius Bassus must almost certainly have possessed, he is known to have had an important agricultural estate near Pula on the Istrian peninsula. Pottery kilns belonging to the estate were brought to light in 1910. Amphorae produced there not only list a minimum of 15 slaves employed in the workshops through the stamps, but also demonstrate that the senator was involved in the commercial production of wine or oil which reached markets in the northern Adriatic zone, the province of Noricum and even Rome. Even if a property at Brindisi cannot be assigned to him with certainty, the estates in two such disparate and productive agricultural areas as were Istria and Campania would seem to represent the tip of a rather large and lucrative iceberg.[12]

The sole example of continuity in land ownership from republican times is perhaps provided by the *gens Caedicia*, in the person of the Tiberian senator C Caedicius Agrippa, quite likely from the area (chap VI *supra*).

Finally, mention may be made of the senator L Burbuleius Optatus L.f. Quir. Ligarianus, consul before AD 138, who appears to have come from Sinuessa or Minturnae and could count amongst his charges *curator rei publicae* of the ports of Terracina, Ancona and Narbo, and *curator viarum* of the Clodia, Cassia and Cimina, before holding various high posts in Sicily, Cappadocia and Syria, where he died. His daughters are attested in a Trajanic dedication at Minturnae.[13]

Some of these properties must have been the subject of confiscations at various periods, thus enriching the imperial patrimony or entering the hands of the emperor's friends and partisans, as seems to have been just the case after Capua's siding with the Vitellian cause against Vespasian.[14]

Imperial property in the ager Falernus is attested by an inscription reading:

[6] Hor. *Ep.* IV, 13: *arat Falerni mille fundi iugera*.

[7] For Apollinaris see Mart. *Ep.* X, xxx, 1–10; for Tigellinus, Plut. *Otho* II, 3, and Tac. *Hist.* I, lxxii.

[8] Farquharson, 1944, 1, 6; *Med.* I, 7.

[9] Sapidius: CIL X 3844. Adiutor: *AE* 1926, 143; Greco, 1927, I, 7; *PIR* 906. Cf CIL X 3851–3852 from Capua, and *AE* 1926, 142, for P. Clodius C.f. Fal., his son? The *Balneum Clodianum* appears in CIL X 4792.

[10] Cebeillac-Gervasoni, 1982, 67 and 86; CIL X 4760. See now Ionta, 1985, n 28, from the area of Minturnae.

[11] De Spagnolis, 1981, 49 and fig 28. McDermott, 1976, especially pp 238–240, discusses the Minturnae inscription in the context of the descendants of Frontinus.

[12] CIL X 5375; Laurent-Vibert and Piganiol, 1907, 497–498; RE IX col. 1486; PIR 16; Callender, 1965, no 365, for the amphorae of Bassus, with a new example now recorded from Zalalovo: Bezecsky, 1983, 154. Cf also the funerary inscription CIL IX 39 from Brindisi, referring possibly to his son. The most up-to-date discussion of the Laecanii is provided by Tassaux, 1982. On the family of Caecina Paetus see Syme, 1983, 106–107. A *libertus* of Caecina Paetus was buried at Ausonia: CIL X 5375. I wonder if the Caecini and the Valerii were also related in some way, as the cognomen Paetus is known to members of both families in the area.

[13] Hopkins, 1983, 158–9; CIL X 6006; Fant, 1976, cited by D'Arms, 1981, 158, no 37. I have not personally examined the study by Fant. For the daughters see Cavuoto, 1982, n 25.

[14] Cebeillac-Gervasoni, 1982, 67; cf also Crawford, 1976, 42.

PORPHYRVS
AVG LIB. PROC
REG. FAL. ET STAT
N. GENIO VOTVM SOLVIT

from the area of the supposed pagus Sarclanus.[15] Within the area was also the *libertus* M Aurelius Felix, *regionarius regionis Statanae*, during the later second century AD.[16] Of higher status was the Flavian *libertus* Graphicus, who was *procurator hereditatium tractus Campaniae et Flaviae*, and may have been concerned with estates around Sinuessa where he was commemorated (pl XV). Yet another freedman, Acastus, was attested on his funerary cippus at Formiae as *procurator provinciae Mauretaniae et tractus Campaniae*.[17] It may also be remembered that the Aquae Vescinae belonged to the *patrimonium*, at least, from the early third century. Aside from the emperor, at least one other member of the imperial family, Matidia, who owned extensive estates around Sitifis in Mauretania which passed directly to the emperor on her death, had interests in the lower Garigliano basin and was presumably a local landowner.[18]

A further change in landownership and organization is indicated by the establishment of numerous veteran colonies throughout the Italian peninsula at the end of the republic and early empire which, in Augustan times, involved the donation of land to some 300.000 men. Northern Campania was included in the schemes with Caesarian and Augustan assignations at Minturnae (pl XVI), Augustan ones in the ager Falernus and possibly in the territory of Suessa Aurunca, and probable Vespasianic assignations at Sinuessa and in the ager Falernus at Urbana, which may have passed to Capua in AD 53.[19] The actual archaeological evidence for the activation of these colonial assignations is slight, in part because it is almost impossible to demonstrate archaeologically the change in ownership of individual pre-existing villas and farms. Furthermore, much of the newly distributed land may have been sold off by disinterested *coloni*, whose only thought was that of returning to their place of origin, to established landowners intent on extending their possessions. The practice is attested by Tacitus in Neronian times.[20] Centuriation of early imperial date has been noticed in the ager Falernus, whilst a very limited number of early imperial sites may perhaps be attributed to the intervention of new

colonial settlers.[21] Yet again, as in earlier times, a number of the new farmers may have dwelt in the towns and the smaller nucleated settlements, such as the Pagus Sarclanus or Forum Popilii, both of which have yielded larger quantities of early imperial finds during survey than either earlier or later material.

Epigraphic evidence for the settlement of veterans is likewise limited, though an interesting inscription from Cellole commemorates L Magius Vrgulanianus, a veteran of the Illyrian campaigns of Augustus, probably settled in freshly centuriated land in the territory of Minturnae, to the south of the Garigliano.[22]

After the early second century textual and epigraphic evidence for ownership in general rarefies until late antique times, when the Church appears as an added and potent factor in possession and exploitation of the land. By this time the social and economic composition of Campania had altered radically, as will be demonstrated in the next chapter.

If we may accept the dating of construction types such as opus reticulatum and opus latericium as essentially early imperial, the evidence for their use would suggest a slump in major rural building activity in period VII. Of over 120 rural sites identified as having been in existence around the first century AD only 8, excluding a bridge and an aqueduct, possess structures in opus reticulatum. Of these eight, 5 may have been new constructions when the reticulate masonry was employed, whilst only 2 of these were built exclusively in the technique and, like the site at Monte Forco in the ager Capenas, may have been small colonial farmsteads or satellites of large estate centres. The remaining 3 'new' foundations consisted of a pottery production plant to the south of Cascano, and 2 large maritime villas. The bridge and the aqueduct are both to be seen as expressions of the planning of urban infrastructures of Suessa Aurunca, where the building technique also found use in an adjustment to the town walls and in three public buildings, the theatre, a fountain/nymphaeum and a presumed bathing complex. The use of opus reticulatum is also found at Minturnae, Sinuessa and Forum Popilii. The pattern agrees with the distribution of the technique plotted by Torelli, with 'epicentres' of usage around the capital and the Bay of Naples.[23]

A technique hardly more common in rural con-

[15] Sementini, nd, 70; Pagano, 1980, whose amendment to Porphyrius seems unnecessary.
[16] AE 1909, 77 = 1919, 69. See, also, Boulvert, 1970, 215.
[17] Graphicus: AE 1922, 122. Acastus: CIL X 6081. Cf Weaver, 1972, chap 21. Crawford, 1976, 68, lists other imperial estates in Campania.
[18] *Supra*; Crawford, *op cit*, 39.
[19] Kuziscin, 1984, chap IV; Keppie, 1983, *passim*.
[20] Tac. *Ann.* XIV, iv, 27.

[21] Cf Vallat, 1984, with bibliography.
[22] Solin, 1984, 130–133.
[23] Torelli, 1980.

texts was the use of bricks, generally triangular in form (*semilateres*), of a kind found produced at the kilns around Casanova di Carinola. The maritime villa at Loc. Treppete, in which reticulate masonry was used, was also partly built of brick, as was that excavated by Johannowsky at Torre S Limato and the site at Le Colonne.[24] It is on occasion found employed for later modifications at large republican villas such as that at S Mauro, built predominantly of opus incertum. The use of reticulate blocks and bricks in the area was, nonetheless, essentially urban and thus gives the impression of a period of urban building expansion and rural building stagnation. As republican villa constructions seem to have been quite robust (they often survive splendidly to this day!), we might view the capital expenditure in towns as an expression of public and private, propagandistic, munificence.

The use of tile or brick as string-courses, as at Forum Claudii and the villa of Corigliano, is also not common and far more difficult to date, though courses of semilateres stamped BILLIE[nus] in the bath-suite of the villa of S Rocco, Francolise, are of first century date. Minor structural adjustments must have taken place on numerous rural sites. Re-roofing is probably indicated by tiles stamped CAL[purnius] CLEM[ens], produced at a first century kiln complex near Forum Popilii, and found on a villa site about three and a half kilometres away, near Casanova di Carinola. The majority of such cases will, however, only come to light through excavation.

The main period of the grand coastal villas in the area seems to have been during the first century of the empire, in contrast to the earlier established villas of the agricultural hinterland, and thus seems to be in accordance with the evidence for the contemporary appearance of new maritime establishments, often with annexed fish-tanks, along the coast of southern Lazio (pl XVII).[25] Their late appearance may, at least in part, be a result of the very real threat posed by pirates, who possessed the capability of sacking Caieta and even pillaging within the port of Ostia. They are recorded as a menace to villas near the coast, and were only finally expunged at the hands of Pompey.[26]

Two suburban villas on the coast by Sinuessa, at Mass. La Signora and Torre S Limato, were decorated with rich mosaics and appear to have been constructed during the first century AD.

Another villa, of first or early second century date, at Loc. Treppete, yielded the bearded head of an emperor in marble, unfortunately looted, columns of grey Egyptian granite and a Greek metrical inscription pertaining to a statue of Aphrodite.[27] A table-leg in Numidian marble (*giallo antico*) feigning a classical Greek kore was found on a site in the area of the supposed pagus Sarclanus, whilst an enormous villa complex (the ?vicus Caedicius), at nearby S Mauro, was embellished with one-piece columns of grey marble. However, it must not be deduced that the rich maritime villas, centres of *otium*, were necessarily non-productive parasites of the hinterland, as the unquestionable extravagance of Lucullus' villa at Bauli must be balanced by Pliny's self-sufficient Laurentine estate.[28]

Whilst the greatest density of rural sites appears, according to survey pottery evidence, to date around the late republic to early first century AD (Fig 19), by the third century less than a third of the sites were apparently still functioning. Impossible though it may be to date the abandonment of a site closely, the phenomenon appears to have already begun by the end of the first century BC, being signaled by the absence of the common aretine or puteolan sigillata on one or two otherwise prolific sites from the point of view of ceramic finds. The pattern is not new, though the chronology may vary through Italy according to local variables. The apex of rural settlement density in the ager Veientanus, in close proximity to the capital, appears to have been around the later first and second century AD. That of the ager Cosanus, as around the Massico, about a century earlier. Afterwards, the abandonment of rural sites seems generally to have been a downhill trend. This may be partly explained as a gradual abandonment of worked land, apparently typical of the *latifundia*, and this may be seen in the context of the growth of some estates at the expense of others, with a concentration of land in the hands of fewer individuals on account of expropriation, policies of dynastic marriage and land sales.[29]

Within this period, various events are discernible as part of a general mutation of the economic pattern of the Italian peninsula. Aside from the decline in rural settlement, the most obvious change in the archaeological record is the decline in the number of amphorae from the area found in the traditional centres of consumption. This presumably equals a decline in surplus production of wine and,

[24] Pagano and Ferone, 1976, 23; Sementini, nd, 26.
[25] Egidi, 1985, 112.
[26] Plut. *Pomp*. XXIV-XXVI; Dio XXXVI, 20–23; Cic. *de imp. Gn. Pomp*. XXXII.

[27] CIG 3, 5956.
[28] Varro *RR* III, xvii, 9; Pliny Ep. II, xvii. For the whole question of *otium*, *amoenitas* and the productive and commercial interests of proprietors in Campania see especially D'Arms, 1970.
[29] Kuziscin, 1984, 180; Potter, 1979, for the ager Veientanus, and Celuzza and Regoli, 1982, 59, for the ager Cosanus.

perhaps, of oil. The trend may already be evident at Ostia in Augustan times, but becomes ever more marked until the early second century AD when Italian amphora production, at least for wide-scale exportation, had all but ceased.[30] A *titulus pictus* on an amphora from Pompeii reading FAVS/TI. CLAVDIO IIII/COS/L.VITELLIO III takes the dating of the exportation of Falernian wine, albeit on a regional scale, to AD 47, although at least as late as AD 43 the wine appears to have reached Britain.[31]

In Augustan times Italian kilns ceased production of the wine amphora of type Dressel 1B in favour of the lighter and more manageable type Dressel 2–4, which had already made its appearance during the third quarter of the first century BC, and which clearly descended from the form of imported Koan containers. At about this time, or slightly later, a series of new amphora production sites developed in the ager Falernus proper, whilst many of the coastal kiln sites ceased production. One of the largest of these new centres adjoined the small settlement of the pagus Sarclanus, on the via Appia, which may indicate the importance of viticulture to the well-being of the site. Other kilns were sited in open country, possibly within estate boundaries, such as that of the villa of the Gran Celsa where production, centered around the late first or early second century AD, also comprised fine and coarse wares for a local market and domestic use.

The appearance of these inland kilns dating from around Augustan times, which is paralleled in south Etruria and the middle Liri valley, may be seen partly in the context of diminishing provincial demand for Italian wine, although improvements in the road system may have facilitated the exploitation of clays for amphora production at some distance from their maritime outlet.[32] For the same period field survey reveals an increment in the number of Italian amphorae (Dressel 2–4) on rural sites in northern Campania, and the kilns start to produce a series, though never in great quantities, of flat-based Dressel 2–4s intended, perhaps, for overland or riverine transport. However, although the earliest of these new kiln sites clearly produced large quantities of amphorae, by the second century their production seems to have become of negligible importance, giving way to expanded production of cooking and table wares destined solely for a regional market. It has indeed been argued that exportation of Italian wine had all but ceased by the first half of the second century, when the Dressel 2–4 type amphora dropped out of circulation, because no successors could be recognized.[33]

Through field survey, a number of unusual amphorae were located on the kiln sites in the ager Falernus.[34] They are probably to be considered the typological successors of Dressel type 2–4 in Campania. Further north, other mid-imperial Italian amphorae have now been recognized as coming from Forlimpopoli, Spello, Santarcangelo di Romagna and Empoli.[35] Even though the vessels from the Falernian kilns vary in their morphological details, they are generally characterized by plain or slightly ribbed oval-sectioned handles and rounded or oval rims. Some may have been flat-based, though the two complete examples known, from Calvi Risorta (antique Cales) and Gricignano, both in Campania, have stubs.[36] There is little stratigraphical dating as yet. That from Gricignano appears in a fourth century cimiterial context, whilst a very precise date is given for a vessel from San Clemente, Rome. This bears a complex *titulus pictus* on the neck which yields the consular date of AD 216. A suggested origin in Campania is strengthened by the results of petrological thin-section analysis, which indicates a similar range of stone inclusions to the wasters from the ager Falernus kilns.[37] Aside

---

[30] Hesnard, 1980; Panella, 1980.

[31] Pompeii: CIL IV 2553; Britain: Sealey and Davies, 1983, for an amphora of type Dressel 2–4 with *titulus pictus* reading FAL/LOLL, from Colchester. The family, in particular a M Lollius, was involved in the manufacture of aretine pottery (and amphorae of type Dressel 2–4?) at Cales: Morel, 1989, 558. For the question of the Lollii in northern Campania see Cebeillac-Gervasoni, 1982, 85.

[32] I owe this last suggestion to Dr Alastair Small. The only inland kiln sites producing Dressel 1 amphorae known to the writer, at Corigliano and Dugenta, are located near navigable sections of the rivers Garigliano and Volturno respectively. I am grateful to Prof W Johannowsky for information regarding the site at Dugenta.

[33] Amongst the latest amphorae of type Dressel 2–4, one might note the examples found in the excavations of Via Gabina (site 10), near Rome, bearing stamps of the *domini* Claudius Claudianus and P Aelius Pollio (?), attested in the later second or early third century AD (*ex inf* J Freed). Cf PIR 2, 834 and 770. Excavations at the Meta Sudans, in Rome, have yielded some 31% of Italian amphorae in contexts dating to AD 140 *ca* (*ex inf* C Panella). The fundamental paper on Italian amphorae of the second century AD is now Panella, 1989.

[34] Arthur, 1982b; Tchernia, 1986, 280–281.

[35] These are probably just the tip of an iceberg. For Forlimpopoli: Aldini, 1978 and 1981; Spello: C Panella, *pers comm*; Santarcangelo di Romagna: Stoppioni Piccoli, 1983; Empoli: Manacorda, 1984. Examples of the Spello type are known at Ostia and Naples. On the whole question see now Panella, 1989.

[36] The example from Cales was unearthed by J-P Morel and awaits publication. That from Gricignano is published in Bencivenga, 1987, 396 and fig 7.

[37] The San Clemente amphora was first illustrated in Guidobaldi, 1978, fig 24. It is now fully published, with thin-section work by David Williams, in Arthur, 1987.

from this example from Rome, two examples of the type appear at Ostia, in a Bay of Naples fabric, and in a context dating to the first half of the third century, and a sole example was found at Neuss.

Transplantation of Falernian vines is recorded, indicating the success of the strain, though one must accordingly be wary in assigning all amphorae referring to Falernian wine to northern Campania.[38] Recently, scholars have insisted on the continuing exportation of Falernian wine through the empire on the basis of literary references. Thus Galen, for example, noted amphorae containing the wine during the reign of Marcus Aurelius, whilst at the beginning of the fourth century Diocletian's edict of maximum prices listed Falernian wine alongside Picentine, Tiburtine, Sabine, Aminean (from the hinterland of Naples), Saitine and Surrentine vintages.[39] Texts continue to cite the wine until the tenth century, although its original topographic meaning is only found used up until the fifth or sixth centuries in the works of Sidonius Apollinaris, Avitus and Venatius Fortunatus. From the time of Gregory of Tours, writing in the later sixth century, the title Falernian appears to have lost its topographic significance, whilst remaining a generic denomination for wine of quality.[40]

All in all, the available information still appears to support a drastic reduction in Italy's wine exportation, which Domitian may have attempted to check with an edict in AD 92 prohibiting the cash-cropping of the vine in the provinces. It was never actually enforced.[41] In northern Campania there is no indication of an ever-increasing importation of provincial and particularly Gallic wines, from the first century, as occurred at Ostia and Rome, and thus it may be suggested that local self-sufficiency was maintained even after the collapse in Campanian

export markets.[42] Furthermore, it may be suggested that the continuing small-scale exportation of wine postulated for northern Campania, on the the basis of the relative costs in Diocletian's price edict where several Italian wines of distinction cost 3.75 times as much as 'vini rustici', was maintained by the world-wide reputation that Falernum had earned for itself. The apparent decline in production of northern Campania's principal crop (at least in apparent importance) would have brought about one or both of two conditions, the spread of alternative crops or the decline in land under cultivation. There is little evidence for either, and the fact that one of the Francolise sites expanded its oil producing capacities around the mid first century AD tells us no more than that.[43] Much later, in AD 328, the texts yield evidence of a toll on Campania of 38.000 modii of grain a year to Rome, sufficient for some 630 people. This was abolished under Gratian and followed by tax-relief under Honorius, on account of an apparent 528.402 iugera of 'agri deserti'.[44] We do not know where the bulk of Campanian grain came from (probably the fields between Capua and the sea), nor whether there was an effective increment in its production during the empire. So much for the concrete evidence for crop diversification after the decline of the wine 'industry'.

Documentation for abandoned land is a little more satisfactory. Aside from the late sources, archaeology reveals a diminution in inhabited sites (supra). We might take this as concentration of land in fewer hands, which would have made available to fewer people a greater choice in exploitable land, greater flexibility in crop diversification, and a tendency to disregard marginal areas. There must have been little motivation to continue extensive exploitation of the hillsides or wetter areas, drained

[38] Pliny NH XIV, 38. The inscription that records P Magnius Q.f. Rufus Magonianus as procurator in charge of transferring and establishing the growth of Falernian wine in Baetica during the second century must now be disregarded, because of correction of a mistaken reading of the text: CIL II 2029. Cf Thouvenot, 1940, 246 and note 3; Pflaum, 1960, 235–236.

[39] Tchernia, 1980 and 1986; Panella, 1980; Kuhn, 1965, XIV, 24–26; Lauffer, 1971, 102–103; edict 2, 1–7.

[40] Greg. Hist. Franc. III, 19; Sid. Ep. II, 13, and IX, 13; Sid. Carm. 15; Avit. Carm. III, 227; Ven. Fort. Carm. III, xiii, 4; V, i, 3, and VII, v, 11. See Brouette, 1949.

[41] Stat. Silv. IV, iii, 11–12. This is a much debated passage. Cf Schnur, 1959, 797. Duncan-Jones, 1980, 77, states that the edict was apparently inspired by a short-term crisis, and that exemption was soon obtained: Philostratus VS 521; VA 6.42. Even the emperor, personally, would have had much to lose with a slump in the market for Italian wine. It may be noted that the price of wine in Italy seems already to have dropped under Nero – Colum. RR III, iii, 10.

[42] For Ostia see Carandini and Panella, 1973, 659ff. The thesis of a more intensive exploitation of Rome's hinterland under the empire, as regards vine-cropping, is now to be added to the discussion: see Purcell, 1985, and now Tchernia, 1986; though I would disagree with Purcell's view of Italian economic well-being which, to my mind, is contradicted by the material evidence. Early to mid imperial Rome-area amphorae are now coming to light: Dressel 2–4s from via Gabina site 10 (supra); 'Aegean-looking' amphorae, in local fabrics, from Fossa della Crescenza (Arthur, 1983), ecc. Panella, 1989, also applies here.

[43] Cotton, 1979, 55–56. Part of the residential area of the complex was sacrificed in period III, from about the mid first century AD, to house a larger press and two separating vats. The same period, however, saw to the extension of the villa terrace with a new plastered floor, possibly as a measure to increase the area devoted to the threshing of grain.

[44] AD 328: Exp Tot Mundi 54; Ruggini, 1961, 152. For AD 395: Cod. Theod. XI, xxviii, 2; Ruggini, op cit, 151, note 423.

during the republic, after Rome and the overseas markets no longer requested or required enormous quantities of Campanian produce, and it may be indicative that the earliest sites abandoned in northern Campania, from the end of the first century BC, lay in the highest or more inaccessible areas. Such, for instance, may be the case of the area around S Croce, in the centre of the Massico range, where no Roman material has been identified as dating after Augustan times. Though this does not immediately presuppose desertion of an area in terms of land use, the abandonment of settlement indicates at the very least a switch away from intensive farming in favour of other regimes such as that of a pastoral economy which, still surviving on a minor scale today, may explain the absence of regenerated woodland and the prevalence of grass, macchia, scrub and wild olives. Much marginal land around the Massico, where terraces and sites are still visibly well-preserved, was never re-occupied and lies beneath the *macchia mediterranea* (pls XIV and XV).

This, however, does not necessarily indicate that mid to later Roman Campania's agricultural yield was wanting as far as regards local needs. Even if it is accepted that there was an increment in the area of unworkable marshland, a steady decline in the number of farm sites occupied and amount of land worked, this is to be balanced against a decline in the number of mouths to be fed and the possible absorption of at least part of a once-exported surplus.

To the scanty evidence so far examined we may add a further hypothetical element. Various scholars would now link the distribution of African Red Slip pottery, produced in the area of modern Tunisia, with the distribution of the *annona* and the commerce in North African grain and olive oil.[45] Grain, olive oil and makeweight cargoes of African Red Slip ware almost certainly travelled together on the same ships though, on arrival at the principal consumer centres in Italy and elsewhere, probably parted company, some goods having already been commissioned and others being free to go onto the open market. Nonetheless, an area well supplied with African Red Slip ware probably depended on a consumer centre to which African grain and oil had been directed. Areas with low quantities of African Red Slip ware may, by extension, have been either areas which were not considered strategically important enough to be furnished with African grain and oil on any regular basis, or areas which were able to survive quite adequately on alternative sources, whether imported or local. I would warrant that Northern Campania fell into the latter cate-

gory, relying on local sources of grain and oil, on the basis not only of the assessed rate of importation of African Red Slip ware, ably imitated by local kilns, but also on the low quantity of late African amphorae found in the region.

The continuing soundness of local productivity may perhaps, in part, be gauged by the number of early and mid imperial functionaries attested in the region (*supra*), as well as high tax demands into the early fourth century, such as the 38.000 modii of grain which Campania, as *cellarium Regnanti Romae*, was made to contribute to the *annona* in AD 328. This was only eventually dropped under Gratian and followed by further tax-relief in AD 395 under Honorius, on account of the apparent 528.402 *iugera* of *agri deserti*.[46] The following year, according to Symmachus, large Campanian landowners needed to import grain on the occasion of a famine.[47] However, the fluctuating ratio of supply and demand will never be quantifiable, and the general well-being of Campania's yield through time will probably remain debatable.[48]

Despite the gradual liberation of land during the course of the empire, there seems little indication of the reappearance of small-holders or peasant farmers in the form of dispersed small farms, although tenant farmers may well have played a significant role on the large estates. It is at this stage that the colonnate system may have begun to make an appearance. The muscle of the large landowners with their significant surplus yields cannot have left much space for the independent small farmer to market his produce. His eventual submission to a patron/*dominus* as a tenant farmer would have provided the best guarantee for his produce in the increasingly difficult economic climate of the later empire.

What effect was all this to have on the urban communities? At the beginning of this chapter, evidence was presented to illustrate an apparent well-being under the early empire, when exportation of surplus products was still balanced by cash-returns leading to speculation and investment in building projects. By the later second century much of this had ceased and our material evidence for substantial improvements in urban development disappears. On the one hand, this may indicate the achievement of an internal stability as regards production/consumption ratios and alternative forms of investment whilst, on the other, it may be suspected that a drastic decline in the quantity of exportable surplus for the open market led eventually to economic involution. This will be explored further in the next chapter.

---

[45] See most recently the important study by Fentress and Perkins, 1988.

[46] AD 328: *Exp Tot Mundi* 54; Ruggini, 1961, 152. For AD 395: Cod. Theod. XI, xxviii, 2; Ruggino, op. cit., 151, note 423.

[47] Symm. *Ep.* IV, 5; Proc. *de Bell. Goth.* II, 4; Llewellyn, 1970, 66–67.

[48] Cf Hannestad, 1962.

Chapter Seven

The End of an Age

By the third century the number of rural sites found to be occupied in the sample area had dwindled to 80, of which 11 were substantial villa sites. About a century later some 27 rural sites were still occupied, 9 of which had been substantial villas. It seems impossible to know what form of activity was conducted at these sites without very careful excavation, although no villa had been built anew; all were late republican foundations. For the sixth century, only four rural settlements have yielded traces of occupation: two large late republican villas (sites M59 and S28), one farm that appears to have been constructed in mid imperial times (site S10) and a possible church (site M151). The inexorable decline suggests, nonetheless, that substantial changes were taking place in the function of sites that survived into the later empire.

Few sites appear as convincing centres of *latifundia*, insofar as none seems to have grown in size through time and, indeed, the late pottery recovered through survey never appears to outnumber the early imperial finds. Furthermore, none has the appearance of the wealthy complexes such as those unearthed in Sicily, at Piazza Armerina, Patti Marina and elsewhere, or even the less sumptuous farms such as S Giovanni a Ruoti, S Vincenzo al Volturno or Quota S Francesco, near Locri.[1] If the farm at Posto is any guide, then late activity of a stable nature may be summed-up archaeologically by modest architectural adjustments, a handful of burials pertaining, perhaps, to a small family group, and enough pottery dating between the fourth and sixth centuries as to indicate continuous occupation based presumably on agricultural pursuits.[2] It seems hard to believe that the farm produced anything like the surplus indicated for earlier times.

In northern Campania there are no indications of the occupation of new sites, unlike the *agri Faliscus et Veientanus*, although the reoccupation of some sites temporarily abandoned during the early or mid-empire is, as yet, an undemonstrable possibility.[3]

As far as concerns the urban sites, municipal activity is rarely attested through textual or epigraphic evidence. Municipal and civic benefactions, building programmes and dedications are con-spicuous by their absence, which implies re-direction of financial interests. Indeed, evidence concurs to suggest greatly reduced populations inhabiting the centres in late antiquity (*infra*).

There is also little evidence to indicate that the countryside supported a large population in the fifth and sixth centuries though, in relation to other rural areas, it may still have sustained a significant, though declining, population. Beloch had estimated some 4 million people in Italy around AD 700, with the south possessing no more than 750.000–800.000 head. On accepting these figures, Galasso suggested that they may be broken down into some 150.000–160.000 families which, divided into the present area of 70.000^2 km for southern Italy, would give a mean average of 1 family per km^2.[4] When the nucleated settlements are taken into account to absorb their due quota, the rural density figure would drop even more. Similar figures have been estimated globally for sixth century England (2 inhabitants per km^2), Germany (2.2) and Gaul (5.5).[5] It is clear that only the last approaches Galasso's estimate, and one may well question whether the monastic revival led indirectly to larger population figures for France than southern Italy in the period subsequent to the seventh century nadir. It may also be suggested that in the seventh century very few people cared to live scattered in the open country. The surviving 'urban' nuclei, providing relative security, were agro-towns *par excellence*, which becomes immediately clear on reading Erchempert's tale of the sack of Capua in 884, when the entire populace, including the municipal aristocracy, had left the walls to harvest the vineyards.[6] This, in turn, may be corroborative evidence for low population figures, the settlement nuclei being incapable of sustaining a significant non-agrarian social group. Admittedly the figures for the fifth to the seventh century are unlikely to have remained constant, it is the latter century that approaches the lowest settlement density and possibly the lowest population figures for the whole period.

The factors leading to a reversion of northern lowland Campania back to the land of the *mazzonari*, the robust but unhealthy marsh-dwellers, are

---

[1] On the late Sicilian villas see Wilson, 1981, 256, and the articles in *Opus* II, 2, 1983.

[2] Cotton, 1979.

[3] Such has been suggested for Posto: Cotton, 1979, 56. See Potter, 1975, 224, for the new sites under the late empire in south Etruria.

[4] Galasso, 1982, 16–18. Lizier, 1907, 71, proposed a figure of 10 inhabitants per square kilometre.

[5] Duby, 1975, 16.

[6] Erchempert, chap 56. It is clear that controlled excavation and publication of these sites is urgently required.

various and complex.[7] Though the land remained essentially fertile throughout historic times, large coastal tracts steadily deteriorated, probably from about the mid first millennium AD and hand in hand with the beginning of a cooler and wetter phase in Mediterranean climate, with rising lake levels, increased stream activity and concomitant erosion and alluviation.[8] This phase led to Vita-Finzi's virtual Mediterranean-wide 'Younger Fill' which, he argues, was a result of climatic deterioration.[9] The '70's and '80's have seen the development of an opposing theory explaining its genesis through the relaxation or desertion of a Classical, 'conservationist', agricultural system, where 'the farmer may withdraw to more fertile fields, and the terraces and slopes are yielded up to the shepherd and his flock. The protective vegetation (on the hills) is then damaged by grazing, walls are trampled, and brush is cut. Runoff excavates gullies along animal trails, the flow of rainwater becomes concentrated, and the precious soil of the terraces washes away to cover the bottom lands in the valley with stream deposits'.[10] The issue is far from resolved, though the effects of an ascertained increase in soil erosion and deposition are becoming apparent.

Sometime during the early middle ages traffic appears to have returned to the proposed original course of the via Appia passing Suessa Aurunca, possibly at the time when Forum Claudii re-asserted itself, and this might be viewed as a result of enroaching marshes alongside the coastal route and the abandonment of maritime towns.[11] Such phenomena were by no means unique to Campania. Uggeri has demonstrated the similar re-routing of traffic from a coastal road to a road some three kilometers inland, bypassing the defunct centre of Egnazia in Puglia, around the seventh century, and further examples could be cited.[12]

Already by the sixth century the rather similar, though more extensive, areas of the Pomptine marshes were in need of care as 'the sea-like swamp, accustomed to impunity through long license, rushes in and spoils all the surrounding lands'.[13] As a stimulus to private drainage operations, given the apparent difficulty of public intervention, Theoderic offered private ownership of all regenerated parcels of land. The same possibly applied to the swamped soil in Campania.

A further factor in the abandonment of rural areas was probably the insecurity brought about by repeated barbarian raids. One of the earliest threats was posed by the Vandals, and various towns circling Campania, such as Naples and probably Terracina, were re-walled. Their occupation of North Africa in AD 429, under Gaiseric, and the curtailment of Rome's traditional annona from *Africa Proconsularis* may have had a double-edged effect. Whilst Campania's productivity ratio may have been forcefully stimulated to meet demands, the additional burden would have been deleterious, requiring severer taxation.[14] Though Rome may not have suffered the great loss in African grain, which Ruggini suggests, given that at least amphora-borne commodities continued to be imported in quantity, a turn to alternative sources of supply, such as Cisalpine Gaul and Sicily, would have avoided an undesirable exportation of cash to the Vandals.[15]

Archaeological evidence now demonstrates that, whatever the case, commercial contact between the Vandals and Rome remained open, to the immediate benefit of the former and long-term deficit of the latter.[16] Even northern Campania possessed its token share of Vandal imports: late African Red slip table ware, a few possible late fifth or early sixth century amphorae and three coins from the bed of the Garigliano at Minturnae.[17] However, the low number of such imports so far recognized may, in

[7]   Greco, 1927, I, 5.
[8]   Lamb, 1977, 270.
[9]   Vita-Finzi, 1969.
[10] van Andel and Runnels, 1987, chap 8. Excavations by Paolo Peduto at Rota, in the valley below Mercato San Severino, have revealed well over a metre of alluvium, above late antique levels, cut by the foundations of an early medieval church. *Ex inf* P Peduto, and Peduto, 1988, 160.
[11] *Supra*. An idea of the re-routing of the Appia may be obtained from the itineraries. The *Tabula Peutingeriana*, the Antonine Itinerary and the *Itinerarium Burdigalense* all give coastal Sinuessa as a stop between Minturnae and Capua. Not so the Ravenna Cosmography and the *Guidonis Geographica*, which both omit Sinuessa and replace the stop with Suesaruntia and Suessa Irunca respectively. The two toponyms, clearly deriving from Suessa Aurunca, indicate a re-routing prior to the editions of the *RC* and *GC*, presumably sometime in the sixth century. See Schnetz, 1940, and Richmond and Crawford, 1949, for the chronology of the itineraries.
[12] Uggeri, 1978, 125.

[13] Cass. *Var.* II, xxxii (translated by Hodgkin, 1886, 188). Cf also the *Variae* II, xxxiii and xxi.
[14] Cf De Robertis, 1948; Hannestad, 1962.
[15] Ruggini, 1964, 271.
[16] Cf Hodges and Whitehouse, 1983, 26–28.
[17] For the coins see Frier and Parker, 1970, 106, and Metcalf, 1974, 49, whilst the amphorae and African Red Slip will be presented by the writer.

contrast to areas like Naples, reflect marginality, continued self-sufficiency or progressive agrarian decline with little production of exchangeable surplus.

One of the problems in assessing the case is the low number of rural sites actually known. Solely 27 rural sites appear to have been frequented until the fifth century, or a little later, and only five are securely dated from the mid fifth to the sixth century, four from the area of intensive survey. Therefore, they are not good indicators of what was actually imported. The two Francolise villas, however, add flesh to the picture. Posto, in particular, has a good range of late pottery which, apart from dating occupation to the fifth and sixth centuries, indicates that African Red Slip ware is only a minor component of the fine ware assemblage and that, furthermore, only one amphora is a Vandal period import.[18]

The local pottery arriving at Posto and San Rocco was produced at a series of kilns distributed within the *ager Falernus*, supplying rural needs, as well as producing amphorae for export up until, at least, the third century. Imitation of African Red Slip wares started in the second century, with form Hayes 8, and continued until the fifth century or later with form Hayes 61. None of the kilns can be proved to have continued to function after the fifth century and the ceramic production that remained in the area seems to have become increasingly fractioned, as may be evinced by the variety of fabrics and treatments involved in post-fifth/sixth century pottery. Their collapse seems not to be attributable to a cessation in demand but, perhaps, to the rising costs in maintaining professional workshops in activity. As population levels dropped and intensive agriculture declined, the quantity of surplus production presumably decreased and consequently became ever more valued as an exchange commodity. Surplus would therefore be used in exchange for cash or prime necessities, whilst pottery could be produced by the household, as indeed later cooking wares seem to have been. Only the more organized social groups (monastic, urban or large rural properties) could afford to support a workforce devoted to non-agricultural pursuits, either directly or indirectly.[19]

Thus, this evident displacement and dispersal may be indicative of a disaggregation in the production of agricultural surplus and fractioning and abandonment of land holdings, as opposed to agglomeration. As will be shown below, some large properties continued to exist, though little may be said concerning their scale of productivity and whether they were exploited through a single bailiff, or let out to various tenants. In any case, even if certain private or ecclesiastical estates yielded a surplus, the eventual profits from its exchange need not have returned to the area but may, instead, have been directed to the seats of landowners or the centres of Church administration.

It is worth examining the rural sites in a little more detail. One villa, on Mt. Finnochiaro, overlooking the *ager Falernus* from over 250m asl, has an early medieval church inserted in a corner of the *basis villae*. The church was constructed largely of re-used stones from the site, including the base for the *arbores* of a press.[20] Further classical sites have yielded late inhumation burials, such as those at Corigliano, at Francolise and at a rural bath-building near Teano. The phenomenon is common both to Italy and France, but is unlikely to have taken place in order to leave unoccupied agriculturally exploitable land, as has been suggested.[21]

It may have been around this time that the south Italian *civiltà rupestre* was in embryonic form. Though late Roman and early medieval troglodytes are rarely attested, their remains have been found by prehistorians with other goals in view. Gregory the Great informs us that the hermit Martin lived in a small cave on the Massico, which has been plausibly identified with a site over 500m asl (*infra*). In about the twelfth century it was converted into a painted chapel. The famous grotto of Tiberius at Sperlonga, long after it had lost its original function, was frequented by people who left behind much domestic rubbish, including late African Red Slip. The excavation of a prehistoric cave in the Marche yielded a significant quantity of African Red Slip, amphorae, a late Roman lamp and coarse ware.[22] The list could be greatly extended, but the trend is obvious even though it never seems to have been purposefully examined in any part of the peninsula.

[18] Cotton, 1979, fig 41, no 4, wrongly identified as a Dressel form 1, probably Keay form LXII.

[19] Recent excavations have shown that a fair quantity of pottery circulating in Naples during the second half of the first millenium AD was produced by full-time or part-time professional potters. Furthermore, a kiln site producing 'broad-line' painted jugs, datable to the sixth or seventh centuries AD, seems to have been active near the amphitheatre at Cuma, one of the few nucleated sites that seems still to have been relatively well-populated at the time in the Bay of Naples. Another contemporary kiln site, with similar products, was active at S Restituta, Ischia.

[20] The *Rationes Decimarum* of the years 1308 to 1310 for Sessa refer to an *ecclesia S Marie ad Castellone*, which was almost certainly a church making use of the structure of a Roman villa: Inguanez, 1942, 103, no 1253.

[21] Small, 1979, 210–212. The Corigliano villa burials are known through the toponym *Campo dei Morti* and the evidence of human bones having been unearthed by the landowner. For Posto, Francolise, see Cotton, 1979, 59–61; for Teano, Gabrici, 1908, 415. A group of such burials found at the Roman villa of Settefinestre in Tuscany indicates a hard-working population with clear signs of malnutrition: Mallegni and Fornaciari, 1985.

[22] For the three caves see respectively De Stasio, 1974, 23; Iacopi, 1963, 157; Radmilli, 1953, 122 and pl I.

Hermitage-caves are attested in Campania from the fifth century, well before the arrival of St Martin, as the dwellings of such figures as St Menna and St Renato.[23] It is quite clear at this point that such small settlements or dwellings were only going to be recorded in the texts if they belonged to religious hermits and presumably, particularly, if the hermits came from prominent families. Any number of cave-dwellings could have evaded documentation in the ecclesiastical or monastic archives from which the bulk of our information derives. At any rate, it may be doubted that there was ever a period when caves were not used as dwellings in southern Italy or Sicily, and indeed they may occasionally be found so used today.[24] In the final analysis, what is important is their relative incidence of use at various periods.

Merely three rural sites have been found which possess both textual and archaeological evidence indicating activity from, at least, the later eighth century. They are the monastic properties of San Martino, Santa Croce and Santa Maria a Fauciano, all dependent on the Benedictine centre of S Vincenzo al Volturno.[25] S Vincenzo's main sphere of influence was to the south of the Garigliano, with land to the north often falling under that of Monte-cassino. It is not known at what dates the three sites were first occupied. The small monastery of S Martino may have developed from an early congregation of acolytes who had grouped around Martin the Holy Man, a contemporary of Pope Pelasgius II (AD 578–590), who sought solitude in the cave on the Massico. In the early eighth century the Duke of Benevento, Romuald II, conceded possession of Mt Marsico (sic) to the monastery of St Martin under the Abbot Albinus.[26]

All three sites appear to be identifiable on the ground. That of S. Martino lies at 556m asl, on a natural platform of relatively difficult access. The substantial remains of bonded limestone walling betray a late date, possibly around the eleventh or twelfth centuries AD, for the monastery above the cave.

S Croce is also of tedious access, lying in a valley within the Massico range and approachable along the narrow defile cut by the Canale Grande. The valley had been exploited during the late republic and Augustan times when it was linked to Sinuessa and the coast by a paved road. No Roman pottery later than the first century AD has been found in the

valley which, whilst suggesting possible cessation of habitation at that time, does not necessarily indicate lapse of land-use. It is to be noted that the area, as now, was more suited to the cultivation of olives and grazing of sheep than the working of fields. The remains in the valley appear particularly confused because of vegetational cover which does not permit easy dating of the structures. One particular building, with an apsidal form visible beneath the grass, may be a church (Fig 20; pl XVIII). Standing remains consist of a substantial terrace wall formed of drystone polygonal limestone blocks of Lugli's type IV, the remains of a rough grey and white mosaic floor, a number of cippolino marble column drums and fragments of possible pentelic and Aegean marble revetment. An early imperial marble capital was recovered from the site in the past. The small amount of pottery found, particularly in the spoil-heaps of clandestine excavators, suggests little if any regular habitation, whilst the obvious use of costly building materials, even if spolia, emphasizes its singular nature. As some of the pottery is early medieval in date (perhaps Xth–XIth century), it seems plausible that the remains represent a church constructed on a republican farm terrace, and re-using marbles looted from Sinuessa.

The last site, in the area now known as S Maria Bocca D'Oro, above Falciano, seems to be the property mentioned in the Chronicon Vulturnense.[27] It is attested in 874 when the entire curtis of a Capuan landowner Galcisius, sited near the church of S Maria a Fauciano, was donated to S Vincenzo for reasons not specified. It is located on the side of a southward-facing slope at about 130m asl and little below a Roman villa which, according to surface finds, was already abandoned. All that is now visible of the early medieval site is part of an apse constructed of mortared grey tuff and irregular limestone blocks with sparse tile fragments, lying in a vineyard. Numerous burials have been found in the past by locals who claim that they were generally devoid of grave-goods, save the discovery of a simple bronze earring. However, the site is strewn with pottery and one or two classical marble fragments including a column base.

The presence of these three monastic properties in the area from, at least, the later eighth century, need in no way imply continuity of agricultural exploitation on any significant scale from late antiquity, particularly in view of the fact that the monastic

[23] Procaccini, 1883; Kalby, 1975, 155.

[24] Cf Arch. Med. VII, 1980, and in particular Francovich, Gelichi and Parenti, 1980, passim; Uggeri, 1974.

[25] Del Treppo, 1955.

[26] See De Stasio, 1974, for a general narrative of the life of St Martin and the later traditions. The concession of Mt Massico to the monastery is documented by the Chron. Vult. III, 127.

[27] Federici, 1925, I, 340–341.

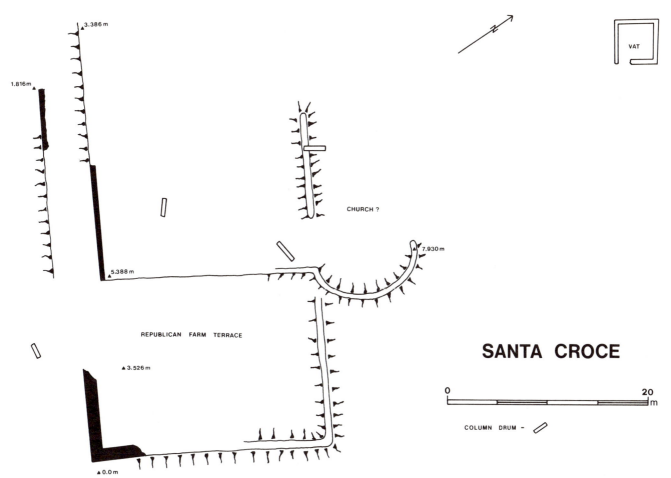

VAT

CHURCH ?

REPUBLICAN FARM TERRACE

SANTA CROCE

0 20
m

COLUMN DRUM - ▱

Fig 20   Plan of part of the Benedictine monastic complex at S Croce (site M11)

orders often provided ideal colonists of *agri deserti* and marginal land where they could obtain their required solitude.[28] S Martino in particular, but also S Croce, were sited in secluded areas of restricted economic potential (pl XIX). Both sites were easily defensible. The site of S Maria a Fauciano, however, was more exposed, lying in the heartland of the old Falernian vineyards. There is no direct evidence that the monastery of S Vincenzo used the property to establish a new satellite monastery though, as the donation comprised vineyards, pastures, forests and marshes, it is most likely that it was fruitfully exploited. For the time being, this is as far as the available evidence will take us, and highlights the need for further work, particularly in the form of excavation.

Unsupported textual evidence for non-monastic properties is equally rare though, from the time of Constantine, an ever-increasing number of lands passed to the Church and, unlike the small fragmented estates more typical of the north, appear to have been organized in large economic units or *massae* worked by peasants.[29] Some of these were imperial gifts, as we learn from the *Liber Pontificalis*, our principal source of information. One such was the *possessio Antonianam* in the territory of Casinum which must have passed into imperial hands under the Antonines and is recorded as Church property under Pope Damasus in the mid fourth century AD.[30] The *Liber* lists four or five ecclesiastical properties from the pontificate of Silvester (AD 314–335) in the Gargliano basin. The sole estate

[28] Cf Delano-Smith, 1979, 109.

[29] Brown, 1984, 198.
[30] Duchesne, 1886, I, 213.

registered in the territory of Minturnae is the *massa Statiliana*.[31] The *possessio Leonis* was probably also located in the territory of the town, but need not be identified with the Leopolis attested in later sources. Little may be said concerning the *possessio in territorio Suessano Gauronica* or *massa Bauronica* and the *possessio Paternum, territurio Suessano*, although both of these presumably lay to the south of the river.[32] Peter the Deacon, in the first half of the twelfth century, also records a *curtem de Lauriana* (mod. Lauro) in the territory of Sessa Aurunca, which may have derived from a certain Laurianus.[33]

The *Liber Pontificalis* further lists a *possessio ad Centum, territurio Capuano*, which Duchesne would not accept in the Garigliano basin on the basis of its textual assignation to Capua.[34] If its name refers to the 100th milestone of the Appia it would fall between Sessa Aurunca and Minturnae. Considering the homogeneity of the list in that particular section of the *Liber Pontificalis*, otherwise referring exclusively to properties between Gaeta and Sessa Aurunca, its location in the basin is plausible and its assignation to Capua possibly an error in transcription. The holding may perhaps be identified with the medieval and modern Centora, which lies within the Garigliano basin and has been tentatively linked with the 100th milestone by various scholars.[35]

Finally, a *massa Gargiliana, territurio Suessano*, is also listed under Pope Silvester. Duchesne, who equated it with the present hamlet of Corigliano, believed that it was later absorbed by the *patrimonium Traiectanum*.[36]

Under the pontificate of Xystus (432–440), the *Liber Pontificalis* lists a *possessio Scauriana, territurio Gazitano* which is presumably to be equated with the present-day area around Scauri, near Minturnae. A further property, the *massa Veneria*, in the territory of Minturnae, seems to have been restored to the abbot Stephen, of the monastery of St Mark, by Pope Benedict in AD 574–578.[37]

On the whole, the references seem to indicate the existence of a significant quantity of ecclesiastical possessions in northern Campania from the reign of Constantine until, at least, the period of the Lombard invasions. Though we have little means of defining the interrelationship of these lands and what agrarian systems they sustained, their mere documentation endorses their importance within the sphere of the Church's own closed economy. Whittaker has recently emphasized their importance as the 'instrument by which (the Church) maintained its army of officials and by which it fed the poor'.[38] Moreover, the revenues, either collected in kind or as monetary taxes from leased land, may have been used on the open market in exchange for goods produced elsewhere. On the physical side, we know little of their size, of their administrative nodes and whether their labour-force was concentrated in large villas/estate villages or in more dispersed forms of settlement, as in south Etruria.[39] The archaeological problem is greatly frustrated by the lack of characterizing elements amongst early medieval ceramics from Campania between the sixth and twelfth centuries AD.[40] In short, we do not yet know what to look for. However, I believe it would be wrong to imagine these properties, by the sixth century, as anything more than pitiful in respect to earlier Roman estates.

In the fourth and fifth centuries most, if not all, of the Roman urban foundations of late republican Campania still existed nominally. By the seventh century a significant number had all but disappeared. By the late ninth century a new set of towns was coming to the fore.

Minturnae provides a well-documented example of the decline and eventual abandonment of a town which, during the first centuries BC/AD, was particularly flourishing. Few inscriptions are known from the site from the fourth century, but include two tetrarchic statue-bases, whilst an interesting bronze *tabula patronatus*, recording a certain Flavius Theodorus, might be attributed to one of the consuls of the same name, for the years 505 and 525, or Flavius Theodorus Pietrus Demosthenes, praetorian prefect in 521 and 525.[41] The tabula appears to have been fixed on display in one of the arcades supporting the *summa cavea* of the theatre.

---

[31] The name is uncommon and appears only once in Italy, at Rome, in the person of *P Aelius Statilianus eq. pub.*, a second century imperial freedman – CIL VI 1589; Kajanto, 1965, 156. For the meaning of *massa* as 'an estate with dwelling-house' or demesne see Souter, 1949, 244. For *possessio*, which does not have to be equated with legal ownership, see Hardy, 1912, 36.

[32] Duchesne, 1886, 174 and 186.

[33] De Santis, 1963, 402.

[34] Duchesne, 1886, 186.

[35] Giarizzo, 1965, 26, note 22; De Santis, 1938, 257.

[36] Duchesne, 1886, I, 184 and III, 77.

[37] Kehr, 1935, 98.

[38] Whittaker, 1983, 167–169; cf also Jones, 1960.

[39] Cf Potter, 1975 and 1979.

[40] The recent series of excavations in Naples and Salerno is helping to sort out the problem, though abraded sherds from surface survey are often totally unrecognizable. It is possible that after the sixth century much of the rural populace subsisted mainly with utensils of organic materials. Naples and large monastic centres were, however, well supplied with competently manufactured ceramics. Cf for example Arthur and Whitehouse, 1982.

[41] Pani, 1987; Johnson, 1936, 491; Cecchelli, 1951, disagrees with Johnson's suggested attributions on the basis of the supposed palaeographical criteria dating the inscription to the late fourth or early fifth century AD. He also claims that the piece is of too crude a workmanship for it commemorate persons of such stature as a consul or praetorian prefect, though this is nonsense.

Concerning the numismatic evidence, 'the fourth and fifth centuries constitute the peak of the Roman series' from the Garigliano. Sixth-century coins were rare, but comprised one example for each of Athalric (526–534), Justinian I (538–544) and Justin II (565–578).[42]

In AD 546, during the Byzantine reconquest, Totila's Goths took Rome and banished the senators and their families to Minturnae. They were released by a Byzantine raiding party later in the same year. It is hard to know how much to read in the event. The number of senators in Rome at the time was probably small, but would have provided a substantial aggregate of people when sent with their families to a country-town such as Minturnae.[43] It is doubtful whether much, if any, new accommodation was built for them, and we might suppose that a substantial amount of the town had already been deserted thus making their lodging particularly easy. The only late building identified in the town is apparently a small basilica in the forum, about which little has been written.[44]

One of the final acts at Minturnae is preserved in a letter of Gregory the Great (590–604). In AD 590 the town, dependant on Byzantine Rome, seems to all intents and purposes to have been abandoned and the Pope consequently conceded its church to Bacauda, bishop of Formia which, in turn, in AD 681 lost its principal citizens and bishop, Adeodatus, through their transference to the promontory of Gaeta further north.[45] It may be no coincidence that in the same year, AD 590, Beneventum was lost to the Lombard king Autharic who made it a duchy, the north-western frontier of which, with the Byzantine Papal State of Rome, appears to have been the river Garigliano. It may also have been around this time that a number of burials were inserted into the area of Minturnae's theatre, leaving eloquent testimony to the town's decay, whilst the port reverted to a stagnant marsh and eventually silted up

completely enough so as to provide the agricultural land which is in use today.[46]

No later evidence for the town exists, whilst just a century later Gaeta (the *civitatis Kaietani*) appears as the principal port and town in southern Lazio and probably the major Byzantine military post or *castrum* safeguarding Rome's southern flank.[47] It is nonetheless quite possible that an extremely reduced population, probably constituting a military garrison, remained at the site, fortifying the amphitheatre. The monument lies in an area today known as *contrada Virilasci* or *Virilassi*, derived from the Lombard term *borlasi* (citadel or fortress), found applied to other Italian amphitheatres, including that at Capua in the form Berelais.

However, with Lando's creation of Lombard gastaldates in northern Campania, in AD 879, including one at Sessa Aurunca, and Pandonolf's intention of claiming Caietam, in 881, which had been promised to him by Pope John VIII, Docibilis I, Duke of Gaeta, in turn, established a garrison of Saracen mercenaries on *Mons Garelianus*.[48] By this time, ancient Minturnae can have been no more than a quarry for the developing centre of *castrum* or *civitas Leopolis*, probably founded by Pope Leo III, in the years 795–816, to safeguard the *patrimonium Traiectanum*, first from the Lombards and then also from the separatist politics of the Duchy of Gaieta. Present-day Minturno lies on the site of Traietto (medieval *Traiectum*), a defensible hill about 140m asl, which in turn, probably covers *Castrum Leopolis*.[49] The town possesses a number of tenth century Romanesque architectural elements and re-used classical pieces.[50]

Less evidence is available for the fate of late urban settlement in the land to the south of the Garigliano which, from 590, formed part of the Lombard Duchy of Beneventum and, from 840, part of the County of Capua. Archaeological research has not confirmed activity at Sinuessa after *c* AD 500. Civic

[42] Frier and Parker, 1970, 106.
[43] Llewellyn, 1970, 72ff; Bury, 1923, 20–21.
[44] De Spagnolis, 1981, 59.
[45] Ewald and Hartmann, 1891, 10; Greg. *Ep.* I, 8; Kehr, 1935, 99. The last recorded bishop of Minturnae, Rusticus, had attended the synod of St. Peter's in Rome in AD 499: Cass. *Acta Syn.*

[46] Johnson, 1935, 14.
[47] Duchesne, 1886, 1, 391; *Cod. Dipl. Caiet.* 24; Galasso, 1975, 71 and note 8.
[48] Aurigemma and De Santis, 1955, 51. *Mons Garelianus* is probably to be identified with the coastal knoll of Monte D'Argento, near Scauri; cf. Fedele, 1899. Archaeological work has now begun on the site, though traces of the Saracen colony have still to come to light. For this, and further references, see Torre, 1988. On the complex events leading to the creation of *Mons Garelianus* see now Rossillo, 1985.
[49] It is possible that the name was altered when the *patrimonium Traiectanum* was absorbed by the independent Duchy of Gaeta, often in conflict with papal interests.
[50] *Cod. Dipl. Caiet.*, 5; Gay, 1904, 503; Nissen, 1902, II, 663; De Spagnolis, 1981, 19 and 63–64.

institutions had continued to function into the fourth century, as L Mamilianus Crispus was *curator civitatis Sinuessanae* at the beginning of the century.[51] The latest case of attested private patronage at the town is documented by a group of tiles stamped with the Latin cross and the name of Viria Marcella. She came from a senatorial family and may have been a fourth century proprietor in the area. Whether the tiles indicate the presence of a new construction or simply restoration of a pre-existing building remains unknown.[52] It is likely, given the evidence from a number of rural sites, that occupation on a reduced scale may have continued until definitive desertion around the sixth or seventh century. The fact that the road from Minturnae to Suessa Aurunca, which still survives on a slightly altered route, outlived that to Sinuessa may indicate the longer surviving importance of the northernmost of the two coastal towns which, prior to the Lombard political imposition on the area south of the Garigliano, may have functioned as principal maritime outlet. Perhaps Sinuessa, in a richer agricultural zone, was one of the towns affected by heavy taxation in kind, which is attested for late Roman Campania. However, as the archaeological evidence is poor even for mid imperial times, it is possible that natural factors in the decay of the town are to be sought, which may include eustatic movements and siltation of the port.[53] As exportation of local wine is attested into the sixth century, certain harbour structures must have continued to function. Indeed, field survey has revealed a substantial late Roman pottery scatter at the site of the Thermae Sinuessanae, on the coast and little over a kilometre to the south of Sinuessa, where docking facilities must have existed in earlier times. Though there is no evidence from the site for continuity after the sixth century, it is probable that it was one and the same as *in Caldanas de Celicias*, whose waters were visited for their therapeutic qualities in 991 by Aloara, wife of Pandulf I of Capua.[54]

Suessa Aurunca has yielded a little evidence for late activity, especially funerary, and is significantly the only one of the three Roman towns around the lower Garigliano basin to have retained its original name through the dark ages. Local tradition has it that its cathedral was erected on the site of a Roman temple, rededicated to the archangel Michael in the (?)fourth century: a strange date and a suspiciously Lombard dedication.[55] An unprovenanced marble funerary inscription commemorating an eleven year old, Salustius, bears the consular date of AD 544.[56] The town has also yielded one of the few sixth century hoards from southern Italy, containing coins of Athalric, Teodatus, Eraric and Balduic (541–552), along with emissions of the Byzantine emperor Justinian I (527–565).[57]

The latest secure historical date known for Suessa Aurunca, prior to the Lombard invasion, is AD 501 when its bishop was in attendance at the Rome synod.[58] In 879 Lando, grandson of Landulf I, established the gastaldate of Sessa, along with others at Caserta, Caiazzo, Carinola, Teano, Aquino, Alife, Venafro, Isernia and Calvi.[59]

Unlike Sinuessa and Minturnae, the evidence appears to point to continuity of occupation through Roman, Ostrogothic, Byzantine and Lombard times. Archaeologically this seems supported by the, albeit partial, survival of the ancient street grid, and well-preserved tracts of the town's enceinte. The much reduced population has left testimony in the shrunken area enclosed by the walls during the middle ages. It is to be noted that the abandoned parts of the town, now occupied principally by market gardens, were first and foremost the low-lying areas to the east of the main settlement nucleus, immediately above the river or Canale Grande, which were not so readily defensible.[60] The aqueduct may have fallen into decay at this time, and water was to be had, one supposes, through a series of cisterns or wells cut through the volcanic tuff.

In the ager Falernus proper, a minor nucleated site of some interest is Forum Claudii, which does not seem to have developed significantly until the later empire when it may have received people migrating from the coast. Though there is no record of the town possessing a bishopric until the eleventh century, unlike Forum Popilii which had a bishop by AD 496, the rich pottery scatter would seem to suggest occupation into the seventh century, if not later, long after its twin may have been deserted. In

[51] AE 1940, no 48; Della Corte, 1938, 202–204. A further, anonymous, *curator coloniae* is also attested: AE 1926, no. 142. Evidence for an ecclesiastical council at the town in AD 303, at which Pope Marcellinus was judged, as well as evidence for the presence of bishops and martyrs, is unsatisfactory: Lanzoni, 1923, 125; *Bibl. Sanct.* VIII, 652 and 938ff.
[52] Melillo Faenza and Pagano, 1983; Pagano, 1985, 85.
[53] For heavy taxation in Campania see *Cod. Theod.* 11, 28, 12. Bishop Ambrose listed a number of 'semirutarum urbium cadavera' in other parts of Italy, provoked by taxation: see Cracco Ruggini and Cracco, 1977.
[54] *Chron. Vult.* I, 15.

[55] Borelli, 1976, 3–4. The mosaic pavement, formed of black tesserae, which recently came to light in the area behind the apses sheds no light on the question: Villucci, 1980c, note 8.
[56] Villucci, 1980c, 39, disregarding the consular date, presumes the inscription to be fourth/fifth century! On similar inscriptions from Teanum see De Franciscis, 1953.
[57] Levi, 1919, 356–358; Mosser, 1935; Miraglia, 1986.
[58] Cass. *Acta Syn.*
[59] Cilento, 1966, 18 and 22.
[60] Valletrisco, 1977, 63.

1071 the episcopal seat of Forum Claudii was transferred to nearby Calenum or Calinula, the modern Carinola. The latter was an expanding centre from at least 980, and is attested as a *civitas* under count Landolf Landi, son of Atenulf, in 1006.[61]

Lesser centres were also developing as part of a new nucleated settlement pattern on both sides of the Massico from, at least, the ninth century, including Scauri (attested *c* 830), Cocciara (855), Fauciano (874), Trimenzulu (945), Garilianum (954)[62] and Cilicie (954), amongst others with less secure dates.[63] It is perhaps noteworthy that none of these hamlets may be considered strictly coastal, and perhaps reflect gradual demographic expansion in the areas where small and fragile family groups had survived the insecure conditions of the preceding centuries. Unfortunately, little is known of the early history of these nuclei and none has ever been excavated, though it might not be amiss to suggest that some found origin in late antique estate villages. However, the fragile archaeology of many is probably now seriously compromised by their development and survival into later medieval or modern times.

Nonetheless, one recently identified hamlet (site M179), in *località* Arivito, near Mondragone, appears to be well preserved because of its brief life span (*c.* eighth to eleventh centuries).[64] This hamlet certainly did not grow out of an estate village, and late Roman pottery is absent. Though not yet excavated, surface remains and the contents of a pit fill have however surrendered a certain amount of information. The material culture seems poor and although the settlement may have existed within the sphere of a regional exchange network, the pottery assemblage is nothing like the far-reaching groups present even on late Roman rural sites. Abundant evidence for iron-working suggests a certain amount of technological self-sufficiency, whilst the animal bones indicate the rural nature of the site, reinforced by the identification of both toad and doormouse pointing to both forested and marshy surroundings.

In synthesis, dispersed settlement, on archaeological evidence, seems to have started thinning-out with the course of the empire and may have become all but absent by the sixth century. Only well-defended nucleated sites, such as Suessa Aurunca and Forum Claudii, and fragile family groups survived, whilst new defended locations were sought for, such as Castrum Leopolis. By the ninth century, at the latest, a new series of villages or hamlets had started to develop, hand in hand with the regeneration or appearance of new urban centres in Campania and Lazio, notably Gaeta, Salerno and Amalfi. Naples, perhaps alone of the coastal Campanian towns, appears to have retained its urban character throughout the late Roman and early middle ages.[65] Though this pattern stands in marked contrast to that available from Molise and other areas of the peninsula, where a number of nucleated settlements, later abandoned, appear to date from the seventh century, it may be argued that the contrast is the result of the success of early nucleated sites in Campania which are still functioning today. Modern settlements will effectively blanket earlier remains whose identification and characterization will only be resolved through careful monitoring of building works and planned excavation.

The reorganization of the countryside was a slow process dependent on the regeneration of cultivable land and the re-establishment of settlement nuclei, the *civitates*, *curtes* and *massae* of medieval Italy.[66] The sources are full of references to marsh and uncultivated land which the monastic centres were already involved in clearing by the ninth century. The introduction and spread of the water buffalo, whether by the Lombards or by the Arabs, may be taken as symbolic of a fresh rural regime, being used to exploit the marshes to which they were accustomed (pl XX).[67] The changes in course during the second half of the first millennium AD in northern Campania had been drastic enough to erase most of the classical traditions of settlement and land exploitation, which nonetheless remain fossilized within the landscape to this day. The painstaking regenesis of the land and the birth of the new regime was eventually to see Italy as one of the leading lights in the formation of later medieval Europe.

[61] *Tab. Cass.* I, 213; Rosi, 1979.
[62] Though the precise location of Garilianum is, to my knowledge, not known, Graevius and Burmannus (1704) place it on the right side of the river Garigliano, more or less at the height of the aquae Vescinae.
[63] Cf in particular De Santis, 1963.
[64] Arthur, Abarella and Wayman, 1989.

[65] See Galasso, 1975, 63ff. in particular, for a stimulating overview of the whole problem of Campanian towns in early medieval Italy.
[66] Cf for example, Sereni, 1979.
[67] Ferrara and Intrieri, 1974, 34; Cantù, 1989. It may be noted that the Campanian environment has now changed sufficiently to necessitate the creation of artificial marshes or *caramoni* for the beasts, which are important to the local economy of areas such as Mondragone and Aversa for the production of mozzarella cheese.

Chapter Eight

Conclusions: Reconciling the Evidence

Interpretations and conclusions which may be drawn from the data now available for northern Campania are manifold, and permit both synchronic and diachronic views of a number of issues. The full data base resulting from the field survey and research which lay the foundations for this study are not presented, though would undoubtedly permit further elaborations. Though I hope to submit all the basic data separately, restrictions of space have dictated a choice in what to present. The primary intentions of the study have been to explain what I think are the major trends in settlement and land-use, in their political, economic and environmental contexts.

The evidence seems rich enough to permit the construction of one or more plausible models of the patterns of human activity in the area, whilst at the same time presenting clear enough lacunae to indicate priorities in future research. I believe that seven major socio-cultural phases may be delineated for the period stretching approximately between the early Iron Age and the onset of a particular south Italian feudal system, that is for a period covering almost two millennia. It should, however, be clear that the periods are to be regarded as nothing more than indicative of general processes, themselves composed of innumerable interrelated, overlapping and gradually mutating trends, by no means easily defined chronologically or otherwise.

That human exploitation of the area was in train by the early upper Palaeolithic has been demonstrated, though for the greater part of pre-history the evidence at present documented is neither of the quality nor of the quantity as to permit much more than tentative generalizations, based if anything on analogy with areas which have been the subject of more intensive research, or more fortunate site recovery rates. In this present work, the evidence for prehistoric activity has been recorded rather than assessed, in the hope that it may contribute in future to the creation of processual patterns with the enlargement of the database for this and other parts of the region. Suffice it to say that it is only with the onset of the final Bronze Age that available evidence appears sufficient (though barely) to attempt models of land exploitation.

I. The first phase dealt with here may be recognized by the early first millennium BC, when a number of cemetery and settlement sites indicate exploitation of the fertile foothills of the Massico and Roccamonfina, and lower-lying areas perhaps previously not cultivated, and may be seen as a period of gradual demographic expansion. Though a number of cemeteries are now registered, dating particularly to the eighth and seventh centuries BC, the proportion of Iron Age settlements known is still disconcertingly low, and there seems to be nothing like the steady build-up of population witnessed in other areas like Etruria, Samnium and even Lucania.[1] Their near-absence needs explaining and is in part due presumably to blanketing geomorphological features. The evidence for a conservative material culture might also suggest that this area remained limitrophal to the ager Campanus and areas more firmly involved in Greek and Etruscan cultural intercourse until the full agricultural potential of the land was discovered in the light of land drainage and imported crop types, particularly at the threshold of the Roman conquest. A poor agrarian regime, based predominantly on mixed seed crops and chestnuts, supplemented by animal husbandry, hardly rising above subsistence level, will have negated the production of a surplus and the creation of capital, stifling population growth and cultural amelioration. The creation of what appears to have been an unsuccessful port of trade does, at least, indicate enough cultural cohesion and the possibility of amassing a unified labour force as early as the eighth century BC. This, in turn, suggests the existence of a defined social hierarchy not yet clearly evidenced through the available settlement or cemetery data.

This phase, dominated by a primitive mode of production, catered to little more than a regional or local market economy, attested by a low percentage of imported pottery, perhaps arriving particularly through Capua and the more closely related Cales.

Towards the end of this phase, with increasing external influences brought about by Roman and Samnite interest in Campania, textual sources indicate the coagulation of the indigenous population into a tribal network known to Rome as the Aurunci. Archaeology demonstrates the appearance of scattered farmsteads and villages of this culture-group though, despite the later references to *pagi* and *urbes* suggesting articulated territorial subdivisions, little in the way of settlement hierarchy. In fact there is little to indicate that the group was approaching anything more than a preliminary stage of state

---

[1] Barker, 1981, 217.

formation with the appearance of that which may be classed as an unsuccessful port of trade at the mouth of the Garigliano, communal sanctuaries and refuge sites, a limited social hierarchy, possibly representing no more than the extension of a family hierarchy or clan system (Livy's Auruncan *principes*?), and a semblance of literacy. All this goes together with the views of scholars such as Lepore, Johannowsky and most recently Talamo, to underline the marginality of the culture-group in late Iron Age Campania.

II. Enforced urbanization and synoecism from the end of the fourth century BC marks the beginning of the second phase, as a direct Roman political and administrative manoeuvre. The move was intended to permit the domination of the subdued indigenous population, the umbellical routes into the ager Campanus, and the sea, which at this time were not yet under strict Roman military and commercial control.

There is, as yet, no indication of a drastic change in the productive output, though an increase in surplus production must have permitted increased labour in other sectors (building, pottery production, commerce, etc), and the nascence of a more hierarchical social structure. This would have been permitted through the reorganisation of properties, more advanced agricultural techniques (vid. centuriation, land drainage, etc.), the integration of indigenous and immigrant populations, bringing about an increase in population figures and in product demand, the creation of a more organised market system (through the colonies and communication networks) and a limited drain of resources from the area by Rome. Telling is the introduction of a partial monetary economy on the ever-increasing Italian, and no longer solely regional, stage.

The stability in the low number of rural sites is not to be seen as stability in the size of population or scale of land-exploitation, but rather a result of synoecism and the newly created nucleated settlements of Suessa Aurunca, Sinuessa, Minturnae and their possible satellites (Cascano, the Fora, etc). In effect, the urban populace was the rural workforce. It is only towards the end of this phase that dispersed settlement may begin to re-affirm itself, but then as a result of more intensive, surplus-oriented agriculture, when it became more efficient to concentrate the means of agricultural exploitation (people, animals and instruments) directly on the individual holdings. The third century probably sees the production of the earliest amphorae in the area, and also the disappearance of the few remaining 'native' sites. This may indicate greater internal stability and an integration of Roman/Italic and native populations, leading to the disappearance of the latter's individuality. *Parri passu*, the three colonies begin to affirm their own identity, with the creation of a spirit of *campanilismo*, and a distancing from mother Rome, as their initial role in maintaining strategic stability around the ager Campanus was eventually rendered redundant.

III. A third phase is marked not wholly arbitrarily by the Second Punic War. Its successful conclusion on the part of Rome signalled not only a premise for overseas expansion, but also a less precarious control of the agrarian resources of Campania, primarily for the benefit of the capital. With assured agricultural surpluses, Rome and her allies were in a position to bring the Mediterranean world to its knees and impose on it a homogenous monetary system to ensure fiscal control.

This phase witnesses the establishment of a predominant slave mode of production. Its tenor seems to have increased steadily from the mid second century as a result of overseas gains, accentuated by the obliteration of Punic Carthage in 146, leading to increments in manpower, in productivity and in market demand. As Carandini notes, wine served to make slaves and slaves served to make wine. However, an exact date for the beginning of the trend cannot be advanced, though it must be significant that few villas may yet be dated earlier than the second half of the second century and that the late Republican amphora *par excellence*, Dressel's form 1, appears little after the mid second century BC. Cato's text *de agri cultura* cannot have appeared that much earlier, around the time that Marcus Aemilius Lepidus constructed a jetty at Terracina for the exportation of produce from his *praedia* and Graeco-Italic vessels are attested as having been produced at Mondragone.

The maritime colonies, at this stage, assume the role of fundamental gateway ports within the expanding Roman economic network. This leads to local investment in the development of urban and commercial infrastructures. Ship-building at Minturnae and the manufacture of specialised agricultural instruments at both Minturnae and Suessa Aurunca are indicative of the significance of the local economy. Only excavation will demonstrate whether or not there was a parallel development in the production of consumer commodities.

Archaeologically the phase is characterised by a proliferation of agricultural estate centres (the villas and farms), often of impressive dimensions and architecture, more akin to those of coastal Etruria and Lazio than to those of the middle Liri valley or Molise, major urban building projects, often privately financed, and the appearance of millions of amphorae, testifying to the agricultural surplus, particularly in wine, which finds expanding markets in Rome and overseas. The process is circular and leads to an ever-increasing pool of cash which, in turn, is reinvested in land, leading ultimately to land-hunger and exploitation of the most intractable soils and marginal areas of coastal Campania, indicated by the presence of more modest, perhaps tenant, farms. To this period may be assigned further reclamation of marsh lands around the Savus and on either side of the Liris, extending thus the quantity of cultivable land. However, both textual and archaeological sources, such as the marked concentration of amphora kilns to the south of the Massico, seem to concur in indicating the southern foothills of the Massico as the prime agricultural area with abundant vineyards. The Garigliano basin was perhaps less specialised, with grain cultivation and polyculture practised in lower-lying areas, and hill slopes bearing olive groves and vineyards.

Epigraphy indicates that the capital was at first divided amongst the local aristocracy (eg the Magii), including descendants of original *coloni* (eg the Paconii). By the first century BC significant land had been further acquired by powerful political magnates from central Italy (eg Pompey, Cicero).

IV. Towards the middle years of the first century BC, a number of changes take place. Smaller farms and villas in the more marginal areas start to disappear, perhaps with a concentration of land in the hands of fewer owners and abandonment of the less fruitful soils. However, absolute numbers of occupied rural sites remains high, indeed there is a slight rise, perhaps around the time of Augustus, due in part to a number of sumptuous maritime villas built from scratch. Indeed, the rise of Octavian to emperor brought about further changes in land possessions with the appearance of his partisans, often *nouveau riche*, and the settlement of thousands of legionary veterans which must have, at least momentarily, increased the ranks of small-holders.

Amphora evidence may indicate that the exportation of local wines starts to wane, though the reputation that they had gained assures them a place on the market, perhaps towards the higher end of the scale. A corollary of the decline in quantity may be the breakdown of centralised amphora production sites along the coast and the creation of new kilns sited on individual properties in the agricultural hinterland, at least from the reign of Tiberius.

In the towns, private local expenditure is still witnessed by donations to building costs, feasts, games and *sportulae*, alongside public building programmes.

This seems to occur almost contemporaneously with the archaeologically-attested investment on the part of Italians in certain western provincial areas, such as southern France and Tarraconensis. In these areas the evidence of villas and locally produced Italian amphora types (Dressel 1B/Pascual 1, Dressel 2–4 and Dressel 28) seems to indicate the importation from western central Italy of an entire productive system.

V. During the course of the early empire the trend in the concentration of land continues leading to the appearance of *latifundia*, often closely linked to the court, if not directly administered by an imperial *procurator*. Figures such as Tigellinus, Frontinus' heirs and Matidia make their appearance.

By the end of the first or early second century AD, wine exportation had severely diminished, and even the inland kiln sites set up a century earlier to produce Dressel 2–4 wine amphorae are abandoned. Only two or three kiln sites continue to produce amphorae, though very much as secondary products alongside a gamut of fine and coarse wares for local use.

On reaching the mid empire (second–third centuries AD) 71% of the rural sites inhabited under the early empire, mainly villas or farms, are gradually abandoned, though without excavation greater chronological precision is hardly possible.[2] We know little about their dependant lands, though some of these must have been absorbed by the imperial *latifundia*. The surplus production of wine continues, although on such a reduced scale that it is hard to envisage anything other than the exportation of luxury vintages. Indeed, only one Falernian type amphora is known from Rome at this time, dated to AD 216.

Both public and private building expenditure is severly curtailed. Recent excavations and survey in the heart of Sinuessa appear to indicate that the town had entered a severe stage of recession, as its role as major gateway port is negated. The town was not a producer, but a consumer, and once its role in the exportation of agricultural produce was denied, it had little reason to continue to exist, apart from its position as administrative centre and the requirements of the diehard urban-culture mentality of its citizens. Furthermore, its port may have suffered serious silting. On a national level, there was just no longer the money, public or private, to pay for simple maintenance, never mind renovation. The (abortive) construction of the *fossa neronis* and the (successful?) realisation of the via Domitiana may both have been occasioned by an early failure in the functioning of Sinuessa, and part of the continuing surplus produce of the ager Falernus may have reached the sea at Puteoli.

Minturnae may have fared a little better, perhaps on account of its more protected port linked directly to the Garigliano, and its role as shipyard and producer of iron artifacts, though even there decline

---

[2]   See the general comments by Tchernia, 1986, 269.

seems to have set-in. We may also recall that the via Appia was forced to reach Minturnae, and not Sinuessa, before veering inland to Suessa Aurunca, linking the inland towns and Capua.

The overall impression gained is that the area's economic base was gradually eroded through competition, and that if internal areas like Suessa Aurunca were more 'successful' during the difficult times of the mid-empire, when compared to Sinuessa, Minturnae and the ager Falernus, it is because their agriculture was more diversified and not over-specialised in meeting the demands of the few large consumer centres such as Rome, Carthage and parts of Gaul.

VI. By the later third or fourth century, as in other parts of Italy, severly reduced and redirected government and municipal expenditure lead to the collapse of part of the economy's infrastructures. Roads and harbours, aqueducts and drains, villas and field systems fall into disrepair. With no substantial break in the trend by the late empire costs of overall rehabilitation escalated well beyond the government's financial resources, which were needed increasingly to be directed towards the frontier provinces. Higher taxation becomes an important factor in the abandonment of land where products find limited marketability. Though this could have led to a growth in the quantity of urban poor, there is yet little archaeological evidence for this from the towns. The consequent drop in the number of food producers and, thus, of food produced may have led to higher prices, limited supplies, unequal distribution, and thus to malnutrition and famine, or rather to a decrease in the number of people who could effectively be supported at subsistence rate.

By the fourth to fifth centuries 45% of the rural sites that had survived into the mid empire were abandoned, giving a mean average of about 0.2 rural sites per km². The countryside seems no longer to be involved in production for extensive commercial exploitation, and the open-market, save on a regional scale, may disappear towards the end of this period. It may also be that surplus production was no longer stimulated by taxation, as the tax-collection mechanisms gradually broke down. Rather, the produce from the diminishing land under cultivation, confirmed also by the continued decline in occupied sites, seems to have been sufficient to meet local needs insofar as there is scant evidence of imported commodities.

Conspicuous late Roman pottery at the Thermae Sinuessanae may indicate that the site had taken over, on a much-reduced scale, the port functions of Sinuessa itself, perhaps serving the one or two major estates. One might further postulate a ruralisation of the, already failing, towns in as far as an increasing proportion of the 'urban' proletariat returned to working the fields thus, in part, offsetting the decline in number of rurally-based agricultural estate centres. Here we might remember Viria Marcella, the *clarissima femina* who invested in construction (of a church?) at Sinuessa and who belonged to the important senatorial family which owned land in fourth century Campania.[3] Figures at the higher end of the social scale who could command substantial wealth were declining in number, and when we eventually hear of the Symmachi, Nicomachi and Melania, we find that their might is based on large holdings spread throughout the empire or, rather, on quite diversified investments. Even these, however, were not to last.

I do not intend to present a catastrophy thesis, though the new economic system cannot have sustained the same population that existed in earlier times and it eventually brought about increased regionalisation. Perhaps paradoxically, the fertile lands of northern Campania were more severely affected by recession than other areas of Italy that under the earlier empire had been lower down on the productive scale and not dependant on the slave mode of production.

VII. With the later fifth-sixth centuries AD rural settlement seems to have all but ceased. Of the four surviving rural settlements noted, two were large late republican villas, one of which may have been the vicus Caedicius. The only site that has yielded abundant evidence of activity at this time is Forum Claudii, lying inland and sited on a knoll, thus perhaps obtaining the function of strategic hamlet or estate village. I would suggest that other such sites existed and will be revealed upon excavation within some of the medieval villages, attested later in the sources and obscured by modern settlement. These may thus have absorbed a certain amount of the population, though a decline in absolute population figures seems inescapable, and is probably to be explained through the effects of plagues and general health deficiency, exacerbated by the worsening environmental conditions and restrictions in food supply. Thus, though no one ever dies of famine, lowered resistance will have helped to lower life expectancy and raise mortality rates.[4]

---

[3]   It is unlikely that her investment at Sinuessa was an example of urban patronage. We might instead propose that the family's estate centre and labour force were based in the town.

[4]   See the interesting papers in Rotberg and Rabb, 1985.

A more decisive move to strategic positions may have ensued the establishment of the Lombards at Benevento in 570, and the creation of a frontier zone along the Garigliano. However, aside from one village, datable to around the eighth century, and three foundations of S Vincenzo al Volturno, there is a dearth of archaeological data taking us to about 915 and the final ousting of the Arabs from Monte D'Argento. The earlier part of this period is clouded, whilst the latter part sees the official foundation of the small medieval hamlets cited above, and a new political organisation based on the Lombard gastaldates.

Population groups were presumably self-sufficient with the drop in standards of living and commodity exchange, although evidence from S Maria a Fauciano suggests that by the later eighth or ninth centuries some settlements, at least, were able to obtain pottery through an exchange system operating at a regional level.[5]

On the one hand, the beginning of this period sees both climatic and environmental deterioration leading to the proliferation of Mediterranean macchia over the old cultivated slopes, regeneration of woodland and the appearance of large tracts of marshland in low-lying areas. On the other hand we glimpse the beginning of a new regime, with deforestation, the recreation of fields and the appearance of the buffalo. Whilst the marshes were only finally abolished this century, the macchia still blankets abandoned classical sites and agricultural terraces.

- - - - * - - - -

A feature common to the entire time-span under consideration seems to be that of the absence of imported primary goods. The only obvious exception, which in fact appears to prove the rule, is the brief period during the late republic when a relative abundance of Tunisian amphorae may indicate scarcity of local olive-oil, not because of land incapacity, but perhaps because of an exaggerated tendency towards crop specialisation and an unprecedented demographic explosion. This period, in fact, sees the vine spreading up the limestone slopes into the 'traditional' habitat of the olive-grove. Thus it may be concluded that favourable environmental conditions permitted a tranquil pattern of self-sufficiency on account of a successful exploitation of the abundant natural resources keeping in line with the

cultural vicissitudes and fluctuating population levels of the area from pre-conquest to late antique times. The eventual causes of recession during the empire are not to be sought directly in local changes, which are but symptoms of the changing political and economic regime of the entire late classical world, further exacerbated by climatic deterioration. It was then only a matter for the area to reach renewed political stability for it to partake in the economic renaissance of the later middle ages, signalled by the appearance of village settlement before the end of the first millennium.

In view of the accelerating rate of destruction of both archaeological sites and the remains of the ancient landscape, the Soprintendenza's policy of safeguarding major recognised archaeological sites through scheduling or rapid excavation of remains is of negligible relevance towards a 'correct' reconstruction of antique settlement patterns and land-use.[6] If anything, this study hopefully will serve to highlight major deficiencies in our knowledge of Northern Campania and act as a springboard for future problem-oriented research. Leaving aside prehistory, about which virtually nothing is known, and later and post-medieval times, which though rich in remains fall outside the competence of the established archaeological institutions and of this volume, it is possible, in summing-up, to outline broad lines of enquiry aimed at patching particular lacunae. It should go without saying that, as various questions are 'satisfactorily' answered, others will arise, thus leading to eventual changes in research design.

On examination, the major socio-cultural phases outlined above beg a number of questions. First of all, a series of well-defined artefact typologies is lacking for virtually the entire period under consideration, which makes close dating and any form of statistical study of material remains quite insecure. This lack has been partially settled through survey, and partly through the creation of archaeological sequences in other parts of Campania (i.e. Pompeii and Naples) which still await publication, but cannot yet be said to have been satisfactorily resolved. The establishment of faunal, floral and geomorphological sequences has only just been initiated, whilst attempts have not yet been made to examine demographic or anthropological problems through skeletal analyses. Environmental archaeology, in sum, does not yet exist in this area.

---

[5] Most settlements probably produced their own wares in a domestic environment. The earliest evidence for renewed 'professional' pottery production in the area dates to the twelfth or thirteenth century, when a kiln was established at Teano, producing jugs with narrow-line decoration. The early medieval sites of S Maria a Fauciano and M179, however, suggest that such jugs were already being produced professionally by the eighth or ninth centuries.

[6] The policy, codified by antiquated legislation passed in 1939, has led to a disproportionate amount of information retrieved for classical villa sites and major Iron Age cemeteries, often of dubious quality and remaining unpublished.

The only major excavation reports for the area regard the two Roman villas excavated by the late Molly Cotton, the early and unsatisfactorily published excavations by Johnson at Minturnae, and the pre-Roman and Roman sanctuary of Marica at the mouth of the Garigliano published by Mingazzini. Phase III is thus, perhaps, best understood, also because of the abundant surface remains surviving throughout the entire area surveyed. Quantitatively, phase III settlement density is also the most substantial, though the striking apex may be partly exaggerated by the insufficient information registered for both preceding and succeeding phases. Evidence for initial occupation of certain villa sites in phase II may be obscured by later remains, and it is to be noted that occasional scraps of third century BC pottery were picked up on a few rural sites, though certainly not of sufficient quantity as to prove a point.

Similarly, continuing occupation of more villas through later phases than has been expressed may be the result of rarity of the main dating element, African Red Slip, and ignorance of alternative chronological guides. It is to be remembered that both the Francolise sites bore traces of late occupation, though the near-complete excavation of the farm at Posto yielded only 69 late ARS sherds. If northern Campania did not need to import significant quantities of North African oil and grain it is possible that ARS, as a makeweight cargo, arrived in negligible quantities. Clearly then, though total villa/farm excavation may not be cost-effective in view of more-pressing historical questions, both foundation and abandonment dates and characteristics require further research.

Slaves pose another problem as they are hard enough to qualify and quantify through excavation, let alone through field survey. Our written sources indicate that they were exceedingly common, in their various guises, through the late republic, and northern Campania's agricultural potential was realised through their use. Productivity decline, villa abandonment and the disappearance of the slave mode of production (though not of all slaves) were all effects of the inability of Italian landowners to discover an economically viable alternative agricultural system so as to undercut the costs which made provincial competition so successful in the decisive years of the early empire. However, I do not wish to make the automatic equation between villas and mass amphora manufacture and slaves as some scholars want to do, despite intimate links. Though the initial economic success of areas such as northern Campania was largely due to the new productive system developed after the Second Punic War, it is hard to judge the true contribution of free or hired labour, and which of the so-called villas were basically family-run. The Caedicii were obviously happy in employing a mass of *coloni* (how many slaves we do not know) on their quite productive northern Campanian holdings.

Moving across the centuries, we are equally uninformed about post-Roman 'towns'. Sessa Aurunca survived the dark ages, but as what? Minturnae and Sinuessa were gradually abandoned, with almost complete desertion arriving possibly by the sixth century, but why and how and where did all the people go? How were the large late and post-Roman estates (*massae* and *possessiones*) managed, and what was their contribution to the economy, both regional and 'national'? If estate-villages existed in the area, one needs to be identified and excavated. The excavation of a site like S Maria a Fauciano should inform us not only about the character of a Lombard estate, but also help to characterise a minor monastic dependency, in this case of S Vincenzo al Volturno, the central place about which we have learnt so much in recent years.

Finally, we possess historical foundation dates of villages in northern Campania (eg Falciano, Carinola, Carano, etc), though primary activity at these sites must have occured earlier, as finds in the centre of Carinola (site C33) might suggest. Perhaps estate villages lie at their origins? As this past decade in Italy was one which saw an increasing awareness of the potentials of urban archaeology, perhaps the next will see the employment of newly acquired methodology to a sample of the myriad of minor centres.

I have attempted to outline certain research possibilities, not to mention archaeology of the landscape (field systems, water control, quarries, and so forth), whilst others will have become self-evident through the text of this work. I end with the hope that the future will see the application of new tactics to both old and new problems before what evidence remains is eradicated forever.

Addenda Epigraphica

The purpose of this appendix is to bring together the texts of inscriptions, mainly not published, monumental and otherwise, found during survey or communicated to the writer. Graffiti and stamps on pottery vessels are excluded and will be published elsewhere.

1. Roman villa. Masseria S. Donato, Corigliano, Sessa Aurunca.

> ... S.SACE ...
> ... VS. ET ...
> ... ISPORV ...
> ...P]ONTEM ...
> ... S.C ...
> ... I]MP.VESPAS[IANO ...

White limestone. The inscribed block appears to be the central part of a three-piece monumental inscription originally mounted on an arch or similarly large structure, possibly over a bridge crossing the Garigliano. In private possession.

2. Minturnae. From within the colony.

> IMP.CAES.L.SEPTIM
> SEVERVS PIVS PERTIN
> AVG.ARAB.ADIAB.
> PERTHIC.MAX.ET.
> IMP.CAES.M.AVREL.
> ANTONINVS.AVG
> PIVS.FELIX./////
> ///////// ////////////
> /////////////////////
> VIA QVAE DVCIT A
> MINTVRNIS AD
> AQVAS VESCINAS
> SVA PEQ STRAVER

White limestone. Length 118cm. Height 175cm. Another similar inscription, missing the last two lines, is also preserved at Minturnae.

3. Northern Roman cemetery, Sinuessa (site M21).

> DM
> PACONIA HELPIS
> CBM
> SEIO SEVERO

White marble. Length 30cm. Height 22.3cm. In private possession.

4. Northern Roman cemetery, Sinuessa (site M21).

> DM
> NANONIAE.GRATAE
> MATER.DVLCISSIMA FECIT

White marble. Length 45cm. Height 20cm. In private possession.

5. Northern Roman cemetery, Sinuessa (site M21).

> ...VNDIO.S[A... or M...

White and grey-veined marble. Length at base 25.5cm. Height 29cm. In private possession.

6. Sinuessa.

> ... .PAL.POLY ...
> ... M.VIRO ...
> ... M.L.PHILA[DELPH ...
> ... NO.ET ...

White limestone. In private possession.

7. Roman villa. Masseria S. Donato, Corigliano, Sessa Aurunca.

> DONATA
> ANN.XIII
> MATER.F
> DVLCE

White marble. Found out of context during excavations by the writer for the Soprintendenza.

8. Between Sessa Aurunca and Avezzano.

> ... F.SÈMERA ...
> ... MPLIVS.DEDI[T ...

White limestone. Re-used as a step in a masseria.

9. Fig. 21, no. 1. Falciano (site M18).

> PEC.EL[..]A

Tile stamp in a rectangular frame, from a *tomba a cappuccina*.

10. Fig. 21, no. 2. Kiln site south of Masseria Pagliare, Casanova di Carinola (site C42).

> CAL[PVRNIVS] CLEM[ENS]

Tile stamp in a rectangular frame.[7] Two other examples come from the Roman villa site S48, in *località* I Greci, Casanova.

11. Fig. 21, no. 3. *località* Cofanari, Falciano (site S72).

> L ..M NO ...

Tile stamp in a rectangular frame.

---

[7] An L Calpurnius Soter is known from Sinuessa: Sementini, nd, 82; Pagano, 1981a, 875.

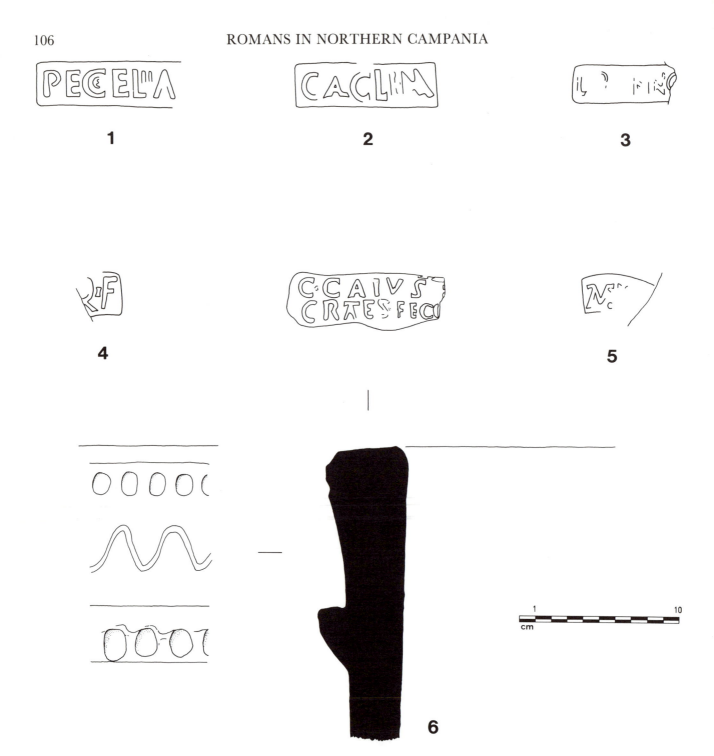

Fig 21   Stamps on tiles (nos 1–5) and on a puteal (no 6) from various sites

12. Fig. 21, no. 4. *località* Santuario della Gran Celsa, Casanova di Carinola. (site S37).

...]Q.F

Tile stamp in a rectangular frame.

13. Fig. 21, no. 5. Kiln site at *località* Mass. Dragone, Casanova di Carinola (site C19).

?MVS[...

Tile stamp in a semi-circular frame.

14. Roman villa at *località* Ponte dell'Impiso/S. Mauro, Mondragone (site M59).

...]MICO

Tile stamp in a rectangular frame. Seen by the local farmer, though not by the writer.

15. Fig. 21, no. 6. Roman villa at Maiano, Cellole.

C.CAIVS
CRATES.FECI[T

Stamp *in planta pedis* on the rim of a *puteal*.

16. Roman cemetery at Casella della Starza, Mondragone (site M123).

L.V.E or L.V.F

Stamp in a rectangular frame on the rim of a terracotta bath found re-used as a sarcophagus for an inhumation burial. Stolen from the farmer who made the discovery, although examined by the writer. The stamp L.V.F is attested on tiles found on two villas to the east of Rome, at Monte Albano and Praeneste (CIL XV, 2370).

According to a letter by Sementini, in the archives of the Soprintendenza (M 2–6, 1952), a vat, possibly containing a female skeleton with corroded bronze jewellery, was discovered against the western wall of an underground funerary chamber constructed of yellow tuff masonry. The chamber was 3 × 3.55m in size and some 3.50m in height with a vaulted ceiling, white plastered walls and a beaten-earth floor. The entrance was formed of a plain architrave supported by two stone uprights and came to light at some 3m below present ground level. Sementini records the stamp STATMARC/LVCIPHERIF on the vat, which thus seems not to be the same as the example examined by the writer. For the stamp, also appearing on mortaria and dating c. AD 70–127, see Hartley, 1973, 53, no. 22.

17. Forum Claudii, Ventaroli (site C21).

C.BR.V (retrograde)

Rectangular bronze seal in private possession.

18. *Località* Ciaurro, Mondragone.

M.NONIVS
REPARATVS (retrograde)

Rectangular bronze seal in private possession.

19. From the Garigliano river, near Minturnae.

IOVIDOLICHENO
SABIDIVSSECVND
INVS IVS DP

Small bronze ansate plaque, probably from the base of a votive statuette. In private possession. The *gens Sabidia* is already attested at Minturnae.

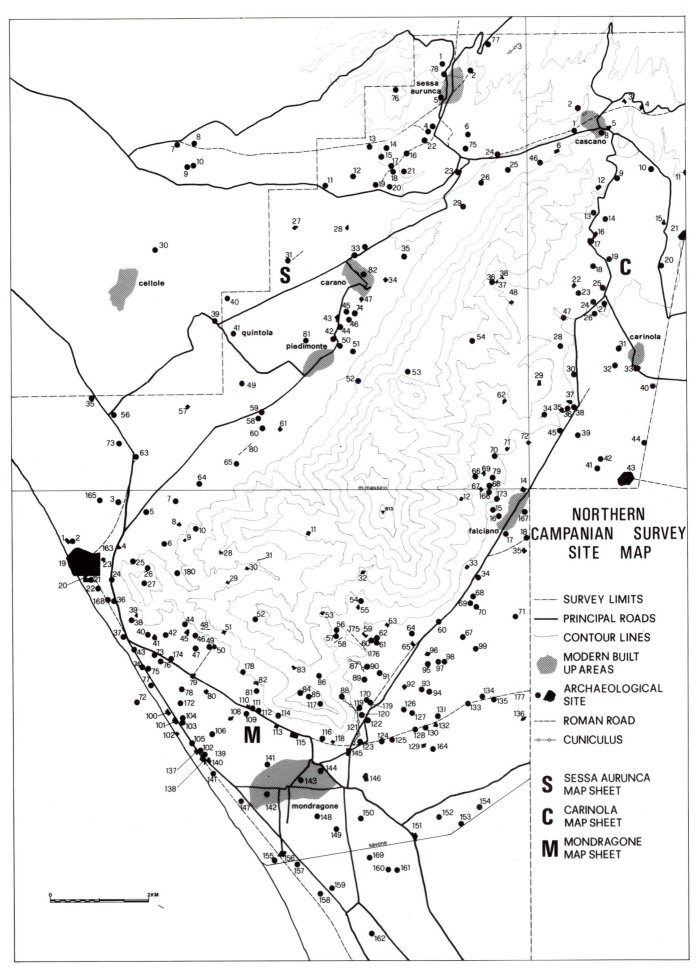

Fig. 22   *The North Campania survey: site distribution*

Appendix: The Site List

The definitions of the various types of sites listed below are given in chapter 2. The chronological span of each period is also provided in chapter 2 and repeated here for ease of reference:

Period   *Time span*
I   Paleolithic–Neolithic
II   Eneolithic–Bronze Age
III   Final BA–primary Iron Age
IV   Proto-historic (C7th–C4th)
V   Roman colonisation–Second Punic War
VI   Late republic
VII Early empire (C1st BC–C1st AD)
VIII Mid empire (C2nd–C3rd)
IX   Late empire (C4th–early C5th)
X   Late antiquity (C5th–C6th)
XI   Early medieval (C7th–C11th)
XII Late medieval (C12th–C14th)

Though attention has been paid to the dating of prehistoric material, details are not presented, and it is hoped that the whole problem of prehistoric settlement and land-use will be picked up by a specialist, to whom details of all discoveries can be made available. Figures in brackets refer to the quantities of material collected during survey.

Abbreviations:
DMV   Deserted medieval village
Amph   Amphora/ae
ARS   African red slip ware (including also Hayes' coarse wares. Letters (A, B, C, D) refer to fabrics. See Hayes, 1972)
BG   Black glaze ware
B-oide One of Morel's black glaze ware classifications. In this case, probably of Calenian or Minturnaean manufacture.[1]
b.s.   Body sherd/s
CW   Coarse ware (wheel-turned unless stated otherwise)
Dr   Dressel
ESA   Eastern sigillata A
ESB   Eastern sigillata B
Fal   Falernian (produced in the ager Falernus)
Fcc   Colour-coated ware from the ager Falernus kilns
frags   Fragments
ITS   Italian terra sigillata
LITS   Late Italian terra sigillata
PRW   Pompeian red ware
r.s.   Rim sherd/s
TWW   Thin-walled ware

The individual sites are presented in the following fashion:

NO.   SITE TYPE   SUGGESTED PERIOD
DESCRIPTION

MONDRAGONE MAP SHEET (IGM F.171 II NE)

M1   Maritime Villa   VII–VIII
Loc. S Limato. Bathing-suite and associated rooms in brick-faced concrete, with black and white mosaic, excavated by W Johannowsky in 1971.[2] CIL X 4736 comes from the site.

M2   Kiln site and cemetery   VI–VII
Loc. S Limato. Dump of amphorae types Dr. 1A (plenty), 1B and 2–4 (scarce). Scattered CW; BG. Tile-tomb revealed by modern building construction.

M3   ?Kiln site   VII
Loc. Baia Felice. Abundant Dr. 1B revealed in road section.

M4   Villa   VI–VIII
Loc. Mass. S Eufemia. Modern buildings covering Roman remains with mosaic pavement. BG (2); ITS (2); ARS A (3); CW; amphorae; tile.

M4bis   Prehistoric site   II–III
Hand-made b.s. (4); flint flake, from area of site M4.

M5   Flint scatter   I
Loc. Mass. Cecere. Abundant worked flints on fossil beach ridge of 16m Minturno level (see fig 2).

M5bis   Pottery scatter   IV
Thin-scatter of heavily abraded Iron Age pottery in same field as site M5.

M6   Roman pottery scatter   Uncertain
Loc. Mass. Molara. Modern building construction has revealed scattered CW and tile.

M7   Pottery scatter and road   V–VI
Loc. Mass. Piombo. White limestone road blocks; BG B-oide; PRW; Dr. 1A; CW; abundant shells of mollusc Donax (serrula) Trunculus.

M8   Villa and medieval fort   ?VI–VIII and XII+
Loc. Castellone. Fort constructed over *basis villae* in polygonal limestone blocks. Local amph.; ARS A Hayes 8 (1); tile.

M9   Villa   III and VI–VII
Loc. Castellone. Levelled area by track leading to Campopiano. Scattered squared limestone blocks; white limestone tesserae; BG B-oide (3); ITS (4); hand-made b.s. (2); glass; tile; painted wall plaster.

M10   Pottery scatter   VI
Loc. Castellone. Bulldozing has revealed BG B-oide (5); Graeco-It. amph. (2); repub. CW (4).

M11   Roman farm and medieval church   VI–VIII; XI–earlyXII
Loc. S Croce. Medieval remains above polygonal limestone block *basis villae* (see fig 20 and pl XVIII).[3] BG B-oide (2); ITS (4); ARS A (2), TWW (1); CW; amph. b.s.; medieval broad and narrow-line painted sherds and a green lead-glazed b.s. Cipollino column drums (5), white marble capital and moulded column base, marble revetment (Aegean and poss. Pentelic) numerous white and dark grey tesserae, may all represent spolia from (?)Sinuessa.

M12   Villa   VI–VII
Loc. Castellone. Polygonal limestone block *basis villae*, opus incertum walls and a cistern. BG B-oide (2); ITS (1); Dr. 1B and 2–4; CW.

---

[1] For the production at Minturnae see Kirsopp Lake, 1935.
[2] See Pagano and Ferone, 1976, 23–24, for a brief description of the site. See also Vallat, 1987b, 328, site Mondragone 1.

[3] Vallat, 1987b, 328, site Mondragone 2.

M13   Void

M14   Cemetery   IV–V
Via Crocelle 45, Falciano. Building works revealed tombs in grey tuff blocks with inhumation burials and pottery vessels.

M15   Flint scatter   II
Above Falciano. Worked flint and obsidian including a flint burin, a flint thumb-nail scraper and a retouched flint blade.

M16   Pottery scatter   III; VII
Near Via Vigna Venosina, Falciano. Building operations revealed abundant pottery collected by local amateurs. I found hand-made b.s. (4), local amph., Roman CW and a first century AD glass base.

M17   Pottery scatter   VI–VII
Loc. Pietragrossa. BG B-oide (3); ARS A Hayes 8 (1); CW.

M18   Road and cemetery   VI–VII
Falciano. Road works in 1981 revealed a Roman road and six tombs (four already robbed):
a-b) 2 rectangular inhumation tombs in squared grey tuff blocks.
c-d) 2 *tombe a ricettacolo* in grey tuff, for cremation urns. One yielded a CW olla with three bosses on the shoulder.
e-f) 2 *tombe a cappuccina*. One was intact and yielded the skeleton of a male in his 20's. Between the tibiae was a one-handled vase containing a local lamp dating to the late first or early second century AD[4], an as of Augustus[5] and a bent iron nail. One of the tiles used in the tomb construction bore a stamp (Addenda epigraphica, no 9).

M19   Sinuessa   For the site of Sinuessa see text.

M20   Sanctuary   V–VI (?) +
Loc. Le Vagnole. Revealed in 1974, looted by clandestini and later excavated by Soprintendenza. Not published.[6] Numerous terracotta heads, human and animal figurines and anatomical members were recovered, along with coins and BG. A terracotta phallus bore the inscription Q.Blatro ... / ... / ... dono/dei mercuri.[7]

M21   Cemetery   VII (?) +
Loc. Baia Azzura. Numerous *tombe a cappuccina* clandestinely excavated in early '70s. Inscriptions 3–5 come from the site (see Addenda epigraphica).

M22   Cemetery   (?)VII
Loc. Baia Azzura. Two mausolea with cylindrical bases, each 3m in diameter.[8] Limestone road blocks were found close by.

M23   Amphitheatre   VII +
Loc. Mass. Morrone. Perimeter visible in air photographs, whilst a *cuneus* in opus reticulatum and semilateres is visible on the ground.[9]

M24   Pottery scatter   VI?
Loc. S Eufemia. Dr. 1A (1); amph. of type Cintas 312–313 (1); republican CW (various); hand-made b.s. (1).

M25   Pottery scatter   VI/VII(?)
Loc. M Cicoli. According to locals terracotta animal figurines were revealed during construction work. I found a few fragments of Roman tile, CW and BG B-oide (1).

M26   Pottery scatter   III?
Loc. M Cicoli, north side. Numerous hand-made sherds, (some with applied cordons, horizontal handles and burnished), eroding out of agricultural terrace.[10]

M27   Structural remains   II(?), late IV–VI; XII
M Cicoli. Drystone wall in large, roughly squared, limestone blocks just below summit. On and below summit: flint waste flake; hand-made b.s. (13); Etruscan amph. (1); BG B-oide (5); Dr. 1A amph.; repub. CW; tile; medieval lead-glazed sherds. For an interpretation see text.

M28   Villa/farm   VI?
Loc. Poggio Le Fosse. On the summit is an L-shaped retaining wall of limestone blocks. Within is a levelled area containing tile and white mosaic tesserae.[11] The absence of pottery is notable.

M29   Farm   VI
Loc. Campopiano. Two-terraced *basis villae* formed by walls of polygonal limestone blocks.[12] Upper terrace yields tile, BG B-oide (1), CW, dolia sherds, terracotta rhombs and a rough limestone basin.

M30   Farm   (?)VI–VII
Loc. S Croce. *Basis villae* revetted on two sides by polygonal limestone block wall. Totally covered with grass, no pottery visible, though ITS (2, including a frag. by the Puteolan N Naevius Hilarus) from the site was presented to the writer by a local shepherd.

M31   Road and (?)bridge (?)VI–VII
Loc. S Croce. Limestone road blocks on an embankment terminating at a stream (rio) where a fragmentary structure in small, bonded, limestone blocks may represent the substructure of a minor bridge.

M32   Villa/farm   VI–VII
Loc. Il Muraglione. *Basis villae* formed of a 15m long terrace wall of polygonal limestone blocks.[13] BG B-oide (3); PRW (1); ITS (1); CW; dolia; local amph.; tile.

M33   Villa/farm   VI +
Loc. Mass. Le Mura. Opus incertum terrace wall. No significant pottery discovered, though access to terrace impeded by vegetation.[14]

M34   Pottery scatter   VI–VIII
Loc. Mass. Le Mura. BG B-oide (5); ARS Hayes 8 (2), 9 (1),

---

[4] Cf Gualandi Genito, 1977, 127–129, pl 40, no 297.
[5] Type RIC I, p 82, 219 – AD 11–12.
[6] For a summary see Pagano and Ferone, 1976, 30–31.
[7] See Sementini, nd, 70, for another dedication to Mercury, by the veteran M Fulvius Faustus, from Sinuessa.
[8] A couple of limestone blocks with decoration in bas-relief may have belonged to one of the tombs: see Ruggiero, 1888, 405; Greco, 1927, I, 8; Pagano, 1981, 876–881.
[9] See also Pagano and Ferone, 1976, 20–23. A member of the gens Caecilia paid towards the construction of its podium: CIL X 4737.

[10] See also Talamo, 1987, 61–66.
[11] This might be Vallat, 1987b, 328 and 334–5, site Mondragone 30, although on his map the site is not placed on the summit of the Poggio.
[12] Vallat, 1987b, 328, site Mondragone 33?
[13] Vallat, 1987b, 328, site Mondragone 45, fig 144.
[14] Vallat, 1987b, 328, site Mondragone 29.

196 (1), 197 (2); Dr. 2–4 r.s. (1); local amph.; abundant CW; tile.

M35   Structural remains   VIII?
Loc. S Rocco. Five walls of mortared rough limestone blocks, local grey tuff and fragmented tile, with associated lens of burnt orange clay (?hearth) visible in road-cutting, over 50m stretch. Little pottery: ARS A (1); dolium b.s.

M36   Pottery scatter   Late IV–V
Baia Azzura. Construction work for holiday flats in 1982 revealed dense pottery scatter and scattered irregular limestone blocks in colluvial deposits. Hand-made CW (8); abundant wheel-turned CW; BG B-oide (3); Graeco-It. amph. (1); Cintas 312–313 amph. (1); ITS (1); loomweight.

M37   Thermae Sinuessanae   VI–IX
Immediately to the SW of Hotel Sinuessa are remains of Roman imperial structures in semilateres fronting onto line of prob. Roman road. East of road are traces of similar constructions. Some 5.000 ex-voto, mainly statuettes, of which some are claimed to have been of pre-Roman date, were looted during construction of the hotel.[15]

Within junction of modern roads are traces of a vaulted structure in opus incertum (?cistern), and other similar walls, though little pottery: BG B-oide (1); PRW (1).

West of via Domiziana are remains of a medieval fort encasing earlier Roman structures and making-use of spolia. Further structures, in semilateres, lie beneath sand at water's edge, associated with water-worn amph. b.s. and tile.

Fields N of hotel contain ploughed-out remains of building in opus incertum and semilateres, as well as marble revetment frags. (white marble, alabaster and porphry) and blue glass paste and white limestone mosaic tesserae. Abundant pottery: BG B-oide (1); ITS (2); ARS Hayes 8 (6), 9 (3), 14 (2), 23 (5), 50 (1), 52 (1), 61A (1), 181 (1), 196 (3); African lamp frags. form Hayes 1 (2); Fcc; CW.

M38   Pottery scatter   VI–VIII
Beneath M Pizzuto. Small limestone blocks from ?opus incertum walls. BG B-oide (3); ITS (1); ARS A (2), C (1) and D (2); abundant CW; tile.

M39   Villa   VII
SW side of M Pizzuto. Construction of holiday apartments in 1980 destroyed part of villa. Bulldozed section revealed two yellow tuff reticulate walls and a wall in semilateres. At the base of the section, cut into bedrock, was a small vaulted structure in rough limestone blocks, without interior lining. White marble cornice moulding; abundant white limestone and blue glass paste tesserae; BG B-oide (2); CW.

M40   Pottery scatter   VI–VII
Loc. Bagni Solfurei. BG (2); ITS (6); Dr. 2–4 amph. (1); CW; tile.

M41   Villa   VI–VII+
Loc. Bagni Solfurei. *Basis villae* in squared and roughly dressed limestone blocks. Behind terrace was an opus signinum pavement, and to its S traces of a hypocaust with square brick *suspensurae*. Other smashed structural remains comprised yellow tuff reticulate blocks, squared flue-tiles, *tegulae mammatae*, white marble and cipollino revetment, and red and yellow painted plaster. Pottery was scarce: BG (1); ITS (1), dolium r.s.; CW.

M42   Pottery scatter   II
Base of M Pizzuto. Apart from Roman CW (2) and ARS Hayes 196 (1), hand-made pottery (8) and 3 flints, including a snapped and retouched blade were discovered.

M43   Pottery scatter and Kiln site VI–VIII
Loc. Bagni Solfurei. Abundant local amph. of forms Dr. 1B, and lesser 1A and 2–4. Further material includes scattered limestone blocks from ?opus incertum structures, white limestone and blue glass paste tesserae; BG B-oide (2); ITS (3); ARS (4: including 1 Hayes 9 and 1 Hayes 51); TWW (1); Roman glass (1); CW.

M44   Enclosure   Not dated
Loc. S Maria Incaldana. A drystone wall of limestone blocks and rare frags. of Roman tile (height 0.50m), and associated (?)quarry ditch, straddle the levelled top of a limestone knoll. Roman pottery was discovered on slopes of knoll: ITS (1); ARS Hayes 8 (1); Dr. 2–4 amph. (1); CW.

M44bis   Pottery scatter   II–III(?)
Loc. S Maria Incaldana. Hand-made pottery (21 frags.) found E of site M44.

M45   Structural remains   Roman
Roman structures are reported close to the chapel of S Maria Incaldana.[16] The area has since been heavily transformed and nothing is now visible.

M46   Pottery scatter   II/III
Loc. Incaldana. Undefined scatter of hand-made sherds (7).

M47   Pottery scatter   VI–VII
Loc. Incaldana. BG B-oide (15); ITS (1); Dr. 2–4 amph. (1); CW; tile.

M48   Road   VI+
Loc. S Anna. Tract of Roman road in white limestone blocks with kerb of small squared blocks, bedded on clay and limestone breccia mixed with abundant frags. of amphorae sherds of form Cintas 312–313. This perhaps led to site M51, on adjacent spur.

M49   Villa/cemetery?   VII–IX
Loc. Le Tre Colonne. Field NW of M50 according to locals revealed a number of *tombe a cappuccina*. I have found signinum frags.; white marble revetment; green limestone rhomb from scutulatum pavement; ARS C (1), D (2); local imitation Hayes 197 (1); CW; dolia; tile; antoninianus of Claudius II, of reverse type CONSECRATIO with eagle. Limestone building blocks and tile dumped in stream bed to N.

M50   Villa   VII–IX
Loc. Le Tre Colonne. Three large pillars of brick-faced concrete masonry with signinum facing, perhaps of cistern, surviving at base of M S Anna.[17] To immediate W is a limestone block wall. ITS (5); ARS A (2; 1 of form Hayes 9); red painted wall plaster; blue glass b.s.

Half way between this site and M79 is a series of limestone road blocks.

M51   Farm   VI
N of Sorgente di Lavinio. *Basis villae* contained by 2 large polygonal limestone block walls on side of hill. Dr. 1A amph. r.s. (1); CW; tile.[18]

[15] Pagano, 1974, 17; Vallat, 1987b, 328, site Mondragone 35.

[16] Sementini, n.d., 25, note 2.
[17] Vallat, 1987b, 328, site Mondragone 24.
[18] This may be the site mentioned by Sementini, nd, 26.

M52   Flint scatter   II
M S Anna. Waste flake and snapped blade by spring. Abandoned agricultural terrace walls and sparse Roman and post-medieval sherds suggest later land-use.

M52bis   Farm   VI–VII
M S Anna. E of M7. Fragmentary opus incertum and a *cuniculus* lie amongst pottery scatter: BG B-oide (4); ITS (2); TSC A (1); local imitation Hayes 197 (1); Dr. 2–4 amph. (1); Roman glass (1); CW; tile.

M53   Villa   VI–VII
N of S Mauro. Squared limestone blocks on side of hill from a *basis villae* (?). BG B-oide (1); ESA (1); ITS (2); LITS (1); Cintas 312–313 amph. (1); dolia; CW; tile.

M54   Pottery scatter   III
Loc. Mass. Cortigiani. Hand-made pottery (24).

M55   Villa   VII–IX
Loc. Canale Storto. Two terraces divided by cryptoporticus in opus incertum. Republican as of 'Janus bifrons' type; BG B-oide (2); ARS A Hayes 3 (1); ARS C (1); ARS Hayes 23 (1) and 181 (1); TWW (1); Dr. 1B and 2–4 amph.; CW, tile.

M56   Pottery scatter   VII
Cava di Marmo. Above quarry and alongside abandoned post-medieval building: BG B-oide (1); Dr. 1B amph. (2); CW; tile. Perhaps evidence for Roman use of quarry.[19]

M57   Pottery scatter/farm   VI
Loc. S Mauro. Fragments of opus signinum; Dr. 1 amph.; dolium lid; CW; tile.

M58   Cuniculus   Roman?
Loc. S Mauro. *Cuniculus* perhaps draining area above Poggio Pianella, marked on IGM as open channel. Of inverted V-shaped section with collapsed vault, and occasional (later?) side rooms with niches for lamp illumination.

M59   Villa   VI–X
Ponte dell'Impiso/S Mauro. *Basis villae* composed of two terraces, lower contained by limestone opus incertum wall and upper by vault/cryptoporticus.[20] Farmers have found various bronze coins: Republican aes of 'Janus/Prow' type to late Imperial. BG (12); ARS A (6), D (4); Pelichet 46 amph. (1); local amph.; Fcc; CW; tile, including stamp (Addenda epigraphica no. 14).

M60   Cuniculus   (?)VI–X
Ponte dell'Impiso. Immediately to E of M59 runs seasonal stream canalized by lined *cuniculus* cut through local tuff. W. side of gulley is surmounted by a wall of semilateres.

M61   Mass burial pit   Roman/medieval?
Loc. Ponte dell'Impiso. Local farmers claim that a large pit containing >20 human skeletons, going by skull-count, was discovered in 1977. Two bronze rings with clasped hands on the bezel were found associated. The area is covered with numerous fragments of Roman tile. The toponym Impiso is an archaic form of the Italian word *impiccato* = hanged, and appears in areas where gallows had been sited.[21] The pit might thus refer to. victims of hanging or, alternatively, derive from the tradition or past discovery of a mass-burial on the spot (thus a plague-pit?).

M62   Villa   VI–VIII
Loc. Ponte dell'Impiso/S Mauro. On the E side of Canale Storto are the remains of a masseria built upon Roman structures in opus incertum, including a vaulted (?)cistern. A fine-grained grey and white-veined marble column (H. 2.90m) lies in front of the masseria. Numerous white limestone tesserae; BG B-oide (5); ITS (2); ARS A (4); CW; tile.

M63   Farm   VI–VII
Loc. Canale della Conca. *Basis villae* formed of large polygonal limestone block retaining walls supports an abandoned masseria built over a structure in opus incertum. Little Roman pottery: Dr. 1 amph. (1); CW; tile.

M64   Pottery scatter   VI–VII+
Loc. Saraceno. Three backfilled Roman wells which, according to a local farmer, led to a subterranean cistern, are visible in a field. White limestone tesserae (3); BG (2); ITS (1); ARS A (2); ARS A Hayes 8 (1); CW.

M65   Pottery scatter   VI–VIII
Loc. Saraceno. Frags. of signinum and opus incertum; BG (2); ITS (1); ARS A (3), C (1); Dr. 1B and 2–4 amph.; Pelichet 47 amph. (1); CW. Abundant limestone road blocks, local amphorae and tile are heaped immediately to N. of modern road.

M66   Pottery scatter   VI?
Loc. Il Cesco. BG B-oide (1); CW.

M67   Pottery scatter   VI–IX
Loc. Mass. Frascarino. Flint waste flake; BG B-oide (14); late Republican lamp; ITS (3); ARS A (5); ARS Hayes form 23 (1); ARS D Hayes 104 (1); Local ARS D imitations (2); CW; glass; terracotta paving rhomb. The scatter covers a slight hump in an otherwise flat field, whilst limestone blocks (from a farm or villa platform?) are re-used in the adjacent abandoned masseria.

M68   Pottery scatter   VI?
Loc. Terragrande. A small scatter of small eroded limestone blocks and undated Roman CW (republican?) may indicate the site of a hut.

M69   Pottery scatter   V–VI
Loc. Terragrande. Fragmentary signinum; BG B-oide (8); CW (including a pedestal base with interior red slip); abundant tile. A couple of limestone road blocks lie to the immediate NW of the site.

M70   Pottery scatter   VII?
Loc. Terragrande. I.A. hand-made b.s. (1); ARS A (1); abundant CW (imperial?); tile.

M71   Pottery scatter/shrine?   VI
Loc. Mass. Torrone. BG B-oide (1); CW (republican); ex-voto: terracotta feet (2), part of a male face and a fragment from the top of a head, displaying locks of hair.

M72   Shipwreck   V
Concentration of fragmented Graeco-Italic amphorae, of Lyding Will's form a1. They are probably not of local manufacture.

---

[19] Cf Arthur, 1985b.
[20] Vallat, 1987b, 328, site Mondragone 41, fig 154.
[21] See, for example, Barillaro, 1976, 183.

M73 Pottery scatter VI–VII
Loc. Mass. Tranzo. Small calcareous blocks probably derive from foundations or a structure in opus incertum. Dr. 1 amph.; CW; tile.

M74 Kiln site VII
Loc. Mass. Tranzo. Abundant fragments of Dr. 2–4 amph. and wasters.

M75 Kiln site VII
Loc. Mass. Tranzo. Abundant fragments of Dr. 2–4 amph. and wasters.

M76 Pottery scatter V–VIII
Loc. Mass. Tranzo. BG B-oide (8; including Morel 1760); ITS (5); ARS A (2); Dr. 1A amph.; Dr. 2–4; African amph. b.s. (1); CW; tile.

M77 Kiln site VII
Via Domiziana 15.2km mark. Abundant fragments of Dr. 2–4 amph. and wasters.

M78 Pottery scatter VI–IX
Loc. Mass. Falco. BG (3); ITS (1); ARS A Hayes 8 (1), 9 (1), 14 (1), D (1); ESB (1); CW; tile.

M79 Structural remains VI–IX
Loc. Incaldana. Structure of mortared limestone blocks with some tile and cipollino marble revetment visible on surface of unpaved track to E. of ancient Via Appia. BG B-oide (3); ARS A (3), Hayes 8 (1); ARS D Hayes 91 (1); Dr. 2–4 amph.; CW; tile.

M80 Villa VII–VIII
Loc. Incaldana. Two fragmentary pavements, one in white mosaic, and one in opus spicatum; opus signinum and opus scutulatum (green limestone rhombs) fragments. BG B-oide (2); ESA (1); ITS (5); ARS A (1), Hayes 8 (1); blue pillar-moulded glass bowl; dolia; local amph.; CW, tile.

M81 Villa VI–VII+
Loc. S Sebastiano. Cryptoporticus in limestone opus incertum. BG B-oide (4); ITS (3); ARS A (3); CW; local amph.; tile.

M82 Villa VI
Loc. S Sebastiano. Cistern in opus incertum with signinum lining, beneath modern farmed terrace/*basis villae* (?). Marble veneer (giallo antico, cipollino and breccia rosa); white mosaic tesserae; red and yellow painted wall plaster; BG B-oide (2); local Dr. 1 and 2–4 amph.; CW; tile.

M83 Farm VI
Loc. Colombrello. Terrace of drystone polygonal limestone blocks. Upon terrace, a dolium base appears to be *in situ*, whilst scattered small limestone blocks may come from destroyed opus incertum walls. The presence of a press is signalled by a limestone base for arbores. Little pottery: BG B-oide (1); local Dr. 1 amph.; CW (republican); tile.

M84 Pottery scatter III
M Petrino, NW side. Dense scatter of hand-made sherds, possibly Bronze Age, in macchia above track leading to castle of Mons Dragonus.

M85 DMV and castle XII(?) +
Village and castle of Rocca Mons Dragonus. Extremely well preserved site with abundant pottery of thirteenth and fourteenth century date. Earlier remains are likely to be obscured, though two local amphora stubs were noted, as well as marble and signinum spolia.[22]

M86 Pottery scatter Later IV
Loc. Pezza di Caso. Hand-made b.s. (10); fifth century BC Attic column-krater (?);[23] probable Etruscan amph. h.s. (1); CW.

M87 Cuniculus Poss. Roman
Loc. Poggio Pianella. The line of a collapsed *cuniculus* is followed by a stream-bed. It was vaulted and a side gallery appears to have had signinum lining.

M88 Pottery scatter III
M. Petrino, NE side. Hand-made CW (27); a stray local Dr. 1 amph. (1). The prehistoric pottery came mainly from the spoil heap of a trench cut to the side of a modern concrete hut.

M89 Flint scatter II
Loc. Arivito. Flint waste flakes (11); obsidian waste flakes (6: at least four are presumably of Lipari obsidian); quartzite frags. (5); tanged and barbed flint arrowhead.

M90 Pottery scatter VI–VIII
Loc. Mass. Combra. Large squared limestone blocks, possibly from a retaining wall, were found dumped to the side of a modern threshing-floor. BG B-oide; ITS; ARS A. The land-owner remembers the discovery of a headless female statuette in white marble.

M91 Pottery scatter VI–VIII
Loc. Arivito. Red and yellow painted wall plaster; BG B-oide (5); ARS A (2); CW; tile; scattered around the remains of a medieval church (site M91bis) built of re-used (?) small limestone blocks. A local shepherd claims that a few tile-tombs were discovered a few metres to the NE of the site and subsequently looted.

M91bis Church XII(?)
Loc. Arivito. See site M91 supra. The site is known locally as S Nazaro.

M92 Villa VI–VII
Loc. Saraceno. Vaulted cistern of opus incertum, partly covered by rubble. Smashed opus incertum masonry and a limestone road block lies to sides of field, whilst a roughly-chiselled limestone column drum lies to the side of a modern hut. BG B-oide (22); ESA (1); ESB (2); ITS (5); ARS A Hayes 9 (1); ARS D Hayes 91 (1); CW; tile.

M93 Hut VI
Loc. Lenze. See text and figure 14. Deep-ploughing (summer 1981) brought to light small and irregular limestone blocks in a rectangular configuration, 7 x 5m in size. Dolium sherds found 5m to NW of structure probably signal dolium emplacement. BG B-oide (3); Graeco-Italic amph. (1); CW (republican types); few tiles.

M93bis Pottery scatter VI
Loc. Lenze. A dense concentration of tegulae were found in same field as site M93, as well as BG B-oide (1); Dr. 1A amph (2); CW (republican types).

---

[22] The site is discussed in Arthur, Albarella and Wayman, 1989.
[23] I should like to thank Dr Robert Guy for having examined this sherd.

M94   Cemetery   IV
Loc. Lenze. Ten distinct pottery scatters, clearly indicating ten
burials, were revealed by deep-ploughing.[24] The pottery is
predominantly of 7th century BC date, whilst the local farmer
claims that two iron swords and a bronze bracelet had been
discovered, only a few days before my inspection, by clandestine
excavators with metal detectors.

M95   Pottery scatter   VIII–IX
Loc. Saraceno. ARS A Hayes 9 (1); ARS D (2; one of form
Hayes 58); CW (imperial); tile.

M96   Villa   VI–VIII
Loc. Saraceno. Various large and roughly squared limestone
blocks probably from the retaining wall of a *basis villae*. Until a
few years ago, a vaulted cistern with signinum lining was visible
above ground. The presence of a press is signalled by a limestone
base for *arbores*. BG B-oide (6); ITS (2); ARS A (1); ARS Hayes
181 (1); mortarium r.s.; Fcc; CW; tile.

M97   Mausoleum?   VII(?)–VIII
Loc. Saraceno. Dense concentration of tegulae, semilateres and
mortar, with no datable pottery.

M98   Pottery scatter   VI(?)–VIII
Loc. Saraceno. Scatter of tiles and CW visible along a 20m
section, cut for a country track.

M99   Pottery scatter   VI–VIII
Loc. Campoli. Abundant tile, mortar and small limestone
blocks, probably from destroyed opus incertum walls. BG B-
oide (3); ARS A (1); ARS C (1); local Dr. 1 and 2–4 amph.;
CW.

M100   Maritime villa   VI–VII
Loc. Treppete. Structures in tile and yellow tuff opus reticulatum of an extensive and elaborate maritime villa, partially
excavated by Dott.ssa Giuliana Tocco in July 1980. The wealth
of the site is indicated by the discovery of a one-piece column in
grey granite, fluted white and coloured marble columns,
abundant frags. of marble veneer and a metrical inscription in
Greek from a statue of Aphrodite Anadyomene.[25] Finds date
from the later first century BC.

M101   Maritime villa   VII–VIII
S of loc. Treppete. Bulldozing revealed and largely destroyed
three pavements in opus sectile, composed of square, rectangular and triangular coloured marble crustae. Beneath one of
the pavements was a tile-built domed structure, whilst other
walls of semilateres were associated. When I visited the site,
most of the spoil had been removed, though labourers showed
me a sestertius of Claudius and various small folded sheets of
lead. Amongst the few objects still lying on the site was a cornice
moulding in white Pentelic marble, the neck of a greenish-blue
glass bottle (Isings form 50/51), Fcc and CW.

M102   Maritime villa   VII?
Sand dunes apparently obscure the remains of a maritime villa,
although only water-worn tile and pottery fragments are visible
on the surface.[26]

M103   Mausoleum   VI–VII
Loc. Mass. Landi. Mortared limestone-rubble core of a square
mausoleum fronts onto the via Domiziana.

M104   Kiln site   Late VI–early VII
Loc. Mass. Landi. Abundant frags. and wasters of amphorae
forms Dr. 1A and 1B, alongside CW and a small number of
amphorae of form Dr. 2–4.[27] Some of the vessels bore stamps. A
single obsidian core was also found on site.

M105   Kiln site   VI–VII
Loc. Ponte dei Tamari. Construction work revealed a dense
concentration of amphora sherds and wasters, mainly of form
Dr. 1B, with lesser numbers of Graeco-Italic (?), Dr. 1A and 2–4.
Also present was: BG B-oide (4); ITS (1); ARS A (1).

M106   Kiln site?   VII
Loc. Padule. A thin scatter of tile and amph. sherds was seen to
E of abandoned building, whilst a concentration of Dr. 2–4
sherds was revealed in the sides of two minor water courses
draining into La Fiumarella.

M107   Kiln site   VII
Loc. Ponte dei Tamari. Many sherds and wasters of amph. form
Dr. 2–4 and lesser numbers of Dr. 1B and CW were found to E of
via Domiziana. Fragmentary walls of tile and amphora sherd
courses, along with signinum, were also noted.

M108   Cemetery and structures   VI–VII
Loc. Padule. Various small concentrations of tile, limestone
blocks and human bones. On N side of field are remains of floor
in opus signinum, which seals a layer of brown soil containing
BG B-oide (5) of third or early second century BC date. Other
finds from the site include: black and yellow and black and
purple painted wall plaster; ARS A (1); dolia; CW; tile.

M109   Cistern   VI–VIII
W of Maria SS Incaldana. Large rectangular, double-vaulted,
cistern in limestone opus incertum, standing in field. There are
traces of associated reticulate masonry. BG B-oide (4; one is
form Lamboglia 1); BG C (1); ITS (4); LITS (1); ARS Hayes
23 (1); Fcc; CW; tile.

M109bis   Flints   II
W of Maria SS Incaldana. Snapped blade and a retouched flake
found to SE of M109.

M110   Farm   VII–VIII
Loc. Maria SS Incaldana. Site fronting onto ancient Via Appia.
Access road to field cuts a *tomba a cappuccina*, recently plundered
though yielding 'a large male adult, not very old' (Rosemary
Powers). Field has yielded smashed frags. of opus signinum; BG
B-oide (1); ITS (3); ARS Hayes 197 (1); local Dr. 2–4; CW; tile.

M111   Flint and pottery scatter   Late II–early III
Loc. Maria SS Incaldana. Numerous hand-made sherds and
flints, including a miniature bifacially-worked axe. Probably
Neolithic.

---

[24] For details of the site and associated finds see Talamo, 1987,
     104–113.
[25] Fiorelli, 1867, 8; CIG 3, 5956 = IG XIV 889; Pagano and
     Ferone, 1976, 37; Vallat, 1987b, 358–9, site Mondragone 27.
     I am grateful to Dott.ssa Tocco for having permitted me to
     visit the excavation on various occasions.
[26] *Ex inf* M Pagano. See Pagano, 1974, 15.

[27] The site has been amply described by Peacock, 1977, though
     see also Panella, 1981; Vallat, 1987b, 359, site Mondragone
     6. Further amphora stamps are to be published by the writer.

M112   Flint and pottery scatter   Late II–early III
Loc. Maria SS Incaldana. Numerous hand-made sherds and flints below the mouth of a large cave now largely destroyed by quarrying.

M113   Cistern(?) and road   VI–VIII
Between base of M Petrino and Padule depression. Vaulted cistern (?) or substructure in mortared limestone blocks and occasional tile, without interior lining. Above and behind the structure runs a stretch of the Via Appia. BG B-oide (1); ITS (6); ARS A (1); ARS A Hayes 8 (1); CW; white limestone tessera.

M114   Pottery scatter   III
M Petrino, W side. Abundant and well preserved pottery and the long bone of a sheep/goat, all with heavy calcareous concretions, in colluvial deposit beneath two small caves/shelters.

M115   Villa   VI–VIII
Loc. S Rocco. Large *basis villae*/criptoporticus in limestone opus incertum. Opus spicatum paving was once visible on the site.[28] BG B-oide (8); BG C (1); Attic BG r.s. (1: prob. second half of fifth century BC); ITS (2); ARS A (4); ARS A Hayes 3 (1); ARS A Hayes 32 (1); ARS Hayes 23 (1); ARS Hayes 197 (1); Cintas 312 amph. (1); CW; tile.

M116   Cemetery   Late IV?; V–VI
Loc. Cave di Tufo. Some twenty inhumation burials were revealed early this century. Majority of finds were BG vessels, including skyphoi, though a CW jar with lug-handles and a late republican lamp were also found.[29]

M117   Pottery scatter   III
M Petrino, SW side. Scatter of hand-made pottery along crest of mountain, and concentrated in a level area.

M118   Villa/farm   VI–VIII
Loc. Mass. Cementaro. Old tuff quarry reveals a tile-lined well leading to a cistern with signinum lining. The cistern is cut by a square adit whose ceiling, due to collapse, revealed an as of Augustus; bronze coins of Cales and Neapolis (2); TWW (2); local amph. Field in front of structures has yielded: BG B-oide (1); ARS A (2); ARS A Hayes 9 (1). Squared limestone blocks (from *basis villae?*) are re-used in masseria, whilst road blocks are in front.

M119   Pottery scatter   III
M Petrino, NE side. Hand-made sherds (58) and an irregular lump of heavy-leaded bronze were found in section and on surface of track leading up mountain.

M120   Structural remains   XII
M Petrino, E side. Construction work revealed drystone and mortared block walls poss. of church of S Michele Arcangelo, reputed to have stood in area. Medieval pottery, some of thirteenth century date; frag. of Roman sarcophagus in Proconnesian marble; frag. of rough limestone inscription: ...]SI[...; plain miniature column frags.; worn tetrarchic bronze coin.

M120bis   Tumulus   IV
M Petrino, E side. Section of building site (see M120) revealed rough heap of limestone boulders covering a black-burnished olla with vertical cordons and human bone. See text, chap 3.

M121   Road blocks   ?VI–VII+
M Petrino, E side. Number of limestone road blocks by side of track leading up mountain. They are close to an abandoned quarry and may represent blocks quarried on site or a road leading up mountain.

M122   Pottery scatter   VI–IX
Loc. S Pietro. In NE part of large tile scatter: BG B-oide (2); ITS (1); ARS D Hayes 52 (1); ARS D (1); African amph. b.s.; green porphyry veneer (1); CW.

M123   Cemetery   VII?
Loc. Casella della Starza. Inhumation cemetery was revealed a number of years ago and yielded, amongst other things, a terracotta vat bearing the stamp STATMARC/LVCIPHERIF, found in an underground funerary chamber.[30] Another vat, seen by the writer, though since looted, bore the stamp L.V.E.

M124   Pottery scatter   V–IX
Cemetery of Mondragone. Building works revealed BG B-oide (1); ARS A (1); ARS D Hayes 67 (1); ARS D Hayes 61? (1); local imitation Hayes 197 (1); Fcc; CW. Labourers claimed that they had recovered various bronze coins. Road blocks are visible running to the south of the cemetery, whilst pottery continues on the other side of the Via Appia: BG B-oide (11); ITS (3); ARS A (1); ARS A Hayes 8 (2); local Dr. 1 and 2–4 amph.; CW; tile.
    Numerous finds have been discovered in the past, including an inscription which suggests that the site is that of the pagus Sarclanus.[31]

M125   Kiln site   VII
Loc. Torone. Large and dense concentration of Dr. 2–4 amph. sherds and wasters to south of Via Appia.

M126   Pottery scatter   Uncertain
Loc. Lenze. Small concentration of tile and CW, perhaps from levelling of site M127.

M127   Villa   VII–IX
Loc. Lenze. Abundant semilateres from brick walls; white limestone tesserae; white marble lozenge-shaped crusta; white marble cornice moulding; Carrara and grey marble veneers; ITS (2); ARS D (4); Africana II amph. (1); Fcc; CW.

M128   Road and cemetery   ?V–VI+
Loc. Spinosa. A sunken road seems to Roman in origin, identifiable with the course of the Via Appia, as the escarpments are revetted with walls of large squared grey tuff blocks and opus incertum. A square-sectioned tile tomb and a *tomba a cappuccina* are visible in an eroded section of the southern scarp.

M129   Cemetery and structures   VI–VIII
Loc. Spinosa. A large rectangular enclosure (*hortus?* or cemetery enclosure) in limestone opus incertum. A local farmer discovered a bronze statuette (H. 9cm) of a youth with a sheep over his shoulders within the enclosure. Pottery includes: BG B-oide (23); ITS (10); ARS A (6; of forms Hayes 8 and 9); ARS C (2); ARS D (2); ARS D Hayes 61 (1); lamp frag. form Dressel 9B; PRW (1); CW. To W of enclosure is a concentration of tegulae, large grey tuff blocks and human bone.

[28] See Sementini, nd, 27–28; Vallat, 1987b, 328, site Mondragone 7.
[29] Pagano, 1974, 36–38; NSA 1911.
[30] Soprintendenza archives M 2–6, 1952: letter by Sementini.
[31] Pellegrino, 1978; Sementini, nd, 32; Pagano, 1980, 8–9; Vallat, 1987b, 328, site Mondragone 10.

M130   Pottery scatter   VI
Loc. Salera. BG B-oide (5) and republican CW eroding out of the southern road section. A human skeleton was found eroding out of a field access road to E of scatter.

M131   Pottery scatter   VI–VIII
Loc. Lenze. BG B-oide (2); ITS (1); ARS A Hayes 8 (2); CW.

M132   Farm   VI–VII
Loc. Mass. Casone. Bulldozing revealed a well and walls in opus incertum, a vat lined with signinum and a limestone threshold block. BG (4); Dr. 2–4 amph.; CW.

M133   Mausoleum   VI–VII
Torre Ballerino. A large rectangular mausoleum with limestone rubble core, stripped of its facing, overlooking the Via Appia. Apparently re-used as a tower in medieval times.[32]

M134   Villa/farm?   Uncertain
Loc. Mass. Ciaurro. The landowner has not permitted access to the property, though locals tell me that abundant remains are visible in the area. A limestone threshold block, of Roman date, is visible by the masseria.

M135   Pottery scatter   ?VI–VII
Mario Pagano informs me that a dense pottery scatter, of Roman date, was once to be seen in the field.

M136   Pottery scatter   VII–IX
Podere S Michele. Structures are indicated by semilateres, purple painted wall plaster and fragmentary blocks of grey tuff. ITS (8); ARS A (5); ARS A Hayes 9 (1); ARS C (1); ARS D (2); ARS D Hayes 91 (1); TWW; CW. A cemetery at the N edge of the site is probably indicated by tile and human bone.

M137   Kiln site   VII?
Loc. Ponte dei Tamari. Construction work in 1977 revealed tile-built structures and amphora waster dump, immediately to W of Via Domiziana.

M138   Kiln site   VI–VII
Loc. Filetti, Mondragone. Building works in 1980 revealed a site fronting onto the via Domitiana subsequently excavated by Mario Pagano. Prior to the excavation, I saw various tile built structures, as well as abundant wasters of Graeco-Italic and Dr. 1A amphorae.[33]

M139   Kiln site   VI–VII
To immediate E of via Domiziana, kiln waste comprises amphorae of form Dr. 1A and CW. Smashed structures are signalled by amph. stubs with mortar and signinum frags.

M140   Kiln site   VI–VII
Loc. Filetti, Mondragone. A dense concentration of Dr. 1A and lesser Dr. 1B amph. frags., CW and wasters was seen immediately in front of the offices of the Guardie di Finanza in 1981, and later destroyed (pl XIII).

M141   Pottery scatter   VI–IX
Loc. Pertecale. BG B-oide (21); ITS (7); ARS A (6); ARS A Hayes 8 (2); ARS Hayes 197 (1); imperial African amph. (1); Fcc; CW; tile; flint waste flakes (2). A local has found a sestertius of Marcus Aurelius on the site.

M142   Pottery scatter   VI–VII+
Mondragone. Building works in the '70s revealed abundant pottery, including BG and sigillata, in the centre of the town.[34]

M143   Pottery scatter   Uncertain
Mondragone. Roman pottery and coins were discovered during building works.

M144   Cemetery   ?VII–?X
Loc. S Angelo. Four tombe a cappuccina were discovered by the landowner during levelling of a garden within the town. Roman tile is still visible on site.

M145   Villa   VI–VII+
Loc. Casale della Starza. Basis villae formed of two terraces of opus incertum, the upper of which is a criptoporticus now supporting a post-medieval casale.[35] Two brick-faced concrete arches, supposed locally to be part of an aqueduct, are visible to the N. No significant pottery has been found.

M146   Villa   VI–IX
Loc. Torone. Building remains comprise frags. of signinum, the footings of a wall in opus incertum, marble veneer (green porphyry, Portasanta, cipollino or pavonazzetto), white limestone tesserae and light and dark blue, turquoise and green glass paste tesserae. Other finds include: a bronze key ward; glass gaming-counters (2); BG A (2); BG B-oide (17); BG C (1); PRW (4); ESB (1); ITS (4); ARS A (14); ARS forms 3 (4), 6 (1), 9B (1), 16 (1), 18 (1), 23 (2), 48 (1), 50 (3), 62 (3) and 197 (1); imitation Hayes 197 (1); Fcc; CW; Tunisian amph. (1); Biv amph. (1).

M146bis   Flint and pottery scatter   II and IV
Same site as M146. Obsidian blades (5); obsidian core and waste flakes (10); flint waste flakes (2); Campanian bucchero (3); hand-made CW (12).

M147   Cemetery   Uncertain
Stabilimento Cirio. A number of tombe a cappuccina were apparently discovered on the site a few years ago.

M148   Pottery scatter   VII–VIII
Near Mass. Cisterna. BG B-oide (3); ARS A (1); ARS Hayes 197 (1); local imitation Hayes 197 (1); glass.

M149   Pottery scatter   ?VI+
Loc. Mass. Lavatoio. Access to the site was impeded, though BG, CW and tile is present.

M150   Pottery scatter   VII–VIII
S of Mass. Fievo. Semilateres, wall plaster and a dark blue glass tessera indicate constructions. Other finds include: BG B-oide (2); PRW (1); ARS A (8); ARS A Hayes 8 (1); ARS A Hayes 9 (1); ARS C (4); CW; hand-made CW (4), and limestone road blocks.

M151   Structures and road   VI–X
Loc. Mass. S Biagio. Ruin in mortared limestone blocks, not examined on account of undergrowth, is poss. church of S Biagio. Finds in surrounding field include: BG B-oide (4); ITS (25); ARS A (5); ARS D (2); ARS D form 105 (1); African amph. (repub.?); CW; tile.

---

[32] See De Caro and Greco, 1981, 228; Vallat, 1987b, 328, site Mondragone 14.

[33] See Hesnard et al., 1989, 27, fig 11.

[34] I should like to thank Gaetano Sperlongano for the information on this and the next two sites.

[35] Sementini, nd, 28–29; Johannowsky, 1973, considers the site the forum of the pagus Sarclanus; see also Vallat, 1987b, 328, site Mondragone 9, fig 151.

A large block of grey tuff and human bones were discovered in field to E during well-digging, whilst limestone road blocks are dumped to side of field and may indicate a road originally coasting the Savus.

M152 Cemetery? ?IV/?V
Loc. Vetterola. Deep-ploughing brought to light rectangular grey tuff blocks, though no pottery.

M153 Pottery scatter VI–VIII
Loc. Vetterola. BG B-oide (3); ARS A (2); CW.

M154 Pottery scatter VI–VIII
Loc. Vetterola. Sparse small limestone blocks may indicate structures in opus incertum. Finds also include: fillet in giallo antico (1); triangular crusta of grey-veined marble (1); grey slate; BG B-oide (13); BG C (3); ESB (1); ARS A (4); ARS A Hayes 3 (2); ARS C (1); CW; Dr. 2–4 amph.; tile. Sparse limestone road blocks may relate to a road coasting the Savus (see site M151 *supra*).

M155 Cemetery ?VI–VII
Numerous finds were unearthed at this site in 1951: structural remains; painted wall plaster; mosaic pavements; coins of Augustus, Claudius and the Flavians.[36]

M156 Villa VI–VII
Macello di Mondragone. A vaulted structure in limestone opus incertum is now re-used as a farmhouse. Other structures prob. lie buried to the E. BG B-oide (5); ITS (3); CW; painted wall plaster; blue glass paste tesserae.
  Stacked amphorae were discovered close to the via Domiziana.

M156bis Pottery scatter VII–VIII
Macello di Mondragone. Yellow and purple painted wall plaster; Dr. 1B and 2–4 amph.; ARS A (3); CW; tile.

M157 Cemetery VII–VIII
Loc. Panetelle. Circular mausoleum of *c* 28m. diam. in opus vittatum. *Tombe a cappuccina* were discovered in the past. The scarce finds include: BG B-oide (7) and a glass rim.

M158 Kiln site VI–VII
Loc. Panetelle. Numerous sherds and wasters of amph. form Dr. 2–4, with fewer examples of Dr. 1B. Slightly to the south of the concentration were: BG B-oide (2); ITS (22); white limestone tesserae.

M159 Sanctuary IV–VII
Loc. Panetelle. Rich sanctuary, partly excavated by Prof W Johannowsky and by Dott.ssa G Tocco, and the object of continuous clandestine excavations.[37] The podium of a small Italic temple in opus incertum is incorporated within a masseria. Material stretches in date from archaic to early first century AD (ITS and a quinarius of Claudius), and includes thousands of terracotta and a few bronze statuettes from the *favissae*.

M160 Pottery scatter VI–VIII
Loc. Fasanare. BG B-oide (3); ARS A (2); CW.

M160bis Pottery scatter II–III
Loc. Fasanare. From the same site as M160: hand-made sherds (30).

M161 Pottery scatter II–III
Loc. Fasanare. Abraded hand-made sherds (8) similar to those from site M160bis.

M162 Pottery scatter VI–VII
Loc. Pineta Vecchia. Buildings are indicated by ?opus incertum building debris, white limestone tesserae, white wall plaster and opus signinum frags. BG B-oide (20); ITS (4); ARS Hayes 196 (1); Dr. 2–4 amph.; CW.

M162bis Pottery scatter ?II–III
Loc. Pineta Vecchia. Hand-made sherds (8) from site M162.

M163 Burial VII
Loc. S Eufemia. According to Mario Pagano, a *tomba a cappuccina* was discovered on this site.

M164 Void

M165 Columns ?VII
Baia Felice. Two marble columns dumped to the side of a building site.

M166 Vineyard ?VII–VII+
Strada Panoramica. Thirteen *sulci* or vine trenches cut into the soft ignimbrite, revealed in a road section. See text and figure 18.

M167 Cemetery ?VII–XII
Via Tiglio 23, Falciano. Several *tombe a cappuccina* were discovered during building works in the 1970s.

M168 Pottery scatter VII
Loc. Mass. Santoracco. BG B-oide (5); PRW (1); local amph.; CW; revealed during building operations.

M169 Cemetery VIII–IX
Loc. Fasanare. Four *tombe a cappuccina* and a burial in a large cylindrical amphora (African?) were revealed by local inhabitants in the 1970's.

M170 Cemetery Late IV–V
Loc. Arivito. Two ploughed-out tombs in grey tuff blocks, with BG (5); hand-made CW (9); CW.

M171 Structures VI–VII
M Petrino, E side. Two walls in opus incertum and a well-head leading to a *cuniculus*, were revealed in the section of a track leading up the mountain. The vaulted *cuniculus* may have brought water from the spring at Colle Pezza di Caso down to the pagus Sarclanus, on a course followed by both a post-medieval and a modern conduit.

M172 Cistern VI
Loc. Mass Falco. Smashed structure in opus incertum with signinum lining which was apparently met by a terracotta pipeline running down from the hills to the NE. Local Dr. 1A amph.; tile.

M173 Pottery scatter II or III
N of Falciano Selice. Hand-made CW (21) and a single BG B-oide b.s. amongst the macchia.

M174 Pottery scatter VI–IX?
Loc. Mass. Tranzo. Abundant eroded tile.

[36] Sementini, nd, 83–86.
[37] Talamo, 1987, 97–103, with bibliography; Vallat, 1987b, 328, site Mondragone 15b.

M175   Road   VI/VII
N of Poggio Pianella. Scatter of limestone road blocks by the side of an open water channel which may once have been a *cuniculus*. The road may possibly have led to the quarry of S Mauro.

M176   Pottery scatter and road   VI–VII+
Loc. Poggio Pianella. Limestone road blocks, some *in situ*, may run in a N-S direction below hill. BG B-oide (11); ITS (2); ARS D (1); local Dr. 2–4 amph.; CW.

M176bis   Pottery scatter   III/IV
Loc. Poggio Pianella. Above site M176: hand-made CW (12); CW with lug-handle (1); fractured flint (1).

M177   Road
Loc. Mass. Marchesella. Limestone road blocks scattered through field.

M178   Villa?/medieval site   VI or XII+
Loc. S Sebastiano. Scattered squared limestone blocks may derive from a *basis villae*, whilst opus spicatum frags. are re-used in a well-head. The abundant pottery on site appears exclusively medieval.

M179   DMV   XI
Loc. Arivito. Eroded pottery on surface and abundant iron-working slag. A pit/silo revealed in a roadside section has yielded an early medieval pottery group and a good faunal assemblage.[38]

M180   Dam   VII
Canale Grande, E of Mt Cicoli. A single high and straight wall, 1.55m wide, stands on the east bank of the Canale Grande, perpendicular to the water-flow. It is smashed as it drops towards the seasonal river. Its facing is composed of alternate bands of grey and yellow tuff reticulate.

CARINOLA MAP SHEET (IGM F.172 IV SO)

C1   Pottery scatter   VI–VIII
Loc. Spirito Santo. To SW of abandoned monastery, in area recently terraced: opus signinum frags.; BG B-oide (1); ESB (1); ITS (1); ARS A (2); ARS A Hayes 7 (1); ARS A Hayes 8 (2); ARS A Hayes 9 (1); Fal. amph. (1); Fcc; CW; tile; frag. of glass bottle handle with moulded signature P CISSI.

C2   Flint scatter   II
Loc. Corbara. Various flints discovered by A Matano.

C3   Villa   VI–IX
Campo sportivo, Gusti. *Basis villae* in limestone opus incertum. White limestone tesserae; denarius of M Antonius; BG B-oide (2); ITS (3); early imperial lamps (2); ARS Hayes 23 (1) and 197 (1); local imitation ARS Hayes 61A (1); Fcc; Dr. 2–4 amph.; Fal. amph. (1); imperial African amph. (3); CW; tile; glass.

C4   Villa   VII–IX
Near Gusti. Cistern(?) in grey lava opus incertum and other structures in mixed semilateres and irregular blocks. BG B-oide (2); ITS (1); TWW (1); PRW (1); ARS A (1); ARS D (1); ARS D Hayes 91 (1); Africana II amph. (1); CW; tile.

C5   Vicus and kiln site   ?V–IX
Cascano. See text. Various objects discovered over the years, including inscriptions.
  Demolition in 1979 revealed wall in squared grey tuff blocks, cistern and walls in semilateres, abundant kiln waste, including imitations of ARS, and an antoninianus of Claudius II.[39] Republican and early imperial pottery was scarce.

C6   Villa   VI–VIII
Mass. Gatta. Masseria built over a series of walls in opus incertum. In front of masseria is a vaulted cistern/*basis villae*(?). Proprietor did not permit detailed survey, though ARS A Hayes 8 (1), Fcc (1) and dolium (1) were seen. A small bronze phallus pendant comes from site.

C7   Cemetery   ?VII–?VIII
W of Cascano. Agricultural levelling destroyed a number of *tombe a cappuccina* in the 1970s.

C8   Pottery scatter   VI–VIII
Campo sportivo, Cascano. BG B-oide (1); ITS (2); LITS (1); ARS A (1); ARS A Hayes 8 (2); CW; tile.

C9   Flint scatter   ?I–II
Loc. Grella. A small scatter of flint flakes was found in an area recently levelled.

C10   Road   VI–VII
Loc. Ponte dell'Epitaffio. Tract of road in grey lava blocks leading towards Rio Pisciarello. BG B-oide (2); Dr. 1 amph.; CW; h.s. of medieval pitcher.

C11   Farm   VI–VIII
Loc. S Paolo. Badly damaged site immediately below church of S Paolo. BG B-oide (1); ITS (1); Rhodian amph. (1); Dr. 2–4 amph.; African amph. (1); ARS A (1); ARS A Hayes 8 (1); ARS Hayes 197 (1); Fcc; CW; dolium with lead 'butterfly' clamp. Locals speak of an intact dolium having been removed from the site and of a buried road surface nearby.

C12   Villa   VI–IX
Loc. Grella. Site extending over *basis villae* composed of three terraces in opus incertum (Fig 15). Uppermost terrace is partly sustained by double-vaulted cistern; reticulate wall composed of red brick and grey tuff on central terrace. BG B-oide (5); ARS A (2); ARS D (4); CW; tile.

C13   Structures   Uncertain
Loc. Selleccola. Vaulted *cuniculus* and rough ?opus incertum wall associated with abundant tile, though no pottery.

C14   Structures   XII+
Loc. S Martino. Roughly mortared wall with irregular limestone blocks, artificial cave and revetted rectangular channel cut through tuff. Narrow-line painted ware (4); lead-glazed ware (2); CW; tile; BG B-oide (1); TWW (1); Dr. 1 amph. (1).

C15   Structures   VI–VII+
Loc. Turriello, Ventaroli. Large opus incertum cisterns with a little brick masonry and signinum lining are all that remain of a destroyed site.[40] Road blocks lie by the masseria.

C15bis   Hoard   II
Large hoard of bronze axeheads and other artifacts was discovered near C15 before WW II. I have been able to locate a sole axehead, of 'Savignano' type, weighing 296gm, with a blunt blade.[41]

---

[38] See Arthur, Albarella and Wayman, 1989.

[39] RIC V, I, Claudius 266 – CONSECRATIO type.
[40] For the site see also Johannowsky, 1976, 37, no 17.
[41] See Peroni, 1971, 73 and fig 73c, for the type.

C16   Farm   VI–VII/VIII
Loc. Sellecola. Limestone opus incertum wall and other destroyed structures to immediate W. of road. BG B-oide (3); ITS (1); ARS A (1); local amph.; CW.

C17·   Pottery scatter   II
Loc. Picozzi. Hand-made sherds, flints and occasional obsidian.

C18   Pottery scatter   V–VII
Loc. Mass Creta. Scattered squared limestone blocks and a roughly hollowed block (?sarcophagus). Hand-made CW (2); BG B-oide (13); ITS (3); Cintas 312 amph. (1); CW; tile.

C19   Kiln site   VII
Loc. Mass. Dragone. Mortared and overfired tiles poss. from kiln structures. BG B-oide (1); ARS D Hayes 61; ARS D Hayes 104 (1); abundant wasters: Dr. 2–4 amph.; Fal. amph;[42] imitation ARS Hayes forms 23, 61, 104 and 197; Fcc; CW; tile. Road blocks lie at bottom of field.

C20   Cistern   VII
Near Ponte S Ruosi. Ploughing has yielded rectangular-sectioned channel connecting with small vaulted cistern. Dr. 2–4 amph.; CW; tile.

C21   Forum Claudii
Near Ventaroli and S Episcopio. See text.

C22   Villa   V–VII
Loc. Cesariello. Various frags. of opus incertum structures, a wall in opus listatum and a poss. antique well, re-used. White limestone tesserae; BG B-oide (29); Calenian BG theatre-mask foot (1); ESA (1); ITS (2); PRW (1); repub. TWW (1); repub. lamp (1); early imp. lamp (1); CW; tile; flint flake.

C23   Pottery scatter   Uncertain
Loc. Campopiano. Dolium lid; few tile.

C24   Pottery scatter   VI
Loc. Campopiano. BG B-oide (6); Cintas 312 amph. (1); repub. CW.

C25   Tumulus   ?III–IV
Loc. Domenico. A tumulus covering a central grave-pit was seen in the section of a building site. All grave-goods and human remains had been destroyed. See text, chap 3.

C26   Cemetery   VII
Loc. Casanova. The spoil from clandestine excavations of burials protruding from the section of a water course revealed: human bone; tile; BG B-oide (1); PRW (2); frags. of a late repub. flagon (5); CW. Other burials probably lie in the field above the water course.

C27   Cemetery   Early IV
Loc. Casanova. Hand-made CW (5); red-slipped wares (2); Italic painted ware (1). The local amateur archaeological group has found two bronze armillae, a small two-handled burnished tazza and a two-handled beaker, all of later seventh or sixth century BC date. A jar with cremated bones and two other bronze armillae are in the Museum of Naples.[43]

C28   Enclosure   Uncertain
Loc. Colle Castelluccio. A large drystone wall formed of small limestone blocks encloses a promontory above Casanova. Though abundant CW was noted, only post-medieval pottery was datable.

C29   Villa and church   VI–VII
M Finocchiaro. Structures in opus incertum on two terraces revetted with polygonal limestone blocks. Threshing-floor or pavement behind upper terrace constructed of small squared calcareous blocks. A small apsed church, possibly palaeo-Christian, has been constructed on corner of upper terrace using spolia, including the base for the *arbores* of a press. Hand-made CW (3); BG B-oide (5); ITS (7); LITS (1); local Dr. 2–4 amph.; two clay rhombs; CW; tile.

C30   Kiln site   VIII+
Loc. Mass. Starza. Construction work revealed rough limestone walls and abundant kiln waste: Fal. amph.; imitation ARS Hayes 196, 197 and lamp form Hayes 1; Fcc; CW. An antoninianus of Probus was also found.[44]

C31   Cemetery   IV
Loc. S Francesco. Heavily abraded Iron Age pottery was found scattered with small blocks of limestone and fragmented grey tuff.

C32   Structures   Uncertain
S of monastery of S Francesco. Large roughly squared blocks and abundant tile was found, though pottery was not noted.

C33   Structures   ?VII; XII
Piazza Municipio, Carinola. Pipe-trench cut in front of town-hall revealed a vat or cistern with opus signinum lining, sealed by a medieval(?) rubble surface or road, whilst a lump of Roman masonry in semilateres was seen on spoil heap. Hand-made jar (1); CW; 12th–13th cent. lead-glazed ware.
Much spolia is to be found in the town, especially in and around the cathedral.

C34   Pottery scatter   Late II–III
Loc. La Piantagone. Hand-made CW (9); a crazed flint pebble; stray illegible bronze coin (3rd–4th cent. AD on module).

C35   Villa + monastery   VI–VIII; XII+
Monastero di S. Salvatore. Monastery encapsulates structures in opus incertum and terrace wall in large polygonal limestone blocks. One squared block bears a phallus in relief. BG B-oide (2); ARS A (1); CW; medieval and later pottery.[45]

C36   Pottery scatter   II, III or IV
Loc. Mass. S Salvatore. Hand-made CW (9) in pockets of earth on limestone along track between the masseria and monastery of S Salvatore.

C37   Villa   VI–VIII
Loc. S Salvatore. *Basis villae* formed of three terraces with opus incertum structures.[46] Central terrace bears mosaic pavement of white tesserae. BG B-oide (2); ITS (3); PRW (1); ARS A (6); ARS Hayes 196 (1) and 197 (1); local imitations of ARS Hayes 196 (2) and 197 (5); early imp. lamps (2); Dr. 1A amph.; Fcc; CW; imbrex moulded into boar's head.

[42] For the amphorae see Arthur, 1982b.
[43] The material found by the local Archeoclub was kindly shown to the writer by Dott. Carmine Di Lorenzo. See also Maiuri, 1925 and 1926.
[44] For the amphorae see Arthur, 1982b. The coin is RIC V, 2, Probus 196: AD 276–282.
[45] For the monastery see Menna, 1848, II, 124–125; Vallat, 1987b, 328, site Carinola 6. This site may have been occupied under the empire (cf Vallat, *loc cit*, p 361).
[46] Vallat, 1987b, 328, site Carinola 1. This site was certainly occupied under the empire, contrary to Vallat's claim (*loc cit*, p 361).

C38　　Pottery scatters　　　　　　　　VII–VIII
Loc. S Salvatore. Three distinct scatters of tile and pottery (representing huts?): clay loom-weight (1); clay rhomb (1); BG B-oide (1); ARS A Hayes 8 (1); Dress. 2–4 amph.; CW; tile.

C39　　Kiln site　　　　　　　　　　　VII
Mass. Zannini. Upstanding triple-vaulted cistern in opus incertum.[47] Abundant amph. waste, partly excavated by writer in August 1980 revealing: 'normal', miniature and flat-based Dr. 2–4 amph. and CW forms produced on site and associated with imported ITS and lamp with Pegasus on discus, suggesting Tiberio-Claudian date for context. Also found was a bone hinge.

C40　　Structures　　　　　　　　　　Uncertain
New Penitentiary, Carinola. Construction work for penitentiary revealed structures, apparently in opus incertum, whilst tombs were clandestinely excavated. I was not able to examine the site closely because of police surveillance.

C41　　Pottery scatter　　　　　　　　III–IV
S of Mass. Pagliare. Hand-made pottery in field recently levelled.

C42　　Kiln site　　　　　　　　　　　VII
S of Mass. Pagliare. Abundant wasters of Dr. 2–4 amph., tile and some CW, protrude from section on W. side of rio Fontanelle. One tile bears the stamp CALCLEM.[48]

C43　　Forum Popilii
Loc. Civitarotta. See text.[49]

C44　　Cemetery　　　　　　　　　　IV–V
Loc. S Guido. In 1925 a cemetery with *tombe a cappuccina* and 2 grey tuff sarcophagi was revealed, one of which contained gold fragments. A bronze bracelet came from one of the tile tombs.[50]

C45　　Cemetery　　　　　　　　　　IV–V
Loc. Cofanari. Apart from the toponym, fragmented grey tuff blocks and tiles seem to reveal presence of burials.

C46　　Pottery scatter　　　　　　　Prob. III
Loc. Mass. Panella. Hand-made CW (29) in section of infilled stream-bed, prob. eroded from site uphill. ARS A (1) and CW found near surface. See text and figure 10.

C47　　Pottery scatter　　　　　　　Uncertain
Loc. S Marciano. Abraded CW and tile, not closely datable (?Roman). Two whole dolia in the nearby courtyard of a house in loc. S Lorenzo come from Forum Popilii.

SESSA AURUNCA MAP SHEET (IGM F.A1 I SE)

S1　　Column　　　　　　　　　　　Uncertain
Loc. Lo Capitolo. Construction works revealed a fluted column drum in yellow tuff, and nothing else.

S2　　Cemetery　　　　　　　　　　VI–IX
Loc. Torricella. A scatter of tegulae, according to the local farmer, derives from a number of *tombe a cappuccina*.

S3　　Aqueduct　　　　　　　　　　VII
Costa Malegrano. Sections of a conduit are visible cut through the tuff and revetted in reticulate with tile courses and a gabled ceiling. This probably led to Suessa Aurunca, crossing the Canale Grande over arches.

S4　　Cemetery　　　　　　　　　　VII–IX
Case popolari. Construction of a housing-estate in the 1960s revealed an extensive cemetery. I have been given photographs of tile-built mausolea, *tombe a cappuccina* and amphora burials.

S5　　Suessa Aurunca
Sessa Aurunca. See text.

S6　　Pottery scatter　　　　　　　　II
Loc. Li Bruni. Hand-made CW (17) revealed during building works in 1981.

S6bis　Pottery scatter　　　　　　　?VI–VII
A Roman site was also destroyed at S6, though all that was recovered includes: green porphyry crusta (1); African amph. (1); CW.

S7　　Church　　　　　　　　　　　XII
Loc. Mass. Volana. Cave-church revealed during deep-ploughing on side of slight hill. Apsidal end bears Campano-Byzantine wall-paintings of six figures: Christ, Mary and saints Thomas, Nicholas, Michael and Peter. Above and behind the cave heaped inhumations have come to light. A minimum of 7/8 individuals of both sexes were represented, at least 3 being immature.

A Roman road passed just to the N of the site.

S7bis　Pottery scatter　　　　　　　VII–VIII
Loc. Mass. Volana. Just to the S of site S7: ARS A closed form (1), Hayes 8 (2), Hayes 9 (5); ARS 23 (2) and 197 (1); ITS (1); CW; dolia; the following amphorae: imperial Rhodian (1); Pelichet 46 (1); Cintas 312–313 (2); Dr. 2–4 (1); Asia Minor Biv (4).

S8　　Cemetery　　　　　　　　　　VIII
Loc. Mass. Volana. At least six *tombe a cappuccina* have been revealed by levelling operations. Finds include: ARS A (1); ARS A Hayes 9 (1); ARS 197 (2); CW.

S9　　Pottery scatter　　　　　　　VII–VIII
Loc. Mass. Volana. ITS (1); ESB (1); ARS A (3); ARS C (1); Fcc; CW; tile.

S10　　Farm　　　　　　　　　　　VIII–X
Loc. Mass. Volana. Semilateres; grey limestone tesserae; ARS A (5); ARS A 8 (1); ARS A 32 or 33 (1); ARS D (1); ARS D Hayes 91 (1); Fcc; CW; late painted ware (2); tile.

S11　　DMV　　　　　　　　　　　?XII +
S Maria della Piana. Though attested in sources, visible remains are of post-medieval date and include a dilapidated church and large pottery scatter.

---

[47]　Vallat, 1987b, 328, site Carinola 4.
[48]　The same stamp is known from site S48.
[49]　See Vallat, 1987b, fig 137, for a proposed plan of the site.
[50]　Soprintendenza archives C.2–33, 1925.

S12   Village   IV–V
Loc. Mass. Irace. Abundant BG, CW and tile, a glass paste
bead, a local bronze coin (Obv: Hel. hd. Minerva l. R: Cock r.
with legend SVESANO), rare Campanian bucchero and reticu-
late-painted lekythoi indicate site of a presumed village.[51]

S12bis Flint scatter   I/II
Loc. Mass. Irace. Scatter of flint flakes and a few retouched
blades on site S12.

S13   Cemetery   Prob. VII
Loc. Il Campo. Several *tombe a cappuccina* were discovered a few
years ago.

S14   Pottery scatter   IV–VIII
S of loc. Il Campo. Iron Age hand-made and wheel-turned CW
(25); early BG B-oide (20); ARS A (1); ARS A Hayes 8 (1);
ARS D (1); late repub. and early imp. CW. It is possible that
there is no continuity between the Iron Age and the Roman
periods of occupation.

S15   Pottery scatter   XI?
Loc. Il Campo. At foot of knoll on which stands masseria: white
marble cornice moulding; ?early medieval CW (several). The
area around the masseria has been bulldozed.

S16   Burial   IV
Near Ponte Ronaco. Pozzolana quarrying in 1964 brought to
light three hand-made vessels which formed part of a later
7th century BC tomb group.[52]

S17   Pottery scatter   IV
Near Ponte Ronaco. Iron Age tazza;[53] CW, possibly from
burials.

S18   Pottery scatter   IV+
Loc. Prop. Valletta. *Tomba a fossa* emerging from S side of road
cutting leading to Ponte Ronaco. It contained frags. of a dolium
and was sealed by one or more blocks of grey tuff. Scatter of
pottery in field above tomb: hand-made CW (12); BG B-oide
(3); ARS A Hayes 8 (1); local Dr. 1 amph.; CW. A 7th century
BC tomb was also discovered in the area.[54]

S19   Mausoleum   VII or VII
Loc. Mass. Irace/Ponte Ronaco. Deep-ploughing has revealed
abundant mortar, signinum, scattered tiles with no pottery, by
side of Roman road.

S20   Flint and pottery scatter   ?Late II
SW of Mass. Fratella. Hand-made CW (13); flint flakes (2);BG
B-oide (2).

S21   Burial/s   Late IV/early V
Near Ponte Ronaco. Leveling in 1980 revealed five BG vessels,
an Italic red-figure krater and a lekythos, and six CW vessels,
datable to end of 4th or early 3rd century BC, from one or more
tombs.[55]

S22   Road and cemetery   VII–IX
Near Ponte Ronaco. Road widening in 1980 revealed three
rectangular brick-faced concrete mausolea and a grey tuff
sarcophagus containing an inhumation and an annular and a
pennanular fibula. Excavations in 1985 by Dott.ssa L Melillo
revealed further burials, some late Roman.

S23   Pottery scatter   VI–VII
Near S Rocco. Bulldozing revealed: BG B-oide (5); repub. CW;
Fcc (1).

S24   Road and cemetery   III; VI–VIII
Loc. Rio delle Cammarelle. Agricultural terracing revealed part
of the road between Suessa Aurunca and Teanum Sidicinum,
flanked by square mausolea and two *tombe a cappuccina*. A
cobbled *diverticulum* was seen to depart from the main road in a
NE direction. The site was subsequently excavated by Dott.
Nunzio Allegro for the Soprintendenza. Survey revealed:
thumb-nail flint scraper (1); hand-made CW (3); BG A (1); BG
B-oide (6); ITS (8); Campanian ITS (2); LITS (1); TWW (1);
PRW (1); ARS A (4); ARS Hayes 8 (2); ARS Hayes 23 (4);
early imp. lamp (1); Fcc; CW; and >20 miniature CW ollae
from a pit.

S24bis ?Kiln site or dump   VIII-IX
Loc. Ponte delle Cammarelle. Red glass paste mosaic tessera;
ARS D (1); wasters of Fcc, imitation ARS Hayes 61A and 91,
tegulae and imbrices.

S25   Pottery scatter   VII–VIII
S of Rio delle Cammarelle. Hand-made CW (1); ARS A (2);
CW.

S25bis Pottery scatter   ?II-III
S of Rio delle Cammarelle. Flint flake (1); hand-made CW (7).

S26   Pottery scatter   VI-VII
Loc. Cerquello. BG B-oide (8); Cintas 312–313 amph. (1); Dr.
2–4 amph.; Africana I amph. (1); early imp. TWW (1); CW.

S26bis Pottery scatter   ?II
Loc. Cerquello. Flint scraper (1); hand-made CW (16).

S27   Villa   VI+
Loc. Mass. Friola. Cryptoporticus of limestone opus incertum in
the midst of a heavily bulldozed area. Repub. TWW; CW.

S28   Villa   VI–IX
E of Mass. Friola. Ploughed-out remains of opus incertum and a
surviving wall with white marble veneer on edge of field. Opus
incertum cistern also survives. BG B-oide (2); PRW (1); ITS (3,
one Campanian?); TWW (3); ARS A (1); ARS D (4); ARS of
Hayes forms 8 (1), 14 (2), 67 (1), 88 (1), 91 (1); Fcc; CW; local
amph.; window glass (1).

S29   Pottery scatter   VII+
Loc. Mass. Palmienti. Flint blade (1); ITS (3); ARS A (1); ARS
A Hayes 9 (1); CW; tile.

S29bis Pottery scatter   ?II-III
Loc. Mass. Palmienti. On agricultural terrace just to S of S29:
hand-made CW (10).

[51] See Talamo, 1987, 10–50.
[52] Villucci, 1980, 46–48; Talamo, 1987, 51–54.
[53] Talamo, 1987, 53–54, no 4.
[54] Talamo, 1987, 53–60; Merolla, 1983, 209–212.
[55] Villucci, 1980, 49–55.

S30   Church   XI+
Loc. S Marco, Cellole. Remains of 8th–9th century wall paintings preserved in the church of St Mark.[56] The Soprintendenza archives (S 12–4) mention classical spolia found in the demolished church of St Lucia, including an inscription recording POMPEIA SECVNDA.

S31   DMV   ?VII–XII+
Loc. Derola. Abundant CW (early med.?); med. lead-glazed ware (2); BG; amph. frags. Roman road blocks, white marble frags. and a decorated architectural terracotta are re-used in revetment walls of a sunken road and in foundations of a casale. The sunken road almost certainly follows the line of a Roman road. Several wells were backfilled by the local farmer.

S32   Pottery scatter   Uncertain
Near Carano. Thin scatter of tile and CW in recently levelled and ploughed field.

S33   Flint scatter   I?
Loc. Mass. Calvisi. Waste flake, flaked pebble and naturally battered piece of flint.

S34   Villa   VI–VIII
Mass. Ponterotto. Two decantation vats for oil or wine paved with terracotta rhombs, re-used limestone threshold block and marble cornice moulding on site of the masseria built over a villa. White limestone tesserae; BG B-oide (2); ITS (4); ARS A (4); ARS of Hayes 23 or 27 (1); early Imp. Rhodian amph. (1); Tripolitana III amph. (1); early imperial lamp (1). Previous finds by Gruppo Archeologico Suessano include an ITS ba.s. with *planta pedis* stamp: C.M.APR.FELIX.[57]

S35   Farm   VII+
Loc. Mass. Vignola. Small rectangular building in yellow tuff reticulate, prob. part of a larger complex. ITS (1); Dr. 2–4 amph.; early Imp. TWW (2); CW; tile.

S36   Pottery scatter   III
Loc. Gran Celsa. Hand-made CW (10), poss. related to similar pottery found in recent quarry cut to SW of site S37.

S37   Villa   VI–VIII
Santuario della Gran Celsa. *Basis villae* constructed in ?two phases: polygonal limestone block wall and criptoporticus in limestone opus incertum, upon which sits an abandoned monastery.[58] Various other structures and elements may be seen, including a signinum-lined vat, a threshold block, column tiles and other walls in opus incertum. A cistern is incorporated within, whilst another lies behind villa. Early imp. kiln dump found behind cryptoporticus including imitations of ARS Hayes 8 and 23, Dr. 2–4 amph., a local amph. type, local TWW and CW.[59] Other pottery from site includes: BG B-oide (2); ARS A (2); CW. A 4th BC Campanian bronze coin with human-headed bull was also found.
    A recent quarry cut to SW of villa has revealed two pits, one lined with mortar, which may be silos.

S38   Villa or farm?   VI?
Loc. Gran Celsa. A tract of wall in polygonal limestone blocks is visible beneath dense vegetation. This may be part of site S37, and no dating evidence was recovered.

S39   Pottery scatter   Uncertain
Sessa Railway Station. Dr. 1 amph. and late repub. CW seen in a roadside section.

S40   Mausoleum   VII
Loc. Mass. Varnella/Falco. Ploughed-out masonry including two blocks with bas-relief probably from a mausoleum, and now in private possession at Carano. Little pottery visible on site: local amph.; CW.

S41   DMV and road   ?XI-XII+
Loc. Quintola. DMV of Quintola stretching W of Mass. degli Aitani, along ridge, and around Roman road signaled by re-used and scattered lava blocks. Dense grass cover permits limited sherding: a few scraps of medieval pottery, the occasional Roman sherd, and a bronze buckle. Four coins have been found by locals:[60]
1) Bronze 'cavallo' of Ferdinand I of Arragon. 1458–1494. CNI XIX, no 1046.
2) As above, though CNI XIX, nos 1021ff.
3) Bronze 'bogattino' of the Republic of Venice. Post 1519. CNI VIII, nos 21ff.
4) Bronze 'follaro' of the Republic of Venice. Zaccaria Salamon (Dalmatia, Albania), 1567–1569. CNI VI, nos 709ff.

S42   Pottery scatter   VII–IX
Loc. Mass. S Elia. BG B-oide (1); ARS A (6); ARS A Hayes 16 (1); ARS D (2); CW; tile; glass beaker rim.

S43   Villa   VI–IX
Loc. Mass. Casarine. *Basis villae* of squared limestone blocks and vaults with opus signinum lining destroyed by agricultural work. Architectural elements signalled by red, purple and yellow striped wall plaster, column tiles and grey limestone tessera. BG B-oide (8); PRW (1); ITS (1); ESB (1); ARS A (3); ARS A Hayes 8 (3), 9 (3); ARS Hayes 23/197 (2), 196 (5); 197 (3); ARS D Hayes 61? (1); Dress. 7–11 amph. (1); Almagro 50 amph. (1); Dress. 28? amph. (1); Dress 1A (1); Fcc; CW; tile; rough limestone mortar.

S43bis Pottery scatter   Late II–III
Loc. Mass. Casarine. Hand-made pottery (9). Neolithic flints were also, apparently, discovered in the area.[61]

S44   Pottery scatter   VI–IX
Loc. Furoni. ?Attic BG (1); BG B-oide (6); PRW (1); ITS (9); ARS A (14); ARS A Hayes 3 (2); ARS A Hayes 8 (4); ARS D (1); ARS D Hayes 91 (1); local imitation ARS Hayes 197 (2); Dr. 1B and 2–4 amph.; late repub. to late imp. CW; tile; blue glass paste tessera; green glass melon-bead.

S45   Pottery scatter   ?VI–VII
Between Piedimonte and Carano. BG B-oide (2); TWW (1); African amph. (1); CW.

S45bis Pottery scatter   III
Between Piedimonte and Carano. Hand-made CW (24).

S46   Pottery scatter   II or III
Between Piedimonte and Carano. Hand-made CW (19).

[56] Bertelli, 1982, 276 and 280, figs 1 and 5.
[57] Villucci, 1979, 56–57.
[58] Menna, 1848, 123; Arthur, 1982b; Vallat, 1987b, 328, site Sessa 12, fig. 147.
[59] For the amphorae see Arthur, 1982b.
[60] I am grateful to Dott.ssa Renata Cantilena for having identified the coins. They have been deposited in the *medagliere* of the National Museum of Naples.
[61] The only diagnostic piece of pottery is published by Villucci, 1981a. For the flints see Borrelli, 1928, 18 and fig 17.

S47   Villa   VI–VIII
Loc. S Maria della Libera. Double-vaulted cistern of opus incertum and tile, and channels cut through local tuff. White and grey limestone tesserae, BG B-oide (3); ITS (2); ARS A Hayes 8 (1); ARS C Hayes 50 (1); CW; tile.

S48   Villa   VI–VII
Loc. I Greci. *Basis villae* of polygonal limestone blocks and remains of vaulted cistern in opus incertum. Column tiles; two tegulae with stamp CALCLE[m;[62] BG B-oide (2); ITS (5); Dr. 20 amph. (1); late repub. and early imp. CW; tile.

S49   Spolia   Post-medieval
Mass. Zacconara. Various limestone blocks, including the base for the arbores of a press, are scattered around the Masseria and presumably were found in the vicinity.

S50   Pottery scatter   Uncertain Roman
Piedimonte-Carano road. Tile fragments and ?imp. CW found in solifluxion deposits.

S51   Flint and pottery scatter   II (Apennine?)
Near Piedimonte Rivoli. Hundreds of hand-made CW, flint (23, including an arrowhead), obsidian (4) and a loom-weight were revealed by agricultural levelling. This seems to be the site of an Apennine village.

S52   Pottery scatter   II
Loc. Pedrale. Hand-made CW (42); irregular baked-clay lump.

S53   Monastery   XI–XII
S Martino. Extensive remains of monastery are preserved, including various walls of irregular limestone blocks, a cistern and St Martin's cave with 12th century and later wall-paintings. No datable pottery is visible. Soprintendenza archives record the discovery of a lead conduit descending from the chapel of St Martin towards Sessa Aurunca.[63]

S54   Pottery scatter   II?
Loc. La Tenuta. Hand-made CW (7) on surface of forest track.

S55   Pottery scatter   VII–IX
Loc. Mass. Fievo. Site cut by via Domiziana with principal remains to W. of road. Tile-column shaft with fluted red-painted plaster; ARS D Hayes 61A (1); ARS D Hayes 91A (1); Cintas 312–313 amph. (1); CW; tile. Farmer claims to have found *tombe a cappuccina* and bronze coins.

S56   Structures   VI–VII
Between Mass. Fievo and Mass. del Medico. Limestone and mortar rubble, opus incertum and signinum, destroyed through bulldozing and leveling. Sole associated sherd: Dr. 1 amph.

S57   Villa   VII
Loc. Le Colonne. Bulldozing and ploughing have revealed: thick spread of tile; limestone blocks from ?opus incertum; tile-column; lava road blocks; ITS (3); ESB (1); Dr. 1 and 2–4 amph.; poss. dolium lid. An inscription is reputed to have been found.

S58   Pottery scatter   VI–VII
Between Mass. Torre Bianca and Scaccia. BG B-oide (3); BG C (1); ITS (1); CW; abundant post-medieval pottery.

S59   Pottery scatter   Uncertain
Loc. Mass. Scaccia. CW; eroded Roman tile.

S60   Villa   VI–VII
Loc. Ciesco Cupo. Vaulted cistern with opus signinum lining, prob. forming part of a *basis villae* and a terrace wall in opus incertum.[64] Hexagonal-shaped paving tiles; BG B-oide (4); Late repub. TWW (1); ITS (1); ARS Hayes 23 (1) and 181 (1); Dr. 7–11 amph. (1); Haltern 70 amph. (1); Africana I amph. (1); Dr. 2–4 amph.; CW; tile.

S61   Villa   VI–VII
Loc. Ciesco Cupo. Cryptoporticus, composed of four parallel vaults in opus incertum, upon which is based a one-roomed post-medieval building re-using Roman structures.[65] Few finds on account of dense vegetation: fluted column drum in yellow tuff; BG B-oide (2); ITS (1); CW; tile.

S62   Villa   VI–VIII
Loc. M Finocchiaro. *Basis villae* contained by wall in squared limestone blocks with rustication. On terrace is a double-vaulted cistern, part of a wall in grey tuff reticulate, a limestone threshold block and a limestone base for the *arbores* of a press. White and mauve tesserae; architectural terracottas with palmettes; ARS A (3); CW; tile.

S63   Pottery scatter and road   VI+
Near Mass. Ulivella. Sparse limestone road blocks across field. BG B-oide (2); Graeco-Italic amph. (1); local amph.; CW.

S64   Structures and road   VII
Loc. S Sebastiano. Well-preserved tract of road in limestone blocks to side of modern villa. Ploughed-out opus incertum with opus signinum lining. Lozenge-shaped tile (1); ITS (2); Dr. 1 and 2–4 amph.; CW; tile.

S65   Pottery scatter and road   VII
Loc. S Lorenzo. Dr. 2–4 amph., CW and tile, revealed on spoil of building works. Landowner claims that during construction a lead pipe was found running beneath a road surface of limestone blocks.

S66   Pottery scatter   II
Strada Panoramica. Hand-made CW (18) revealed in bulldozed section for agricultural terracing.

S67   Villa/Farm   VI–VIII
Strada Panoramica. Large polygonal limestone blocks (from *basis villae?*) re-used in modern terrace walls. BG B-oide (6); LITS (1); ARS A (6); ARS A Hayes 8 (1); ARS Hayes 196 (1); ARS Hayes 23/197 (1); repub. TWW (1); terracotta rhombs (2).

S67bis Flint scatter   Prob. II
Strada Panoramica. Three flints revealed on site S67.

---

[62] See site C42 for the kiln site that produced these tiles.
[63] S.8–6, 1940.

[64] Vallat, 1987b, 328 and 341–2, site Sessa 4. Contrary to his conclusions, the site seems to have remained in use until, at least, the second century AD.
[65] Vallat, 1987b, 328 and 341–2, site Sessa 3.

S68   Church/monastery   XI–XII+
Loc. S Maria Bocca D'Oro. See text. Walls, including an apse, in mortared irregular limestone and grey tuff blocks.[66] Below the structures is a concentration of human bones, a white marble column base, part of a fluted column drum and fragments of Pentelic marble and porphyry veneer. Local farmers had unearthed a number of burials generally devoid of grave goods save a bronze earring and a bracelet. Flint waste flake (1); Graeco-Italic amph. (1); BG B-oide (2); abundant CW and early medieval painted pottery; frags. of red, light blue and white painted plaster.

S69   Villa   VI+?
Loc. Querce di Santoro. Standing structures in opus incertum heavily obscured by vegetation. BG B-oide (15); BG A (1); PRW (1); repub. CW.

S70   Pottery scatter   VI–VII
Loc. Mass. Casella. Levelling has revealed a concentration of Dr. 1A and 1B amph., not, apparently, kiln waste.

S71   Villa   V–VII
Loc. Cas. Zannini. *Basis villae* composed of a section of squared limestone blocks and a section of a cryptoporticus in opus incertum. Upon the terrace are structures in opus incertum and several late repub. mosaic floors.[67] BG B-oide (44); PRW (2); ITS (9); African amph. (1); Dr. 20? (1); CW; tile.

S72   Farm   VI–VIII
Loc. Cofanari. A vaulted gallery is visible below ground in field.[68] Limestone tessera; BG B-oide (5); PRW (1); LITS (1); ARS A (1); ARS Hayes 196 (1); Fcc; CW; local amph.; tile.

S73   Pottery scatter   VI–IX
Loc. Mass. Schitoli. Limestone blocks prob. from opus incertum. BG B-oide (2); ARS A (2); ARS A Hayes 14A (1) and 14B (1); ARS D (1); Dr. 1B and 2–4 amph.; Fcc; CW; late Roman painted CW.

S74   Pottery scatter   Late IV–V
Between Piedimonte and Carano. Hand-made CW (10); BG B-oide (6); CW.

S75   Pottery scatter   VI–VII
Loc. S Agata. BG B-oide (2); PRW (1); ARS A (1); Dr. 1 amph.; CW; tile, in a colluvial deposit below a quarry.

S76   Pottery scatter   VII–VIII
M Ofelio. BG B-oide (1); ARS A Hayes 5C (1) and 8 (1); ARS Hayes 197 (1); ARS D (1); CW. Local farmer claims that a tile-built structure exists nearby in a heavily overgrown area.

S77   Pottery scatter   VI
Loc. Torricelle. BG B-oide (4); CW; on dirt-track in heavily disturbed and overgrown area, prob. from site in vicinity.

S78   Pottery scatter   VII–IX
Loc. Palombarella. Building works have revealed a rough mortared wall and pottery: BG B-oide (2); PRW (1); Campanian ITS (1); repub. TWW (1); ARS Hayes 23 or 197 (3); ARS D Hayes 91 (1); Fcc; CW; tile.

S79   Pottery scatter   III?
Via Panoramica. Hand-made CW (19).

S80   Pottery scatter   VI–VII
Loc. Mass. Pozzili. BG B-oide (1); ITS (2); Graeco-Italic amph. (1); Africana I amph. (1); dolium; CW.

S81   Uncertain   I
Loc. Furoni. Worked palaeolithic flint found associated with charcoal beneath ignimbrite exposed in northern section of Piedimonte-Carano road by Prof J Sevink.[69]

S82   Cemetery   Uncertain
Carano. Numerous inhumations reported during construction of the house of Avv. Santilli in early 1970's.

---

[66] This site is almost certainly the dependancy of S Vincenzo al Volturno known as S Maria a Fauciano in the *Chronicon Vulturnense*. It eventually became the parish church of Falciano, to be finally abandoned in favour of a church in the centre of the town in 1640 (De Stasio, 1975, 55–56).

[67] Johannowsky, 1975, site 8; Vallat, 1987b, 328, site Sessa 10. The site has been the subject of excavation by Dott. N. Allegro, though remains unpublished.

[68] Vallat, 1987b, 328 and 352, site Carinola 9/Sessa 11.

[69] See Remmelzwaal, 1978, fig. 2.14, for a drawing of the roadside section. I thank Prof. Sevink for the information.

BIBLIOGRAPHY

Periodicals, when possible, are referred to by the abbreviations adopted by L'Année Philologique. Standard reference works are cited in the notes using the following abbreviations:

CIL   Corpus Inscriptionum Latinarum
CNI   Corpus Nummorum Italicorum
EE   Ephemeris Epigraphica
CIG   Corpus Inscriptiones Graecae
ILLRP   Inscriptiones Latinae Liberae Rei Publicae
ILS   Inscriptiones Latinae Selectae
PIR   Prosopographia Imperii Romani
RE   Realencyclopädie der Altumwissenschaft. Ed. Pauly-Wissowa.
RIC   The Roman Imperial Coinage. Eds. H. Mattingly, E.A. Sydenham and others.

ACERBO, G. (1934), La economia dei cereali nell'Italia e nel mondo, Milano.

ADRIANI, A. (1938), "Minturno", NSA, 159–226.

AFAN DE RIVERA, C. (1845), Del bonificamento del lago Salpi coordinato a quello della pianura della Capitanata, delle opere eseguite e dei vantaggi ottenuti, Napoli.

AFZELIUS, A. (1944), Die römische Kriegsmacht wahrend der Auseinanderstzung mit den hellenistichen Grossmachten, Copenhagen.

ALBORE LIVADIE, C. (1979), "Le bucchero nero en Campanie. Notes de typologie et chronologie", Le bucchero étrusque et sa diffusion en Gaule Meridionale, Coll. Latomus 106, 91-110.

ALBORE LIVADIE, C. (1983), "Sur les amphores de type étrusque des nécropoles archaiques de Nuceria: aspects et problemes de l'etrusquisation de la Campanie", RSL XLIV, 4, 71-135.

ALBORE LIVADIE, C. (1985), "La situazione in Campania", Il Commercio Etrusco Arcaico, Quad. Centro Stud. Arch. Etrusco Italica 9, CNR, Rome, 127-149.

ALDINI, T. (1978), "Anfore Foropopiliensi", ArchClass XXX, 236-245.

ALDINI, T. (1981), Fornaci di Forum Popili, Forlimpopoli.

ALDRIDGE, J.L. (1978), Mediterranean Pilot 11, 10ᵗʰ Ed., Admiralty, Taunton.

ALESSIO, G. (1977), "Il nome di Terra di Lavoro", ArchStor Terra di Lavoro V, 9-14.

ALMAGIA, R. (1966), Lazio, Le regioni d'Italia II, TCI, Roma.

AMAR, G. and LIOU, B. (1984), "Les estampilles sur amphores du Golfe de Fos", Archeonautica 4, 145-211.

AMARI, M. and SCHIAPARELLI, C. (1883), "L'Italia descritta nel 'Libro del Re Ruggiero' compilato da Edrisi", AttiRAccLinc VIII, ser. 2.

AMPOLO, C. (1980), "Le condizioni materiali della produzione. Agricoltura e paesaggio agrario", DdA 1, 2, 15-46.

ANDERSON, P. (1974), Passages from Antiquity to Feudalism, London.

ANDREI, S. (1981), Aspects du vocabulaire agricole, Roma.

ANDREWS, D. (1978), "Medieval masonry in northern Lazio: its development and uses for dating", H. McK. Blake, T.W. Potter and D.B. Whitehouse (Eds.), Papers in Italian Archaeology I, pt. ii, BAR S41, Oxford, 391-422.

ANTONINI, R. (1977), "Iscrizioni osche inedite", SE XLV, 343-344.

ARTHUR, P. (1976), "Some recent finds from Ostia", NCirc, March 1976, Spink's, London, 3.

ARTHUR, P. (1982a), "Considerazioni su una probabile divisione agraria nell'agro di Suessa Aurunca", ArchClass XXXIV, 175-178.

ARTHUR, P. (1982b), "Roman amphorae and the Ager Falernus under the Empire", PBSR L, 22-23.

ARTHUR, P. (1982c), "Notiziario – Campania – Provincia di Caserta", RSP XXXVII, 1-2, 1984, 317.

ARTHUR, P. (1985a), "Naples: notes on the economy of a dark age city", C. Malone and S. Stoddart (Eds.), Papers in Italian Archaeology IV, pt. iv, BAR S243, Oxford, 247-259.

ARTHUR, P. (1985b), "The marble of Mondragone", StMisc 26, 97-98.

ARTHUR, P. (1986), "Problems of the urbanization of Pompeii", AntJ 66, pt. 1, 29-44.

ARTHUR, P. (1987), "Precisazioni su di una forma anforica medio-imperiale dalla Campania", in El vi a l'antiguitat. Economia, produccio i comerc al Mediterrani occidental, Badalona, 401-406.

ARTHUR, P., ALBARELLA, U. and WAYMAN, M. (1989), "M179: An early medieval lowland site at Loc. Arivito, near Mondragone (Caserta)", ArchMed XVI, forthcoming.

ARTHUR, P. and GUALTIERI, M. (1987), "Rapporto preliminare sugli scavi a Sinuessa", Civiltà Aurunca 5, 417-422.

ARTHUR, P. and WHITEHOUSE, D.B. (1982), "La ceramica dell'Italia meridionale: produzione e mercato tra V e X secolo", ArchMed IX, 39-46.

ASTROM, P. (1969), "Iter populo debetur ped. tot", ORom VII, 83-88.

AUBERT, R. (Ed.) (1971), Dictionnaire d'Histoire et de Geographie Ecclesiastique 17, Paris.

AURIGEMMA, S. and DE SANTIS, A. (1955), Gaeta-Formia-Minturno, Itinerari dei musei e monumenti, Ist. Polig. dello Stato, Roma.

BADIAN, E. (1971), "Roman politics and the Italians (133-91 B.C.)", DdA V, 373-409.

BADIAN, E. (1973), "Marius' villas: the testimony of the slave and the knight", JRS LXIII, 121-132.

BAILO MODESTI, G., D'AGOSTINO, B., GASTALDI, P. and JOHANNOWSKY, W. (1976), "La Protostoria", La Voce della Campania 1, 23-38.

BALDACCI, P. (1969), "Le principali correnti del commercio di anfore romane nella Cisalpina", G. Bermond Montanari (Ed.), I Problemi della Ceramica Romana di Ravenna, della Valle Padana e dell'Alto Adriatico, Bologna, 103-131.

BARATTA, M. (1901), I Terremoti d'Italia, Forni, Torino.

BARKER, G. (1981), Landscape and Society. Prehistoric Central Italy, Academic Press, London.

BARKER, G., LLOYD, J. and WEBLEY, D. (1978), "A Classical landscape in Molise", PBSR XXXIII, 35-51.

BARKER, G. and SYMONDS, J. (1984), "The Montarrenti survey, 1982-1983", ArchMed XI, 278-289.

BARNISH, S.J.B. (1987), "Pigs, plebians and potentates: Rome's economic hinterland, c. 350-600 A.D.", PBSR LV, 157-185.

BASANOFF, V. (1950), "M. Caedicius de Plebe...et...Q. Caedicius Centurio", Latomus IX.

BATICLE, Y. (1974), L'Elevage Ovin dans les Pays Européens de la Mediterranée Occidentale, Dijon.

BELOCH, K.J. (1926), Romische Geschichte bis zum Beginn der punischen Kriege, Berlin and Leipzig.

BENCIVENGA, C. (1987), "Sulla diffusione delle anfore tardo-imperiali in Campania: il complesso di Gricognano (Caserta)", in El vi a l'antiguitat. Economia, produccio i comerc al Mediterrani occidental, Badalona, 395-401.

BERARD, J. (1941), La Colonisation Grecque de l'Italie meridionale et de la Sicile dans l'Antiquité: l'Histoire et la Légende, Paris.

BERGOMI, C., CATENNACI, V., CESTARI, G.,

MANFREDINI, M. and MANGANELLI, V. (1969), Note illustrative della carta geologica d'Italia, Foglio 171, Gaeta e vulcano di Roccamonfina, Roma.

BERGOMI, C. and MANGANELLI, V. (1971), "Vulcano di Roccamonfina", F. Scarsella, Note illustrative della carta geologica d'Italia, Foglio 172, Caserta, Roma, 67-123.

BERNARDI, A. (1943), "Roma e Capua nella seconda metà del quarto secolo a.C., II", Atheneum XXXI (n.s. XXI), 21-31.

BEZECZKY, T. (1983), "Roman amphorae from Zalalovo", MittArchInstUngAkadWiss 12/13, 153-166.

BIDDITTU, I. and SEGRE NALDINI, E. (1981), "Insediamenti eneolitici e dell'antica età del bronzo nella Valle del Sacco, a Silva dei Muli e Ceccano (Frosinone)", ArchLaz IV, 35-46.

BLOK, A. (1969), "South Italian agro-towns", Comp. Stud. in Soc. and Hist. 11.

BOAK, A.E.R. (1955), Manpower shortage and the fall of the Roman Empire in the West, Ann Arbor.

BOGNETTI, G.P. (1927), Sulle origini dei comuni rurali nel medioevo, Pavia.

BONGHI IOVINO, M. and DONCEEL, R. (1969), La Necropoli di Nola Preromana, Napoli.

BORRELLI, F. (1976), Appunti di Storiografia Aurunca, Sessa Aurunca.

BORRELLI, N. (1916), L'Agro Vescino, Maddaloni.

BORRELLI, N. (1921), "Le monete dell'antica Suessa Aurunca", MiscNum II.

BORRELLI, N. (1935), "Osservazioni e chiarificazioni intorno alla monetazione degli Aurunci", RassNum, 9-10.

BOULVERT, G. (1970), Esclaves et affranchis imperiaux sous le haut empire romain. Role politique et administratif, Paris.

BRANCACCIO, S. (1980), "Il sisma e l'incuria: nuovi e antichi mali del patrimonio artistico", StudSuess II, 11-20.

BRAUDEL, P. (1975), The Mediterranean and the Mediterranean World in the Age of Philip II, 2 vols., London.

BRAUN, R. (1964), Quodvultdeus: Livre des promesses et des predictions de Dieu, Sources Chretiénnes 101-2, Paris.

BREGLIA, L. (1946), "Rinvenimento monetale di Sessa Aurunca", Numis 1-2, 1-5.

BREISLAK, S. (1798), Topografia Fisica della Campania, Napoli.

BROOKES, A.C. (1974), "Minturnae: The Via Appia Bridge", AJA 78, 41-48.

BROUETTE, E. (1949), "'Vinum Falernum': Contribution à l'étude de la sémantique latine au Haut Moyen Age", C&M X, 263-273.

BROWN, F.E. (1980), Cosa. The Making of a Town, Ann Arbor.

BRUNT, P.A. (1971), Italian Manpower 225 B.C.-A.D. 14, OUP, Oxford.

BURY, J.B. (1923), History of the Later Roman Empire, 2 vols., London.

BUTLER, H.C. (1901), "The aqueduct of Minturnae", AJA V, 187-192.

CALLENDER, M.H. (1965), Roman Amphorae with Index of Stamps, OUP, London.

CAMODECA, G. (1981), "Ricerche su Puteoli tardoromana (Fine III-IV secolo)", Puteoli IV-V, 59-128.

CANTILENA, R. (Ed.) (1981), Sannio, Pentri e Frentani dal VI al I secolo a.C., Napoli.

CANTU', C.M. (1989), I bufali in Italia dall'alto medioevo ad oggi, Edizioni Lativa.

CARAFA, R. and COLLETTA, T. (1978), "Proposta di restauro a Sessa Aurunca, Gli ambienti romani di Piazza Tiberio", Antiqua 10, 62-66.

CARANCINI, G.L. (1979), "Alcuni aspetti della metallurgia nel corso dell'età del bronzo", ArchLaz II, 177-184.

CARANDINI, A. (1970), "Produzione agricola e produzione ceramica nell'Africa di età imperiale", StudMisc 15, 95-119.

CARANDINI, A. (1980), "Prefazione: Quando la dimora dello strumento è l'uomo", in J. Kolendo, L'Agricoltura nell'Italia Romana, Riuniti, Rome, ix-lx.

CARANDINI, A. (1989), "La villa romana e la piantagione schiavistica", in Storia di Roma 4, Caratteri e morfologie, Einaudi, Turin, 101-200.

CARANDINI, A. and PANELLA, C. (Eds.) (1973), Ostia, Terme del Nuotatore, Saggio nell'area S-O, StudMisc 21, Ostia III.

CARANDINI, A. and SETTIS, S. (1979), Schiavi e padroni nell'Etruria romana. La villa di Settefinestre dallo scavo alla mostra, Bari.

CARNEY, T.F. (1961), "The flight and exile of Marius", G&R VIII, 98-121.

CAROTTI, A. (1974), Gli Affreschi della Grotta delle Fornelle a Calvi Vecchia, De Luca, Roma.

CARRINGTON, R.C. (1931), "Studies in the Campanian 'villae rusticae'", JRS XXI, 110-130.

CARTER, J.C., COSTANTINI, L., D'ANNIBALE, C., JONES, J.R., FOLK, R.L. and SULLIVAN, D. (1985), "Population and Agriculture: Magna Grecia in the fourth century B.C.", in C. Malone and S. Stoddart (Eds.) Papers in Italian Archaeology IV, BAR S246, Oxford, 281-311.

CASSANDRO, G. (1969), "Il Ducato Bizantino", Storia di Napoli vol. 2, tome 1, Naples.

CASTAGNETTI, A. (1979), L'organizzazione del territorio rurale nel medioevo. Circoscrizioni ecclesiastiche e civili nella 'Langobardia' e nella 'Romania', Torino.

CASTAGNOLI, F. (1944), "Le formae delle colonie romane e le miniature dei codici dei gromatici", AttiRAccIt ser. 7, IV, 83-118.

CASTAGNOLI, F. (1955), "I più antiche esempi conservati di divisioni agrarie romane", BCAR LXXV, 3-9.

CASTAGNOLI, F. (1956), Ippodamo di Mileto e l'urbanistica a pianta ortogonale, De Luca, Roma.

CASTAGNOLI, F. (1978), "La Carta Archeologica d'Italia", PP CLXXVIII, 78-80.

CASTREN, P. (1975), Ordo Populusque Pompeianus, Polity and Society in Roman Pompeii, Acta Ist. Rom. Fin. VIII.

CAVUOTO, P. (1982), "Le iscrizioni latine di Minturno", VIII misc. greca e latina, 489-585.

CAZZELLA, A., MARAZZI, M., MOSCOLONI, M. and TUSA, S. (1981), "La preistoria dell'isola", Vivara, Oasi di Protezione Naturale, Napoli, 105-152.

CEBEILLAC-GERVASONI, M. (1982), "Ascesa al senato e rapporti con i territori d'origine: la zona di Capua e di Cales", Tituli 5, 59-99.

CECCHELLI, C. (1951), "La Torre di Pandolfo Capodiferro al Garigliano ed uno scomparso cimelio della sua raccolta", ArchStorPat, LXXIV, 1-26.

CEDERNA, A. (1951), "Carsoli – scoperta di un deposito votivo del III secolo av. Cr. (Prima campagna di scavo)", NSA Ser. VIII, vol. V, 169-224.

CELUZZA, M. and REGOLI, E. (1982), "La Valle d'Oro nel territorio di Cosa; ager Cosanus e ager Veientanus a confronto", DdA 4, 1, 31-62.

CERLESI, E.E., CERLESI, L.L. and CERLESI, F.G. (1984), Cavità sotterranee e sollecitazioni sismiche, Rome.

CHASTAGNOL, A. (1953), "Le ravitaillement de Rome en viande au Ve siècle", RH 210, 13-22.

CHERUBINI, G. (1981), "La 'civiltà' del castgno in Italia alla fine del medioevo", ArchMed VIII, 247-280.

CHOUQUER, G. and FAVORY, F. (1983), "Cadastrions antiques de Campanie, du Latium méridional et de Romagne", in M. Clavel-Léveque (Ed.), Cadastres at Espace Rural, Table ronde de Besancon, Mai 1980, Paris, 318-324.

CHOUQUER, G., CLAVEL-LEVEQUE, M., FAVORY, F. and VALLAT, J-P. (1987), Structures agraires en Italie centro-méridionale, cadastres et paysage ruraux, Coll.EFR 100.

CIASCA, R. (1928), Storia delle Bonifiche del Regno di Napoli, Naples.

CICALA, S. e LAO, F. (1958), "Ricerche subacque per l'ubicazione di Vescia", Atti II° Conv. Int. Arch. Sub., Albenga, 110-116.

CILENTO, N. (1966), Italia Meridionale Longobarda, Milan and Naples.

CLUVERIUS, F. (1624), Italia Antiqua II, Lyons.

COARELLI, F. (1977), "Public building in Rome between the Second Punic War and Sulla", PBSR 45, 1-23.

COARELLI, F. (1982), Lazio, Bari.

COARELLI, F. (1983), "Il commercio delle opere d'arte in età tardo repubblicana", DArch I, 1, 45-53.

COARELLI, F. (Ed.) (1989), Minturnae, Rome.

COCOZZA, F. (1981), Indagine preliminare per uno studio topografico del territorio di Teano, Univ. of Naples, unpublished undergraduate thesis.

COLACCIO, G. (1955), La Bonifica del Tavoliere, Foggia.

COMFORT, H. (1943), "Terra Sigillata from Minturnae", AJA 47, 313ff.

COMFORT, H. (1976), "Minturnae", Princeton Enciclopedia of Classical Sites, Princeton, 582-583.

CONTA HALLER, G. (1978), Ricerche su alcuni centri fortificati in opera poligonale in area Campano-Sannitica (Valle del Volturno – Territorio tra Liri e Volturno), Naples.

COTTON, M.A. (1979), The Late Republican Villa at Posto, Francolise, BSR, London.

COTTON, M.A. and METRAUX, G. (1985), The San Rocco Villa at Francolise, BSR, London.

CRACCO RUGGINI, L. and CRACCO, G. (1977), "Changing fortunes of the Italian city from late antiquity to the early middle ages", RFIC 105, 448-475.

CRAWFORD, D.J. (1976), "Imperial estates", in M. Finley (Ed.), Studies in Roman Property, Cambridge, 35-70.

CRAWFORD, M.H. (1969), Roman Republican Coin Hoards, London.

CRAWFORD, M.H. (1974), Roman Republican Coinage, CUP, Cambridge.

CREMA, L. (1933), "Marmi di Minturno nel Museo Archeologico di Zagabria", Boll. Ass. Int. St. Med. IV, nos. 1-2, 25-44.

CRESCE, G. (1914), Sessa Aurunca nel periodo antico, Naples.

CUOMO, L. (1974), "La colonia di Urbana", RAAN XLIX, 29-36.

CUOMO, R., D'ABROSCA, A., D'ABROSCA, G., MENERELLA, C., NERONE, A., PAGLIARO, A., PALMIERI, M. and SPERLONGANO, F. (n.d., around 1981), Un territorio da salvaguardare: recupero delle memorie storiche, Mondragone exhibition catalogue, Scauri.

D'AGOSTINO, B. (1974), "La civiltà del ferro nell'Italia meridionale e nella Sicilia", Popoli e Civiltà dell'Italia Antica, Vol. II, Rome, 11-91.

D'ARMS, J. (1970), Romans on the Bay of Naples. A social and cultural study of the villas and their owners from 150 B.C. to A.D. 400, Harvard University Press.

D'ARMS, J. (1974), "Puteoli in the Second Century of the Roman Empire: a social and economic study", JRS LXIV,

D'ARMS, J. (1977), "M.I. Rostovtzeff and M.I. Finley: The status of traders in the Roman world", J.H. D'Arms and J.W. Eadie (Eds.), Ancient and Modern, Essays in honour of Gerald F. Else, Ann Arbor, 159-179.

D'ARMS, J. (1981), Commerce and Social Standing in Ancient Rome, Harvard.

DE AZEVEDO, M.C. (1947), Interamna Lirenas vel Sucasina, Italia Romana, Municipi e Colonie ser. II, vol. II, Rome.

DE FRANCISCIS, A. (1953), "Iscrizioni sepolcrali da Teano", RAC XXIX, 227-230.

DE FRANCISCIS, A. (1983), "Tito e la Campania nella documentazione archeologica", in Atti del Congresso Internazionale di Studi Flaviani, Rieti, 147-159.

DELANO-SMITH, C. (1978), Daunia Vetus, terra, vita e mutamenti sulle coste del Tavoliere, Foggia.

DELANO-SMITH, C. (1979), Western Mediterranean Europe, A Historical Geography of Italy, Spain and Southern France since the Neolithic, Academic Press, London.

DELLA CORTE, M. (1923), "Pompei – Scavi eseguiti da privati nel territorio pompeiano", NSA XX, 271-287.

DELLA CORTE, M. (1938), "Le iscrizioni graffite sul criptoportico del teatro", Campania Romana I, Naples, 189-201.

DEL TREPPO, M. (1955), "La vita economica e sociale in una grande abbazia del Mezzogiorno: S. Vincenzo al Volturno nell'alto medioevo", Arch. Stor. Prov. Nap. LXXIV, 31-110.

DE MASI, T. (1761), Memorie Istoriche degli Aurunci, Naples.

DE ROBERTIS, F.M. (1948), "La produzione agricola in Italia dalla crisi del III secolo all'età dei Carolingi", Ann. Fac. Econ. Comm. Univ. Bari 8, Bari, 67-271.

DE ROSSI, G. (1980), Lazio Meridionale, Rome.

DE SANTIS, A. (1938), "La numerazione dei fuochi a Sessa nel 1447", Latina Gens 9-10, 248-261.

DE SANTIS, A. (1945), "Appunti di toponomastica della bassa valle del Garigliano", Arch. Dep. Rom. Stor. Pat. LXVIII, n.s. XI, 257-299.

DE SANTIS, A. (1963), "Centri del basso Garigliano abitati nel medioevo e abbandonati nei secoli XVI e XVII", Bull. Ist. Stor. It. Med. Evo. e Arch. Mur. 75, Rome, 391-408.

DE SPAGNOLIS, M. (1981), Minturno, Itri.

DE STASIO, L. (1974), S. Martino, eremita del Monte Massico, Scauri.

DE STASIO, L. (1975), Alle Origini di Falciano del Massico, Falciano.

DEVOTO, G. (1952), Gli Antichi Italici, Florence.

DEVOTO, G. (1965), "Lacustrine pleicestocene in the lower Liri valley", Geol. Rom. 4.

DIAMARE, G.M. (1906), Memorie critico-storiche della Chiesa di Sessa Aurunca, Naples.

DIEBNER, S. (1979), Aesernia – Venafrum, Rome.

DIEBNER, S. (1983), "Un gruppo di cinerari romani del Lazio meridionale", DArch ser. III, no. 1, 65-78.

DILKE, O.A.W. (1971), The Roman Land Surveyors, Plymouth.

DI PORTO, A. (1984), Impresa collettiva e schiavo 'manager' in Roma antica (II sec. a.C. – II sec. d.C.), Milano.

D'ONOFRIO, M. (1980), "La 'Turris ad Mare' al Garigliano", Stud. Suess. II, 29-32.

D'ONOFRIO, M. and PACE, V. (1981), La Campania, Italia Romanica 4, Milan.

DRESSEL, H. (1891), "Instrumentum Domesticum", CIL XV.

DUBY, G. (1975), Le Origini dell'Economia Europea, guerrieri e contadini nel medioevo, Laterza, Rome-Bari.

DUCHESNE, L. (1886-1957), Le Liber Pontificalis, 3 vols., BEFAR, Paris.

DUNBABIN, K.M. (1978), The Mosaics of Roman North Africa, Oxford.

DUNCAN JONES, R.P. (1974), The Economy of the Roman Empire, Quantitative Studies, London.

DUNCAN JONES, R.P. (1980), "Demographic change and economic progress under the Roman Empire", Tecnologia, Economia e Società nel Mondo Romano, Como, 67-80.

DYSON, S.L. (1978), "Settlement patterns in the ager Cosanus: the Wesleyan University Survey", JFA 5, 251ff.

DYSON, S.L. (1983), The Roman Villas of Buccino, BAR S187, Oxford.

EGIDI, R. (1985), "Il Lazio meridionale costiero. Le villae maritimae", Misurare la Terra: centuriazione e coloni nel mondo romano. Città, agricoltura, commercio: materiali da Roma e dal suburbio, Modena, 110-112.

ESCHEBACH, H. (1970), Die stadtebauliche entwicklung des antiken Pompeji, MDAI(R) Supp.

EVANS, J.K. (1981), "Wheat production and its social consequences in the Roman world", CQ XXXI, no. 2, 428-442.

EWALD, P. and HARTMANN, L.M. (Eds.) (1981), Gregorii I Papae, Registrum Epistolarum vol. I, Berlin.

FABRE', G. (1981), Libertus, Recherches sur les rapports patron-affranchi à la fin de la république Romaine, Rome.

FANT, J.C. (1976), Curatores Rei Publicae in the Roman Empire, Univ. of Michigan, unpub. Ph.D thesis.

FARQUHARSON, A.S.L. (1944), The Meditations of Marcus Aurelius, 2 vols., Oxford.

FEDELE, P. (1899), "La battaglia del garigliano dell'anno 915 ed i monumenti che la ricordano", Arch. R. Soc. Rom. Stor. Pat. XXII, 181-211.

FEDELE, P. (1958), Minturno, Storia e Folklore, Naples.

FEDERICI, V. (Ed.) (1925-1938), Chronicon Vulturnense del Monaco Giovanni, Fonti per la Storia d'Italia, vols. I-III, Rome.

FENTRESS, L. and PERKINS, P. (1988), "Counting African Red Slip Ware", in L'Africa Romana, Atti del V convegno di studio Sassari, 11-13 dicembre 1987, 205-214.

FERRARA, B. and INTRIERI, F. (1974), "La bufala in Italia", Atti del 1o Convegno Internazionale sull'allevamento bufalino nel mondo, Caserta, 35-47.

FEUGERE, M. (1981), "Découvertes au quartier de Villeneuve, Fréjus (Var), la mobilier métallique et la parure", Doc. D'Arch. Mer. 4, 137-168.

FICCADORI, G. (1983), "I frammenti iscritti", in G. Bermond Montanari (Ed.), Ravenna e il porto di Classe, Univ. Press, Bologna, 238-241.

FINLEY, M.I. (1958), Review of Boak, 1955, JRS XLVIII, 156-164.

FINLEY, M.I. (1975), Storia della Sicilia Antica, Laterza, Bari.

FINLEY, M.I. (Ed.) (1976), Studies in Roman Property, Cambridge.

FINLEY, M.I. (1980), Ancient Slavery and Modern Ideology, London.

FIORITO, E. and VILLUCCI, A.M. (1980), "Ricognizione di una variante dell'Appia nel tratto Suessa-Teanum", Stud. Suess. II, 33-37.

FORABOSCHI, D. (1984), Preface to Kuziskin, 1984, pp. vii-xxii.

FORTI, L. (1950), "Terracotte del santuario della dea Marica", RAAN XXIV-X-XV, 349ff.

FOSS, C. (1977), "Archaeology and the 'Twenty Cities' of Byzantine Asia", AJA 81, 469-486.

FRACCHIA, H., GUALTIERI, M. and DE POLIGNAC, F. (1983), "Il territorio di Roccagloriosa in Lucania (Provincia di Salerno)", MEFRA 95, 1, 345-380.

FRAENKEL, E. (1957), Horace, Oxford.

FRANCOVICH, R., GELICHI, S. and PARENTI, R. (1980), "Aspetti e problemi di forme abitative minori attraverso la documentazione materiale nella Toscana medievale", Arch. Med. VII, 173-246.

FRANK, T. (1933), An Economic Survey of Ancient Rome: vol. i: Rome and Italy of the Republic, John Hopkins U.P., Baltimore.

FREDERIKSEN, M.W. (1959), "Republican Capua: A social and economic study", PBSR XXVII, 80-130.

FREDERIKSEN, M.W. (1971), "The contribution of archaeology to the agrarian problem in the Gracchan period", DArch V, 330-357.

FREDERIKSEN, M.W. (1976), "Changes in the patterns of settlement", in P. Zanker (Ed.), Hellenismus in Mittelitalien, 341-355.

FREDERIKSEN, M.W. (1977), "Una fonte trascurata sul bradisismo puteolano", in I Campi Flegrei nell'Archeologia e nella Storia, Accad. Linc., Rome, 117-129.

FREDERIKSEN, M.W. (1979), "The Etruscans in Campania", in D. and F. Ridgeway (Eds.), Italy before the Romans. The Iron Age, Orientalizing and Etruscan Periods, London, 277-311.

FREDERIKSEN, M.W. (1981), "I cambiamenti delle strutture agrarie nella tarda repubblica: La Campania", in A. Giardina and F. Schiavone (Eds.), L'Italia: Insediamenti e forme economiche, Società Romana e Produzione Schiavistica I, Laterza, Bari, 265-287.

FREDERIKSEN, M.W. (1984), Campania, Ed. with additions by N. Purcell, BSR, London.

FRIER, B.W. (1969), "Points on the topography of Minturnae", Historia 18, 510-512.

FRIER, B.W. and PARKER, A.J. (1970), "Roman coins from the river Liri", NC X, 89-109.

FUGAZZOLA DELPINO, M.A. (1976), Testimonianze di cultura appeninica nel Lazio, Sansoni, Florence.

FULFORD, M. (1980), "Carthage: Overseas Trade and the Political Economy", c. A.D. 400-700", Read. Med. Stud. 6, 68-80.

GABBA, E. (1967), Appiani Bellorum Civilium Liber Primus, Florence.

GABBA, E. and PASQUINUCCI, M. (1979), Strutture Agrarie e Allevamento Transumante nell'Italia Romana (III-I sec. A.C.), Pisa.

GABRICI, E. (1908), "Teano – avanzi di un grande edificio termale dell'antico 'Teanum Sidicinum' sorgente in contrada S. Croce", NSA, 399-415.

GAGGIOTTI, M. (1983), "Tre casi regionali italici: Il Sannio Pentro", in M. Cébeillac-Gervasoni (Ed.), Les 'Bourgeoisies' Municipales Italiennes aux IIe et Ier Siecles av. J-C, Rome, 137-150.

GAGLIARDO, G.B. (1814), Dell'Agricoltura di Sessa, Naples.

GALASSO, G. (1975), Mezzogiorno Medievale e Moderno, Turin.

GALASSO, G. (1982), L'altra Europa, Per un'antropologia storica del Mezzogiorno d'Italia, Milan.

GALLINA, A. (1971), "Via Appia", Fasti Arch. XXII, no. 4268.

GAY, J. (1904), L'Italie meridionale et l'empire byzantin, Paris.

GENTILE, A. (1955), La romanità dell'agro campano alla luce dei suoi nomi locali, Naples.

GIANFROTTA, P.A. (1981), "Archeologia sott'acqua: rinvenimenti sottomarini in Etruria meridionale", BA 10, 69-92.

GIANNETTI, B. (1979), "The geology of Roccamonfina caldera", Giornale di Geologia, Ann. del Mus. Geol. di Bologna XLVIII, 2, 187-206.

GIARDINO, L. (1983), "Il porto di Metaponto in età imperiale, topografia e materiale ceramico", Stud. di Ant. 4, 5-36.

GIARIZZO, A. (1965), "La piana del Garigliano", Boll. Soc. Geog. It. ser IX, vol. VI.

GIGLIOLI, G.Q. (1911), "Note archeologiche sul Latium Novum", Ausonia VI. 39-87.

GOETHE, J.W. (1886), Viaggio in Italia (It. ed. Novara, 1973).

GORGES, J. (1979), Les villas Hispano-Romaines. Inventaire et problematique archeologiques, Paris.

GOUDINEAU, C. (1968), La céramique arétine lissé, Rome.

GRAEVIUS, G.J. and BURMANNUS, P. (1704), Thesaurus antiquitatum et historiarum Italiae, Neapolis et Siciliae I, Lyons.

GRECO, B. (1927), Storia di Mondragone, 2 vols., Naples.

GRENIER, A. (1959), Manuel d'Archeologie Gallo-romaine IV, 2, Paris.

GROS, P. and TORELLI, M. (1988), Storia dell'Urbanistica. Il mondo romano, Bari.

GUADAGNO, G. (1976), "Vie commerciali preistoriche e

protostoriche in Terra di Lavoro", Antiqua 2, 55-68.

GUADAGNO, G. (1979), "Sui centri fortificati preromani nell'Alto Casertano", Arch. stor. Terra di Lavoro VI, 261-279.

GUADAGNO, G. (1987), "L'ager Falernus in età romana", in G. Guadagno (ed.), Storia, economia ed architettura nell'ager Falernus, Minturno, 17-58.

GUAITOLI, M. (1984), "Urbanistica", Arch. Laz. VI, 364-381.

GUIDOBALDI, F. (1978), Il complesso archeologico di S. Clemente, Rome.

GUIDOBONI, E. (Ed.) (1989), I terremoti prima del Mille in Italia e nell'area mediterranea, Bologna.

HAMMOND, M. (1957), "Composition of the Senate. A.D. 68-235", JRS 47, 74-81.

HANNESTAD, K. (1962), L'evolution des resources agricoles de l'Italie du 4eme au 6eme siecle de notre ere, Copenhagen.

HARDY, E.G. (1912), Roman Laws and Charters, Oxford.

HARTLEY, K. (1973), "La diffusion des mortiers, tuiles et autres produits en provenance des fabriques Italiennes", Cah.D'Arch.Sub. II, 49–60.

HATZFELD, J. (1912), "Les Italiens resident a Delos", BCH XXXVI, 5-218.

HATZFELD, J. (1919), Les Trafiquants Italiens dans l'Orient Hellenique, Paris.

HAYES, J.W. (1972), Late Roman Pottery, BSR, London.

HAYES, J.W. (1980), Supplement to Late Roman Pottery, BSR, London.

HEITLAND, W.E. (1921), Agricola, Cambridge.

HESNARD, A. (1980), "Un dépot augustéen à la Longarina, Ostie", in J.H. D'Arms and E.C. Kopff (Eds.), Roman Seaborne Commerce: Studies in Archaeology and History, MAAR 36, Rome, 141-156.

HESNARD, A., RICQ, M., ARTHUR, P., PICON, M. and TCHERNIA, A. (1989), Aires de production des gréco-italiques et des Dr. 1", in Amphores romaines et histoire économiques, dix ans de recherche, Rome, 21-65.

HEURGON, J. (1942), Recherches sur l'histoire, la religion et la civilisation de Capoue préromaine, Paris.

HODGES, R. (1985), "S. Vincenzo al Volturno", Conoscenze I, 228-233.

HODGES, R. and WHITEHOUSE, D.B. (1984), Mohammed, Charlemagne and the Origins of Europe, Duckworth, London.

HODGES, R. and WICKHAM, C. (1981), "The evolution of hilltop villages in the Biferno valley, Molise", in G. Barker and R. Hodges (Eds.), Archaeology and Italian Society, Papers in Italian Archaeology II, BAR S102, Oxford, 305-312.

HODGKIN, T. (Ed.), (1886), The Letters of Cassiodorus, London.

HOPKINS, K. (1978), Conquerors and Slaves, Cambridge.

HOPKINS, K. (1980), "Taxes and Trade in the Roman Empire (200 B.C. to A.D. 400)", JRS LXX, 101-125.

HOPKINS, K. (1983), Death and Renewal, Cambridge.

HOUSTON, G.W. (1980), "The administration of Italian seaports during the first three centuries of the Roman Empire", in J.H. D'Arms and E.C. Kopff (Eds.), Roman Seaborne Commerce: Studies in Archaeology and History, MAAR 36, Rome, 157-171.

IACOPI, G. (1963), L'Antro di Tiberio a Sperlonga, Roma.

INGUANEZ, M., MATTEI-CERASOLI, L. and SELLA, P. (Eds.) (1942), Rationes decimarum, Campania, Vatican.

IONTA, A.C. (1985), Ricognizioni epigrafiche nel territorio di Minturnae, Formia.

IPPOLITO, G. (1930), La bonifica idraulica in destra del Volturno, Naples.

JASNY, N. (1944), The Wheats of Classical Antiquity, Baltimore.

JOHANNOWSKY, W. (1961), "Relazione preliminare sugli scavi di Cales", BA XLVI, 258-268.

JOHANNOWSKY, W. (1963), "L'occupazione etrusca in Campania", in A. Alfoldi, Early Rome and the Latins, Ann Arbor.

JOHANNOWSKY, W. (1965), "Problemi di classificazione e cronologia di alcune scoperte protostoriche a Capua e Cales", SE XXXIII, 685-698.

JOHANNOWSKY, W. (1971), "La Campania", DArch V, 460-471.

JOHANNOWSKY, W. (1973), "Note sui criptoportici pubblici in Campania", Les Cryptoportiques dans l'Architecture Romaine, CollEFR 14, Rome, 143-165.

JOHANNOWSKY, W. (1974), "La situazione in Campania", in P. Zanker (Ed.), Hellenismus in Mittelitalien, Gottingen.

JOHANNOWSKY, W. (1975), "Problemi archeologici campani", RAAN L, 3-38.

JOHANNOWSKY, W. (1978), "Importazioni Greco-Orientali in Campania", Les Ceramiques de la Grece de l'Est et leur diffusion en Occident, CNRS, Naples, 137-139.

JOHANNOWSKY, W. (1983), Materiali di età arcaica dalla Campania, Naples.

JOHNSON, J. (1933), Inscriptions at Minturnae I, Republican Magistri, Pennsylvania.

JOHNSON, J. (1935), Excavations at Minturnae I, Pennsylvania.

JOHNSON, J. (1936), "Minturnae" in RE, 458-494.

JONCHERAY, J-P. and ROCHIER, Y. (1976), "L'Epave de la Roche Fouras, coque du navire, estampilles sur amphores", Cah. D'Arch. Sub. V, 167-180.

JONES, A.H.M. (1960), "Church finance in the fifth and sixth centuries", JThS 11, 84-94.

JONES, A.H.M., MARTINDALE, J.R. and MORRIS, J. (1976), The Prosopography of the Later Roman Empire, Cambridge.

JONES, G.D.B. (1963), "Capena and the ager Capenas. pt. II", PBSR 31, 100-158.

KALBY, G. (1975), "Gli insediamenti rupestri della Campania", La Civiltà Rupestre medioevale nel Mezzogiorno d'Italia. Ricerche e Problemi, Atti del I convegno, Genova, 153-172.

KALBY, G. (Ed.) (1982), Terremoto. Memoria Storica, Salerno.

KAJANTO, I. (1965), The Latin Cognomina, Soc. Sc. Fenn. Comm. Hum. Litt. XXVI, 2, Helsinki.

KEAY, S.J. (1984), Late Roman Amphorae in the Western Mediterranean. A typology and economic study: the Catalan evidence, BAR S196, Oxford.

KEHR, P.F. (1935), Italia Pontificia, Berlin.

KEPPIE, L. (1983), Colonisation and Veteran Settlement in Italy 47-14 B.C., BSR, London.

KING, A. and HENIG. M. (Eds.) (1981), The Roman West in the Third Century, BAR S109, Oxford.

KING, R.L. (1973), Land Reform. The Italian Experience, London.

KIRSOPP LAKE, A. (1935), "Campana Supellex – The Pottery deposit at Minturnae", Bull. Ass. Int. St. Med. V, 97-136.

KORNEMANN, E. (1905), "Polis und Urbs", Klio, 72–92.

KUBITSCHEK, W. (1889), Imperium Romanum tributim discriptim, Vienna.

KUHN, C.G. (Ed.) (1965), Claudii Galeni Opera Omnia, repr. Hildesheim.

KUZISKIM, V.I. (1982), "L'espansione del latifondo in Italia alla fine della repubblica", in L. Capogrossi Colognesi (Ed.), L'Agricoltura Romana. Guida storica e critica, Bari, 43-63.

KUZISKIN, V.I. (1984), La grande proprietà agraria nell'Italia romana, Rome.

LACHMANN, C. and RUDORFF, A. (Ed.) (1948), Gromatici

Veteres, Berlin.

LAFON, X. (1979), "La voie littorale Sperlonga-Gaeta-Formia", MEFRA L, 399-419.

LAMB, H.H. (1977), Climate, Past, Present and Future, 2 vols., London.

LAMBOGLIA, N. (1961), "La nave romana di Spargi", Actes du IIᶜ Congrès International d'Archeologie sous-marine, Albenga, 1958, 143-166.

LAMBRECHTS, P. (1936), "La composition du Senat romain de l'accession au trone d'Hadrien à la mort de Commode (117-192)", Werken uitgegeven door de Faculteit van de Wysbegeerte en Letteren 79, Antwerp.

LANZONI, F. (1927), Le diocesi d'Italia dalle origini al principio del secolo VII (an. 604), Faenza.

LA PENNA, A. (1971), "Discussione", DArch V, 359-360.

LA REGINA, A. (1970), "Note sulla formazione dei centri urbani in area Sabellica", in G. Mansuelli and R. Zangheri (Eds.), La Città Etrusca ed Italia Preromana, Bologna, 191-207.

LAUBENHEIMER, F. (1985), La production des amphores en Gaule Narbonnaise, Parigi.

LAUBENHEIMER, F., ODIOT, T. and LECLERE, H. (1989), "Sous Auguste, un atelier de potiers italianisant à Saint-Just (Ardèche)", Mélanges P. Léveque, 295-329.

LAUFFER, S. (Ed.) (1971), Diokletians Preisedikt, Berlin.

LAURENT-VIBERT, R. and PIGANIOL, A. (1907), "Inscriptions inédites de Minturnes", MEFRA XXVII, 495-507.

LECCISOTTI, T. (Ed.) (1972), I Regesti dell'Archivio VII, Abbazia di Monte Cassino, Rome.

LEHNER, H. (1930), "Romische Steindenkmaler von der Bonner Munsterkirche", BJ CXXXV, 1-48.

LEPORE, E. (1977), "Gli Ausoni e il più antico popolamento della Campania: leggende delle origini, tradizioni antiche e realtà culturali", Arch. Stor. Terra di Lavoro V, 81-108.

LEVI, A. (1919), NSA, 356-358.

LEWTHWAITE, J. (1981), "Plains tails from the hills: Transhumance in Mediterranean Archaeology", in A. Sheridan and G. Bailey (Eds.), Economic Archaeology, BAR S96, Oxford, 57-66.

LINDSAY, W.M. (Ed.) (1913), Sextus Pompeius Festus. De Significatione Verborum, Leipzig.

LIZIER, A. (1907), L'economia rurale dell'età prenormanna nell'Italia meridionale, Studi su documenti editi dei secoli IX-XI, Palermo.

LLEWELLYN, P. (1970), Rome in the Dark Ages, Oxford.

LLOYD, J.A. (1981), Review of Cotton, 1979, AntJ LXI, 136-137.

LOESCHCKE, S. (1942), "Die Römische und belgische Keramik", in Ch. Albrecht, Das Romerlager in Oberaden, II, Dortmund.

LUGLI, G. (1957), La Tecnica Edilizia Romana, Rome.

LYDING WILL, E. (1979), "The Sestius Amphoras: a reappraisal", JFA 6, n. 3, 341-350.

LYDING WILL, E. (1982), "Greco-Italic amphoras", Hesperia 51, 3, 338-356.

LYDING WILL, E. (1984), "The Spargi wreck: a reconsideration", AJA 88, 264.

LYDING WILL, E. (1987), "The Roman Amphoras", in A.M. McCann (Ed.), The Roman Port and Fishery of Cosa, Princeton, 171-220.

MACGEACHY, J.A. (1942), Quintus Aurelius Symmachus and the Senatorial Aristocracy of the West, Chicago.

MAGNAGUTI, A. (1940), La Fauna in Virgilio e in altri poeti antichi e moderni, Padua.

MAIURI, A. (1925), "Oggetti sporadici di epoca preistorica", NSA, 90.

MAIURI, A. (1926), "Armille di bronzo preromane dell'Italia meridionale", BPI XLVI, fasc. 1, 3-9.

MAIURI, A. (1928), "Cuma – nuovi tratti messi in luce della 'Via Domitiana'", NSA, 181-185.

MAIURI, A. (1934), "Del sito di Vescia nel territorio degli Aurunci", Atti Accad. Nap. n.s. XIII, 295-315.

MAIURI, A. (1938), Passegiate Campane, Milan.

MAIURI, A. (1961), "Il criptoportico di Suessa Aurunca", RAAN 36, 55-62.

MAIURI, A. (1973), Alla ricerca di Pompei Preromana, Naples.

MAIURI, A. (1975), Ercolano, new ed., Rome.

MALLEGNI, F. and FORNACIARI, G. (1985), "Le ossa umane", in A. Ricci (Ed.), Settefinestre, Una villa schiavistica nell'etruria romana. La villa e i suoi reperti, Modena, 275-277.

MANACORDA, D. (1977), "Anfore spagnole a Pompei", in A. Carandini (Ed.), L'Instrumentum Domesticum di Ercolano e Pompei, Rome, 121-133.

MANACORDA, D. (1977b), "Testimonianze sulla produzione e il consumo dell'olio tripolitano nel III secolo", DArch IX-X, 542-601.

MANACORDA, D. (1981), "Produzione agricola, produzione ceramica e proprietari nell'ager Cosanus nel I sec. a.C.", in A. Giardina and A. Schiavone (Eds.), L'Italia: Società Romana e Produzione Schiavistica II, Bari, 3-54.

MANACORDA, D. (1982), "Il frantoio della villa dei Volusii a Lucus Feroniae", I Volusii Saturnini, Bari, 55-82.

MANACORDA, D. (1984), "L'identificazione dell'anfora di Empoli", in Archeologia del territorio di Empoli, Empoli, 23-28.

MANACORDA, D. (1985), "L'interpretazione della villa. Dai Sestii agli Imperatori", in A. Carandini (Ed.), Settefinestre, Una villa schiavistica nell'etruria romana. La villa nel suo insieme, Modena, 101-106.

MANACORDA, D. (1985b), "Schiavo 'manager' e anfore romane: a proposito dei rapporti tra archeologia e storia del diritto", Opus IV, 141-151.

MARTIN, T. (1986), Montans. Centre potier Gallo-Romain, Montans.

MARUCCHI, O. (1897), "Conferenze di archeologia cristiana", Nuovo Boll. di Arch. Crist. III, 131-144.

MARZOCCHELLA, A. (1980), "Le tombe eneolitiche di Napoli – Materdei", RSP 35, 147-164.

MATTINGLY, D.J. (1988), "Oil for export? A comparison of Libyan, Spanish and Tunisian olive oil production in the Roman empire", JRA 1, 33-56.

MAZZA, M. (1973), Lotte sociali e restaurazione autoritaria nel III secolo d.C., Bari.

McCAIL, R.C. (1978), "P.Gr. Vindob. 29788C: hexameter encomium on an un-named emperor", JHS XCVIII, 38-63.

McDERMOTT, W.C. (1976), "Stemmata qui faciunt? The descendants of Frontinus", Anc. Soc. VII, 229–261.

MEIGGS, R. (1980), "Sea-borne timber supplies to Rome", in J.H. D'Arms and E.C. Kopff (Eds.), Roman Seaborne Commerce: Studies in Archaeology and History, MAAR 36, Rome, 185-196.

MELILLO FAENZA, L. and PAGANO, M. (1983), "La senatrice Viria Marcella in un singolare bollo laterizio da Sinuessa", RAAN LVIII, 371-377.

MENNA, L. (1848), Saggio istorico della città di Carinola, 2 vols., Aversa.

MEROLLA, M. (1964), "Allifae, le mura e il criptoportico", AClass XVI, 36-48.

MEROLLA, M. (1983), "Suessa Aurunca, Cales, Calatia, Suessula", in W. Johannowsky, 1983, 209-286.

METCALF, W. (1974), "Roman coins from the river Liri II", NC XIV, 42-52.

MICHELE, S. (1968), "Alla scoperta di Sinuessa", Vie Nuove.

MILLAR, F. (1981), "The world of the Golden Ass", JRS LXXI, 63-75.

MILLER, K. (1916), Itineraria Romana, Stuttgart.

MINGAZZINI, P. (1938), "Il santuario della dea Marica alle foci del Garigliano", MonAL XXXVII.

MIRAGLIA, G. (1986), "Ricerche sulla tarda antichità nei Campi Flegrei. Un tesoretto monetale del VI secolo d.C. da Cuma", in P. Amalfitano (Ed.), Il Destino della Sibilla, Naples, 235-252.

MOELLER, W.O. (1976), The Wool Trade of Ancient Pompeii, Leiden.

MOMMSEN, T. (1908), "Die italischen Regionen", Gesammelte Schriften V, 268-285.

MORANI, M. (1933), "Per migliorare l'olivicoltura nell'agro di Sessa Aurunca", Boll. Aur. I, 80-89.

MOREL, J-P. (1976), "Aspects de l'artisanat dans la Grande Grèce romaine", La Magna Grecia in Età Romana, Atti di Taranto XV, 263-324.

MOREL, J-P. (1981), Ceramique Campanienne: Les Formes, BEFAR 244, Rome.

MOREL, J-P. (1983), "Les productions de biens artisanaux en Italie à la fin de la République", in M. Cébeillac-Gervasoni (Ed.), Les 'Bourgeoises' Municipales Italiennes aux IIe et Ier Siecles av.J.-C., Rome, 21-39.

MOREL, J-P. (1989), "Un atelier d'amphores Dressel 2/4 à Cales", in Amphores romaines et histoire économiques, dix ans de recherche, Rome, 558-559.

MORITZ, L.A. (1958), Grain Mills and Flour in Classical Antiquity, Oxford.

MOSS, H.St.L.B. (1937), "The economic consequences of the barbarian invasions", Econ. Hist. Rev. VII, 209-216.

MOSSER, S.Mc.A. (1935), A Bibliography of Byzantine Coin Hoards, New York.

MUNZER, F. (1935), "Zu den magistri von Minturnae", MDAI(R) 50, 321-330.

MUSTILLI, D. (1962), "La documentazione archeologica in Campania", Greci ed Italici in Magna Grecia, Atti di Taranto I, Naples, 163-194.

NAPOLI, M. (1957), "L'Afrodite di Sinuessa", RAAN XXXII, 183ff.

NEWELL, E.T. (1933), Two Hoards from Minturnae, New York.

NICOTERA, P. (1950), "Sulle rocce laviche adoperate nell'antica Pompei", Pompeiana. Raccolta di studi per il secondo centenario degli scavi di Pompei, Naples, 396-424.

NISSEN, H. (1883), Italische Landeskunde II, Berlin.

NORTH, J.A. (1976), "Conservatism and change in Roman religion", PBSR XLIV 1-12.

OGILVIE, R.M. (1965), A Commentary on Livy Books 1-5, Oxford.

OXE, A. and COMFORT, H. (1968), Corpus Vasorum Aretinorum, Bonn.

PAGANO, M. (1974), Una città sepolta: Sinuessa, Naples.

PAGANO, M. (1980), "Due iscrizioni latine da Mondragone", RAAN LV, 5-12.

PAGANO, M. (1981a), "Note epigrafiche e archeologiche Sinuessanae", MEFRA 93, 2, 869-881.

PAGANO, M. (1981b), "Tracce di centuriazione e altri contributi su Sinuessa e Minturnae", RAAN LVI, 105-124.

PAGANO, M. (1983), "Nuove iscrizioni dall'agro Falerno", RAAN LVIII, 363-370.

PAGANO, M. and FERONE, C. (1976), Sinuessa, Ricerche storiche e topografiche, Naples.

PAIS, E. (1908), "Intorno all'estensione degli Ausoni", Ricerche Storiche e Geografiche sull'Italia Antica, Turin.

PALLARES, F. (1986), "Il relitto della nave romana di Spargi", BollD'Arte Supp. Archeologia Subacquea 3, 89-102.

PALLOTTINO, M. (1976), "Inquadramento storico", in Civiltà del Lazio Primitivo, Rome, 37-55.

PALMIERI, R. (1977), "Nuove iscrizioni di Capua, Sinuessa,

Suessa e revisione di 'Ephemeris Epigraphica' VIII 566", MGR V, 315-338.

PANELLA, C. (1973), "Le Anfore", in A. Carandini and C. Panella (Eds.), Ostia, Terme del Nuotatore, Saggio nell'area S-O, Ostia III, StudMisc 21, 460-633.

PANELLA, C. (1977), "Anfore Tripolitane a Pompei", in A. Carandini (Ed.), L'Instrumentum Domesticum di ercolano e Pompei, Rome, 135-149.

PANELLA, C. (1980), "Retroterra, porti e mercati: l'esempio dell'ager Falernus", in J.H. D'Arms and E.C. Kopff (Eds.), Roman Seaborne Commerce: Studies in Archaeology and History, MAAR 36, Rome, 251-259.

PANELLA, C. (1981), "La distribuzione e i mercati", in A. Giardina and A. Schiavone (Eds.), L'Italia: Società Romana e Produzione Schiavistica II, Bari, 55-80.

PANELLA, C. (1989), "Le anfore italiche del II secolo", Amphores Romaines et Histoire Economique: Dix ans de recherche, Rome, 139-178.

PANI, G.G. (1987), "Il recupero della tabula di Flavius Teodorus, patrono di Minturno (= AE 1954, 27)", ArchLaz VIII, 308-317.

PATERSON, J. (1982), "'Salvation from the Sea': Amphorae and Trade in the Roman West", JRS LXXII, 146-157.

PATTERSON, J.R. (1985), "Il vicus di epoca imperiale nella tenuta presidenziale di Castelporziano: contesto storico", in Castelporziano I, campagna di scavo e restauro, 1984, 67-69.

PEACOCK, D.P.S. (1978), "Recent discoveries of Roman amphora kilns in Italy", AntJ 58, 262-269.

PEACOCK, D.P.S. (1980), "The Roman millstone trade: a petrological sketch", World Arch. 12, no. 1, 43-53.

PEDRONI, L. (1986), Ceramica a vernice nera da Cales, 2 vols., Naples.

PEDUTO, P. (1988), "Dalla città di Rota al Castello di Sanseverino: un progetto di scavo territoriale", Rassegna Storica Salernitana 9, 155-160.

PELLEGRINO, A. (1977), Terra di Lavoro in età preromana e romana, note topografiche, Naples.

PELLEGRINO, A. (1978), "Iscrizioni da Mondragone", MGR VI, 383-394.

PELLEGRINO, C. (1651), Discorsi sulla Campania Felice, Naples.

PENSABENE, P. (1979), "Doni votivi fittili di Roma: Contributo per un inquadramento storico", Arch. Laz. II, 217-222.

PERONI, P. (1971), L'età del bronzo nella penisola italiana, 1, L'antica età del bronzo, Florence.

PERROTTA, G. (1737), La sede degli Aurunci, Naples.

PERROTTA, P. (1980), "Un sarcofago con resti umani scoperto nell'antica Sinuessa" (sic), Roma, Friday June 6th., Naples.

PETTERUTTI, B, (1983), Gli Aurunci nella Campania Felix (Storia e Monetazione), Gaeta.

PFLAUM, H-G. (1960), Les Carriers Procuratoriennes Equestres sous le Haut-Empire, vol. 2, Paris.

PIRAZZOLI, P.A. (1976), "Sea level variations in the northwest Mediterranean during Roman times", Science 194, 519-521.

PIRENNE, H. (1939), Mohammed and Charlemagne, London.

POCCETTI, P. (1982), "Sul toponimo Rocca Monfina (Caserta)", L'Italia Dialettale XLV (n.s. XXII), 221-227.

POLLINO, A. (1975), "L'épave de la Fourmigue, dans le golfe Juan", Cah.D'Arch.Sub. IV, 71-81.

PONTECORVO, C. (1979), "Ritorna alla luce dopo duemila anni il nome della superba città di Vescia", Il Golfo 10, 31 December, Gaeta.

POTTER, T.W. (1975), "Recenti ricerche in etruria meridionale: problemi della transizione dal tardo antico all'alto medioevo", Arch. Med. II, 215-236.

POTTER, T.W. (1979), The Changing Landscape of South

Etruria, London.

PRATILLI, F.M. (1745), Della Via Appia riconosciuta e descritta da Roma a Brindisi, Naples.

PROCACCINI, F. (1883), Gli atti di S. Menna eremita, Naples.

PUGLIESE CARRATELLI, G. (1962), "Santuari extra-murani in Magna Grecia", PdP XVII, 241-246.

PUGLIESE CARRATELLI, G. (1980), "Platonopolis a Cuma?", PdP CXCV, 440-442.

QUILICI GIGLI, S. (1970), "La valle del Sacco nel quadro delle comunicazioni tra Etruria e Magna Grecia", SE 38, 363-366.

RADKE, G. (1971), "Viae publicae romanae", RE Supplementband XIII.

RADMILLI, A.M. (1953), "Scavi nella Grotta dei Baffoni presso S. Vittore di Frasassi", Bull. Palet. It. VIII, pt. V, 117-130.

RADMILLI, A.M. (1961), "La preistoria in Campania", L'Universo, 715-736.

RANDAZZO, U. (1982), "A Sinuessa evitare una seconda Spargi", La Tribuna VII, no. 4, April 7th., 17.

REECE, R. (1980), "Town and country: the end of Roman Britain", World Arch. 12, no. 1, 77-91.

REMMELZWAAL, A. (1978), Soil genesis and quaternary landscape development in the Tyrrhenian coastal area of South-Central Italy, Amsterdam.

RENFREW, C. (1975), "Trade as action at a distance: questions of integration and communication", in J. Sabloff and C.C. Lamberg-Karlovsky (Eds.), Ancient Civilisation and Trade, Alburquerque, 3-59.

RICCARDELLI, F. (1873), Minturno e Traetto, svolgimenti storici antichi e moderni, Naples.

RICHARDS, J. (1980), Consul of God. The Life and Times of Gregory the Great, London.

RICHMOND, I.A. (1933), "Commemorative arches and city-gates in the Augustan age", JRS XXIII, 149-174.

RICHMOND, I.A. (1935), Review of Johnson, 1935, JRS XXVII, 291-292.

RICHMOND, I.A. and CRAWFORD, O.G.S. (1949), "The British section of the Ravenna Cosmography", Archeologia XCVIII, 1-50.

RICKMAN, G. (1971), Roman granaries and store buildings, Cambridge.

RICKMAN, G. (1980), The corn supply of ancient Rome, Oxford.

RIDGEWAY, D. (1973), "The first western Greeks: Campanian coasts and southern Etruria", in C. and S. Hawkes (Eds.), Greeks, Celts and Romans, London, 5-38.

RILEY, J.A. (1979), "Coarse pottery", in J. Lloyd (Ed.), Excavations at Sidi Khrebish, Benghazi (Berenice) II, Tripoli, 91-465.

RIZZELLO, M. (1980), I santuari della media valle del Liri, IV-I sec., Sora.

ROBERTS, P.C. (1964), "The Pirenne Thesis, economics or civilisations, towards reformulation", C&M 25, 297-315.

RODRIGUEZ ALMEIDA, E. (1984), Il Monte Testaccio, Ambiente, Storia, Materiale, Rome.

ROMANELLI, D. (1819), Antica topografia istorica del Regno di Napoli, Naples.

ROSI, G. (1989), "Il territorio di Scauri", in F. Coarelli, 1989, 97-119.

ROSI, M. (1979), Carinola, Pompei quattrocentesca, Naples.

ROSSILLO, O. (1985), La colonia musulmana del Garigliano, Scauri.

ROSS TAYLOR, L. (1960), The Voting Districts of the Roman Republic, Rome.

ROTBERG, R.I. and RABB, T.K. (Eds.) (1985), Hunger in History, Cambridge.

RUEGG, S.D. (1983), "The underwater excavation in the Garigliano river: final report 1982. The Roman port and bridge at Minturnae, Italy", IJNA 12, 3, 203-218.

RUGGIERO, M. (1881), Degli scavi di antichità nelle province di Terraferma dell'antico Regno di Napoli dal 1734 al 1876, Naples.

RUGGINI, L. (1961), Economia e società nell'Italia Annonaria, Milan.

RUGGINI, L. (1964), "Vicende rurali dell'Italia antica dall'età tetrarchica ai Longobardi", RSI LXXVI, 261-286.

RUOCCO, D. (1965), Campania, Le Regioni D'Italia 13, Turin.

RUOCCO, D. (1970), Memoria illustrativa della carta della utilizzazione del suolo della Campania, Rome.

RUOFF-VAANANEN, E. (1978), Studies on the Italian Fora, Hist. Einzelschriften 32, Rome.

SACCO, L. (1640), L'antichissima Sessa Pometia. Discorso istorico, Naples.

SALMON, E.T. (1967), Samnium and the Samnites, Cambridge.

SALMON, E.T. (1982), The Making of Roman Italy, London.

SAMBON, A. (1903), Les Monnaies Antiques de l'Italie, Paris.

SAVARESE, G. (1856), Bonificamento del bacino inferiore del Volturno, Naples.

SCARSELLA, F. (1971), Note illustrative della carta geologica d'Italia, Foglio 172, Caserta, Rome.

SCHERILLO, A., FRANCO, E., GIROLAMO, P. di. and STANZIONE, D. (1968), "Precisazioni sulle 'forme crateriche' dell'agro Falerno", Atti. Accad. Pont. XVII, 1-20.

SCHEUERMEIER, P. (1943), Il Lavoro dei Contadini, Milan.

SCHMIEDT, G. (1972), Il livello antico del Mar Tirreno, Florence.

SCHMIEDT, G. (1981), "Les viviers Romaines de la cote Tyrrhenienne", Hist. et Arch. 50, 28-45.

SCHNETZ, J. (Ed.) (1940), Itineraria Romana II, Ravennati anonymi cosmographia et Guidoni Geographica, Leipzig.

SCHNUR, H.C. (1959), "The economic background of the Satyricon", Latomus, 790-799.

SCHULZE, W. (1904), Zur Geschichte Lateinischer Eigennamen, Berlin.

SEALEY, P.R. and DAVIES, G.M.R. (1983), "Falernian wine at Roman Colchester", Britannia XIII, 250-254.

SEMENTINI, A. (no date; around 1975), Sinuessa – Ricognizioni archeologiche lungo l'Appia e la Domiziana, Naples.

SERENI, E. (1979), Storia del paessaggio agrario italiano, Bari.

SERENI, E. (1981), Terra nuova e buoi rossi, Turin.

SEVINK, J. (1985), "Physiographic soil surveys and archaeology", Papers in Italian Archaeology IV, pt. i, BAR S243, 41-52.

SEVINK, J., REMMELZWAAL, A. and SPAARGAREN, O.C. (1984), The Soils of Southern Lazio and Adjacent Campania, Amsterdam.

SHATZMAN, I. (1975), Senatorial Wealth and Roman Politics, Brussels.

SHAW, B.D. (1981), "Rural markets in North Africa and the political economy of the Roman Empire", AntAfr 17, 37-83.

SIRAGO, V.A. (1957), L'Italia agraria sotto Traiano, Louvain.

SKYDSGAARD, J.E. (1969), "Nuove ricerche sulla villa rustica romana fino all'epoca di Traiano", ARID V, 25-40.

SMALL, A. (1983), "Gli edifci del periodo tardo-antico a San Giovanni", in Lo scavo di S. Giovanni di Ruoti ed il periodo tardoantico in Basilicata, Bari, 21-37.

SMITH, W. (1873), A Dictionary of Greek and Roman Antiquities, London.

SOLIN, H. (1984), "Zu Inschriften aus den Nordlichen Kampanien", Arctos XVIII, 127-139.

SOMMELLA, P. (1978), "Forma e urbanistica di Pozzuoli romana", Puteoli II.

SOMMELLA, P. (1988), Italia antica. L'urbanistica Romana, Rome.

SORDI, M. (1965), "Sulla cronologia Liviana del IV secolo", Helikon V, 3-44.

SOUTER, A. (1949), A Glossary of later Latin to 600 A.D., Oxford.

STAEDLER, E. (1942), "Zu den 29 neu aufgefundenen Inschriftstelen von Minturno", Hermes LXXVII, 149-196.

STAERMAN, E.M. and TROFIMOVA, M.K. (1982), La schiavitù nell'Italia Imperiale, Rome.

STANZIONE, D. (1966), "Il tufo campano dell'agro Falerno, Mondragone", Rend. Acc. Sc. Fis. Mat. ser. IV, vol. XXXII, 163-190.

STOPPIONI PICCOLI, M.L. (1983), "I materiali della fornace romana di Via della Resistenza, a Santarcangelo di Romagna", Studi Romagnoli, 29-46.

SYME, R. (1939), The Roman Revolution, Oxford.

SYME, R. (1983), "Eight consuls from Patavium", PBSR LI 102-124.

TABACCO, G. (1967), "Problemi di insediamento e di popolamento nell'alto medioevo", RSI 76, 67-110.

TALAMO, P. (1987), L'area aurunca nel quadro dell'Italia centromeridionale. Testimonianze archeologiche di età arcaica, BAR S384, Oxford.

TASSAUX, F. (1982), "Laecanii – Recherches sur une famille sénatoriale d'Istrie", MEFRA 94, 1, 227-269.

TATA, M.B. (1981), "Discussione", Arch. Laz. IV, 224-225.

TCHERNIA, A. (1964), "Amphores et marques d'amphores de Betique à Pompéi et à Stabies", MEFRA 76, 419-449.

TCHERNIA, A. (1971), "Les amphores vinaires de Tarraconaise et leur exportation au debut de l'Empire", AEA 44, 38-85.

TCHERNIA, A. (1980), "Quelques remarques sur le commerce du vin et les amphores", in J.H. D'Arms and E.C. Kopff (Eds.), Roman Seaborne Commerce: Studies in Archaeology and History, MAAR 36, Rome, 305-312.

TCHERNIA, A. (1986), Le Vin de l'Italie Romaine, BEFAR 261, Rome.

TCHERNIA, A. and VILLA, J-P. (1977), "Note sur le matériel recueilli dans la fouille d'un atelier d'amphores à Velaux (Bouches-du-Rhone)", in Méthodes Classiques et Méthodes Formelles dans l'Etude des Amphores, 231-239.

THIELSCHER, P. (1963), Des Marcus Cato Belehrung uber die Landwirtschaft, Berlin.

THOMSEN, R. (1947), The Italic Regions from Augustus to the Lombards, Copenhagen.

THOMSEN, R. (1947), "The Iter statements of the Liber Coloniarum", C&M IX, 37ff.

THOUVENOT, R. (1940), Essai sur le province Romaine de Baetique, BEFAR 149, Paris.

THREIPLAND, L.M. (1963), "Excavations behind the northwest gate at Veii, 1957-1958, pt. II, the pottery", PBSR 31, 33-73.

THULIN, C. (Ed.) (1913), Corpus Agrimensorum Romanorum, Leipzig.

TOCCO SCIARELLI, G. (1981), "Teano (Caserta) – necropoli in loc. Torricelle", SE XLIX, 519-520.

TOCCO, G., BOTTINI, A., PICA, E. and MOLES, P.G. (1982), Testimonianze archeologiche nel territorio di Tolve, Matera.

TOMMASINO, G. (1925), La denominazione degli Ausoni in Campania, Santa Maria Capua Vetere.

TOMMASINO, G. (1942), Aurunci Patres, Minturno.

TORELLI, M. (1980), "Innovazioni nelle tecniche edilizie romane tra il I sec. a.C. e il I sec. d.C.", Tecnologia, Economia e Società nel Mondo Romano, Como, 139-162.

TORRE, P. (1988), "Monte D'Argento: Indagini preliminari", ArchLaz IX, 432-440.

TOYNBEE, A.J. (1965), Hannibal's Legacy: The Hannibalic War's Effects on Roman Life, 2 vols., Oxford.

TOZZI, C. (1974), "Il mesolitico della Campania", Atti XVII Riun. Sc. Camp., Florence, 33-48.

UGGERI, G. (1969), "Kleroi arcaici e bonifica classica nella chora di Metaponto", PdP XXIV, 51-71.

UGGERI, G. (1978), "Sistema viario e insediamento rupestre tra antichità e medioevo", in C. Damiano Fonseca (Ed.), Habitat-Strutture-Territorio, Galatina, 115-136.

VALLAT, J-P. (1979), "Le vocabulaire des attributions de terres en Campanie, analyse spatiale et temporelle", MEFRA 91, 2, 977-1011.

VALLAT, J-P. (1980), "Cadastrations et controle de la terre en Campanie septentrionale (IVᵉ siècle av. J.-C. – Iᵉʳ siècle ap. J.-C.)", MEFRA 92, 1, 387-444.

VALLAT, J-P. (1984), "Studio del catasto dell'Ager Falernus (IV a.C. – I d.C.)", in S. Settis (Ed.), Misurare la terra: centuriazione e coloni nel mondo romano, Modena, 227-230.

VALLAT, J-P. (1987), "Les structures agraires de l'Italie républicaine", Annales ESC 1, 181-218.

VALLAT, J-P. (1987b), "Le paysage agraire du piedmont du Massique", in Chouquer et alii (1987), 315-377.

VALLETRISCO, A. (1972), "Su un corredo etrusco ritrovato a Cales", RAAN XXXIII, 221-240.

VALLETRISCO, A. (1977), "Note sulla topografia di Suessa Aurunca", RAAN LII, 59-73.

VALLETRISCO, A. (1980), "Note aggiuntive sulla topografia di Suessa Aurunca", Stud. Suess. II, 39-44.

VAN ANDEL, T.H. and RUNNELS, C. (1987), Beyond the Acropolis, A Rural Greek Past, Stanford.

VAN DER WERFF, J.H. (1978), "Amphores de tradition punique à Uzita", BABesch 52-53, 171-200.

VERRENGIA, F. (1920), Vescia capitale degli Ausoni, Naples.

VETTER, E. (1953), Handbuch der italischen Dialekte, Heidelburg.

VILLUCCI, A.M. (1979), "Note di presenza romana nell'agro di Suessa Aurunca", Stud. Suess. I, 41-59.

VILLUCCI, A.M. (1980a), "Testimonianze archeologiche nel territorio di Suessa Aurunca. Di un rinvenimento a Sinuessa", Stud. Suess. II, 45-66.

VILLUCCI, A.M. (1980b), Di alcune nuove testimonianze archeologiche a Suessa Aurunca e nel suo territorio, Sessa Aurunca.

VILLUCCI, A.M. (1980c), I Monumenti di Suessa Aurunca, Scauri.

VILLUCCI, A.M. (1981a), "Testimonianze del Gaudo nel territorio di Suessa Aurunca", Atti I Conv. G.A. Camp., Rome, 145-147.

VILLUCCI, A.M. (1981b), Atti I Conv. G.A. Camp., Rome, 153-174.

VITALE, N. (1939), "Condizioni idrauliche della bassa valle del Garigliano nell'epoca classica e le cause geografiche di disbonifica", Abissi I, no. 4, 239-248.

WARD-PERKINS, B. (1978), "Luni – The decline and abandonment of a Roman town", in H.McK. Blake, T.W. Potter and D.B. Whitehouse (Eds.), Papers in Italian Archaeology I, pt. ii, BAR, Oxford, 313-321.

WARD-PERKINS, B. (1984), From Classical Antiquity to the Middle Ages. Urban Public Building in Northern and Central Italy A.D. 300-850, Oxford.

WARD-PERKINS, J.B. (1964), Landscape and History in Central Italy, Oxford.

WEAVER, P.R.C. (1972), Familia Caesaris, Cambridge.

WHITE, K.D. (1967), "Latifundia", BICS 14, 62-79.

WHITE, K.D. (1970), Roman Farming, London.

WHITTAKER, C.R. (1976), "Agri deserti", in M.I. Finley (Ed.), Studies in Roman Property, Cambridge.

WHITTAKER, C.R. (1983), "Late Roman trade and traders",

in P. Garnsey, K. Hopkins and C.R. Whittaker (Eds.), Trade in the Ancient Economy, London, 163-180.

WICKHAM, C. (1981), Early Medieval Italy. Central Power and local Society, 400-1000, London.

WIDRIG, W. (1980), "Two sites on the via Gabina", in K. Painter (Ed.), Roman Villas in Italy: Recent Excavations and Research, London, 119-140.

WIGHTMAN, E.M. (1981), "The lower Liri valley: Problems, trends and peculiarities", in G. Barker and R. Hodges (Eds.), Landscape and Society, Papers in Italian Archaeology II, BAR S102, Oxford, 275-287.

WILKES, J.J. (1969), Dalmatia, London.

WILSON, R.J.A. (1981), "The hinterland of Heraclea Minoa (Sicily) in classical antiquity", in G. Barker and R. Hodges (Eds.), Landscape and Society, Papers in Italian Archaeology II, BAR S102, Oxford, 249-260.

WISEMAN, T.P. (1970), "Roman Republican road building", PBSR XXXVIII, 121-152.

WISEMAN, T.P. (1971), New Men in the Roman Senate, 139 B.C. – A.D. 14, Oxford.

WISEMAN, T.P. (1983), "Domi nobiles and the Roman cultural élite", in M. Cébeillac-Gervasoni (Ed.), Les 'Bourgeoisies' Municipales Italiennes aux IIe et Ier Siecles av. J-C, Rome, 299-307.

WITTFOGEL, K.A. (1956), "The hydraulic civilisation", in W.L. Thomas (Ed.), Man's Role in Changing the Face of the Earth, Chicago, 152-164.

ZEVI, F. (1966), "Appunti sulle anfore romane", AClass XVIII, 208-247.

PLATE I *De Rossi's map of 1714 showing the lagoons near the mouth of the Garigliano (Biblioteca Nazionale, Napoli).*

PLATE II *November floods: the Garigliano in spate in 1979*

PLATE III *The rich lands of the ager Falernus: view to the SE from S. Mauro. All three masserie to right of centre are built over Roman villas*

PLATE IV *The northern cemetery of Sinuessa devastated by clandestine excavations in 1976 (Photo: M Marzano)*

PLATE V *Modern agricultural terracing below the Casanova–Cascano road*

PLATE VI *The hollowed way of the via Appia*

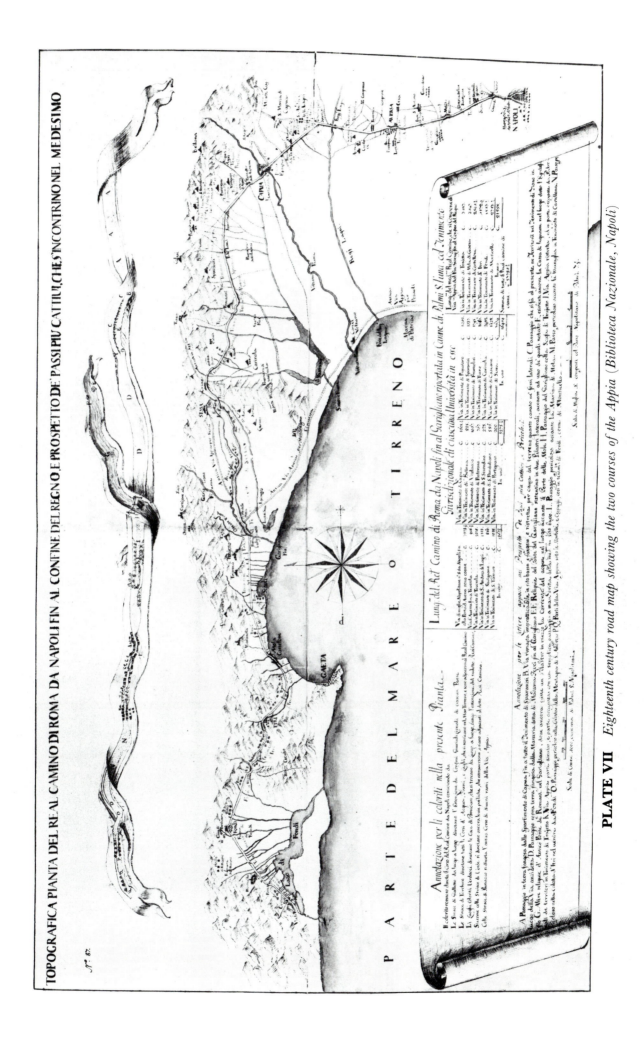

PLATE VII *Eighteenth century road map showing the two courses of the Appia (Biblioteca Nazionale, Napoli)*

PLATE VIII   *Wealth in the late Republic: remains of a fortified villa at Scauri – second century BC limestone-block basis villae*

PLATE IX *Wealth in the late Republic: remains of a fortified villa at Scauri – early first century BC cryptoporticus*

PLATE X *The Roman dam east of Mt Cicoli (site M180)*

PLATE XI *The landowners: Caedicii and Papii — the inscription from the bell-tower of Carinola cathedral*

PLATE XII *Wealth in the late Republic: the 'Venus of Sinuessa' (Soprintendenza Archeologica, Napoli)*

PLATE XIII *The scale of production: late Republican wine amphorae from a kiln dump at Mondragone (site M140)*

PLATE XIV *Imperial presence: Portrait of Titus from Sinuessa (see De Franciscis, 1983)*

PLATE XV *Imperial presence: the tombstone of Graphicus,* procurator hereditatium tractus Campaniae, *from Sinuessa*

PLATE XVI   *Tombstone of Lucius Magius, veteran of the Illyrian campaigns of Augustus, at Cellole*

PLATE XVII   *The harbour of the Roman villa at Gianola, near Scauri*

PLATE XVIII *Abandoned Republican farm terrace re-used as a basement for the Benedictine monastic site at S Croce (site M11)*

PLATE XIX *Agri deserti: the deforested wilderness of S Croce*

PLATE XX   *A new regime: buffaloes in northern Campania*